Eng Lang
2.-

Heroes and Villains

Heroes and Villains

SELECTED ESSAYS

R. W. Johnson

The University of Georgia Press
Athens

Published in the United States of
America in 1990 by the University of
Georgia Press, Athens, Georgia 30602

First published in Great Britain in 1990 by
Harvester Wheatsheaf,
66 Wood Lane End, Hemel Hempstead,
Hertfordshire, HP2 4RG
A division of
Simon & Schuster International Group

© R. W. Johnson, 1990

All rights reserved. No part of this publication may be
reproduced, stored in a retrieval system, or transmitted,
in any form, or by any means, electronic, mechanical,
photocopying, recording or otherwise, without the
prior permission, in writing, from the publisher.

Printed and bound in Great Britain by
BPCC Wheatons Ltd, Exeter

Typeset by Witwell Ltd, Southport
in Goudy 10/12pt

Library of Congress Cataloging in Publication Data

Johnson, R. W. (Richard William)
    Heroes and villains : selected essays/R. W. Johnson.
      p.   cm.
    "First published in Great Britain in 1990 by Harvester
Wheatsheaf" — Galley t.p. verso.
    Includes bibliographical references and index.
    ISBN 0-8203-1272-X
    1. Politicians — Biography. 2. World politics — 20th
century.
I. Title.
D412.7.J64   1990
909.82'092'2—dc20   90-36443
[B]   CIP

For Becky, my best girl, and Dicken, my best boy

Contents

Acknowledgements ix

Introduction: Individuals and Politics 1

I *Politicians*

1 Mendès 15
2 Dreyfus: Their Affair and Our Affair 24
3 Doriot: Le Grand Jacques 34
4 Doctor Feelgood 47
5 Tony Benn, Neil Kinnock and the Travails of Labour 56
6 Thatcher's New Order 68
7 Waiting for Chirac 80
8 Le Pen and his Legions 91
9 The Revolution is Over 98
10 The Battle for the Mairies, 1989 107

II *Intellectuals*

11 Paul Johnson 119
12 Conor Cruise O'Brien 127
13 Raymond Williams and E. P. Thompson 136
14 Tom Nairn and the Monarchy 147
15 A. J. P. Taylor 157
16 French Intellectuals, May '68 and All That 166

III *Spies, Merchants of Death and Other Monsters*

17 Edgar Hoover: Public Enemy 179
18 Rising Moon 193
19 Living with Terrorism 204
20 Collaborators and the Purge 214

21	The Price of *Indépendance*	222
22	Making Things Happen	228
23	Subversions: The Shadowy History of MI5	238
24	Spycatching	252
25	Rainbow Warriors	259
26	The Age of the Vampire	270

IV Blacks and Whites

27	South Africa 1980: The Last 'Good Year'?	279
28	South Africa in the Era of 'Reform'	287
29	Scenes from South African Life	298
30	Laughing Till It Hurts	307
31	Black on Black	310
32	Via Mandela	321

Index 333

Acknowledgements

I am grateful to a number of journals and editors for the original publication of various of these essays (or versions of them). In particular I should like to thank Karl Miller and Mary-Kay Wilmers of the *London Review of Books* who have been a continuous source of encouragement and stimulus. Their achievement in creating and sustaining the LRB has been a good deed in a naughty world.

New Society

'The Age of the Vampire' first appeared as 'The Myth of the Twentieth Century' on 9 December 1982; 'Le Pen and his Legions' on 21 March 1985; 'South Africa 1980' on 28 August 1980.

Times Literary Supplement

Parts of 'French Intellectuals, May '68 And All That' first appeared as 'The Intelligentsia Goes Pop' on 31 July 1987; 'The Price of Indépendance' first appeared on 15–21 April 1988.

The Guardian

Parts of 'The Battle for the Mairies, 1989' first appeared as 'Powers in the Land', 6 March 1989.

The Independent Magazine

'Laughing Till It Hurts' appeared as 'News from Elsewhere', 26 November 1988.

London Review of Books

'Mendès' appeared on 20 June 1985, 'Dreyfus: Their Affair and Our Affair' on 23 April 1987, 'Doriot: Le Grand Jacques' on 9 October

1986, and 'Doctor Feelgood' on 3 March 1988; while 'Tony Benn, Neil Kinnock and the Travails of Labour' draws on articles published on 23 July and 10 December 1987. 'Thatcher's New Order' appeared on 20 April 1989, 'Waiting for Chirac' on 23 January 1986, 'The Revolution is Over' on 16 February 1989, 'Paul Johnson' on 4 July 1985, 'Conor Cruise O'Brien' on 2 June 1988, 'Tom Nairn and the Monarchy' on 7 July 1988, 'A. J. P. Taylor' on 8 May 1986, 'Edgar Hoover: Public Enemy' on 26 November 1987, 'Rising Moon' on 18 December 1986, 'Living with Terrorism' on 9 July 1987, 'Collaborators and the Purge' on 5 March 1987, 'Making Things Happen' on 6–19 September 1984, 'Subversions: The Shadowy History of MI5' on 4 June 1987, 'Spycatching' on 3 September 1987, 'Rainbow Warriors' on 5 June 1986, 'South Africa in the Era of "Reform" ' on 3 July 1986, 'Scenes from South African Life' on 13 October 1988, 'Black on Black' on 24 November 1988, and 'Via Mandela' on 5 January 1989.

Introduction: Individuals and Politics

In the post-war England where I spent my early years, no one had much doubt that individuals counted in politics. The war had been started by Hitler, who was directly responsible for the bomb sites which still littered the landscape. The Germans were a bad lot on their own, I learnt, but Hitler had made them even worse. Hitler was that truly satisfying creature to a child, a bogy-man, a mighty personification of pure evil. Luckily, we had had Churchill. His individual greatness had trumped Hitler, and lingering in the background there had, besides, been Roosevelt and Stalin. But one's fantasy life included only Hitler and Churchill, and of these Hitler was by far the stronger image. (Today, English children still often have a strong image of Hitler but none at all of Churchill.) Later, I learnt about the previous great bogy-man, Napoleon, and about a whole string of characters who had led up to Churchill in making England great. Mainly there were Nelson, Shakespeare and Drake, but Wolfe, Marlborough, Wordsworth and Wellington were, so to speak, mentioned in dispatches. There was also William Wilberforce, who had single-handedly abolished slavery as far as British lands were concerned, thus usefully proving us superior to the Americans, who had persevered with it for a while longer. There was no doubt that they were Great Men of History, indeed History was basically the story of Great Men.

Later, I learnt this was all wrong, not just because Great Men invariably had feet of clay but because they basically did not count anyway. This was because individuals just were not important in the way I had been taught they were. What mattered were the large forces of history – wars, revolutions, famines, demography, economic depressions and the like. Individuals became significant and men became great simply by happening to be in the right place at the right time for the tide of history to let them surf inevitably in. And they were not really individually great, because if they had not existed there would have been someone else much like them. Indeed, the whole category of 'greatness', as also that of 'heroes', was bogus. Someone might commit a fleeting act which you could term 'great' or 'heroic', but that was as far as it went; there was no permanent status beyond that. Which meant that the great and heroic might, on occasion, also act in a small-minded or even villainous way.

The people who preached the 'forces of history' side of things were often Marxists. They were rightly critical of 'history from above', of history being reduced to a list of kings, queens and prime ministers. It wasn't just historical forces that were important, they said, but the masses too. One could not help but notice, though, that the same people were also wont to speak of the fundamental role of Lenin, Stalin, Mao, Castro and so on. When it came to certain key figures on the Left, individuals did seem to count. Marx himself counted hugely, it was clear. And it was hard not to notice that the cult of personality was carried to its greatest extremes under regimes of the Left – not just in straightforwardly Communist states but in Nkrumah's Ghana, Toure's Guinea, Nyerere's Tanzania and so on. It was striking, too, that it was under left-wing regimes, where the role of the masses was claimed to be greatest, that this personality cult was given its logical extension into dynastic, indeed quasi-monarchical, rule – in Mao's China, in Ceaucescu's Rumania, in Kim Il-Sung's North Korea, in Mrs Gandhi's (later Rajiv Gandhi's) India, and in the Pakistan of the Bhuttos, father and daughter. A lot of those who claimed in theory not to believe in the significance of individuals in history seemed not to mean it in practice.

I have come to believe that individuals do matter, at least within certain limits. Clearly the impersonal forces of history are more powerful than any individual; and the Great-Men-of-History approach is wrong, just as all personality cults are dangerous; but none of that stops individuals from making a difference. As the essays in this book attest, my attention has tended to concentrate on three countries – Britain, France and South Africa. It is fairly clear that individuals have mattered in each of those countries. I could not but be aware, for example, that Enoch Powell had decisively swung the elections of 1970 and 1974 in Britain; that the development of the Bantustan concept derived from Verwoerd in a fairly personal sense; and that de Gaulle's return to power in 1958 had not only led to the speedy independence of Algeria but had changed the whole course of constitutional and political development in France. Such individuals, at least, had mattered a great deal. Of course, one could deny their centrality by attempting to prove that it was not important that this or that election was won, or that Algeria was decolonised when it was, or that South Africa's Native Reserves became quasi-independent states. But whoever takes this side of the argument has clearly got an uphill task, arguing against the significance of an ever-growing list of historical events, and with only hypothetical non-facts to appeal to. So at what one might term the heroic level, individuals do indeed count. Most of the essays in the first section of this book, as also the essay on Nelson Mandela, are about individuals who have counted in that sense.

The question of whether individuals really make a difference becomes easily conflated with them being famous. But, of course, public fame is not in itself a reliable indicator of political efficacy – it is a truism in many countries that enormous power is often wielded by relatively faceless bureaucrats. But beyond that there is, too, a covert world – reflected in the second section of this book – the world of the secret police, of arms merchants, terrorists, spies, crooks, hustlers, hucksters and so forth, whose power is exercised with deliberate secrecy. Here too, individuals can matter a great deal – not just men like J. Edgar Hoover and Sun Myung Moon – but men and women of whom one never hears. It is worth remembering that Kim Philby – 'the spy who betrayed a generation' – did not defect until he was over 50. Had he not been found out, had he made it through to retirement, we would have known his name only as one among hundreds of similar entries in the civil service section of the Honours List.

Most politicians do not act at the heroic level where their individual actions can make a real historical difference. And, of course, most people who take an active role in politics do so for fairly mundane motives – because they enjoy telling other people what to do and getting applauded for doing so, because they hate people in the opposing party and would like public opportunities of saying so, because they would like to 'be somebody', especially a 'somebody' in the party with which they identify, because they think they can use political power to advance their other interests, because they want to get patronage for themselves or would like to have it to distribute to their clients, sometimes because of strong feelings of local attachment. Such reasons would doubtless describe most politicians the world over, whether they be Chicago congressmen, São Paolo city councillors, British MPs or French mayors. Of course, many will lay claim to an altruistic concern for the public good, just as dentists will often proclaim an overwhelming concern for oral hygiene. This is not to say such professional concerns are insincere, but simply that they are professional concerns. Politics is, among other things, just a career. Politics at this level is commonly despised but there is no more reason to despise it than to feel contempt for dentistry, accountancy or any other profession. And, for the same reasons, most individuals who enter politics will not end up making more real difference to the world than if they had gone in for accountancy, dentistry or even academic life.

But if individuals usually do not make any difference, whence all the anguished debate over 'commitment', about the importance of having to choose sides and so on? Anyone who reads the passionate discussions of post-war French intellectuals about how one ought to be *engagé* will quickly realise that the sort of politics they are talking about is a world away from the more workaday politics-as-a-profession that our Chicago congressman or São Paolo city councillor is involved in. The literature of 'commitment' is all about having to make extremely stark and risky moral choices, a view of life which came fairly naturally to those who had just lived through the Nazi Occupation: the choice then had been about whether to join the Resistance and risk torture and death or to play safe and feel guilty. Happily, moral choices as tough as those have been fairly unusual in most Western countries. But outside the West politics has quite normally involved extremely tough choices indeed – in large parts of both the Communist and the Third World the dissident has had to choose between real personal danger, exile or silence. It is worth remembering that the anguished Western intellectual knows little of what 'commitment' really means compared to a critic of the government in, say, China, Ethiopia or Turkey.

So why have Western – rather than Eastern or Third World – intellectuals produced a literature about 'commitment'? It is not the whole answer, but one is bound to say that there is something very satisfying about politics viewed as a stark moral choice. This sort of choice is both so clarifying and so dramatic that there is a strong temptation, when once you have had to view politics in that way, to keep on doing so. The fact is that there are certain pleasures in the opportunity for melodrama and self-dramatisation which politics-as-moral-choice affords, and once tasted these are not easily given up. And since moral choices are normally made by individuals – some would say, can only be made by individuals – this sort of politics puts the individual right at the centre of the frame. Growing up in South Africa, this was also how I first learnt to think about politics – a fact to which the last section of this book stands witness. Just being white made one feel guilty and compromised and there was thus a lot of anguished discussion among people like myself about what to 'do', it being understood that draconian laws and a ruthless police force made doing anything at all pretty risky. Later on, in England, one would meet up again with some of one's old South African acquaintances. They would, to a man, profess a complete incomprehension of how British politics worked: all these passionate arguments about interest rates, the trade deficit, the management of nationalised industries and so forth. How could you argue about things like that, let alone feel passionate about them? There was, they felt, hardly a moral issue in sight. Like me, they had been impelled into politics by an overwhelming sense of moral guilt and had used political action – in South Africa a high-adrenalin business – to assuage that guilt. Politics without that was like smoking without nicotine. Although they would have been amazed at the thought, the fact was that they were not really functioning politically at all. Their political antennae had been dulled by an endless diet of moral melodrama. It was, though, not uncommon to find some of these friends virtually priding themselves on their incomprehension of workaday politics. But they were the poorer for it: an appreciation of how and why people behave politically, the deals and pay-offs, the webs of patronage, favours, clientage and the rest are essential to the understanding of any politics, even that sort of politics which invariably dresses itself up in moral clothes.

When faced with a situation like that in South Africa there may not, though, be any satisfactory individual moral choice open to one. I found that out fairly definitively as a teenager, in the week after Sharpeville. Trudging home from school in Durban in the stifling, dusty heat I was hailed by a motorist who drew level with me and wanted to know the way to the nearest police station. The driver – a burly, middle-aged white man – gestured indignantly at the little Zulu *umfaan* crying his eyes out on the back seat of the car. He told me that he had 'found the little bastard reading an ANC leaflet', and wanted to turn him over to the police. The little boy – he must have been twelve at the most, I can see his face now – had clearly already been beaten and was doubtless aware that far worse was in store. I knew I could not be a party to helping that far worse thing happen and so gave the driver false directions. He thanked me and drove off with a cheerful wave, leaving me with a bad conscience over the incident which, nearly thirty years later, I have still got. I hated the idea that the little Zulu boy had seen me as a willing accomplice to his fate. Of course, I would like to think the driver lost his way and gave up looking for the police in the end. Probably he asked directions again and found the police quite easily. For all I know, my getting the driver lost merely enraged him and made things even worse for the boy.

In trying to come to terms with choices like that I found two things to be useful. The first was the thought that while I could not escape responsibility for my own actions there was also the danger of my turning such an incident into something primarily about my feelings of guilt, my moral anguish, seeing it as my problem. It was all really about the little Zulu boy, not about me, and it was wrong to make oneself too important. Compared to what that little boy had to endure my anguished feelings were as nothing and I could damn well put up with a bit of guilt and suffer in silence. I still think this is a healthy response. I have also come to feel that political actions born of guilt are always likely to be a failure for the same reason – that they involve making one's own feelings of guilt far too important. Political action has to be directed towards its own proper external objects; its goal should not just be making the actor himself feel better.

Jan Kadar's famous film, *Shop on the High Street*, also sheds a useful light. The film, set in the Nazi-occupied Slovakia of 1942, is dominated by the interaction between the little Jewish shopkeeper, Mrs Lautmann, who keeps a button shop on the high street, and Tono, the somewhat good-for-nothing brother of the local fascist leader, who is appointed Mrs Lautmann's 'Aryan Controller'. But the shadowy figure of a lone Resistant flits in and out of the action too. His presence poses the question, what does the good man do in an impossible situation? For the Nazis and their local collaborators are wholly in charge, the Resistance is weak, help is nowhere near, and measures are being put in place which will lead to the Final Solution for the Jews. What the Resistant actually does is to seek out ways here and there of making the situation just a little better than it might have been – he leans on Tono, when he is appointed Aryan Controller, to make sure he treats the little old lady well, and he does favours for the old lady himself, like fishing for carp so that she can keep a Jewish holiday. If you think in the context, it is an act of surpassing political courage to fish for that carp; but at the end all he has got for that courage is a cold, wet fish. What he does, in a word, is bits and pieces, things that do not matter at all in the larger scheme of things. He does what he can. In a sense it is more than enough: at the end of the film we see the Resistant at death's door. He has been beaten to death by the local fascists and is wearing a notice, pinned to him by his tormentors, with the legend 'I am a White Jew'. Meanwhile the Jews have been rounded up into cattle wagons – he has failed entirely to stop the horror.

The film is, of course, typically Czech – Czechoslovakia is a country in an impossible situation, sandwiched between the

Germans and the Russians, trying to offend neither of them but getting occupied by both, the country of the good soldier Schweik. The Czechs are the world experts at the impossible situation – so it is worth listening to them on this. I first saw the film in South Africa and its message seemed clear: you do what you can, even though it changes nothing. That was the second part of the answer, I decided. If you are an individual in an impossible situation you make sure not to let your feelings of guilt play too central a role and you do what you can.

To talk of 'an impossible situation' is another way of saying that not all moral or political choices an individual may face are individually soluble. Which is why, even if one starts from the standpoint of politics-as-moral-choice individualism, one has to confront the question of political organisation. In practice, that is what all the talk of 'commitment' is about: whether to join this or that organisation to help the oppressed and downtrodden, and if so, what attitude to adopt towards it. For belonging to political organisations is hardly unproblematic – they have imperatives of their own and are fashioned around collective, not individual, needs. Intellectuals – to whom the second section of this book is devoted – have dominated the resulting debate over 'commitment'. Or at least, to be quite specific, Western left-wing intellectuals have: Stalinist, Maoist and most Third World nationalist regimes did not really admit of intellectual debate at all, while right-wing intellectuals in the West, with the Establishment rich and powerful already on their side, have not found the problem of organisational loyalty particularly pressing.

The single greatest influence on the discussion of intellectuals and 'commitment' has been the work of Antonio Gramsci. In part, no doubt, intellectuals responded warmly to Gramsci because he thought they were important. For Gramsci, the French Revolution was won not on the barricades but long before, in the years of the Enlightenment. That is, the storming of the Bastille was in a sense a necessary outcome, a dotting of the 'i's, a crossing of the 't's – it was the preceding cultural victory which was decisive. Gramsci distinguished several different types of intellectuals – traditional intellectuals, relating essentially to an established high culture; organic intellectuals of the ruling class, who articulated and rationalised the dominance of the classes from which they themselves had sprung; and finally, the revolutionary intellectuals who attempted to carry out the same functions for the proletariat, developing its consciousness of itself into an alternative, and ultimately hegemonic, culture.

This last type (of which Gramsci was an example himself) was the veritable prototype of the committed left-wing intellectual, but Walzer (1989) is surely right to point out that this made the intellectual (and the Party) a missionary – calling workers 'comrade' but being anything but brothers under the skin. Like Christian missionaries before them, these activists – preaching friars, clerks militant – knew the real Truth and were concerned to get the masses to recognise it, if necessary by heroic self-sacrifice. There was no doubting the extraordinary devotion and selflessness of many such clerks militant of the Left, but it has to be admitted that such a posture often bespoke a certain arrogance and tended to make a fraud of any profession of egalitarianism, let alone democracy. It is customary to think of the 'brave days' of commitment as the intellectuals' popular-frontism of the 1930s. But what were the organisational monuments of all those bright spirits recruited by Willi Munzenberg and his ilk, if not the ossified autocracies of the Comintern, Cominform and the now mouldering hulks of the Western Communist Parties? Similarly, once all the debate about 'commitment' was finished, what it often boiled down to in practice for many French intellectuals was signing up on the dotted line to become a loyal follower of Maurice Thorez or even, heavens above, Guy Mollet.

And where did that Truth really come from? Individuals making a major, possibly courageous, commitment to a Cause were prone to say that once the Truth – whatever the political ideology in question – had been revealed to them, they felt they had little choice. But this, as Ignazio Silone pointed out, was an evasion: 'We proclaim ourselves revolutionaries . . . for motives, often ill-defined, that are deep within us, and before choosing, we are, unknown to ourselves, chosen. As for the new ideology, we learn that, usually, at the (Party) schools.' (Walzer, 1989.) (The citations from Silone and Breytenbach, below, are also taken from Walzer's invaluable book.)

One uses the past tense for all this because, although one recognises any number of twentieth-century Communist and socialist intellectuals in this portrait, it is surely difficult to see this as a model for the future. It is not just that we have reached, in Hobsbawm's phrase, 'the end of the classic labour movement' in the West; in any case, the post-Mao and Gorbachev era has pulled the rug out from under organised political Marxism. Both these developments suggest that the day of Gramsci's revolutionary intellectual is over. There was, moreover, always something terribly wrong about the role of the missionary bringing the Truth to the poor. No wonder this role so often led its practitioners into political cul-de-sacs. The South African writer, Breyten Breytenbach, reflected how his revolutionary group, for all its talk of 'power to the people', had been as sure as all the rest that it, and not the people, had the exclusive rights to the Truth:

> Maybe we ought to settle for the slower processes; maybe we must, very paradoxically, extend our confidence to the people and whatever mass organizations the people may throw up. Ah, but that means that we have to accommodate the notion that our way . . . may be diluted or changed completely . . . since we shall be losing control over the evolution that we become part of. Isn't that what 'power to the people' implies?

This strikes a sympathetic note but where does it actually lead? Clearly, it will take Breytenbach towards some form of populism, but it will be surprising if it is really 'the people' he ends up losing control to; more likely it will be to some well-organised élite with fewer scruples than him. That's the way it usually goes, after all.

For the choices are really not easy. If the old missionary role of the radical intellectual is rejected, there are only so many alternatives. One can become a mystic populist, like Tolstoy who 'against every social evil, summoned up the primitive but sublime goodness of the Russian peasant'. But this is really rather silly. Silone was admirably frank about it: 'I haven't the illusion that the poor possess the truth', he wrote. 'I know that their spiritual poverty . . . is often as great as their material misery.'

A second alternative is to do what Silone did – to plunge oneself back into the world of the peasant village, to savour not the peasant's intrinsic goodness or wisdom but his cunning, his humour, his discontents, jealousies and parochial rivalries, his land-hunger – his sheer earthy naturalness, in a word; to become 'one more weary radical wrapping himself in the shroud of organic connection'. There is something vastly satisfying about this. But it is difficult to see the absorption into these little worlds of Don Camillo as representing an alternative political choice. Usually it means giving up political choices for the pleasures of becoming a participant-observer.

A third possibility, faced with the evident exhaustion of the classic labour movement – and, with it, the exhaustion of the classic Gramscian role of the radical intellectual – is simply to pretend nothing has happened. A surprising number of left-wing intellectuals have opted for this and go emptily banging on as if the clock has stopped at 1968 or even earlier. They resemble those cartoon characters who run over the edge of a cliff and hang suspended for a while, their feet spinning in mid air. A fourth possibility is to become a right-wing renegade. Usually this means giving up an instinctive sympathy with the poor and oppressed – sometimes by arguing that the poor will always be with us, sometimes by denying that such categories even exist.

There is also, though, the uncomfortable path charted by Orwell. Both Right and Left have claimed him, the Left pointing essentially to his pre-war writings, the Right pointing to *1984* and *Animal Farm*. But there is no need to choose: the post-war Orwell never reneged on what he had written earlier. And there was no reason to do so. It is perfectly possible to detest both the British class system *and* Stalinism. But the crystal quality of Orwell's writing comes not from his dislike of this or that political dispensation but from his simple detestation of untruth.

Interviewed in 1940 on the subject of 'The Proletarian Writer', for example, Orwell simply denied that there was such a thing as proletarian literature – all it could be, he said, was 'bourgeois literature with a slightly different slant'. This sort of uncomfortable truth-telling does not make friends. Raymond Williams's reaction to *1984* is a typical example of the fury created by the discomforting Orwell: 'As for *1984*, its projections of ugliness and hatred . . . onto the difficulties of revolution or political change, seem to introduce a period of really decadent bourgeois writing in which the whole status of human beings is reduced.' Walzer is surely right in suggesting that Williams's reaction is itself an example of the failure of English political writing and that the phrase 'the difficulties of revolution' is as dishonest a gloss as Auden's 'necessary murder', a line which, Orwell correctly observed, could never have been written by anyone who had actually seen a man murdered. But the real point is surely that *1984* contains a number of important truths about the nature of totalitarianism, just as *Animal Farm* contains some important truths about the fate of revolution. You cannot write those truths out of the script just because they make you feel uncomfortable. Nor is it fair to saddle Orwell with responsibility for the 'decadent' writing which followed him or with what political use others made of his writings.

In theory, of course, everyone will tell you they believe in telling the truth. In practice, Orwell's path is a hard one to follow, and yet he is the first really modern intellectual, the first to achieve a transcendence of the classic Gramscian categories. What Orwell is saying is that you have to be committed and you have to tell the truth. And telling the truth is not just not telling lies about your enemies: it is talking straight to your friends. It means the avoidance of bad faith. What makes this so hard is the politics of solidarity which applies quite equally on Right and Left. What solidarity politics means is that you have to stay on the same side as this or that group and that therefore you must not say anything which might embarrass that group or which could possibly be of use to its enemies. Crucially, it means observing certain necessary silences and not being right too soon. The Gramscian intellectual, facing a moral dilemma over truth-telling within a political organisation, will feel that the cause and the organisation come first. But the Orwellian will feel that the truth must always come first. Orwell was no fool and he knew a white lie when he saw one; and he also knew that compulsive truth-telling for its own sake can be naïve and destructive. But he also knew that once you had agonised over the problem you still had to tell the truth. Because the truth will come out in the end anyway. Because you betray people by not telling them the truth. Because perhaps you can head off worse in the future by telling the truth now. But finally you tell the truth not for any instrumental reason but just because the truth is sacred and covering up an untruth is squalid. Since political organisations do not feel comfortable with individuals who tell uncomfortable truths and ask awkward questions, the individual who decides to adopt this Orwellian stance may ultimately be forced into a lone wolf role. But if so, so be it.

So individuals can count, and anyway we have to act on the moral assumption that they do. However collectivist one's aims and objectives may be, the argument for a political commitment to such a cause must necessarily be addressed to the individual's sense of moral responsibility. The argument that one should side with the majority, the poor and the oppressed rests not just on notions of elementary humanity but on the assumption that one feels or should feel a moral responsibility towards that wider humanity. And once one accepts that notion of individual moral responsibility, one cannot but judge people in terms of it, heroes and villains and all the rest. The only moral framework for judgement is that you have to do the best you can and you have to try to tell the truth.

Such rules look simple but are actually extremely tough. Perhaps too tough: looking through the essays in this book it will be clear that there are far more villains than heroes. Part of the reason for this is probably that I am more drawn to villains, more suspicious of heroes. Who, after all, is a hero to himself? And, anyway, what do we think of men who are heroes to themselves? No one wants such a man as a friend, let alone as a leader. Better, perhaps, to accept that we are all at least partly villains, that the political causes and organisations we commit ourselves to are all imperfect, and that we are going to be in permanent hot water with our friends for telling them truths they do not want to hear. But that is no excuse for giving up. Again, Orwell is the best guide. In his essay on Arthur Koestler, Orwell acknowledges the awful truth of Koestler's accusations against the Communist cause to which he had once given his loyalty, and acknowledges that the revolution he had followed had led to purges, murders, deportations and torture. But despite agreeing with all that Koestler says, Orwell reproves him for his retreat into 'short-term pessimism'; that is, his retreat from politics into a little personal oasis of sanity. The only basis for such a retreat, Orwell points out, is hedonism, the same hedonism which had originally led Koestler into finding the notion of an Earthly Paradise so desirable:

> Perhaps, however, whether desirable or not, it isn't possible. Perhaps some degree of suffering is ineradicable from human life, perhaps the choice before man is always a choice of evils, perhaps even the aim of Socialism is not to make the world perfect but to make it better. All revolutions are failures, but they are not all the same failure.

Thus the answer to short-term pessimism is long-term pessimism – a steady awarenes that it's an imperfect world, that there are far more villains than heroes, that revolutions will always fail in some sense, that there will always be suffering, perhaps even that the poor will always be with us. But none of that excuses us. We have to know about those different failures, analyse and describe them, tell the truth about them: we have to understand because we have to go on, just as the world goes on. And, whatever creed we espouse, if we cannot make the world perfect we still have 'to make it better'.

References

Walzer, Michael (1989) *The Company of Critics. Social Criticism and Political Commitment in the Twentieth Century* (London: Peter Halban)

PART I
Politicians

Chapter 1
Mendès

Mendès was a man of principle who found it peculiarly difficult to judge where the dictates of practical politics had to be respected and, in particular, where principles alone are not enough. In the end he bowed the knee to the Fifth Republic by running as Gaston Defferre's vice-presidential candidate in the presidential campaign of 1969. This was absurd: if he was going to run, the 1965 nomination was the one to seek; it was ridiculous to accept second place to an old fixer like Defferre – whose 1969 presidential bid was a predictable disaster, achieving the lowest vote for a Socialist in French history; and there is not, in any case, such an office as Vice-President in the Fifth Republic. It was an old man's folly, but no matter: his stature remained undiminished. After I had written this piece I met Mme Marie-Louise Avril, once Mendès' secretary. During the Algerian War Mme Avril's connection with Mendès had brought upon her an OAS attack, the door of her apartment being blown off with plastic explosive. (The OAS – Organisation de l'Armée Sécrête – was the far-right terrorist organisation mounted by the Algerian settlers against those favouring a liberal or independent solution to the Algerian problem.) The neighbours complained that it was bad enough worrying that the old lady at the other end of the corridor might attract an attact from Left extremists, without worrying about the OAS as well. On enquiry, Mme Avril discovered that the old lady at the end of the corridor was none other than Mme Pétain . . . I was delighted to find that when Mme Avril talked of 'le Président' she meant not Mitterrand but her old boss, Mendès, as 'le Président du Conseil' (a French prime minister's formal title).

It is difficult to communicate to those too young to remember Pierre Mendès-France ('PMF') the passionate enthusiasm his name generated. For a whole post-war French generation he was the de Gaulle of the Left: a man of total integrity, a beacon of intelligence and republican principle in the darkest hours. Yet he was Prime Minister for just 245 days. George Holoch's fine translation of Jean Lacouture's excellent journalistic biography is thus especially welcome (Lacouture, 1984).

Mendès was born of a family of Portuguese Jews (the original name was Mendo Franca) who fled to France from the tortures of the Inquisition. His father, a travelling salesman and shopkeeper, was a fervent admirer of the Commune, who wrote a poem to call down the curses of the common people on Thiers. The great affair of his father's life – a prosperous textile merchant – was, inevitably, Dreyfus. Mendès *père*, a secular, radical republican, rallied to Dreyfus as a passionate democrat more than a Jew and, as a furious anti-Prussian, had the honour to serve in the First World War under . . . Colonel Alfred Dreyfus. For all his sophistication PMF never strayed far from these roots: he was the classic scion of the progressive republican bourgeoisie.

He was also the classic – perhaps slightly spoilt – Jewish bright boy, top of every class, a furious worker, always dashing off to libraries while his fellow students dawdled. '"You have time to lose", he would say to us', one of his contemporaries recollects: 'He didn't.' It was as a student that Mendès first encountered a force with which he had not had to contend before – the rabid anti-semitism of the French Right. The militant student sections of Action Française and the Camelots du Roi mounted direct and violent action against republicans, socialists and Jews, and even for the studious young Mendès the need to fight this wave took priority over his books. He became the national leader of the Ligue d'Action Universitaire Républicaine et Socialiste, which turned out to be a veritable nursery of the French political élite: alongside Mendès in LAURS were to be found Léo Hamon, Maurice Schuman, Léopold Senghor, Jacques Soustelle and George Pompidou (then a militant young socialist). Already Mendès had joined Herriot's Radicals and was determined on a political future – 'dreaming of a career like Disraeli's'.

Even in such a talented generation Mendès was a phenomenon. When he qualified at the age of 19, he was the youngest lawyer in France. His thesis on Poincaré's fiscal policy immediately became a successful book; and by the time he was 23 he had trained as an Air Force navigator and published a second successful book, on international finance – calling for a united Europe and the creation of a world bank. To the utter stupefaction of his family, he then forsook Paris to become a country lawyer in Louviers in Normandy, simply because he had been promised the Radical nomination in this hopelessly conservative constituency. After overcoming the predictably anti-Semitic campaign of the Right, he defeated the entrenched local political boss to become, at 25, the youngest Deputy in France. Within three years he was also Mayor of Louviers and the financial oracle of the Left in parliament. His brilliance was breathtaking, and years later even the brightest civil service technocrats were to agree that in the sheer quality of his intellectual grasp PMF was the ablest man they had ever served.

In parliament Mendès quickly became a leader of the radical young Turks discontented with Herriot's conservatism, and a keen supporter of the Popular Front. Given the nature of his constituency, this was a bold stand to take and in the 1936 election he faced a furious right-wing campaign against him whose tenor may be judged by the fact that his supporters were reduced to chanting: 'Long live the Jews!' He was triumphantly re-elected and was the only Deputy in parliament to vote against French participation in the Berlin Olympics, on the grounds that they were bound to be a Nazi propaganda ramp (even the Communists did not dare thus to offend the patriotic sporting enthusiasms of their voters). Mendès was furiously critical of Blum's failure to devalue the franc on his accession to power in 1936 – a failure which doomed the Popular Front. In 1937, Blum, acknowledging his error, took over the Ministry of Finance himself and appointed Mendès and his lifelong friend, Georges Boris, as under-secretaries. The sight of three Jews in charge of the French Treasury amply fulfilled the Right's expectations of socialist government.

With the Government's collapse and the coming of war Mendès enlisted in the Air Force. Once France had fallen, the Vichy regime pounced on him and sentenced him to jail on a series of trumped-up charges. In a ludicrous trial before the magistrate who had just sentenced de Gaulle to death *in absentia*, Mendès refused to 'confess' and passionately attacked the judge for 'doing Hitler's work', an act which must have required extreme physical bravery. Resourceful as ever, Mendès managed to saw through his cell bars and escaped, cleverly but dangerously, into the Nazi-occupied zone. (While underground and in disguise, he saw the catalogue of the anti-Jewish exhibition organised by Vichy at the Berlitz Palace: it included a wax dummy of himself representing all that was evil in French Jewry). He eventually escaped to Switzerland (smuggling his wife and children out to America), and, in 1942, finally ended up with de Gaulle in London. De Gaulle was keen to use PMF's talents in an administrative role, but Mendès, wanting only to fight, joined a Free French bomber squadron as navigator.

As the war progressed, de Gaulle desperately wanted strong French representation at the world financial summit at Bretton Woods. When Gaston Defferre urged the name of Mendès on him, de Gaulle assented with a sigh: 'Another Jew!' At Bretton Woods PMF worked with Keynes, a man whose lonely French disciple he had long been, and returned at the Liberation to become de Gaulle's Economics Minister. Almost immediately he was at odds with Pleven, the Finance Minister, who favoured a far less rigorous anti-inflation policy than PMF was resolved upon. De Gaulle took the politically easier way out and sided with Pleven, whereupon PMF promptly resigned. This was in April 1945. In the years of galloping inflation which followed, PMF's judgement came to seem less quixotic than it did at the time. Pleven never forgave him for being right and his enmity was to dog PMF down the years. Meanwhile, PMF, re-elected Deputy and Mayor of Louviers, went off to lecture at the newly-founded Ecole Nationale d'Administration (ENA), where the young Giscard d'Estaing was among his pupils.

For the next eight years, the name of Mendès was repeatedly canvassed for the premiership or Ministry of Finance, but to no avail. He had become a loner: his links with the Radicals were tenuous and he seldom attended their congresses, while his post-war refusal to join the Freemasons isolated him from almost all other left-wing politicians. It was clear, too, that he would only accept power if he was free to pursue his own unbending economic policies. He was widely admired, but the party bosses and notables of the Fourth Republic could hardly trust such a man – particularly given the 'scandal' of his views on Indo-China.

From 1950 on, Mendès endlessly repeated what otherwise only the Communists were willing to say: that France's war in Indo-China was doomed and that the only thing to do was to give in to Ho Chi Minh and make peace. He even dared to suggest that similar sweeping concessions would have to be made in North Africa. To his opponents on the Right (including the US Embassy in Paris) this meant that he was no better than a Communist fellow-traveller, while the political leaders of the Centre and Left threw up their hands at such total 'unrealism'. In 1953 he was summoned to form a government, but created a sensation by spelling out quite bluntly in his nomination speech exactly what he would do in power. The Assembly, used to premiers who wrapped even generalities in smoke-screens, panicked and refused him a vote of confidence.

By this time Jean-Jacques Servan-Schreiber had founded *L'Express* with the sole aim of bringing PMF to power, and when Dien Bien Phu fell the following year, the crisis of Indo-China had become the crisis of the Republic itself. Only in such circumstances could PMF come to power. Knowing his own parliamentary naïvety, he recruited the most brilliant young man in the Assembly to help him, François Mitterrand, whom Lacouture describes as a 'parliamentary zoologist of incomparable skill'. 'No one', Lacouture says, 'was more knowledgeable about the deputies, their talents and their weaknesses, their past performances, their secret aspirations, and their connections.' Mitterrand was a great strength, but PMF did not entirely trust him.

To gasps of astonishment, PMF announced that he was setting a target of one month to make peace in Indo-China: if it was not achieved by then he would resign. This was a clever move. The French Army was on the point of collapse and large-scale desertions were feared. The message was clear: to the Army – hang on for one more month, and the horror will stop; to Ho Chi Minh – if you do not negotiate with me now you will have to deal with someone else who will be less sympathetic to your cause. Later, the Vietnamese were to claim that the gamble worked only because of the brutal pressure the Chinese were putting on them, but Lacouture shows that it was Molotov who overruled Vietnamese objections and settled the key issues on terms PMF could sell to his countrymen. The agreement was a triumph. Laos and Cambodia were to become independent non-Communist states and France was to retain control in South Vietnam with elections delayed for two years. Had this agreement been faithfully respected, there would have been a united (and Communist) Vietnam by 1956, no second Vietnam War, and Laos and Cambodia would still be neutral, independent states. Unfortunately Dulles never accepted the agreement, with the results we know: three Communist states and thirty years of awful bloodshed which has still not come to an end. None of this was the fault of PMF – indeed, he constantly warned Dulles of the evil consequences his simple-minded anti-Communism was bound to have.

Eleven days after meeting his deadline on Indo-China, PMF announced a scheme for self-government in Tunisia which brought another bitter colonial war to an end. To the fury of the colonial lobby, the decision and the speed with which it was made were wondrously popular in France. Even *Le Canard Enchaîné* admitted, with embarrassment, that this was a government it supported ('Finally, an Opposition Government', the headline ran). A month later another issue was settled. The European Defence Community had long engendered bitter political divisions within France. PMF was ambivalent, but decided to let it come to a vote. Parliament threw it out and the European lobby never forgave PMF for the 'crime of 30 August'. PMF then shot off to the UN, where he called for the neutralisation of Austria, *détente* between the superpowers and a nuclear test ban. These proposals met with icy hostility from the US Administration – such notions were only to be expected from the crypto-Communist PMF, as the US Embassy in Paris depicted him.

In November the Algerian insurrection began. PMF was appalled and announced that a sweeping programme of reform and a complete halt to the (now revealed) use of torture by the police were indispensable if a tragedy was to be averted. By now, however, he had too many enemies; not just the colonial lobbies and the Europeans, but the sugar and alcohol interests he had so offended with his public campaign against alcoholism and the symbolic bottle of milk he always placed on the Assembly podium before speaking. He was also feared and hated by the party bosses and dignitaries. He was too direct, too presidential, he bid right over their heads to the party rank and file and the country at large. Indeed, he hardly seemed to care about party at all. The Government was thrown out after just eight months. PMF was never to hold power again.

Mendès now belatedly realised that he needed a party and threw himself into organising the Mendèsiste Radicals, forming the so-called Republican Front with Mollet's Socialists. PMF was by far the most popular man in the country and used his authority principally to get Radicals to stand down in favour of Socialists. The result was that, despite a huge surge of popular support for PMF, almost all the benefit went to Mollet, who used his power to block PMF from the premiership or even a senior ministry. He ended us as minister without portfolio with Mollet as premier, and resigned in disgust when Mollet used his power to step up repression in Algeria. He was vehemently opposed to the Suez expedition – a courageous act given the predictable Israeli fury his position elicited – and then further infuriated the European lobby by voting against the EEC Treaty: as a passionate Anglophile from wartime days, he could not accept Britain's exclusion. Engulfed in waves of hatred from all directions, he continued to denounce torture in Algeria – the fact that he had been right about so many things seemed only to infuriate his enemies all the more.

Despite his admiration for de Gaulle, PMF was deeply offended by the Fifth Republic, which he saw as a reincarnation of the Second Empire. Swept out of his Louviers seat by the Gaullist wave and expelled from the Radical Party, he none the less remained the dominating personality of the Left: the Left's presidential nomination in 1965 was his for the asking but he spurned any gesture which might legitimate the new presidential regime, so offensive to his republican spirit. In May 1968, PMF alone was 'with the students'. Speculation that he might somehow return to power did not really cease until the 1974 election made it clear that the leadership of the Left had passed irrevocably to Mitterrand. PMF gave Mitterrand his unconditional support at every turn, but Mitterrand never quite overcame his fear that PMF might somehow return to steal his thunder. Even though the two men fell upon one another like two weeping brothers when Mitterrand finally won power in 1981, PMF waited sadly and in vain for a minor job in the new administration. When he died in 1982 Mitterrand immediately issued a special stamp to commemorate him.

PMF was a man of great achievement, but what made him a truly lasting presence was his shining integrity. He was, too, naïve, vain and spoilt, tending to see political opposition as mere personal dislike, and never seeming to realise that his own entirely presidential disposition was more in tune with the Fifth Republic than the Fourth. His refusal to be a wheeler-dealer was admirable, but also blind: politicians who did him favours were outraged by his 'ingratitude' when he did no favour back. He never seemed to care about the repercussions of his actions, provided they seemed right to him: he spent a good deal of time in his later years closeted with left-wing Israelis and the PLO, more in the belief that reconciliation was a good thing than in any real hope that he could effect a change in the Middle East. Zionists were infuriated by his refusal to support Israel unconditionally, religious Jews by his happy confession that the only thing that made him feel Jewish was anti-semitism. Above all, his attitude to parties was perverse: in a mass democracy one cannot be politically serious if one spurns party organisation, discovering its importance only after one had become prime minister.

Inevitably, PMF, as the providential man of the Left, was compared with de Gaulle; and as the Fourth Republic neared collapse the country was bound to turn to one or other of them as its saviour. In part, de Gaulle won and PMF lost simply through luck and circumstance, but it also has to be said that de Gaulle was, at bottom, shrewder and had a depth of historical sense which PMF could not equal. This is evident from the exchanges between the two cited by Lacouture. When, in March 1944, PMF asked de Gaulle if future economic planners might not consider the possibility of a united Europe, de Gaulle replied:

> Europe! Of course, it has to be set up. With Belgium, Holland and

Italy to begin with. Spain will follow when they have got rid of Franco. Germany? There will no longer be *one* but *several* Germanies. We shall see. . . . England? No, I don't see it participating in a European enterprise.

There, three months before D-Day, was a vision of the Europe that was to unfold over the next thirty years. Neither PMF, nor anyone else, could equal that.

Here again, is de Gaulle explaining why PMF's anti-inflation policy of 1945, however technically correct, was historically wrong:

In economics, as in politics or strategy, there does not exist, in my view, any absolute truth. But there are circumstances. The country is sick and wounded. Why throw it into dangerous convulsions when in any event it is going to recover its health?

De Gaulle was right: French post-war economic growth was extremely rapid. If higher inflation made the political cost easier to bear, it was a price well worth paying. Finally, listen to de Gaulle explaining to PMF in 1954, when the latter was at the height of his power, that his premiership could not last:

The regime does not permit you to have a government . . . No one can act within this system. . . . From time to time people may very well cheer you as you pass by . . . but when you have got rid of what troubles the regime, the regime will get rid of you at the first opportunity.

Within months it had happened. PMF could not really compete with that superior *realpolitik* – a fact which he reluctantly acknowledged when he admitted that de Gaulle, whom he endlessly opposed, was also the man he had most admired. Typically, de Gaulle's comment on Mendès was less direct and more brutal: 'I respect only those who resist me, but them I cannot tolerate.'

On the other hand, it is also wrong to compare PMF with de Gaulle, the colossus of *realpolitik*. What made PMF memorable, and makes him so still, is sheer quality of intellect wedded to a crystalline integrity. Through all the many dark hours France had known since the 1920s – Depression, the threat of Fascism, Vichy, Indo-China, the horrors of Algeria – the voice of Mendès could be heard, always on the side of humanity, time and again right before his time. He had had to brush aside the most outrageous anti-semitism in order to speak at all, but once he had done so he was ready to act with dispatch and decision and to take whatever the consequences might be. Alongside de Gaulle, with his unmistakable echoes of Bonaparte, PMF sometimes seemed merely the supreme example of a modern technocrat, but he was more than that: the heir of Danton, Victor Hugo and Jaurès, the voice of republican conscience in the twentieth century, the voice of the Dreyfusards. While that spirit lives, Mendès will be remembered.

References

Lacouture, Jean (trans. George Holoch) (1984) *Pierre Mendès France* (New York: Holmes and Meier).

Chapter 2
Dreyfus: Their Affair and Our Affair

The Dreyfus Affair has the timeless appeal of a morality play. It is the complex moral story of how a powerful Establishment sought to subvert democratic rules in order to scapegoat an individual, banking on the cover of popular prejudice against him as a member of an unpopular minority: how the tireless campaigning of an originally small band brought that Establishment to heel and secured justice for that individual; but also of how the humiliation of that Establishment produced an angry cloud of anti-democratic poison which lingered for decades after in the bloodstream of the Third Republic, ultimately eventuating in the triumphant reaction of Vichy. Writing about the Affair in the looming shadow of a third Thatcher victory in 1987, one could not but be aware of a similar cloud of poison working its way through the British system, puffed on by a scabrous press and eventuating in a similar triumph of reaction.

John Weightman, reviewing Jean-Denis Bredin's monumental work (Bredin, 1987) in *The Observer*, wrote of the Dreyfus Affair that

> it was perhaps a good thing for France that the abcess burst when it did, because this brought tensions out into the open and revealed the 'undeclared civil war' which would need to be resolved in the twentieth century.

It is, perhaps, a curious notion that there could be *any* time when it would be 'a good thing' for a country to experience a racking political scandal which, over a twelve year period, led to the unparalleled expression of group hatreds, brought about suicides, the ruination of careers and the fall of governments, and which produced anti-Semitic riots without number in which Jews were robbed, vilified and killed. But it is worth pausing over Weightman's judgement, for it encapsulates a marvellously Anglo-Saxon misunderstanding not only of the Dreyfus Affair but of the ways in which social cleavages operate and opinion is formed and crystallised.

Crudely, the model is this. There was a Jewish officer working for the French General Staff, Captain Alfred Dreyfus, who in 1894 was falsely accused and imprisoned for being a German spy. Once Emile Zola had written his famous '*J'accuse*' open letter there was a great taking of sides, with the forces of the republican and anti-clerical Left ranged against the forces of the conservative Establishment, especially the Army and the Church. In the ensuing twelve year social explosion, ended only by the freeing of Dreyfus and the conferment on him of the Legion of Honour, the French gave themselves over to a frenzy of ideological confrontation. In so doing, they 'burst the abcess' of the bad feeling which had dwelt at the heart of French society ever since the Revolution. For these battles concerned essentially nineteenth or even twentieth century matters – the monarchy versus the republic, clericals versus anti-clericals – and these issues just had to be 'resolved' before France could get on with living in the twentieth century. The paradigm is clearly that of the naughty child who has to vent his burst of bad temper before he can settle down and sensibly adapt himself to living his life according to the Whig interpretation of history. While he has still got those bad feelings, he simply can't get on with things, you see, and we have to be indulgently parental about his having a jolly good scream and kick because this is what it is to 'work something out of your system'.

The Dreyfus Affair was no more like this than any social explosion great enough to change people's lives ever can be. Paradoxical though it may seem, the lasting importance of the Affair was not all that much to do with Alfred Dreyfus, who, after his release, fought well in the war and then lived a quiet and unremarkable life until his death in 1935. Jean-Denis Bredin has provided us with what will probably stand as the definitive account of the Affair and of its impact on the politics of the period: there is not that much that is new that can be said of the Affair itself, but the political context has never been better or more fully treated. Even that is only part of the story, however. The really difficult project is to descry the long-term impact of the Affair and, through that prism, to understand how ideas and alignments feed through and inform a long-running social and political climate.

At the turn of the century, France was a society bearing the psychological scar of a quite unbearable defeat. Frenchmen, used to the idea that the country of Charlemagne, Louis XIV and Napoleon was the dominant power of continental Europe, had to face the fact that Prussia had comprehensively vanquished them in just a few weeks in 1870, inflicted huge reparations payments, and detached the sacred lands of Alsace and Lorraine from the motherland. Worse, the new and mighty state of united Germany continued to outstrip France in wealth, production, population and power at a quite terrifying rate. It was intolerable that France should accept such a permanently diminished status, but no one could feel truly confident that France could match the ever-strengthening German juggernaut, particularly since the democratic regime installed in France after 1871 threatened continuously to teeter over, through weakness, instability, and corruption, into a mere banana republic. The implications of the situation were too painful to be faced: instead, there was a collective averting of the eyes, a determined insistence that the French Army was still Europe's finest, a refusal to accept that the era of France's greatness might be behind her. The fact that such assertions of national greatness rang somewhat hollow, that they involved a collective act of bad faith, that the underlying sense of defeat could never really be disposed of, gave a fragile, febrile quality to the political climate. Moreover, lurking within the body politic was an army whose *armour propre* had been desperately wounded, a Catholic bloc far from reconciled to the new Republic, and a republican Left which would need little provocation to have a further go at its traditional enemies.

The Dreyfus Affair derived much of its power from the fact that it tapped into this unexpressed, indeed well-nigh inexpressible, sense of national defeat. When Barrès sought to explain what the anti-Dreyfusards were fighting for, he mentioned not only the nation, the Army, Honour and God. What was at stake, he said, was 'the house of our fathers, our land, our dead'. It is worth reflecting long and hard about that 'our dead'.

The real problems were very different. The issue of social reform had to be confronted if the burgeoning and desperately alienated proletariat was to be integrated into the nation. French agriculture was in a lamentable state of backwardness, and urgent measures for its modernisation were clearly required. Above all, a modern French industrial state had to be built. The convulsion of the Dreyfus Affair ensured that none of these problems was adequately addressed. Instead, whole new generations were educated into seeing politics as essentially a battleground between clerical anti-republicans and anti-clerical republicans. Thus the Affair did not lance an abcess but greatly prolonged its life – and the renewal and reinforcement of all the old oppositions and hatreds which it brought about bear a considerable responsibility for the stagnation of the Third Republic.

This effect was achieved despite the fact that the main impact of the Affair was confined almost exclusively to the literate, opinion-forming élites. There was, as Bredin notes, little evidence that the peasant masses were much touched by it, and probably the same was largely true of factory workers. This was almost necessarily so, for the Affair was the true father of Watergate in that it was fought out exclusively in the press (parliament playing no role). The Dreyfusard press was massively outgunned. *L'Aurore*, which printed Zola's famous 'J'accuse', had a sale of only 25,000 (though for a few weeks after this salvo its sales rose to 150,000). Only eleven per cent of newspaper sales in Paris and fifteen per cent in France overall were of Dreyfusard papers. It was not the case that all the others were hostile – the mass-circulation papers such as *Le Petit Journal* (one-million-plus sales), *Le Petit Parisien* (700,000 plus) and *Le Journal* (450,000) paid little attention to the Affair. But the real long-term damage to the political and social climate was done by the Catholic press, *La Croix* (170,000), *La Libre Parole* (100,000) and their innumerable provincial counterparts. Bredin argues that while the Dreyfusard press had a powerful impact on procedure, the Catholic press had a far deeper and more insidious effect

> ... nurturing and cultivating the state of mind of the impoverished or irritated middle classes, stirring up the anti-Judaic traditions of Christianity, encouraging hatred for foreigners, Jews, parliament and all those who disturb the traditional balance and its peaceful order.

There is a direct sense in which this press prepared Catholic and middle class opinion to adopt an attitude of benign equanimity towards the anti-Jewish atrocities carried out under Vichy. Moreover, the Affair played a key role in welding together a coherent right-wing faction of the intelligentsia which was insistently influential throughout the inter-war period, continuously pushing anti-democratic, xenophobic, nationalist and Fascist themes into the bloodstream of public debate.

But the Affair had a fundamental effect on the French intelligentsia as a whole. While artists, poets and writers had long been in the habit of making sporadic individual interventions in French public life, the Affair saw, as Bredin puts it, 'the coming together of intellectuals into a collective involvement with the life of the *polis*'. At the Affair's end, matching the intellectuals of the Right, there was for the first time a coherent liberal and Left intelligentsia ready to play its part in the French political arena.

The emergence of this Left intelligentsia has been one of the decisive facts of French life in the twentieth century. Throughout the inter-war period the group sparred endlessly with its rightist counterpart, but while the rightist intelligentsia hailed Vichy as the triumph of the anti-Dreyfusards – and thus went down with the Vichy ship – the Left intelligentsia threw in its lot with the Resistance. And since the triumph of the Resistance was, as Maurras bitterly observed, the revenge of the Dreyfusards, the Left intelligentsia came wholly into its own after 1945 and ruled the cultural scene almost unchallenged until the late 1970s. It makes some sense, indeed, to see Sartre, not only as the direct cultural descendant of Zola, but as his beneficiary: Zola had brought together the Left intelligentsia for the first time, but under Sartre there was virtually no other sort of intelligentsia – and Sartre's influence thus extended right across the cultural continuum. The whole style of Sartre's intervention – the fierce commitment to the Left, the determination to expose 'bad faith' however uncomfortable the results, his siding with the Algerian Revolution against the tide of a furious French nationalism (and, once again, the French Army) – was that of the victorious Dreyfusard intellectual let loose on the world of the 1950s and 1960s. The 1980s have seen the re-emergence of the rightist intelligentsia, and it is clear that the Affair lives on there too – for example, in the figure of Louis Pauwels, the editor of *Figaro* magazine, Maurras, Lemaître and Barrès would have recognised themselves only too well in the xenophobic nationalism of Pauwel's anti-immigrant campaigns, his flirting with the integrist themes of Le Pen's Front National and the venom of his attacks on his cultural opponents – student resistance to Chirac's abortive university reform was characterised as 'a form of mental Aids'.

Before the Affair it was not uncommon to find anti-Semitic references in the anti-capitalist rhetoric of the Left, though Jews such as the Rothschilds were held up as symbols of capitalism rather than as an ethnic scourge in their own right. The Affair put such rhetoric beyond the pale: henceforth anti-Semitism was not just mainly the preserve of the Right, but its exclusive preserve. And there were further beneficial effects for the Left. The Affair brought to an end the absolute dominance of committees of notables over political life, as unions, co-operatives, academic associations and professional societies burst into the political debate – thereafter regarding themselves as permanent participants in public life. The

Affair also pulled the first generation of women into political life: during the Affair the first group of socialist women was founded; a Dreyfusard feminist newspaper, *La Fronde*, was launched; and thanks to the initiative of the Dreyfusard Viviani, the legal profession was opened to women for the first time in 1898. But the Affair had more paradoxical results for the Left too. By rallying to the defence of Dreyfus and thus the Republic, the Left moved decisively towards the integration of itself and its proletarian supporters into the same bourgeois republic. And for all that the Dreyfusards found themselves struggling against the overweening claims of an integrist French nationalism, rallying to the Republic meant that they were, in effect, rallying to the national idea themselves. As always, the notions of national security and national crisis provided treacherous ground for the Left (when Dreyfus was first convicted as a spy, the Socialist leader Jaurès waxed indignant that he had not been shot). Adopting the cause of Dreyfus meant forging links with men like Clemenceau – most fiery of the Dreyfusards – who was to have no scruple in ordering out the Army to repress workers in 1906.

There is a straight line from the Left's *ralliement* to Dreyfus and its *ralliement* to the flag in 1914. The resulting *union sacrée* with the likes of Clemenceau was thereafter seen on the Left as a tragic betrayal of the French working class. The *union sacrée* was an exaltation of the nation, and Dreyfusards and anti-Dreyfusards were joined in a blind and ultimately murderous patriotic fervour. Such was the climate that even the arch anti-Dreyfusard Barrès attended the funeral of Jaurès. The Socialist Minister of War, Millerand, astonished even the anti-Dreyfusards by authorising the summary execution within twenty-four hours of suspected spies: the Army's morale demanded nothing less, he claimed. The fact that precisely this form of argument had been so execrated by the Left during the Affair, and that the whole institution of special military tribunals had been discredited by the Affair, now counted for nothing. (The Dreyfusard hatred of such tribunals remains potent. When, in 1981, the Mitterrand Government finally abolished special military tribunals, the conservative deputy Olivier Stirn infuriated his right-wing colleagues by openly congratulating the Government: he is, after all, the great-nephew of Dreyfus. Stirn has since joined the Socialists.)

On Jews, too, the Affair had a mixed impact. Prominent French Jews were so assimilationist that there was no Jewish community as such, and the wealthy Jewish bourgeoisie – Dreyfus's peers – tended to shun him. Indeed, Léon Blum was to speak of their 'cowardly neutralism', inspired by the fear of attracting anti-Semitism upon themselves. The Affair did not halt the drive towards assimilation. As Bredin points out, it is likely that the Affair's impact was stronger upon poorer Jews, for whom assimilation was anyway a difficult option. It certainly had a decisive effect on the thinking of Theodore Herzl, and thus provided Zionism with its major dynamic. Having been the victims of nationalism, Jews would seek to appropriate the nationalist idea for themselves. Given that Dreyfus always refused to speak of himself as a Jew or to react against anti-Semitism as such, his role as an effective founding father of the State of Israel is not without an irony of its own.

Bredin's work overlaps at many points with Sternhell's magisterial survey of Fascist thought in France (Sternhell, 1986), his third large book on this theme. (Bredin and Sternhell have, incidentally, each been well served by their translators, though in both cases there is a tendency to over-literalism). Sternhell provides a comprehensive and subtle guide to the writings and thought of the whole pantheon of the French Far Right – not just Barrès, Maurras and Péguy, but Valois, Mounier, de Man, Déat and many others. Inevitably, the effect is encyclopaedic and beyond summary, and there is the further difficulty of differentiating truly Fascist thought, given that sociologically its proponents tended to shade off into a more traditional conservatism. Parting company with those who have somewhat simplistically seen extreme nationalism as the necessary ideological ground floor of any Fascist movement, Sternhell suggests that Fascism and Communism derive their common revolutionary character from their unusual willingness to defy the nationalist imperative in the last resort.

> 'Nationalism', he argues, 'far from being a factor that brings fascists and conservatives together, is precisely the factor that divides them .... Pure, quintessential nationalism was a doctrine of moderates: the radical right, for whom nationalism was the revolutionary factor *par excellence*, engaged in a war that was an ideological war *par excellence* – a war in which the defeat of the nation would not be too high a price to pay for the victory of certain ideas.

Like all distinctions based purely on ideas, this is neat but historically somewhat difficult to referee. The cry 'Better Hitler than Blum' was, after all, a fairly common one among conservatives who loathed the Popular Front: but does that imply that French conservatives had all been captured by Fascism? The privileging of domestic social enmities over national solidarity is not all that unusual, even if it does carry heavy significance. How many

Conservatives would have rallied to the Union Jack in 1940 if Nye Bevan, not Churchill, had been prime minister? And was not the deep objection to the Falklands War among many on the Left rooted in the fact that acceptance of the war meant accepting, at least temporarily, the leadership of Mrs Thatcher?

Sternhell is at his best in describing how the intelligentsia of the Far Right, though always a radical minority, were able to exercise a long-run cultural influence out of all proportion to their numbers. As he points out, the effective function of the small-circulation intellectual journals of the Right – *Combat*, *L'Ordre Nouveau*, *Plans*, *Revue du Siècle* and the *Revue Française* – was to act as forcing houses for an ideology which, in suitably bowdlerised form, then fed through into the popular right-wing press. All these little reviews put together sold only 12,000 copies, but the ideological material they generated was recycled in the 1930s by such papers as *L'Ami du Peuple* (an organ of the popular suburban Right, with sales of 600,000) and by the scabrous *Candide* (300,000) and *Gringoire* (600,000). Then, as now, the Left had no real counter-weight to such papers.

All this might have come to nothing: after all, the *Daily Mail* campaigned against allowing German Jewish refugees into 1930s Britain at the same time as *L'Ami du Peuple* was campaigning against Albert Einstein being invited to join the Collège de France. The difference was that in 1940 France experienced a national crisis which gave such poison its chance. The work of the Far Right reviews and the yellow press suddenly then became of great moment, for an ideological substructure to the Vichy regime already existed in incubation. Sternhell argues persuasively that the Vichy revolution

> would probably never have been possible without the fascist impregnation and the respectability acquired by anti-democratic ideas . . . fascism owed its real success to the support it received from outside its ranks, to that fact that its main concepts – as opposed to its methods – aroused the sympathy of vast sections of the public.

It is difficult to argue with this, for, as Sternhell points out, nobody forced one million French men to go to the cinema to see the Nazi epic, *Jew Süss*, or to buy Fascist papers by the hundreds of thousand, or to make a best-seller of Rebatet's *Les Décombres*. Similarly, no French publisher was obliged to sign a censorship agreement with the German authorities in Paris, but all did so, and there was no German pressure brought to bear on Vichy to bring itself into line with Nazi racial legislation in October 1940 – the regime did so because it was putting into practice ideas which already had an autonomous legitimacy in France. 'Far more than the presence of the occupying power', says Sternhell, 'it was the delegitimisation of French democracy that explains Vichy legislation'.

It is impossible to ponder such questions without reflecting on the obvious and contemporary British parallels. Taking at random merely the single issue of a newspaper appearing on the same day that this article was written, I find stories of a further government bill to strip local authorities of their powers, of the removal of all bargaining rights from an entire occupational group, of a consultant physician in a major London hospital, who had voiced concern about the rundown of the NHS, being threatened with the loss of his contract in a phone-call from Downing Street, of the cancellation of an entire BBC TV series that might have embarrassed the Government, of the Prime Minister's refusal to allow an inquiry to be made into nothing less than an alleged attempt to destabilise the preceding Labour Government, and, finally, of moves to impose a new set of model rules on all Conservative Associations without prior consideration by those Associations, which would make it impossible for Tory Party members to call a special meeting of the Party's Council, and remove the right of reply from 'debates' at Tory Party Conferences. All this from just one day's newspaper.

How can such profoundly anti-democratic trends be explained in Britain, the 'land of the free'? The biggest culprit is the selfish, indeed suicidal unwillingness of the three main anti-Thatcherite parties, which collectively constitute a large electoral majority, to stand together in the face of the clear threat to liberty represented by the Thatcher Government. The potential erosion of all our freedoms under five more years of Thatcherism threatens to give the petty disagreements between these parties the dimensions of a historical tragedy.

To understand the weakness of popular resistance to this anti-democratic tide one must look at the way extreme right-wing and authoritarian views have percolated downwards from the 'little reviews' to the now predominantly Far Right 'quality press' and thence to the mass-circulation yellow press. The past decade has seen continuous saturation campaigns by this press, with all manner of xenophobic and racialist themes to the fore, with a degradingly deferential and voyeuristic pursuit of royal and other celebrities, with a casual, day-by-day degradation of women, with invented stories, with, indeed, the whole panoply of devices employed by

Candide and *Gringoire*. The slow seepage of this poison into our body politic goes a long way to explain how protagonists of quite ordinary liberal causes have been thrown onto the defensive.

We too are a country which, like France after 1870, is feeling a profound sense of psychological defeat. For the notion that we lost our empire without pain must surely be revised. That loss is now reinterpreted as our 'national decline', and in Thatcherism we are experiencing the full fury of the dispossessed imperial backlash. Our government even feels indignation that it cannot make Australian judges behave as tamely as the thoroughly domesticated British species.

And we, too, have the spy mania which tends to characterise such periods of defeatedness. The difference is that while Fin-de-Siècle French spy mania found its ultimate target in the Jews, our endless recycling of Burgess, Philby, Maclean, Blunt *et al*. – villains from all of thirty years ago, for heaven's sake – has a rather different target. The story, in its endless retelling, fastens ever more compulsively not on the spies themselves but on their social milieu: inter-war Cambridge, the foppish upper classes, the leftish intelligentsia. What is under attack is the world of Keynes, of intellectuals in general, of anyone who ever sympathised with the Spanish Republic or was a 'premature anti-Fascist', even the wettish Tory gentry of the Macmillan era who are now reviled for leading us into national decline. If Burgess, Maclean and the rest had not existed, the Thatcherite press would invent them, for the interminable recycling of these clapped-out spy sagas undoubtedly does Thatcher's work. The huge popularity of the Le Carré books, with their pursuit of the enemy within rather than the enemy without, has a parallel cultural significance.

There are, then, many lessons for us in the French experience, and it little becomes us to react to that experience with an arrogant English particularism. The Dreyfus Affair still has a contemporary significance for the French – and if one reflects about it, for us. It is our affair too.

References

Bredin, Jean-Denis (trans. Jeffrey Mehlman) (1987) *The Affair: The Case of Alfred Dreyfus* (London: Sidgwick & Jackson).
Sternhell, Zeev (trans. David Maisel) (1986) *Neither Right nor Left: Fascist Ideology in France* (Los Angeles: University of California Press).

Chapter 3

Doriot: Le Grand Jacques

Doriot was a monster but he was also a tragic and herculean figure, a proletarian who hauled himself upwards to prominence and power against all odds, but never quite achieving the position he sought. Deprived of that focus, he was a man adrift, conscious of his talents and abilities and determined not to play second fiddle to those he despised. As he grew older and more frustrated he made first one and then many compromises, not only with those he despised but even with those whom he had once – and not unreasonably – seen as the personification of evil. In the end he simply pigged himself – morally, politically, financially and sexually, let alone gastronomically. One marvels at what that must have cost: to drive oneself upwards so far, against so many obstacles, required an overwhelming sense of self – and yet, by the end, there must have been an abandonment of self, certainly of self-respect. And do what he might, Doriot, in his second incarnation as Fascist leader, could never quite shake himself free of his earlier career as Communist militant. It was not just the picture of Lenin by the bed; he still felt aggrieved that he had not been picked as the leader of French Communism. And the bourgeoisie could not forget that either, so that even in his most right-wing phase he was never really trusted by fellow reactionaries.

All this, it should never be forgotten, stemmed from the turmoil and industrialised bloodletting of the First World War. Those few short years shaped the century. They plucked up workers and peasants by the million, tearing them out of the parochial world of their slums and villages, and those that survived were flung back into the civilian world utterly changed. They could never really 'go back home' for home could never be quite the same thing to them as once it had been; indeed, reality was never the same quantity for them again. Doriot was one of those millions: the years 1917–19 tore his world apart and he was never comfortable again. In the end he became a virtual personification of evil, positively volunteering to commit atrocities, venal, disgusting and gross. And yet there were things in him as a youth – an élan, a drive, an emotional and self-sacrificing loyalty to a *cause, and an extraordinary courage – which lend a genuine pathos to thinking about the man he might have become.*

When Mussolini was making his last desperate flit from Milan in April 1945, Nicola Bombacci, his old comrade – the two men had been revolutionary socialist schoolteachers together thirty years before – climbed into the *Duce's* car carrying only a small suitcase. 'What else would I need?' he said, 'I am an expert in such matters. I was in Lenin's office in Petersburg when the White troops of Yudenitch were advancing on the city and we were preparing to leave, as we are doing today.' In the space of a quarter-century, Bombacci, an old Communist and Comintern hand, had progressed right across the ideological spectrum, beginning as an intimate of Lenin's and ending as an adviser to Mussolini: by fluke he stood next to both men in their supreme hour of crisis.

Probably only the twentieth century, with its rapid and immense revolutionary convulsions, has produced biographies as extraordinary as this. But even in our century, floaters who drifted across from Communism to Fascism were oddities. On the other hand, how *does* one understand the process by which a major Communist leader became a major Fascist leader? To anyone who has pondered this question the career of Jacques Doriot has always had a special fascination. Now Jean-Paul Brunet has ransacked just about everything – including police files – in order to put the full story together (Brunet, 1986). He has an amazing story to tell.

Doriot was the only child of a working-class family, his father a blacksmith forced into factory work and a man of anti-clerical views, his mother a devout Catholic who ensured that her son became an altar boy. Jacques, a tall, painfully thin boy, left school early to become a factory worker in St Denis, the most proletarian suburb of Paris. This perfectly ordinary career was changed for ever by his call-up in 1917. He fought heroically at the front – an experience which scarred his life – and was then retained in the Army after the war, to be sent with a French expeditionary force to put down Bela Kun's Soviet republic in Hungary (and instal the noxious Admiral Horthy in power), to help D'Annunzio in Fiume, and then to put down partisans in Albania. By this stage he had had more than enough and was jailed for a month for indiscipline.

Returning to St Denis, Doriot became a moderate member of the Young Socialists, but his strong autodidactic urge found expression in an endless diet of Western penny dreadfuls rather than in the political classics. Politicised by war, but also confused by it, he earned a greater reputation for a love of adventure and drama than for radicalism. When the Socialist Party voted to become the Communist Party, Doriot moved with the majority and, growing prominent in the Young Communists, was sent to Moscow in 1921 for the Comintern Youth Congress. The experience transformed him. He met Lenin, received extensive training in Marxism, learnt speech-making, German and some Russian, and generally went through an accelerated Communist higher education. Selected as a promising young cadre, he spent twenty months in Moscow, working closely under Trotsky, who became his friend. Above all, Doriot venerated Lenin and took it very much to heart when Lenin chided him in fatherly fashion for becoming too dogmatic. When Lenin died Doriot cried publicly and unashamedly.

By the age of 23 Doriot was a member of the Presidium of the Comintern Executive. Zinoviev, harassed by the endless leadership squabbles of the French Communist Party (the PCF), looked on the ascetic young Doriot as a dependable revolutionary, commendably tough and cynical in his involvement with the covert side of the Comintern's activities, and quite understanding about difficult comrades who had to be 'disappeared'. Here was the PCF leader of the future – a view Doriot shared.

Returning to France, Doriot devoted himself to a series of anti-militarist campaigns, first among French troops in the Ruhr and then in the Rif. These campaigns – aimed at getting soldiers to desert and to show solidarity with the occupied populations – earned him considerable notoriety, the unrelenting hatred of the French military establishment, and a series of prison sentences for treason. He became, as it were, the Scarlet Pimpernel of the PCF – leading the PCF Youth, sitting on the Party's Politburo and addressing meetings, all while on the run from the Police, using a series of aliases and sleeping where he could. Finally caught and sentenced to thirty-four months' jail in 1923, he continued to write incendiary anti-military articles (earning him further sentences) until the PCF put him up as a candidate in the 1924 elections. An embarrassed President had to release him when the working-class voters of the Paris *banlieu*, among whom he was already a popular hero, elected him by a very large majority. He immediately became a parliamentary *enfant terrible*, proudly announcing that he considered himself a soldier of the Red, not the French Army, and generally seeking every occasion to provoke paroxysms among bourgeois Deputies and the non-PCF press. A powerful and charismatic speaker, he gloried in sheer intransigence, drew large crowds wherever he went, and, noticeably more than any other PCF leader, was always in the midst of the violent confrontations which quite routinely occurred in the course of PCF marches and demonstrations. On one such occasion Doriot was so badly beaten by the police that he had to be hospitalised while in jail – but one policeman also died after, so it was claimed, Doriot had kicked him.

Doriot raised eyebrows within the PCF as well. His revolutionary fervour was exemplary but his style was undeniably self-advertising and his ambition was clear. It was noted, too, than when, in between jail sentences, he got married (to a PCF *militante*), the ceremony – amazingly for a PCF leader – took place in church. He moved his now widowed mother into the new marital home, where she became a Catholic materfamilias to his two daughters.

Besides running the PCF Youth section, Doriot had responsibility for colonial questions, exercising a wide influence on young revolutionaries throughout the French Empire. One young Vietnamese who came under his wing carried the alias of Nguyen O Phap ('the peasant who hates France'). Doriot suggested that this be changed to the more diplomatic Nguyen Ai Quoc ('the patriot'). This protégé became better-known as Ho Chi Minh.

Doriot himself had originally been a protégé of Trotsky, but transferred his loyalties to the Comintern chief, Zinoviev, as Trotsky's star waned. Returning to Moscow in 1925, he was quick to abandon Zinoviev for Stalin, who invited him to a private supper in the Kremlin and advised him to build a political base of his own. It might seem that being high up in the Comintern was enough, said Stalin, but one had to realise that in Soviet eyes Comintern operatives were mere employees. A man who could command the loyalties of a whole town or district was bound to count for more. Doriot returned home in cynical mood, reflecting that his meteoric career in the Comintern was counting for less than he had hoped and that the PCF leadership to which he aspired would be settled by men in Moscow with their own peculiar set of criteria.

The turning-point probably came with Doriot's trip to China on a Comintern mission in 1927. Loyally toeing Stalin's pro-Kuomintang line, the mission deliberately failed to warn the Chinese Communists that it had come across hard evidence that the Kuomintang was about to turn on them. The Shanghai massacre took place shortly afterwards and Doriot, on his return to Moscow, incautiously told friends that Stalin's policy in China had been an utter disaster and the mission a disgrace. This seems to have got back to Stalin, who never fully trusted him again. An icy reception awaited him on his return to France, and the next year Thorez was confirmed as the PCF leader. Doriot was furious. Emerging from yet another spell in jail, he now openly attacked the Politburo's new 'class against class' line and questioned whether Stalin had any idea that this policy was ruining the PCF, causing both its membership and its electoral support to plummet. The Comintern representative who secretly attended this meeting of the Politburo was arrested straight afterwards on a tip-off which must have come from a Politburo member. The finger of suspicion points at Doriot: the Police said he had been the source and certainly he had a powerful interest in curtailing Comintern influence within the PCF.

From this point on, Doriot fought a sustained campaign against the Comintern line within the Politburo. Publicly he remained a loyal defender of 'class against class', for he was (rightly) certain that the policy was so suicidal that either it would destroy the PCF utterly or it would have to be reversed: in either case the fact that he alone had stuck out strongly for something more sensible would surely enable him to take over the PCF leadership. Thorez and his supporters fought back against this unwonted opposition, even at one stage forcing Doriot into a humiliating public autocritique. Meanwhile Doriot was still battling with the Police: he fought the 1928 elections while on the run, eluding the Police for four months while popping out of hiding to address election meetings. He was caught, jailed again, but again elected as deputy for St Denis from jail. This time there was no remission. He emerged from jail to find that the Party had stripped him of his colonial and youth responsibilities and he offered his resignation from the Politburo. This the PCF refused. It had lost over half of its membership in only a few years, Doriot was publicly loyal and he was the Party's only real star. He was too valuable to lose.

What Doriot wanted was to become mayor of St Denis: as député-maire of this proletarian redoubt he would have the base he needed. But the PCF made him campaign for faceless yes-men instead. A year later, the ruling PCF administration of the town split, causing fresh elections. Again, Doriot threw his huge popularity into getting another yes-man elected to the mayoralty he so badly wanted himself. This mayor too, only lasted a year before being dismissed for financial fraud. This time there could only be one choice: in 1931 Doriot at last took possession of 'his' town.

The result was astonishing. While the PCF's vote and membership slumped everywhere else, in St Denis they soared. A massive social welfare and education programme was launched and the municipal payroll hugely expanded. Doriot's benevolent but authoritarian figure was everywhere. He ran his own local paper, reinstituted civil baptisms (which he himself performed), had youth groups named after him, hob-nobbed with the local *curé*, got on famously with local businessmen and allowed White Russian exiles and the local Fascist leagues to use municipal facilities. He was everyone's friend. The Politburo ground its teeth. In Parliament Doriot now became so pally with Socialist and bourgeois Deputies that he got special government help for St Denis's huge budget deficit. Suddenly the lean ascetic was no more: he developed a taste for good restaurants, wine, Paris night-life – and became fat. His striking height was now matched by corresponding width: to one and all, he became Le Grand Jacques. The Politburo made him take a Thorez yes-man (i.e. spy) Marcel Marschal, as deputy mayor. Marschal immediately fell under Doriot's sway, becoming his loyal retainer and drinking partner. He was simply irresistible. Though publicly still loyal to the PCF line, in private he was bitterly cynical about Stalin and the Comintern. Not only did he tell the Politburo that Stalin's policy was 'imbecile and absurd': he went to Moscow to repeat this blasphemy at a Comintern meeting. But he was the PCF's star, and the Party endlessly used him as its major draw. He continued to brawl with the Police at demonstrations – a great, earthy proletarian giant who packed an awesome punch – and his personality cult grew apace. In Parliament, where he preached a national Keynesianism, Socialist Deputies promised him a 'brilliant future' if only he would switch to their side. He in turn was careful only to criticise the Socialists on such issues as their plan to limit the number of immigrant workers: 'For me the word "foreigner" has no sense', he proudly declared. An unhappy Thorez had to watch as Doriot was elected leader of the PCF parliamentary group, head of the federation of PCF mayors and boss of the Party's Central Control Commission.

In February 1934 Doriot made his break. At wildly enthusiastic mass meetings he urged that the Fascist danger was too great to allow the suicidal 'class against class' policy to continue. The fatal split between Communists and Socialists which had helped Hitler to power in Germany must not be repeated in France: there must, at all costs, be a popular front. The PCF leadership publicly condemned him for 'crimes against the working class'. A worried Comintern summoned Thorez and Doriot to Moscow. Doriot insultingly replied that he was too busy with a municipal by-election to come. The Comintern was so eager to keep him on board that it swallowed even this. So Doriot demanded a public Comintern disavowal of the whole PCF leadership before he would come. This time he was expelled.

The PCF moved quickly to isolate Doriot in St Denis, where the local Party stuck solidly by him. For a while he still went on PCF demonstrations in Paris, but these were now a calvary where he was hooted, booed and needed bodyguards to protect him. His great trump card was that his call for a broad anti-Fascist front was immensely popular, but only a few months later the PCF swung round and adopted this tactic as its own, signing a pact with the Socialists and Radicals and warning their partners that any collaboration with Doriot would threaten the new alliance. He was frozen out. The Popular Front, for which he had so courageously campaigned, was now a threat to his political survival.

Under this pressure, Doriot's political position evolved rapidly. Although the St Denis *mairie* still flew the red flag and Doriot still called himself a 'national communist', his attacks against the PCF, Stalin and the Comintern became increasingly bitter. When the Franco-Soviet Treaty was signed in 1935, Doriot attacked it as a scheme on Stalin's part to lure France into a European war. Lenin, he said, had been a revolutionary genius, but Stalinism was merely Pan-Slavism in modern guise. What Stalin really wanted was dominance over Asia. He therefore needed a free hand for a war against Japan, which in turn meant that he needed France to keep Germany under threat. France's own interests lay, above all, in keeping out of war. What mattered most was a *rapprochement* with Germany. So why not talk to Hitler? Those who wanted to place Hitler beyond the pale, who made everything conditional upon a doctrinaire anti-Fascism – i.e. the Popular Front parties – were simply playing Stalin's game. The Popular Front had made itself Doriot's enemy: it was not difficult for him to decide that it had become the enemy of France as well. Not surprisingly, French businessmen, frightened of the growing threat of the Left, began to see Doriot as a barrier against the Popular Front, and to make contributions to his cause. One of them even introduced him to Colonel La Rocque, leader of the biggest of the Fascist leagues. Doriot found La Rocque 'politically naïve', but 'a patriot, a fine French officer'.

Doriot's rightward drift was probably constrained by the need to hold St Denis, the reddest part of the red belt. The PCF knew that without this base, Doriot would pose no threat and made every effort to dispossess him of it. An orthodox PCF branch had been founded there straight after Doriot's expulsion and gradually ate into his working-class support. In 1935 Doriot had been triumphantly re-elected as mayor – right-wing voters flocking to him to compensate for the fact that he had held only fifty-five per cent of his old Communist voters. In 1936, despite the huge tide of Popular Front enthusiasm, Doriot just managed to hang on to his parliamentary seat – an astounding achievement – but the orthodox PCF candidate took over forty-eight per cent of the vote: Doriot was now very much the candidate of the Right.

Financial support for him now poured in. Le Roy Ladurie, head of the Worms bank, was a notable contributor, but the Verre, BNCI and Dreyfus banks chipped in, as did Rothschilds, Lazard Frères, the Banque de l'Indochine, all manner of employers' associations and business pressure groups, the De Wendel empire, the Comité des Forges, Rhône Poulenc, Mazda Lamps, and so on. All this money was poured into Doriot's Parti Populaire Français (PPF), founded straight after the 1936 elections. The PPF claimed that its main enemies were the PCF and social conservatism: in practice, it evolved rapidly towards a pure form of Fascism. Even at its founding congress Doriot boasted that he 'knew *Mein Kampf* well', and he was soon soliciting (and getting) a large and regular flow of funds from Mussolini and, probably (though the evidence is less clear), from Hitler.

The PPF claimed, above all, to be socialist and national, demanding a strong national state as the arbiter between corporately represented professional groups. It was staunchly for the 'defence of the working class' – but also for the peasantry and the middle class 'which constitute the very essence of the nation'. It favoured ambitious programmes of public education, hygiene and sport 'in order to fashion a stronger, healthier race'. Doriot demanded a sweeping reinforcement of the French state and empire and French neutrality abroad under the banner of 'France first'.

Above all, though, the PPF was built around Doriot. He was an electrifying orator. His clear and brutally factual style was reinforced by his awesome physical presence – in hot weather, sweating profusely, he would take his shirt off to speak, and his huge arms and body gave rhythm and cadence to his sentences. People often said that it was only by listening to him that they learnt what they had really been thinking. 'One had the impression', said one admirer, ' of being present at an enormous collective rape, effected by a power of elemental virility'. A number of talented young men of the right – Drieu La Rochelle, Bertrand de Jouvenel, Alfred Fabre-Luce, Maurice Duverger[1] – clustered round him, mingling oddly with the considerable number of working-class and PCF militants he had carried with him: Marcel Marschal, once Thorez's trusty agent, was now only one of six former Communists sitting on the PPF Politburo. The PPF's secretary-general was Henri Barbé, who had succeeded Doriot as head of the Communist Youth section. From the outset the PPF was a party of leader-worship: members took an oath to the Leader, who was also mentioned in the party hymn ('listen, O child of France, to Doriot, who calls you towards the noblest goal'). A Nazi-style salute was adopted to greet the Leader and party ceremonies made great play with a swastika-like emblem. The PPF exalted action, the necessity of violence, and instinct ('the spontaneous force of life') – all of which Doriot was taken to exemplify. Doriot never appeared now without large numbers of body-guards – usually drawn from the PPF Action Groups (i.e. street-fighters) who in turn were recruited heavily from unemployed workers (especially North African migrants). By January 1938 the PPF claimed 295,000 members: it was probably the largest French Fascist party with genuine proletarian roots, though it became steadily more middle-class all the time.

Initially Doriot made a point of saying the PPF was not anti-semitic: it had 'better things to do' than fight the Jews. The PPF was, after all, receiving large funds from three Jewish banks – Rothschilds, Lazards and Worms – and Bertrand de Jouvenel (the key bagman for PPF funds from Mussolini) was half-Jewish. But the PPF had naturally attracted fierce anti-Semites into its leadership, and its large following among the Algerian *colons* was furiously anti-Semitic. Inevitably, the PPF's anti-Semitism became steadily more pronounced, and by 1938 Doriot was regularly referring to the phenomenon of 'Judaeo-Bolshevism'. Business funds still poured in, but he also solicited secret contributions from the Police, in return for 'special services'.

The PCF meanwhile, had pressured the Blum Government into investigating Doriot for municipal fraud. This was to produce a wonderfully French political comedy. The inquiry revealed school heating bills for St Denis which were up to ten times the normal level – and corrupt arrangements with two local businessmen to whom the heating contract had been given. This had been going on ever since 1931, when St Denis had been under PCF rule, so the PCF must have known only too well what an inquiry would reveal. Doriot was revoked as mayor, resigned in a rage, and stood again in the by-election – but this time the PCF won. Doriot, utterly dashed, resigned as Deputy on the spot. The PCF won the parliamentary by-election even more resoundingly. However, Doriot's revocation as mayor was then set aside on procedural grounds. Doriot naturally trumpeted this as a complete vindication of his innocence (which it was not), and his cronies happily announced that Le Grand Jacques would become mayor once again. But to do that Doriot would have to win election to the council again – and it was clear he could not win another election in St Denis. So, prudently announcing that he had a national destiny instead, Doriot refused to run. He put Marschal in as mayor instead and ruled through him.

Although Doriot had become steadily more sympathetic to Hitler, he readily joined up in 1939: to fight, he said, not against Nazism, but as a good French nationalist against Germany. Blessed with a commander who was a PPF sympathiser, Doriot returned home in 1940 with a Croix de Guerre. He immediately rallied to Pétain and eagerly sought a position in the new Vichy Government. To curry favour with the Germans he unleashed PPF toughs on a (premature) campaign of smashing up Jewish shops and hanging Freemasons in effigy.

Thereafter it was downhill all the way. Doriot was made a member of the Vichy National Council, but was always kept at arm's length both by the Germans and by Pétain (who had never forgiven him for his anti-militarist agitation in the Twenties). Frustrated, Doriot turned to the SS and Gestapo as the 'most revolutionary' elements among the Germans, and sought to prove himself by continuously outbidding Vichy in extremism. When French Jews were deprived of their citizenship, Doriot denounced the law as insufficient and demanded that Jews be made to 'cry tears of blood': 'scientific' means and concentration camps were needed, he said, to 'cleanse' France of the Jews. In time he got his wish and the PPF eagerly volunteered to do work too dirty even for the French Police. From soliciting contributions Doriot moved to outright protection rackets and extortion and used the PPF as a spy network for the Gestapo, denouncing members of the Resistance in return for cash. He grew fat on the proceeds, indeed he had become steadily more obese, more and more addicted to night-life, to mistresses (by one of whom he had a child), and to brothels.

His great day came with the German war on Russia – Doriot cried tears of joy at the news. Against Vichy's wishes, he organised the Légion des Volontaires Français to fight Russia and went off to war with them in 1941, hoping to emerge as the new (and this time successful) Napoleon, carrying the French flag on a great victory parade through Moscow. This dream took an initial knock when the Germans insisted that the LVF, Doriot included, should wear German uniform. Worse still was to come. The LVF, by the winter of 1941, found itself, ironically, at Borodino, where they suffered much the same fate as Napoleon. Within a month the Russians and the cold had killed half of them. The rest had to be pulled back from the front. Thereafter the LVF was only used against partisans, alternating between cosy unofficial agreements with their opponents and spasms of unspeakable atrocity against civilians. Doriot hurried back to Paris after just a few months, lighter by three stone, and only once appeared at the front again.

Doriot's great hope was that the PPF – now really just a few thousand thugs, barely able to protect Doriot from the repeated assassination attempts mounted by Communist Resistants – would be declared the single party of the Vichy regime. Failing that, he hoped, at least, to be made Minister of Jewish Affairs. But the Germans realised only too well that Doriot was now probably the best-hated man in France: he was accorded the sublime accolade of a visit to Hitler in the Wolf's Lair, but that was all. After D-Day he and his remaining followers fell back over the Rhine with the retreating Germans – during the train ride PPF militants competed for the favour of their German fellow-travellers with lovingly detailed accounts of the atrocities they had committed (some had been helping Klaus Barbie). Doriot was convinced that his moment had at last come. A Committee of National Liberation was set up to plan the Fascist restoration in France. (Doriot was furious at the German suggestion that they set up their headquarters in the Schloss Stauffenberg. How could he feel at home in a castle confiscated from the leader of the July plotters against the Führer?) His days were spent in frantic intrigues over the composition of the future Fascist government of France and tugging at the sleeves of all who would listen to tell them that Hitler's secret weapons would still win the war. Did they not know that there was a V3 rocket which could bombard New York? In the Reich's death agony Doriot had somehow procured unlimited supplies of fine wine and food. He was still living extremely well when, in March 1945, the car in which he was travelling was strafed to bits by Allied planes. The faithful Marschal delivered the funeral oration over the almost unrecognisable corpse.

How to explain the career of a man who went from the extremes of militant Communist self-sacrifice to this Götterdämmerung in the twilight of the Third Reich? There are three clues. One is sheer ambition: Doriot believed most of all in his own star. He would take second place to no one. What he wanted most of all was to be leader of the PCF – long after he had left the Party he would regale crowds of right-wing extremists with accounts of how he had been unjustly thwarted in that ambition. His systematic tactic for achieving his ends was the dramatic outflanking movement. He would show Thorez up by going endlessly to jail, by getting into street fights, by being more militant than anyone. Then he would outflank him by calling for a popular front when he knew the Comintern was not ready to allow Thorez to do the same. When Thorez did follow suit, the alternatives of submission or leaving to become a junior oddity in the Socialist Party were equally demeaning and thus unacceptable. He had to found the PPF, he had to be leader of a party, that immense ego had to be gratified. Later, he tried to outflank Pétain and Laval by displays of Hitlerite enthusiasm he knew they could not match. He was always consumed by the injustice of the fact that sheer militancy was never quite enough.

The second point is that Doriot was a classic inter-war political boss. As one reads of his rule in St Denis, one is irresistibly reminded of the political machines which ruled New York, Chicago, Huey Long's Louisiana or even Leningrad in the same period. The pattern of rackets, extortion, jobbery through expanded municipal services, the ubiquitous bully-boys, the populist cult of the man of the people who had become the Boss, has a wide resonance. One wonders, even, how necessary politics was to it all. How different was Doriot's little empire in St Denis from Capone's in Cicero?

The final clue is surely Doriot's size. While he was a revolutionary militant he was ascetically thin: when he became a Communist boss he became fat; as his career veered frenetically away from its origins, he became grossly obese. Food and drink are metaphors as well as necessities. Doriot's increasingly rapacious intake of both must have been part-compensation, partly a matter of in for a penny, in for a pound: as one reads of the grossness of his later years one wonder whether sheer self-disgust may not also have played some part. But surely, too, it was a simple matter of self-fulfilment, of gratification of ego? We are told that inside every fat man there is a thin man trying to get out. Doriot may have been a case of the opposite: inside the ascetic revolutionary there was a corpulent high-liver dying to get out. What we know of Doriot's sexual habits suggest a similar progression from puritan self-denial to grotesque over-indulgence. One wonders, too, about the significance of that early religious childhood, the marriage in church, the willingness to have his children brought up as Catholics, his friendship with the local *curé* even while a Communist, his Vichy-period glorification of the Church as the essential spirit of France . . ..

Probably Doriot himself did not know the answers to these questions. Late in his career as Fascist leader, he still kept a portrait of Lenin at his bedside. Perhaps Lenin was the father he wished he had had. And despite all the grotesquerie of his later days, the memory of Doriot the heroic proletarian militant dies hard. Going round the Parisian Red Belt in 1967, I found that more than one

Communist home still had pictures of him on the wall. Amazed, I asked a PCF organiser how this could be. He shrugged. 'It's not so unnatural', he said: 'A une certaine époque il était une grande figure. Il était Le Grand Jacques.'

Note

1. Fabre-Luce writes today in *Le Monde*, and has done for many years, while Duverger is still one of the great luminaries of French political science. He was bitterly disappointed that Mitterrand did not appoint him a member of the Constitutional Council. But everyone on the Left holds against him the fact that one of his earliest academic articles was an examination of the Vichy law to deprive French Jews of citizenship. It was a prelude to what followed: once they were not citizens, you could do anything to them. Duverger, in his article, took the attitude that the law was no bad thing. This will never be forgotten. So while he is the author of a best-selling book on political parties and of another now on *Cohabitation*, the shadow of his PPF period has scarred his whole life. Most French academics think it is a great shame and that a young man should be forgiven his follies – a view not shared by French Jews.

References

Brunet, Jean-Paul (1986) *Jacques Doriot: Du Communisme au Fascisme* (Paris: Balland)

Chapter 4
Doctor Feelgood

It is already getting to be quite difficult to believe that Ronald Reagan was ever America's President – but then, of course, it was always quite difficult to believe at the time. The fact that such a man could also be politically the most successful President since Eisenhower, perhaps even since Roosevelt, was both an extraordinary fluke and an interesting comment on the American political system. It ought by now to be clear that the whole literature spawned by Richard Neustadt's Presidential Power, *which encourages us to think of the Chief Executive as the key activist influence on the whole political system – is simply wrong. The fact is that it does not seem to matter too much if the President has Mafia connections and spends too much of his time screwing around (JFK), is a psychopathic bully who enjoys humiliating advisers by making them advise him while he sits on the lavatory (LBJ), is organising burglaries and having a nervous breakdown (Nixon), is a complete idiot who uses the Presidency mainly as a springboard towards his chosen career of golf commentator (Ford), is a man so obsessive about delegation that he ends up being the man who has to arrange the bookings for the White House tennis courts (Carter) – or is even an ignorant, superstitious old actor. The fact is that America goes on whoever is in the White House.*

Reagan was wise enough to know this, adopted a noticeably 'hands off' style of management, and always kept his sleep and his holidays high on the agenda. The world began his presidency alarmed that he might start a war. It took some time for the realisation to sink in that Ronnie was not only temperamentally unsuited to war-making but that his whole management style precluded anything requiring too much sustained attention or concentration. Many dreadful things did happen under his Administration – from the Korean airliner affair through literally hundreds of CIA interventions in the Third World to the mounting debt problems (Third World debt, Savings and Loan debt, Budget debt, Consumer debt,

Corporate debt and cumulative Trade Deficit debt, all save one at record levels) – but the first question for later historians will always be, how much did the President even know about his own Administration?

'Would you believe', asked Ronald Reagan, opening his campaign for Governor in 1966, 'that 15.1 per cent of the population of California is on welfare?' A pretty shocking figure, you might think, for the Golden State in the midst of the Vietnam War boom: no wonder Reagan's well-heeled backers were so righteously indignant about all their tax money going to all those layabouts. But we have not answered the question: would you believe it? Well no, actually – the real figure was 5.1 per cent. Unfazed, Ronnie's backers simply redoubled their efforts and their campaign contributions. The expert handler put in to manage him discovered that 'he knew zero about California when we came in, I mean zero'. Instead, everything had to be reduced to little memorisable gobbets on 5- x 8-inch cards and, above all, Ron had to have a handler with him at every waking moment: 'goofproofing Reagan was a task that called for eternal vigilance.'

Riding a tide of conservative money, Ronnie was duly elected. Then, discovering that the Chief Justice who had to swear him in was a liberal, Ronnie simply broke with precedent, dispensing with the Chief Justice and promoting a conservative Associate Justice in his place. Although Ronnie was, even then, not famous for intellectual (or other kinds of) effort or hands-on management, the swearing-in ceremony was to be staged at ten past midnight after his predecessor's last day in office, to dramatise the urgency with which Reagan was keen to set about fulfilling his campaign promises. But Ronnie swears by astrology and his astrologer warned that the hour of 12.10 was astrally unfavourable. No matter, 12.01 would suggest even greater breathless urgency for the cameras. Unable to understand the California budget, our man Ron then carried out a simple 10 per cent cut in everything. This produced chaos, U-turns, and an out-of-control financial process, from which Reagan was rescued by the arrival, at long last, of a competent finance director, one Caspar Weinberger . . ..

Almost all the key elements of the Reagan Presidency were already evident: the cheerful invention and trumpeting of 'facts' which turn out to be, at best, factoids, the happy ignorance of the world about him, even the local world he had been living and working in for years; the complete reliance on, and thus the authority of, the handlers and men of any competence; the utter primacy of public relations over substance; the application of ideological simple-mindedness to an intransigent reality, and the consequent need for sharp U-turns. Send the Marines to Lebanon, pull the Marines out of Lebanon, hooray photo opportunities with the heroes as they set out, sombre and moving photo opportunities with them as they come back in body bags, just keep those cameras whirring. Above all, as Garry Wills points out, Reagan not only tells fairy-tales (informing the Israeli premier of how he had seen the terrible suffering of the Jewish people while filming, the concentration camps at the end of the war – when in fact he'd never left America) but lives in a sort of fairyland of his own.

Garry Wills has established a well-deserved reputation as one of the most acute and literate observers of the American past and present, and his volume (Wills, 1988) is a delightful read, often very funny, sharply thoughtful and analytical, always telling: it will have a deservedly large success. (I hope, though, that Wills changes his publishers, I would not stay with someone who fulfils a classic author's nightmare by getting his name wrong on the dust-jacket.) But it is important to say what the book is and is not. It is not, or not very much, about Reagan's America or the Reagan Presidency. It is a lengthy biography of Ron (and Jane and Nancy), in which each episode – sportscaster, movie star, company propagandist, Governor, and so on – is examined in the light of the President Ron we have come to known and boggle at. The result is the definitive analysis of a personality and a career – and the fact that Wills is often kind and forgiving towards his subject makes his softly-spoken conclusions all the more ineluctable and devastating.

That said, the danger in these elaborate dissections of personality is that the secret is not there. There is a tendency to believe that, when someone is, like Reagan or Thatcher, greatly successful or even, like Nixon, a spectacular failure, there must be something special, almost magical about them as a person. In the wake of Reagan's second and Thatcher's third election victory we had to endure a surfeit of this sort of thing. And yet the truth is so prosaic. Mrs Thatcher is an extremely limited woman, energetic and ruthless, but seldom able politically to see very far ahead, innocent of economic knowledge, and equipped only with the right-wing suburban views common on the Tory back-benches in the 1950s when she entered Parliament. She owes her success to the normal, ordinary reasons – determination, energy, luck and circumstance. The nearest thing to a 'secret' in her career is that she managed, in her youth, to come across a millionaire somewhat older than herself who was seeking consolation from a failed marriage to another blonde, also called Margaret. Lo, the grocer's daughter became a millionairess. What Mrs Thatcher preaches is that we should all go out and make money by hard work: what she actually did herself was to marry money, give up paid work, hire others to work for her, and dedicate herself to becoming first an MP, then a minister, and so on. Without Denis's money her whole career would have been simply inconceivable. This is the truth of the matter – though you will wait a very long time indeed if you want to hear anyone admit this on radio or television.

Similarly, to conduct an endless quest for the secret depths of Reagan's 'Doctor Feelgood' personality is a bit like searching through the *Reader's Digest* for great literature: if you are not careful, you end up discussing the literary merits of 'The Most Unforgettable Character I've Ever Met'. It makes more sense to see Reagan as merely a living monument to the banal power of the media in politics. If you are going to have, as the Americans do, a political system which makes television performance the key to political success, which allows the richer party to buy unlimited TV time and which effectively allows no limit to the money that can be spent in pursuit of office, it is fairly predictable that the winning combination will be a screen pro standing for the Rich Man's Party. And in this class, Reagan achieves a sort of perfection, because, for him, only the media is real. To be fair, this is a perception which is more and more widely shared. Look how our own newspapers and airwaves are nowadays saturated with endless non-news about the non-real world of the media and entertainment. The death of a minor character actor, or even, god save us, a news announcer, will get far more airtime than the demise of a major scientist or philosopher. In the world of the media, a Jack Benny or an Eamonn Andrews are far bigger men than Sartre. Similarly, the media are a thousand times more interested in *Dallas* and *Dynasty*, *Coronation Street* and *Eastenders*, than in anything that actually happens in Texas, let alone working-class Liverpool and London. Only the non-real is important and thus, in the end, real. In the United States, this sort of thing is old hat, and Ronnie, living and working in radio and films all his life, internalised all this long ago. For him, reality was always plastic, particularly since his only excursion into highbrow culture was the *Reader's Digest*. How many more clues do we have to have when a President explains his foreign policies to us by saying: 'Now I've seen *Rambo*, I'll know what to do?' The vulgar trash of pop culture is what this man looks to for explanation and inspiration. Again, no deep secrets here.

Wills is perceptive about the way in which the Reagan Presidency has involved the use of Ronnie's beliefs by people who do not really share them, perhaps the best example being SDI. There seems little doubt that Ronnie has the complete Disneyland view of this project, that he really believes that lasers which can destroy things from space somehow do not have offensive capability, and that he has wholly failed to understand how the project threatens the strategic balance. But he could be allowed to bumble happily on in this fashion – while those around him grasped SDI as a way of moving up to the next phase of weapons technology, pushing huge sums to arms contractors, establishing military supremacy in space, threatening the Russians and frightening them into weakening their own economic system through military overspending. 'All these motives', writes Wills, 'were jostling along together under the cover of the Reagan fairy-tale, each gaining advantages so long as the fairy-tale was neither questioned nor taken seriously'. Every now and again Ronnie would break free of his handlers and make jokes about launching a nuclear war, or suggest that the United States made a present of SDI technology to the Russians, or reveal that he believed submarine-launched missiles could be recalled in midflight, or that trees were a major source of pollution. There would then be a rush by aides, and if necessary, by Ron, to say that he had been 'misunderstood', 'misquoted', or, if you got right down to it, that he had plain 'misspoke' – a telling admission that policy statements were seen merely as lines or script that Ron had to get through. Mainly our man hams his way through very satisfactorily, but occasionally, like any other actor, he misspeaks. So what's the big deal? We'll do SDI again now, Ron, this time without the 'Let's give it all away to the Russians' line. Uh, well, Mr President, in the next scene you have this line about maximum security being necessary for all European and Japanese work done on SDI and the desperate importance of preventing high-technology transfers to the USSR. Sorta confuses the fans if you're offering the highest tech of all to 'em as a kinda present. OK? OK. Lights. Action. Take Two!

It is, though, high time we all stopped just having fun with the largely unfunny Reagan Presidency and began to ask what it all means. The first thing to notice is what the Reagan phenomenon says about America's lack of a true ruling class. The heart and guts of any Republican administration in the old days generally derived from Northern, Ivy League Wasps, frequently from 'old money' New England families. This class has been mocked and pilloried, but it remains true that it was often well-educated, sophisticated, and had a genuine ethic of public service. After Eisenhower, the Republican Party has slipped further and further beyond the control of such groups.

The early 1960s saw the rise of Goldwater, a Jewish supermarket millionaire from the far West, while the Nixon Administration brought to Washington a veritable mafia of get-rich-quick Floridans and Californians who, to put it mildly, were not overly weighed down by a public service ethic. Henry Cabot Lodge had give way to Bebe Rebozo. Watergate scattered this group in all directions (including jail) and it took some imagination to believe that much the same group would take over power again just six years later – but this is exactly what happened. Reagan re-installed such Nixon stalwarts as Haig, Shultz, Weinberger and Casey, while Ed Meese and Larry Speakes gave imitations of John Mitchell and Ron Ziegler which had all but the *cognoscenti* fooled. This time, however, there were no residual concessions to the Eastern Establishment – no Harvard professors like Kissinger (indeed, virtually no eggheads or Jews), and this time the constraints of the old public service ethic were virtually non-existent. These get-rich-quick, self-made men from the South-West brought to politics the same instinct for corner-cutting that they had shown in their business careers, and the Administration was quickly acknowledged as the most corrupt since Harding's. The extraordinary resilience of this group suggests it is here to stay in future Republican administrations. A group that can bounce back so quickly from a Watergate can ride right through an Irangate.

It is, though, difficult to talk of this group as a new class. There is, perhaps, some comparison with the more petty-bourgeois tone of Thatcher's Tory Party, but the truth is that the main impression is of a group of pushing, hustling, huckstering individuals with very little sense of the institutional or social continuities necessary to the constitution of a class. Instead, such men appear virtually as naked brokers for powerful interests, selling themselves and their services to the highest bidder. There is very little mediation of commercial interest through the prism of class in such a situation. As one reviews the saga of Irangate, chronicled in Leslie Cockburn's *Out of Control* (1988), one is struck by the way in which this cast of cocaine-dealers, thugs, arms salesmen, retired generals, right-wing nuts, Third World guerrillas and many other bizarre characters simply flows through the 'policy-making process'. Who owns whom is never easy to say, particularly since most of the cast are always available for rent. Eisenhower's Administration – the last one to stand up successfully against the pressure for increased military spending – seems part of a lost age now. Ike could even warn publicly of the 'military industrial complex' – though only on leaving office, with no more elections to finance and fight. It is difficult indeed to imagine any administration bringing such interests to heel now, or indeed to imagine such words so much as crossing the lips of aspiring Presidential candidates.

On the whole, of course, the haves have in a general way – particularly employers – done well out of the Reagan period, but there is no doubt that the dominant interest has been that of the arms manufacturers. Never before in peacetime has an administration been so peopled with the products of the arms industry: never has the Pentagon been so much under the thumb of its main suppliers; and never before in peacetime have the demands of the Pentagon been so binding on an entire administration. It is best to avoid the normal jokes about the $100 spanner, or the $1,000 toilet seat, or about having an Assistant Secretary of Defense (Paul Thayer) in jail – these are the mere ephemera of an administration utterly devoted to pouring hundreds of billions of dollars towards Lockheed, Boeing, Rockwell, General Dynamics, Martin Marietta and so on. Even though there is no money to pay for it. Even though this means a huge budget deficit, means cutting back on education and social spending, means borrowing abroad, means becoming a debtor nation, means the collapse of the currency. Whatever the consequences, the 'defence' industries have got to have their monetary fix. The armourers have never thrived like this before.

The irony is that this extraordinary arms build-up was begun with the chuckling intent that the Soviets would have to match it, could not afford to, and would thus spend themselves into economic collapse. In fact, there was no answering surge in Soviet military spending, for the Soviet economy was collapsing of its own accord. The entire Soviet threat had been grotesquely exaggerated. The US is now left with vast heaps of useless weapons and a mountainous debt. What should not be forgotten is that the rationale for the whole exercise was provided by a sudden, enormous and false re-estimating of Soviet military potential in 1976. The more or less openly crazed Team B, led by Richard Pipes, was invited by the CIA to rework the Agency's established estimates of its rival's strength in such a way that the only possible thing for the United States to do was to conduct a massive and feverish arms build-up. The figures arrived at by Team B are now acknowledged to have been nonsense – indeed, a wholly ideological construct. This was, actually, perfectly obvious at the time, but the CIA director who allowed Pipes and his merry men to get their hands into the cookie jar was a weak man, less concerned with doing his job properly than with staying on the right side of the powerful conservative lobbies. This, rather than anything to do with Irangate, is the real reason why that CIA director, George Bush, would probably be no improvement on

Reagan as President, and could well be worse.

There is little doubt that the fundamental force which put Reagan into office was a growing sense of public unease at American imperial decline. (Already in 1976 Gerald Ford's posters had read 'Don't Follow England Down the Drain!') But the real meaning of Reaganism is that instead of recognising the inevitability of that decline and attempting, Kissinger-like, to manage it, Dr Feelgood thought the fans would like it better if you just insisted the whole phenomenon did not exist and acted as if that were so. You got better lines to speak that way. When Jimmy Carter spoke worriedly of a 'national *malaise*', or Walter Mondale spoke about the inevitability of higher taxes, people thought it was all a bit sombre and downbeat. And only deadbeats are downbeat – always better, especially in America, to be upbeat. The fans like it more. And the fans did like it more – they liked it four more years more. In effect, they were invited in to share Ron's warm little fantasy world with him and were happy to do so. Garry Wills cites the reaction of one of Ron's fans faced with some of his more overtly crazy statements: 'Well, even Jesus spoke in parables' – truly the cry of someone keen to stay a believer.

Reagan's childlike refusal to face realities has greatly accelerated American decline, and even some of the fans have begun to wake up to that. America is moving rapidly towards trillion-dollar debtor status; the country has lost its high-tech lead in industry after industry; the dollar is at an all-time low; and Reagan will bequeath to the nation an enormously increased military establishment – such as Navy Secretary John Lehmann's famous 600-ship fleet, designed to be capable of fighting three different wars in separate theatres simultaneously. Just to maintain this establishment is going to be ruinously expensive – and of course the tidal wave of expenditure lavished on the defence industries has only made them richer and more powerful players of pressure politics. Whatever happens, there will have to be some very painful choices.

Reagan has, in a sense, been a poor man's Harold Macmillan. Macmillan disposed of most of the British Empire in a few years and led us down the slope to complete nuclear dependence on the United States. But he did all this with such panache, and with so many brave words about Europe, the future, the Commonwealth and never having had it so good, that he was lauded as Super-Mac and the whole process of decline was carefully disguised as its opposite. The difference is that Super-Mac knew very well what he was doing, while Ron will be the last person in America to realise what he has done. But if you only bother about the media you will never know what is going on, especially since American predominance at the level of popular culture and the media seems to wax ever greater even as American economic power wanes.

It may not, in fact, matter very much who wins the next American Presidential election, or indeed the one after that. Maybe we should be thinking, not of 1988 or 1992, but of 1996. America has no real alternative to continuing imperial decline: the big questions are simply how fast and how peacefully. The problem is that the arms industries will fund any and every Presidential candidate and, whoever wins, those industries will demand to be fed. It is unclear, though, whether Americans at large are willing to accept the sacrifices this may entail. As the American debt grows, the choice will become stark: paying off the debt – or, more realistically, never paying more than just the interest on the debt – will require either large tax increases, or a deep recession, or a huge inflation. The American public will vote for inflation as the least painful solution: somewhere out there in the years to come there is a giant inflation of almost Weimar proportions waiting to happen. But the banks will hate that, as will virtually all the other business interests (including the arms manufacturers) who are full voting members of the American democracy. The people's candidate, if such there be, will thus find him or herself fighting for inflation against a probably unbeatable coalition of the haves. We have seen all this before, of course – in the great Populist crusade of 1896, when William Jennings Bryan unforgettably complained that the American people were being crucified on a cross of gold. The candidate of 1996 is more likely to phrase his lament in terms of ECUs or Yen than of gold, but if he is a literate man or woman he/she will surely nurse a special grievance against the man who spoke of his country as that 'shining city on the hill', when in fact he was rushing it towards a ravine. Ah well, he misspoke.

References

Cockburn, Leslie (1988) *Out of Control: The Story of the Reagan Administration's Secret War in Nicaragua, the Illegal Arms Pipeline and the Contra Drug Connection* (London: Bloomsbury).

Neustadt, Richard E. (1980) *Presidential Power. The Politics of Leadership from FDR to Carter* (New York: Wiley).

Wills, Garry (1988) *Reagan's America: Innocents at Home* (London: Heinemann).

Chapter 5
Tony Benn, Neil Kinnock and the Travails of Labour

People read what they want to in an article. Depite all my disclaimers, what I wrote below was widely received as a snobbish insistence that you had to go to Oxford to be Prime Minister and that those who had not been to Oxford were not good enough. This earned me a certain amount of populist abuse. Sadly, perhaps, nobody else up to that point had been quite as brutal in print as I was below about Neil Kinnock. In the months that followed there was an avalanche of similar criticism about this essentially nice man, and I felt a little guilty about apparently having started all that snow into motion.

The Opposition is at a low ebb. Labour consoles itself for its third defeat, in 1987, with the thought that at least its leader put up a good show and the Party was well prepared and ran a good campaign. None of these things was true: Kinnock trailed Thatcher massively in the leader polls and was far less popular than his party; the campaign, largely a matter of a few videos and avoiding the London press, was good only in comparision with Foot's; and the Party was so ill-prepared that, despite four years of reflection, it was still chronically unsure even about such key issues as its taxation policy. For some years now, the most impressive intellectual input to the Kinnock camps has been that of Eric Hobsbawm, who is actually a member of quite another party, a fact which is surely comment enough in itself. But Labour still exists, which the Alliance no longer does. In their different ways all the members of the old Gang of Four have effectively admitted that it was 1987 or bust. Three of them have moved purposefully towards retirement while the fourth seems to have gone mad. The resulting collapse in

Alliance support has seen the Tories reach 50 per cent in the polls, a fact which, like the tremors from the Stock Exchange, is uncomfortably reminiscent of the 1930s. Why has the Opposition done so badly? Two recent books afford a clue (Benn, 1987, and Wainwright, 1987).

Tony Benn's diaries are full of interest, in many ways the more so because we already have such plentiful diaristic accounts of the 1964–70 Labour Government. (Benn reveals, incidentally, that Harold Wilson promised that he would publish posthumously the *real* inside story of his government). Many of the incidents and personalities that Benn describes are now of historical interest only, as indeed is the great battle he fought for the right to disclaim his title. This, together with his struggle as Postmaster-General to have stamps issued without the Queen's head, occupies no little part of these diaries, and in both cases Benn argues that, though the issues were small, they provide a chilling insight into the machinations of the Establishment and the dense and pervasive network which operates in this country to throttle democratic impulses.

Benn's attempt to hype up the significance of these two battles in the anti-Establishment struggles seems almost deliberately naïve. Few passages are more unconsciously telling than that in which he describes how his triumphant re-entry to the Commons as a commoner in October 1963 was spoilt by the ironical cheering of Tory MPs celebrating Lord Home's appointment as premier, made possible only through Benn's Act. This, he records, 'discomfited the Labour Members and confused the nature of the victory'. I am not sure it did confuse it. After all, such an Act was always likely to be most useful to the Tories, enjoying as they do the support of the overwhelming bulk of peers, and the new phenomenon of life peers spawned by Benn's Act has simply breathed fresh life and respectability into the whole institution of the peerage. And surely the true significance of the battle of the stamps was that it symbolises so exactly the way in which those full of zeal to abolish private schools, redistribute wealth or bring about rapid economic growth end up by doing nothing whatsoever about such things while getting enormously waxed up about matters like hare-coursing, motorway speed limits, British policy towards Anguilla or Antigua, and whether or not the sovereign's head is on stamps. It is all very well for Benn to inveigh against the way in which the Establishment deflects reforming politicians, but for this to work such politicians, in the last analysis, have to be willing to be deflected. As these diaries only too copiously show, Benn was willingly deflected into all manner of things.

Whether or not he realises it, he emerges from these diaries as an earnest, good-natured man of a naïvety so complete as to verge, occasionally, upon stupidity. If one puts that together with the unforgettable picture of Benn which emerges from Susan Crosland's biography of Tony Crosland – Benn ringing up at all hours with phone pranks, practical jokes, impersonations and Goon Show voices – one realises that the common strand is a good-hearted boyishness. Far from being the sinister ogre of the hard Left, Benn is, simply and irretrievably, an honourable schoolboy. One senses that his later radicalism springs from the same source. Early on, he seems to have swallowed the whole school prospectus and everything the Head said on speech days, a reaction to which the son of a Labour MP sent to a private school was more vulnerable than most. He set out to serve his constituents with a truly rare unselfishness and worked with an even rarer zeal as a minister for what he saw as the national good. But late in the day – long after the period covered by these diaries – he seems to have realised that the Head was not quite the Arnold he presented himself as, that the prefects were smoking behind the cricket pavilion, that the teachers were trying to seduce the boys, and that the whole prospectus was a fraud. His reaction was an outraged sense of honour, a righteous indignation knowing no bounds, and a root-and-branch denunciation of the school in terms of the rather pious school ethic, now clung to more fiercely than ever. God knows what actually happened to Benn at Westminster to explain all this.

But the real drama, of course, is the fate of the 1964–70 Government, which remains, far more than that of 1974–9, the real turning-point for Labour. For Labour came to power in 1964 with the most talented team it had ever had, with an economy rolling along in the midst of a world boom, with full employment, and a winning set of policies. Power over long-term economic planning had to be taken away from the Treasury, which, in the crunch, always sacrificed everything to protect the pound, and given to a new ministry which would make growth the watchword. To ensure that this growth did not lead to wage inflation, an incomes policy would be imposed from the start; and to ensure that industry became more competitive, a strong attack would be made on overmanning by means of a payroll tax. The basic assumption – surely correct – was that you could shake out labour and even hold wages back provided you could maintain steady growth – which would mean that there were always other jobs to go to and that wages would be rising nicely anyhow. The unspoken assumption was that if the currency had to take the strain, so be it. There was nothing particularly socialist about this, but if you could get growth you could spend more on schools, pensions, housing, and all the other things socialists like making speeches about. These were almost certainly workable policies – and they were effectively abandoned by Wilson, Callaghan and Brown on the night of the election victory when it was decided to give top priority to defending the pound. With that fateful decision went the best chance Labour may ever have; after thirteen years of waiting and planning and passionate commitment, the Party simply blew it. The shock-waves from that awesome failure are still with us.

What one looks for in vain in Benn's book is any recognition of the great turning-points of that government. He had greeted the news of Wilson's victory in the leadership contest as 'wonderful and incredible', but even by June 1964 he relates how he, Crossman, Balogh and Shore had 'discussed fully Harold Wilson's complete failure to consult with us collectively . . . .. The disillusionment with Harold has set in quite firmly now.' This disillusionment gathered pace as the sheer triviality and day-to-day nature of Wilson's management was born in upon the government as a whole. And yet nothing happened. At no stage did any member of the Government resign because the Party had abandoned its entire economic project, because it had done the very opposite of all it had promised, or because the situation was irremediable while Wilson remained Prime Minister. The nearest anyone came to this was George Brown in July 1966, when, to save the pound, the Government launched a wage freeze and a great wave of deflationary measures in the full knowledge that this would lead to higher unemployment. But even Brown, who was always resigning about everything, could not manage to do it on the one occasion it would really have counted – for a resignation by a senior minister at that stage would soon have made him or her an irresistible leadership candidate. Benn frequently mentions in his diaries that this or that minister is talking about resigning, but he always says that he is against anyone resigning, and while he shares the general opinion that Wilson is hopeless, he seems to regard him as a cross which just has to be borne. This curiously passive attitude seems to have gripped the whole government – and utterly doomed it.

Why was this? Partly, of course, love of office: all these ministers had been out in the cold for a very long time and were enormously enjoying their brief place in the sun. But there *were* some resignations, just never on the central issue of the economic U-turn. The awful truth is that this caused fewer flutters than worries over Rhodesia, policy east of Suez, cutting the Navy too much or even the god-damned stamps. On the very last page of Benn's diary we see, perhaps, the reason why: 1967, he records, 'was the year of devaluation, when we finally realised that we couldn't hold the exchange rate and later wondered why we had ever tried to do so'. The comment is so flip that it seems clear that Benn – and his case was far from unusual – had simply not understood properly either what Labour's economic policy was supposed to have been or quite what a dreadful betrayal the top priority for sterling had been. The fateful decision by Wilson, Brown and Callaghan revealed that none of the party leaders had believed very much in the policies they had just been elected on: Benn's comment shows that they were hardly alone. Later on, Mr Callaghan, when leading the next Labour government, made a positive virtue out of the fact that he did not much believe in *anything*.

The real lessons of all this do not, as Benn seems to think, relate to the cunning and sophistication of the Establishment, but to a more general point about seriousness of purpose. Mrs Thatcher has been handing out an object lesson for years now in how an economic strategy – thoroughly understood and internalised by *all* government members – can change the whole shape of the political realm if it is consistently deployed over a period of years and forced through against all difficulties. The electorate has shown, too, that it is not necessary for Mrs Thatcher to be liked, not necessary for her to play it week by week like Wilson – she can survive her Westlands and her banana skins, because she retains widespread respect for her determined seriousness of purpose. She knows what she believes in; she believes in it passionately; she will not be deflected. The way in which both Labour and the Alliance have already begun to indicate that they no longer feel much commitment to a lot of what they were exhorting us all to vote for just a few months ago suggests that this point has still not been taken.

So great was the failure and disappointment of the 1964–70 Government that the whole Labour coalition began to unravel and fragment – a process which still continues today. Some crossed to the Tories or Liberals, some retreated into abstention, others left to form the SDP, others to virtually independent factions – Militant, feminist groups, black groups, the UDM/Eric Hammond 'realists', CND, and, in all the major cities, a whole series of strongly differentiated local party factions. The fundamental mistake in Hilary Wainwright's book is that she mistakes this fragmentation – a sort of slow dying – for a new birth. The two parties of her title are 'old' Labourism, on the one hand, and a vital, vibrant new party which is emerging 'subterraneanly', to use the equally new adjective that she herself favours – a presumed coalition of women, blacks,

CND, left-wing councils and so forth. What she clearly foresees is a complete take-over of the Labour Party by these new forces, or perhaps their formation into a separate socialist movement, the very themes surprise, surprise, of the Bennite's alternative party conference at Chesterfield. Given that Ms Wainwright was one of the organisers of the Chesterfield conference – apparently to become an annual event – one might have thought that she would have realised that for a party to stage two separate annual conferences was about the most extreme sign of fragmentation one could get. Similarly, one wonders whether her easy presumption of an effective coalition between the warring fragments of the Labour Left has not encountered certain factual difficulties.

To put it mildly, Ms Wainwright's book is not strong on fact. Its interest lies simply in its being a sort of wondrous compendium of myths currently prevalent on the Labour Left and the way in which inconsistencies in argument go simply unnoticed. Past Labour governments are berated by her because they did not stick to their manifestos – but Ms Wainwright, until recently in charge of something called the Popular Planning Unit at the GLC, is blithely approving about the way in which parts of the London Manifesto were abandoned as impractical. The growth of black and women's sections is greeted with such enthusiasm as a sign of renewal that it passed without notice that the Labour Party membership is still falling overall, with the likely corollary that black and women's membership is falling too. There is, amidst the approving quotes from Sharon Atkin, no mention of the fact that a discernible fringe of Asian voters trickled over to the Tories for the first time in 1987. Or again, Ms Wainwright makes much of the fact that a council as Left as Liverpool could twice, in 1983 and 1984, get as much as 46 per cent of the vote, and yet, like Arthur Scargill, she also supports proportional representation and talks blithely of the day when Labour will win an absolute majority under PR. The fact that Labour has never in its entire history won 50 per cent of the vote or that PR would have kept the Left out of power in Liverpool goes unremarked. Whenever she meets a poser of this sort Ms Wainwright retreats into furious denunciation of the Labour leadership for 'failing to challenge the terms of public debate', which often seems to mean that the right use of words could somehow have changed the facts.

But this is nothing compared to the treatment of those two great myths, the miners' strike and the GLC. The former is treated as a great socialist crusade which failed largely due to the treasons of the Labour Right, but which had an enduring effect in bringing a new popular consciousness to birth, particularly among the Women's Support groups. At one point the electricians' union is chastised for failing to support the strike, and the fact that the EEPTU 'went through the formality of a ballot' on the issue is seen as the final cynicism. At no point is there any mention of the NUM's failure to hold a ballot, nor, in this version, does the UDM exist. There is also no mention of the fact that the NUM, though one of the richest unions in the country, refused, throughout the strike, to give strike pay, despite the terrible suffering of miners' families – but carried on paying its officials, such as Mr Scargill, quite normally. Similarly, one would never guess that the union was simultaneously playing ducks and drakes with huge sums in the Euromarkets, ultimately losing much of their money, or that the strike was financed quite largely from loans taken out from other unions, creating debts that the NUM had signally failed to honour. After the strike was over, the NCB quietly admitted that it had been much influenced by the constant in-depth polling it had done of miners' families, which had, *inter alia*, shown that throughout the strike a clear majority of miners' wives always wanted their husbands to return to work. The Miners' Wives Support Committees no doubt put on a bonny show but they were never representative: the prolongation of the strike has to be seen as a victory, not for socialist feminism, but for the male chauvinism of miners willing to ignore what their wives thought. There is no room for such uncomfortable facts here.

It is much the same with the GLC. Ms Wainwright assumes throughout that the Livingstone regime was a major political success, winning large numbers of converts for its brand of radical socialism. It is a pity she, and Ken Livingstone for that matter, did not bother to study how Herbert Morrison first turned London into a Labour stronghold. Having captured London for Labour for the first time in 1934, with a campaign of textbook thoroughness, Morrison insisted that Labour must, in its first term, avoid flamboyant symbolic gestures. Instead, it must make London a showcase of its capacity to govern – which meant winning the trust of the middle ground simply by being the most efficient, decisive and energetic administration London had ever seen. Only after you had won people's trust on that basis, Morrison believed, could you hope to attract their support for more partisan causes dear to your heart. After three years of this, Labour had so consolidated its hold that although the Tories mounted a tremendous assault to recapture London in 1937 – claiming that it would be an insult to the Crown if the capital of the Empire were in socialist hands in Coronation Year – Labour almost doubled its majority on the LCC and, in the next twenty-seven years of the LCC's life, never again lost it.

The Livingstone regime had no respect for this sort of political horse-sense. Despite his distinctly fragile base in popular support – the London electorate was offered one Labour leader but, after a post-election coup, got another – Livingstone immediately launched a series of initiatives (e.g. talks with the IRA) calculated to offend the majority of Londoners and with a doubtful relevance to the capital's problems. At the same time, even circles highly sympathetic to the GLC were scandalised by the large grants and fancy salaries being handed out to left-wing groupies attracted to the GLC like wasps to jam. (Hilary Wainwright has the good grace to admit to the 'fat salary' she drew from the GLC, apparently for her work in connection with planning, a subject in which she had no training or qualification.) This brought such great unpopularity to the GLC that Mrs Thatcher felt emboldened to propose its outright abolition. The threat of abolition enabled the Livingstone administration briefly to ride the inevitable wave of popular indignation it caused, but it has been clear for a while now that Mrs Thatcher has got clean away with it. Not only has the collapse of London services constantly predicted by the GLC not taken place, but the general election results in London showed clearly enough how shallow and conditional Livingstone's popularity had really been. Labour, for its part, was so aghast at the whole episode that it has firmly refused to commit itself to re-creating the GLC in the future. Ms Wainwright fails entirely to realise that this is a pretty fair catalogue of political disaster and cheerfully recommends Labour to take the GLC path. It is rather like a Tory activist suggesting that the best way ahead for the Conservatives would be to invade Suez or restage the Profumo Affair.

If the Left wants to get out of its current mess it will have to set aside such deliberate naïvety and wishfulness and concentrate on the facts as they are. One might start with two key sociological facts which emerge from the 1987 election. At a mass level the most striking feature of the election was the highly differential way in which the sexes behaved. Among men the pro-Labour swing from the Tories was a mere 0.5 per cent, but among women it was nine times greater, at 4.5 per cent. (All figures here are based on the vast MORI sample of 23,396 voters interviewed in the course of the campaign, weighted to the actual outcome.) Further analysis of that swing shows peculiar age differences among women: among the 35–54 age-group women moved only 2 per cent towards Labour; the 25–34s swung 6.5 per cent; and the 18–24s a massive 11 per cent. (The shift among men aged 18–24 was only 1.5 per cent to Labour.)

The real peculiarity is that women aged 55–65 also moved 4.5 per cent to Labour and women over 65 showed a 7 per cent Labour swing. That is to say, it was the middle-aged who were the odd women out: not only did far more younger women swing to Labour, but so did many more older women. Without doubt, most of these middle-aged women who stuck with the Tories lived in the South: Southern women showed a pro-Labour swing only one-third as great as that of Northern women. Even so, women in the South did show a pro-Labour swing, while the men swung clearly towards the Tories.

This sex difference remains striking even when one holds class constant. Male trade-unionists actually showed a 0.5 per cent swing from Labour to the Tories, while among women trade-unionists there was a 6 per cent pro-Labour swing. Among the unemployed, men moved 5.5 per cent to Labour, but women swung twice as much (11 per cent) in that direction. The result of all this was that the normal Tory advantage among women was completely wiped out, but that was all: the proportion of women who voted Labour was no greater than the proportion of men who voted Labour – the big change is simply that there is no longer a statistical difference in the way the sexes vote. But if there is no gender gap now, there soon could be. Among the 18–24s – the face of the future, perhaps – the Tories had a healthy 5 per cent lead among men, while Labour had a huge 11 per cent lead among women. In other words, if the electorate had consisted entirely of young women aged 18–24 there would now be a Labour Parliamentary majority of over a hundred. That all this should be happening under the first woman Prime Minister is not the least ironic aspect of the situation.

But the question is, how do we explain this trend? How does it relate to the gender gap opening in the Left's favour in other Western industrialised states? How does it relate to the decline both in the absolute size of the working class and in Labour's share of the remaining working-class vote? Why is Labour doing so badly among men, and particularly young men? Historically, these latter have tended to be one of the most pro-Labour groups in the whole population: a Tory lead in this group is psephologically staggering. And why, against all expectations, does Labour do worse among working-age women than among those too young or too old to work? Only a great deal of further thought, analysis and research will answer such questions.

One can be rather more definite about the new sociological profile of Labour's élite as it emerges from the election. In the 1960s Labour's Front Bench was dominated by Oxford graduates – often by Oxford dons. Over the last two decades that élite has been progressively squeezed out, so that in 1987, for the first time in over half a century, Labour went into the election with a leader and deputy leader both of whom were recruited from outside Oxbridge. Anyone who is, like me, an Oxford don has been perfectly aware for some time of what has been happening. In the first two decades after the war, the cream of the Oxford PPE School (Wilson, Healey, Jenkins, Crossman, Crosland, etc.) tended to gravitate to the Labour benches, lending the Party an intellectual authority which was crucial to its appeal beyond the traditional working-class. Whether or not such men were any good in government, they had the decisive effect of making Labour appear and sound socially legitimate in this acutely class-conscious country – and in making the Tories seem the 'stupid party'. (The substantial Oxbridge intake on to the Tory benches always contained a far smaller proportion of the intellectual high-flyers.) When, by the early 1970s, it was clear that Oxford's best and brightest were no longer heading in Labour's direction, only fear of being accused of intellectual snobbery prevented one from saying that trouble lay ahead for Labour. The reason they stayed away was largely instinctual: they no longer felt at home with Labour, and some tried their luck there only to find that holding an Oxford degree was now a positive disadvantage in many CLPs. One bright and strongly Labour young graduate of West Indian origin I know applied for a job in a Labour-ruled South London local authority on going down. At his interview has was accused of having betrayed both his race and his class by having attended Oxford. Had he not been black, his reception might have been worse.

By the early 1980s it was clear that Oxford's best and brightest had found a new home – the Alliance, especially the SDP. Indeed, the SDP was *the* Oxford party: three of the Gang of Four were Oxford graduates (the fourth came from Cambridge); the rumpus over the Thatcher honorary degree made the same point, which Roy Jenkins' election as the University's new Chancellor only confirmed. Up and down the country, the SDP adopted Oxbridge graduates in large numbers. Had the 1987 election marked the Alliance breakthrough which only a few weeks before had seemed quite possible, we would have seen the massive re-entry into Parliament of the Oxbridge élite deflected from Labour. In a hung Parliament they would, no doubt, have renegotiated the old terms of alliance with Labour's proles and petty bourgeois, this time making sure they could never be squeezed out again.

It was not to be. On the Opposition side the sole Oxford don to remain in Labour's ranks, Bryan Gould, rose like a rocket to effective number two or three status in the Party. The young Oxbridge SDP hopefuls were scythed down in their scores and now find their party in ruins. Politically, they are a homeless group. A lot will depend on where they turn in pursuit of their political future. It is far from clear that Labour can win without them.

Thirdly, there is the question of Neil Kinnock. The one thing all commentators agreed upon as Labour went down to defeat in 1987, was that at least Kinnock's presidential-style campaign had been a considerable success. If this was true, it was so only in the sense that it may have helped change Kinnock's leadership ratings from the appalling to the merely abysmal. The polls show that, overall, Thatcher emerged with a leadership rating (*pros* minus *antis*) of + 8, while Kinnock scored −13: a gap of 21 points as compared to the 11-point gap which separated the Tory and Labour Parties. Whatever the media slickness of the Kinnock campaign, the fact is that he was a large net drag on his Party. At the risk of all the obvious accusations, I would venture the opinion that a man who needed to resit his exams in order to gain a Pass degree from Cardiff is never going to carry intellectual conviction and authority with the British electorate. For better or worse (worse, I would say), that electorate is used to its figures of authority speaking from the background of an Oxbridge education. The same is true, *a fortiori*, of that key constituent of all winning coalitions, the young Oxbridge best and brightest. They might well turn to a Labour Party led by Bryan Gould: a slick media campaign is not going to cause them to discover virtues in Neil Kinnock. It may be sad or even wrong that it is so, but it is so.

This is not, of course, to suggest some sort of educational determinism – that only an Oxbridge-educated leader can win: there are plenty of stupid and unelectable people produced by Oxbridge and there are also plenty of clever and electable people who have never been anywhere near Oxbridge. But there is a Kinnock problem, partly because he is so far from being the best that even non-Oxbridge produces. He is, let it be said, clearly a very nice chap, a decent human being with a warm sense for people and a charming Welsh sense of humour. But he is also, and quite irretrievably, just a student union politician. He is vacuous, verbose and comprehensively not up to it. The notion of him at Number Ten has much the same surrealist feel as the idea of Jesse Jackson in the White House. Labour has never won with a leader who runs behind his Tory counterpart in the polls and Kinnock will be out-polled by almost whoever the Tories put up. If Labour is serious about winning, Kinnock has to go. But Kinnock will not go. He does not want to; there is no obvious alternative; the leadership election rules give the incumbent an overwhelming advantage; and Labour is too conservative and sentimental a party to face up to reality like this.

Having looked at the difficulties, the reaction within the Opposition parties is to say that all this talk of pacts and changing leaders, let alone having policies they actually believe in, is too difficult and best left alone. Which means 'let's return to a provenly losing strategy, muck around with our policies a bit, and hope we get lucky'.

Getting lucky, in this context, has to mean nothing less than a thunderous economic crisis – a crisis so great that the electorate willingly votes for a non-credible Opposition simply in order to punish the Government. It could happen, just as the phenomenon of the own-goal happens in soccer matches. But what would we think of a soccer team manager whose strategy for winning the championship relied solely on his team's opponents scoring own-goals? Would we take such a manager seriously? Or, of course, Labour could wait to get crushingly defeated yet again in 1991 or 1992 and then face up to some of these problems. Both options actually mean choosing defeat as the lesser of two evils and the problem is that the electorate is *never* going to confer victory on a party that shows a preference for defeat. Surely even the horror of facing up to some hard facts is better?

References

Benn, Tony (1987) *Out of the Wilderness: Diaries 1963–1967* (London: Hutchinson)

Wainwright, Hilary (1987) *Labour: A Tale of Two Parties* (London: Hogarth Press).

Chapter 6
Thatcher's New Order

Almost all the essays in this book were written in the shadow of the Thatcher regime. Interestingly, Mrs Thatcher herself uses the word 'regime' to describe her government. At the time of writing most political commentators have been so intimidated by the political success of Thatcherism that they are actually quick to list the regime's virtues before essaying even the mildest criticism. The virtues of Thatcherism lie simply in the thorough bashing it has given to a large number of pressure groups which had laid themselves open to such treatment; a decidedly ambivalent heritage since all these victories were achieved by the brute exertion of state power against weaker elements in civil society. To cheer these triumphs is to cheer the victory of Goliath over a number of admittedly rather ill-behaved Davids. Thatcherism has also inflicted untold misery upon the legions of the unemployed, single mothers, the poor – especially poor children, ethnic minorities, the sick, the homeless and all the other groups unable to help themselves. As I write, the tenth anniversary of Thatcherism is being celebrated – Hugo Young's biography of Thatcher (Young, 1989) reviewed below, was part of that celebration. I take the risk, in this hour of Thatcherite triumph, of predicting that we will come to look back on Thatcherism in much the same rueful, wryly acknowledging, but ultimately ignominious way that Spain now remembers Franco.

In February 1981 Mrs Thatcher made an ecstatic pilgrimage to Washington to commune with the new President, Ronald Reagan, about such then modish topics as supply-side economics and the evil empire. Hugo Young recalls the 'patronising astonishment' with which her Foreign Secretary, Lord Carrington, witnessed this jejune and effusive display. Asked by a colleague, on his return, how the visit had really gone, Carrington replied, 'Oh, very well indeed. She liked the Reagan people very much. They're so vulgar.'

The story illustrates the major problems of writing a biography about Margaret Thatcher: personally, she is neither nice nor interesting. She has immense energy, remarkable tenacity and stamina, and a good brain. But she has a shallow mind, little imagination and an immense, bullying ego. One cannot empathise with a subject like that and as she goes ramping on and on and on through these pages, just as she has gone ramping on and on and on through the last decade of British life, it is hard not to feel a sort of appalled boredom. There is, too, simply no end to her presumption: to the various quotations about 'I as a government' and 'We are a grandmother', one can add another culled by Young who finds her measuring 'My performance against that of other countries in the real world'. And while it added something to one's assessment of, say, Macmillan, to know that he sought solace in his private hours with the works of Livy and Jane Austen, what can one say about someone who, after spending much of her day ranting at her Ministers, her civil servants and the Opposition about the evils of socialism, likes to relax, as her confidant, John Vaizey, put it, by 'exciting herself with books about the horrors of Marxism'. 'At the moment I'm re-reading *The Fourth Protocol*', she happily tells a journalist. *Re*-reading. Of the various verdicts on her Young offers, the pick is probably that of the playwright, Jonathan Miller: 'loathsome, repulsive in almost every way . . . her odious suburban gentility, and sentimental, saccharine patriotism, catering to the worst elements of commuter idiocy'.

Hugo Young is the best political journalist writing in Britain today and he has done a dutiful, indeed fluent job which will doubtless become the standard work for some time to come. Some things were new to me. I had not known that as Minister for Education under Heath Mrs Thatcher had fought to preserve the Open University or that she regretted her measure to abolish free milk in schools (characteristically blaming the Civil Service for her mistake), or that she had fought against the idea of abolishing the rates when it was proposed by Heath. It was also something of a shock to hear that she had toyed with the idea of inviting Roy Jenkins back from Europe to be Chancellor of the Exchequer in 1979. But otherwise it is pretty much the story as we know it – one can, reading Young, get the feeling of reading ten years of *The Guardian* again. It is very much a political correspondent's book, not only in that there is far more on political scandals like Spycatcher and Westland than on the economic factors which determined the government's life, but in the way that insider-ish factors are sometimes rather questionably assumed to be the ones that really count. Thus, for example, Young seems to think that the 1987 election began to tip away from Labour when Kinnock was caught having telephone chats with the Australian lawyer acting against the British government in the Spycatcher case. Yet the polls do not suggest that this fact ever registered very widely outside Westminster – and they do suggest that far more important was the long and blazing row over defence policy staged by the Alliance, which had the effect of shedding a merciless (and, because it was a row within another party, peculiarly unanswerable) light on Labour's weakest point. Young is, in fact, not at his best with opinion polls and electoral data: examining the 1987 result, for example, he speaks of the rise of the Tories' share of the working-class vote in 1987 and the fall in their share of the middle-class vote as purely a product of eight years of Thatcherism. In fact this trend of class de-alignment had been visible (and extensively written about by academics) for years before the advent of Thatcher. The real question is not whether Thatcher has pulled workers over to the Tories but whether Thatcherism is not in part the product of an already de-aligning working class.

One or two things seem to have eluded Young. He mentions the young Margaret Robert's election campaign in Dartford in 1950, but neglects the best part of it. Ms Roberts insisted throughout the campaign that she would win. As they neared the last lap her agent advised her to drop this line. She had, he said, fought a bonny campaign, but the Labour majority was 19,000 after all, and it would be best not to risk looking ridiculous in a few days' time. Only at that stage did it emerge that Ms Roberts was so full of naïve self-belief that she really did believe she would win, and would not hear a word more of this defeatist talk. (She lost by 13,600).

The second point is far more significant. Young notes that Mrs Thatcher has developed a close relationship with the large Jewish component of her constituency, Finchley, and remarks that 'she had special need to do so, since shortly before her first election (1959) Tory forces had combined to exclude Jews from membership of the Finchley Golf Club. This presented her with no difficulty . . .' . This is to gloss over an utterly critical moment in Mrs Thatcher's career. Golf club anti-Semitism is, even today, a fairly common part of English life, and the Finchley row of 1957 took the not unusual form of the club committee which excluded Jews being largely made up of Tory worthies wearing, so to speak, their golfing hats. The Liberals took the issue up (ultimately righting it) and in 1957 the first Liberals gained election to the Finchley and adjoining Friern Barnet councils. Mrs Thatcher's arrival in Finchley in 1959, replete with golfing husband, did not, however, see the end of the matter. In

1961 the Liberals, riding the wave of Jewish protest, attacked every ward in Finchley for the first time and in 1962 they won every single ward there, as well as three of the five Friern Barnet wards. It was suddenly clear that Mrs Thatcher was in real trouble: whereas she had been elected in 1959 with a majority of 16,260, the Liberals had now polled 51 per cent right across her constituency. Worse still, in 1963 the Liberals repeated their clean sweep – on the Finchley council they now held nineteen of the twenty four seats. Six of the nineteen were Jews, including the new mayor and deputy-mayor, and there was just one issue – 'the Jewish question', as it was baldly called. Feeling was running extremely high – there was a nearly 60 per cent poll – and the possibility looked that Mrs Thatcher's political career might be abruptly terminated in an angry wave of Jewish anti-Tory protest. Finchley, wrote Bernard Donoghue in 1964, 'was the Liberal party's greatest and most publicised hope of "another Orpington" in the South East of England', and the Liberals even arranged two special TV campaign appearances for their candidate, John Pardoe.

All of this must have been fairly panic-inducing for a young Tory hopeful, a woman at that, who had only found this winnable seat after nine years' search. Mrs Thatcher can have been in no doubt that if she lost Finchley she would never get another chance – and to hear that the Liberals had made her their top target in the whole country, drafting in a huge team of outside helpers, can hardly have helped her sleep at nights. But somehow, in the course of 1963–4, the tide was turned. No biographer has ever told us how Mrs Thatcher managed this or even exactly what her role in the row was, but Young is surely wrong to dismiss the whole incident with the statement that the situation 'presented her with no difficulty': mediating between enraged Jewish erstwhile supporters and the traditional Tory worthies on the nineteenth green can hardly have been easy, and it is not certain that Denis would have been altogether an asset. All we really know is that a new Tory agent was hired in 1962 with the mission of rebuilding the constituency party organisation almost from scratch and that in 1964 Mrs Thatcher managed to hold the anti-Tory swing among Jewish voters down to 20 per cent, thus clinging on to her seat with a majority cut in half. What is certain is that she has taken extreme pains never to find herself on the wrong side of the Jewish vote again.

In fact things have been strikingly the other way. Mrs Thatcher comes from the sort of provincial suburban background in which a mild, social anti-Semitism has traditionally been quite pervasive, but one of the most attractive things about her is the entirely warm and open-hearted way she has related to the Jewish community. This clearly stems, moreover, from something far deeper than local electoral convenience – Mrs Thatcher instinctively warms to the Jewish *nouveaux riches* of north London and seems to see Judaism as an exemplary religion of capitalism. The Chief Rabbi, Immanuel Jakobovits, has done much to encourage this symbiosis – indeed, he seems to have the ambition, as Young puts it, of becoming 'the spiritual leader of Thatcherite Britain'. He has certainly acted more like the old-fashioned head of an established church than has Archbishop Runcie. Not only are his sermons Samuel Smiles homilies, attacking trade unions and preaching the gospel of work, advising the blacks to pull themselves up by their own bootstraps like the Jews, and so forth, but he has strongly attacked the Anglican document *Faith in the City* as, in effect, a charter for the welfare-scroungers and the work-shy. This being Thatcher's Britain, these rather brutal sentiments have earned him a place on the Honours List.

To a degree that is really very striking – though utterly unwritten about – Thatcherism has seen the old Jewish identification with Labour stood on its head. In the old days a Jewish Tory MP, if not quite a contradiction in terms, was likely to be a Sir Gerald Nabarro – converted away from his Jewish faith and attempting to be a sort of caricature of the Tory squire. In the 1970s this changed, sharply. Harold Macmillan's alleged retort on seeing the first Thatcher Cabinet list – 'there are more Old Estonians than Old Etonians in this government' – must have been symptomatic of what many Old Guard Tories felt. There was a record Jewish presence not only in Mrs Thatcher's Cabinet – including, at its peak, Joseph, Lawson, Young, Rifkind and Brittan – but among those on whom Mrs Thatcher leant for private advice – Joseph, Lawson and Alfred Sherman and the Saatchi brothers. Able young Jewish MPs (and there are now quite a few on the Tory benches) were natural recruits to the Thatcherite cause not only because they often came from market-oriented careers, but because they were, to put it mildly, free of all ties to the more traditional Tories that Thatcher was displacing.

Resistance to this historic change in élite composition has been happily muffled, but one can see something of the strains between the old guard and the new in the relationship between Nigel Lawson and Willie Whitelaw; the brash young financial journalist and the hereditary landowner and grandee. Whitelaw regarded Lawson as fast, flash and 'thoroughly unsound'. In Young's words, of Whitelaw's 'myriad managerial tasks, keeping Lawson out of high places had not been the least important'. Thatcher was, however, determined to get Lawson to the Treasury. She finally overcame Whitelaw's opposition, but Whitelaw went around making it clear that he could never be comfortable with the fact. 'Nigel Lawson is unfortunately almost entirely without friends', he was wont to remark. 'I have therefore made a very conscious effort to become his friend. People tell me this is a doomed enterprise.' One doubts if such shafts pierced Lawson's armour. It is in the nature of their being Jewish that men like Lawson have to get used to people like Whitelaw thinking, in the famous phrase, that they are 'too clever by half'. Later, of course, Whitelaw was to stage a long and successful rearguard action against Lord Young being allowed to take over the chairmanship of the Tory party. Again, the terms of the dispute were revealing – Young, the millionaire property developer arguing that since the Tory party had an annual turnover of only £5 million any really business-like Minister could run it in one day a week, Whitelaw retorting that it would not be proper for a Minister of Trade and Industry to be soliciting party contributions from those he was supposed to be regulating; the corollary being that Young's business-cum-political ethics left much to be desired if it was necessary not just to point out such rules to him but to have actually to impose them on him.

All of this was, however, pretty coded stuff. Only with two members of the government, Leon Brittan and Edwina Currie, did their Jewishness become a cause for comment. In their very different ways these two ministers had personalities which rubbed their colleagues up the wrong way, a fact which was, in the usual mysterious manner, put down to their Jewish origins. When they slipped up, the Labour party, as if sensing the strain, was in both cases able to hound them out of office. (We have just seen Paul Channon, the Transport Minister, brazen out the constant run of transport 'disasters, thanks to sold back-bench support. Would it have been the same if he were Jewish?) One Tory back-bencher greeted Thatcher's sacrifice of Brittan with the furious demand that at least his replacement should be a 'proper red-faced, red-blooded Englishman'. Despite her conversion from Judaism, similar mouthings about Mrs Currie could recently be heard from certain red-faced, red-blooded Englishmen on the Tory back-benches. It was this sort of thing, which did not require much decoding, that had created all that trouble at the Finchley Golf Club back in 1957. . . .

Young's biography does not, unfortunately, directly broach any of the major analytic questions about Thatcherism. But three questions are inescapable: from what did Thatcherism originate?

what distinguishes it from traditional Toryism? and will it work?

Mrs Thatcher is keen that we turn back the page to those interwar figures, Ludwig von Mises and Friedrich von Hayek, and see things through their lens. Ironically, the best place to start in understanding Thatcherism is the collapse of German conservatism in the 1930s and the concomitant rise of Nazism. Nazism grew in response to two major threats: the exploitation and immiseration of Germany at an international level, and the threat of the Left at the domestic level. German conservative voters not only felt terrified by these two threats but, losing all confidence in the traditional ruling class to protect them, turned instead to the radical *petit bourgeois* leadership of the Nazis. The result was, ultimately, the re-formation of the old conservative bloc under subaltern leadership: quite literally the old *Junker* class and its generals found they were now commanded by a former corporal. If we strip this model of all the inevitable ideological baggage which attaches to Nazism, what we are left with is that the last resort of conservatism faced with a domestic and international crisis is its own social re-formation. In this model, the old structure of the conservative coalition suffers a radical inversion so that the leadership is seized by a tough-minded parvenu group willing to take utterly extreme measures to save the day. Typically, the old leadership group proves socially incapable of taking its rivals seriously enough so that it underestimates the parvenu challenge until too late, or nourishes wishful illusions that it will get rid of the parvenus after a year or two. The old group of vanquished notables then either quits the field altogether or is grumblingly reintegrated into the coalition at a lower level, on terms set by the new, upstart leadership. However, since the leadership of this group is socially so unnatural, it needs to shore itself up by a greatly strengthened leadership principle and a sweeping centralisation of command. Typically, too, the Left also underestimates the parvenu challenge – in the German case not only was the Left locked in fratricidal battle but some Communists even thought that the Nazi seizure of power would ultimately benefit the revolution.

Thatcherism is not, of course, Nazism; and Britain has not had to face a crisis remotely as great as did Germany after 1929. But the model is clear enough, and clearly enough it fits. The two dangers threatening the British middle classes – relative international decline at the international level, the trade union challenge at a domestic level – were, however, experienced as being truly acute only by a fraction of the old conservative coalition. This fraction was hardly uniformly *petit bourgeois* but it did, perforce, have to look to outsiders within the conservative camp and it did work by centralising command and the erection of the leadership principle to unparalleled heights.

Faithful to the model, we find that the re-formation of the conservative bloc under Thatcher took many of its victims unaware. Over and over again in Young's pages the Priors, Gilmours and Pyms reproach themselves for having comprehensively misconstrued and underestimated the advance of the whole Thatcherite phenomenon. Whitelaw early on reflected that 'being a woman, added to being an outsider, imposed on her an irresistible need to assert herself at every opportunity'. Which is to miss the point that in terms of the old paradigm of Tory leadership, being a woman was itself the extreme form of marginal, outsider status. And that it was natural that she promoted and sought the company of other marginalised men – cranks like Alfred Sherman and Paul Johnson, mystics like Laurens van der Post and the born-again Brian Griffiths, embittered outcasts like Enoch Powell and Ray Honeyford, men like Bernard Ingham and John Hoskyns whose previous Labour sympathies made them oddities in the Tory camp, *émigrés* from Britain like Alan Walters, Ian MacGregor and Robert Conquest – the list is endless. Her Jewish Cabinet members were definitionally marginal men within the Tory party – which had the useful extra twist that they would be properly grateful for their preferment and could probably never become rivals for the leadership. (Can one imagine a Tory gentile being a successful Chancellor of the Exchequer for six years on end without ever being seriously discussed as a future leader? Such is Lawson's position.) It was natural, too, that within the Cabinet Mrs Thatcher should promote the likes of Norman Tebbit. Young writes of Tebbit's bitter scorn for the Left, 'the well-heeled whigs personified by Roy Jenkins, whom he considered to have been the agents of national corruption', and 'the old Conservative establishment, epitomised by Macmillan and Heath, whom he considered to be responsible for keeping the likes of himself out of power. By a narrow margin, the latter group probably headed the catalogue of infamy.' Such, pretty well exactly, were the feelings that the Brownshirts harboured towards their Left, their over-comfortable centrists and the old *Junker* class who had kept them out of power. But traditional Tories like Prior and Pym were slow to realise what was happening. Of Pym Young writes that 'gentleman though he was, [he] wasn't lacking in corridor savagery' and illustratively cites his remark that 'The trouble is we've got a corporal at the top, not a cavalry officer'. But this was actually just sociological description. One doubts if the German General Staff were as slow to wake up to the fact they too had a corporal in command. Many of the assessments of Thatcher cited by Young reflect a belated patrician fury as the fact of their dispossession sinks in, though Young himself sometimes fails to realise this. Thus he instances Lady Warnock feeling a 'kind of rage' as she sees Mrs Thatcher on television, choosing her clothes at Marks and Spencer, and feeling there was something 'obscene' about it 'in a way that's not exactly vulgar, just *low*'. Lady Warnock is here adduced by Young as representing a paradigm of the intellectuals' rejection of Mrs Thatcher. This is to miss the point entirely. Lady Warnock is an old-style mandarin who at first gained considerable preferment under Thatcher – a peerage and numerous appointments to royal commissions and the like, so that as late as 1985 Lady Warnock was campaigning energetically in favour of the Oxford honorary degree for Mrs Thatcher. At this point, for some reason, Lady Warnock lost favour and she now seems to be furious at being dropped by someone who stoops to shopping in Marks and Spencer. Her response to Mrs Thatcher cited above, bespeaking not intellectual rejection but a pure class disdain, merely typifies the wounded rejection of an older class of notables who find themselves downgraded under Thatcher's New Order.

Thatcher was, in a way, right to accuse the Tory old guard of defeatism. They did not like national economic decline any more than the next man but tended to assume that it was somehow written in the tides of history, that it was something you banged on about but did not really expect to reverse. Similarly, you banged on about the outrageous presumption of the trade union barons but at bottom you felt that trade unions were just a bloody nuisance you could not do much about. This defeatism was easily perceptible to the trade unions who accordingly expected things to go on much as before and were thus taken unawares by Thatcherism just as much as the Tory old guard were. Alan Fisher, the NUPE leader during the 1978–9 'winter of discontent', challenged with the damage he was doing to Labour prospects, replied that it didn't much matter because no government could be worse than the Callaghan one they had already got. A similar, wrong-headedly cavalier attitude was apparent across wide sections of the Labour movement, which accordingly felt free to indulge in fratricidal strife, just as the German Communists and Social Democrats had in the early 1930s. For in looking back to the late 1970s under Callaghan we are looking back at our own Weimar, our own Hindenberg.

Among Mrs Thatcher's coterie the trade union issue was viewed with a quite surpassing bitterness. As early as 1977 John Hoskyns and Norman Strauss, acting at Keith Joseph's behest, produced a report for Mrs Thatcher entitled *Stepping Stones* which asserted that 'The one precondition for success will be a complete change in the role of the trades union movement', by which was clearly meant nothing less than the movement's rapid and complete emasculation. The danger, they warned, was that a Tory government would be tempted to 'get on with' the unions – which, they insisted, would mean selling the country down the river. 'We may have to take greater political risks than we had anticipated' warned the report, whose apocalyptic and alarmist language meant that it stayed secret. Mrs Thatcher, Young tells us, was 'tremendously excited by what she read'. Thereafter, the trade union theme recurs insistently and within the Thatcherite camp one's attitude on this issue was treated as the benchmark of true conservative purpose. This brought enormous pressure to bear on the Tory spokesman on the unions, James Prior, who clung to obstinately moderate views. The tenor of that pressure is best judged by the way Tebbit, to applause from Thatcher, 'likened Prior's softness on industrial relations and especially the closed shop to "the morality of Pétain and Laval"'.

Drifting back comes Jonathan Miller's telling phrase, 'commuter idiocy'. Who in the 1960s and 1970s did not find themselves at one time or another standing miserably on a station platform waiting for trains which, due to industrial action, were endlessly late or might not arrive at all? Among one's fellow passengers there was always at least one furious business gent who wanted the railway sold off on the spot and the strikers dispatched, within about the next ten minutes, to Botany Bay. Tebbit's comparison of Prior giving in to the unions with Pétain and Laval giving in to Hitler was just the sort of language those furious business gents would talk. The fact is that those who staged those endless guerrilla actions in the public sector – the protest stoppages, go-slows, work-to-rules and demarcation disputes, as well as the straightforward strikes – very seriously underestimated the extent to which they were playing with fire. That furious business gent on the platform was a thoroughly noxious chap, a bullying Home Counties, *Telegraph*-reading snob, but if you drove the other passengers mad for long enough, in the end they would, in their frustration, line up behind him, commuter idiocy and all. Which is pretty much what happened.

Surprisingly (to me) Hugo Young seems to take Thatcherism's assessment of its economic record pretty much at face value. I am much less sure that Thatcherism is working. It is perfectly true that many British companies and institutions became leaner and meaner as a result of the 1980-1 recession, but it is also true that many died and that many more live on in a state of fragile anaemia. At the same time, the wilful undermining both of state schools and universities and the almost complete neglect of industrial training and retraining are producing a work-force which is falling behind those of our competitors in education and skills. And two of the biggest positive influences were sheer luck: the fall in world commodity prices brought inflation down and made industry more profitable, while the coming on stream of North Sea oil removed – for a while – the old balance of payments constraint to growth.

At the moment, we are told, we have almost an *embarras de richesse*, with a budget surplus of £14 billion. And we have had a protracted boom. The government boasts that it has launched one state industry after another into the private sector, that it has set enterprise free, that conditions for the private sector have never been so good. So why did the private sector run at a £14 billion trading loss last year? And why is it projected, even by the Treasury, to run up another £14 billion deficit this year? It certainly does not sound as if the private sector is really so healthy. Relative to the size of the two economies, our trade deficit is already bigger than the American one, itself considered a major threat to world financial stability. And what in God's name is our deficit likely to be as North Sea oil production winds down? To finance these huge deficits we have to borrow foreign money and to suck that in we have to offer very high rates of interest. These interest rates hurt investment and they keep the currency too high, hurting exports and favouring imports. So we attract loans to finance our trade deficit by means which only worsen that trade deficit. Is this really successful management?

The pound is now 70 per cent higher against the dollar than it was in 1983 and considerably higher against other currencies too. Quite clearly this makes us uncompetitive – but we push interest rates right up to make sure we stay that way. Why do we keep the currency so ludicrously high? Well, you see, that forces the private sector to keep wage increases down to our competitors' level, so that we don't become uncompetitive. But it doesn't: wages are increasing at an annual 9 per cent at present (14 per cent for company directors), far above our competitors' rates, and we are losing market share sharply. Is this really successful management? But we do have a nice, fat budget surplus. Yes, but when we ran a budget deficit we borrowed by issuing Gilts – at relatively low interest rates because they were backed by the State itself. Now we have a trade deficit the same size as the budget surplus and this we finance by attracting hot money, not backed by the State and so at much higher rates. So all we have really done is to substitute short-term borrowing at high rates for long-term borrowing at low rates – the classic recipe leading to the bankruptcy courts: except we are now told that this is part of 'the economic miracle'. As part of this 'miracle', by the way, we are told that we are even doing better than West Germany now. Strange that our trade deficit with the West Germans was £12.7 billion last year . . ..

Meanwhile, ahead, we are promised, lie yet further income tax cuts. But we know that such cuts are import-intensive in their effects in a way that extra public spending is not, and so all that such cuts can do is to add to the already mountainous trade deficit. Is that good management? Thanks to the oil boom of the past decade we have at least built up a huge portfolio of overseas investments which yield a major invisible inflow of dividend payments. But if we go on running up huge trade deficits we will end up making ever greater interest payments on the cumulative trade debt thus created. In the end this will wipe out the net benefit of those foreign dividend payments – indeed we could end up running down that stock of overseas assets to finance our domestic consumption. It seems clear that, one way or another, the approach of 1992 will see the crunch. A variety of scenarios exist but they all lead in the end to the denouement of a major sterling collapse and a consequent inflationary surge. Of course, when that happens that furious business gent on the station platform will have some fresh commuter idiocy to explain it all. But fewer of the sensible passengers will be listening to him by then. And some may even be sidling away.

References

Young, Hugo (1989) *One of Us. A Biography of Margaret Thatcher* (London: Macmillan)

Chapter 7
Waiting for Chirac

Though living in Paris as a visiting professor at the Sorbonne when I wrote the article below, in January 1986, I was also making frequent trips back to England and could not but be struck by the very different nature of the discussions one heard in these two countries on the merits and demerits of proportional representation. The fact is that the British have a very crude, blunt-edged political system: there is one ballot, with first past the post wins all, and then all power is handed over to a single party which rules without constitutional let or hindrance or democratic restraint for five years. In particular, power is held by that party's leader who has been elected in a safe seat and thus has little sense of accountability, let alone any real national mandate. And this leader will decide on his/her own when is a good time for the electorate to have their say again. Indeed, if the leader can get a majority in parliament to agree, then it may be decided to put off elections for years on end, as happened between 1935 and 1945. This political system having been in place for a very long time, the British regard it as a matter of simple patriotism to claim that it was the best system there could be and happily imposed it on numerous former colonies. One boggles now not just at the imperial confidence of such an attitude, but at its sheer wooden stupidity.

The French, on the other hand, have at one time or another tried almost every conceivable electoral and political system, with the happy result that few Frenchmen would ever go very far in the defence of any particular set of arrangements. There is, as Mitterrand puts it, no sense in treating the choice of electoral system as a question of religious belief – and a similar happy secularism pervades the discussion of other elements of the system too.

Things turned out much as the first paragraph below suggested: Chirac won the election and Le Pen captured thirty-five seats. Chirac formed a government and changed the electoral system back to its old two-ballot single member format. Mitterrand clung on by nerve and cunning for two years and then swept Chirac away in a fresh presidential and parliamentary triumph for the Left.

After the first five years of left-wing government the Fifth Republic has known, the result of the March 1986 parliamentary elections is already, and quite universally, taken for granted. The Left will lose its majority and without much doubt the next government will be formed by the leader of the RPR (Gaullists), Jacques Chirac. This result seems so inevitable that pollsters are amusing themselves by asking such questions as whether voters would object to voting for a candidate who was two-timing his wife with another woman (78 per cent would not object), while political sophisticates are already turning their minds to the real showdown, the Presidential election of 1988. Without much doubt Mitterrand hopes to neutralise a Chirac government via his considerable Presidential powers and then secure the election of another Socialist President in 1988 – who would dissolve the Assembly and hope to sweep in a Left-Centre coalition, thus reducing 1986–8 to the proportions of a brief interregnum. Chirac, naturally has other ideas and since no one knows what will happen in 1988 there has been a Gadarene rush towards him by key élites. The RPR boasts that every single head of a nationalised industry has already been in touch with them. This is unlikely to save many of their jobs. The heads of TV channels are equally unlikely to survive.

The pre-electoral period is dominated not by the usual who-will-win question but by two concerns which are threatening a wholesale *bouleversement* of French political life: the introduction of proportional representation, and immigration. Speculation continues as to why Mitterrand has introduced PR. To be sure, the Communists demanded it and the President is thus fulfilling a promise to them: and defensively it has ensured that though Socialist losses will be heavy, the party will have about a quarter of the Deputies in parliament. But it also means that the PS (Parti Socialiste) can never again hope for the sort of absolute majority it won in 1981 and that it will not in future have the same leverage to force the Communists into supporting a PS Presidential candidate. The real reason probably goes deeper: it is Mitterrand's revenge on de Gaulle. For with PR every future President will face the likelihood of shifting, conditional parliamentary majorities. The President will thus need to coax and curry favour with the Assembly, and the Bonapartist Presidency of the Fifth Republic will at last be cut down to size. It is the revenge of the Third and Fourth Republics on the Fifth.

The introduction of PR has already profoundly changed the political environment. It has, above all, transferred enormous power to the national party bosses and the select circle of cronies who fill their smoke-filled rooms, for it is they who will decide who is to carry their parties' colours on the ninety-six departmental lists and, more important, who is to get the 'eligible' places on those lists – that is the list positions likely to result in them being elected. Thus a reform supported by the rhetoric of a wider, fairer democracy has immediately resulted in the key decisions being taken more secretively and by fewer people than ever before.

The best way to understand the anomalies thus created is to take the case of a hypothetical department with, say, ten seats. In 1981, let us imagine, the combined vote of the Left parties was 55 per cent and that of the combined Right 45 per cent. However, since the PS was the dominant party within the Left, and the RPR within the Right, the final result produced by the majoritarian system in force in 1981 was six PS and four RPR Deputies (a perfectly typical result). In 1986, however, the polls point towards a 60–40 per cent majority for the Right in terms of the popular vote. With ten seats up for grabs and the small parties (Ecologists, Trotskyites, Independents, etc.) bound to take up to 10 per cent between them, it seems likely that 8–9 per cent of the popular vote will be enough to win a seat for one of the major parties.

Everyone does their sums – and panic ensues. The PS knows that the Left can get only four seats. But even though the Communists are weak, they can surely get 8–9 per cent and take one seat – leaving the PS with just three. This means that only the first three places on the PS lists are of any serious interest, which means that three of the six sitting PS Deputies have to be dumped: virtual war between the six and their clients ensues. On the Right the situation is no easier. Le Pen's Front National (FN) is bound to take 8–9 per cent and thus one of the seats, but the Giscardian Centre-Right, the UDF, will run its own list and probably get 20 per cent and thus two seats. This leaves only three seats for the RPR, which has four sitting Deputies . . . . And nobody can be fobbed off with the offer of fourth place on either the PS or RPR lists, for everyone can see that it will take an electoral swing of enormous – and thus highly unlikely – proportions to make these of more than academic interest. To offer such a place to a sitting Deputy is an insult.

The situation has been further complicated by a (helpful) increase in the total number of seats from 491 to 577 – but also by the first proper redistribution along population lines for twenty-seven years.

This means that many departments have suffered a sharp drop in their number of seats – Paris has gone from 31 to 21 seats and the infighting in the capital is the fiercest of all, especially since Le Pen is standing here and is bound to be elected with at least one other FN candidate.

The party bosses have priorities of their own. Thinking ahead to the key parliamentary battles of 1986–8, they all want their strongest teams in the Assembly – which means parachuting front-bench figures into leading positions in favourable departments, thus increasing the squeeze on the (highly indignant) sitting Deputies. There is also the pressure to broaden the parties' appeal by including allegedly non-partisan 'personalities' here and there. But not a few of such notables have realised that Le Pen's FN offers the best chance of all. Under the present majoritarian system he has no Deputies at all but under PR he will have several dozen. Although the early expectation that the film star Alain Delon might figure on a FN list has been disappointed, there has been a considerable flocking of local celebrities on to FN lists – thus creating furious ructions among the FN's *militants de première heure* who had begun to preen themselves as future Deputies but now find their ambitions indefinitely deferred.

PR has robbed the election of any element of surprise it might still have had. Although it is clear that the parties will spend as never before – £50,000 per party, for each of the ninety-six departments seems a likely figure – not only the overall result but that for most individuals is already assured. In our hypothetical department, for example, the top two men on the PS, UDF and RPR lists are, effectively, already elected. Similarly, numbers four to ten on their lists are there only for the ride. All of these candidates can sleepwalk their way through the election. Only the marginal third man on the list is likely to break sweat. Similarly, while a swing of 2–3 per cent could well settle the whole election under a majoritarian system, under PR it will only modify the overall result very slightly: PR, as the Italian example shows, means almost complete immobility, and the campaign itself becomes a largely bogus form of popular entertainment.

One talks of the top 'men' on the various lists advisedly, for once the party bosses get down to the nitty-gritty of allocating the 'eligible' list positions, it is usually the women who get squeezed out. Realising what was happening, the Minister for Women's Rights, Yvette Roudy, led a uniquely cross-party campaign to shame the (male) party bosses into concessions. This was not wholly disinterested – Madame Roudy was finding herself left out of the 'eligible' places in one department after another. The PS has responded by trying hard to impose at least its women Ministers on usually very reluctant departments. Mme Roudy, having been rejected in Hauts-de-Seine, seems likely to find a place in Calvados. The Minister for Social Affairs, Georgina Dufoix, has been parachuted into Gard – but is being fiercely resisted by the local party. The Minister for Foreign Trade, Edith Cresson, is having a similarly difficult time after being parachuted into Vienne. The Minister for the Environment, Huguette Bouchardeau, has trekked all over France, being angrily resisted by local (male) vested interests everywhere. The Right has reluctantly doubled its number of 'eligible' places for women – from three to six. Only the Communists have a really strong feminine representation on their lists, but given the Party's poor prospects, few of these will get elected. Overall, it is already clear that PR will be a disaster for women: from 27 Deputies out of 491 they will diminish to 24 or 25 out of 577. Shirley Williams please note.

What is true for women is also true for the young. The party bosses are naturally more susceptible to the powerful pressure of the senior sitting Deputies than to the claims of younger hopefuls with less bargaining power. It already seems clear that PR will have a strongly ossifying effect, entrenching the old political class, more able to elbow its way into 'eligible' places. As the weekly *Le Point* put it, 'on the right the lists resemble the court of Louis XVIII, a veritable Restoration, replete with old powdered marquises, their hair-pieces whitened with the passage of time, and with great local feudatories.' On the Left the difference is one only of degree.

The exception to this rule, of course, is that new faces are welcome if they belong to the rich, the powerful and the well-connected. With a handful of men in all the parties making the crucial decisions behind closed doors, money and influence can buy their way in as never before. One sitting PS Deputy has angrily resigned from the party altogether after finding 'his' eligible place assigned to a 28-year-old who happens to be Mitterrand's grand-nephew. In Indre-et-Loire, a split in the RPR seems likely after the imposition of Bernard Debré, a son of de Gaulle's first premier. In Eure, Chirac's imposition of another of Debré's sons has led to similar trouble. In Deux-Sevres, Chirac has had less difficulty in imposing the young Jean de Gaulle: no one in the RPR is very keen to opposed – publicly at least – the General's grandson.

The most remarkable case, though, is that of the press tycoon, Robert Hersant – the third richest man in France. Hersant's Vichyite and anti-Semitic past does not make him an attractive candidate: the last time he stood in a parliamentary election in one of the safest conservative seats in France, he was roundly defeated. That, though, was under the old majoritarian system. With the coming of PR Hersant has gobbled up 'eligible' places not only for himself and his son but for another thirteen of his collaborators and assistants as well. The only real question is whether Hersant will use his leverage to become a minister or will prefer to buy one of the public TV channels the Right is promising to sell off.

The introduction of PR also has a great deal to do with the fact that the election campaign is likely to be disfigured by a good deal of anti-immigrant racism. Under the old majoritarian system Le Pen could have said what he liked on this theme, got his 10 per cent of the first-round vote, and then watched his support flock towards orthodox conservatives on the second ballot without ending up with much leverage or a single seat. Under PR, however, every vote Le Pen takes is a direct loss for the RPR and UDF – and he will get lots of seats. His leverage is, accordingly, enormous: he can even dream of making and unmaking governments. The result is an alarming and escalating auction in racist promises and threats as the orthodox Right engages with Le Pen in a fierce competition for every last racist vote. Already Chirac has made it clear that he personally would like to see all unemployed immigrants expelled from France – which would give employers virtual power of deportation over many of their workers. Even official RPR policy calls for continuous street-corner identity checks by the police to clamp down on illegal immigrants (*clandestins*), and for the discontinuation of family allowances to immigrant families for their third and subsequent children. The assumption that more French children are a good thing and more immigrant children a bad thing is quite openly racist. This amounts to the almost complete adoption of the FN platform by the man who will be the next prime minister. It is no good, of course: Le Pen is only too happy to go further. The FN is now calling for the total abolition of *all* family allowances to immigrants; their deprivation of free education and of all trade-union and works-council voting rights; and the stripping of French citizenship from the most recently naturalised.

The atmosphere engendered by this auction is, as they say, something else. The Hersant press, with its apocalyptic warnings that French national identity will soon be lost, has become more and more openly racist – particularly *Figaro*, whose editorial staff includes an unashamed FN clique which reportedly 'terrorises' the more orthodoxly right-wing journalists on the paper. Le Pen's meetings are increasingly anti-Semitic as well as anti-Arab and anti-black. On TV the question put to all aspiring politicians is 'What would you say to an Arab becoming prime minister of France one day?' (As one looks round at the miserable Arab street-cleaners and reflects on the absence of naturalised Arabs from all the party lists, one wonders how these French variants on Anna Ford and Selena Scott manage to look so pertly relevant while posing such ludicrous questions.) Even 'liberals' such as ex-President Giscard make ponderous remarks about immigrants having to 'remember that they may have rights, but they have duties too' – as though suggesting that immigrants are falling down on their duties in some unexplained way. But the key mechanism is PR: it forces Chirac to compete with Le Pen; Giscard with Chirac; even the Socialist premier, Fabius, can be heard boasting on TV of the 'exceptional firmness' the Government would display against *clandestins*. PR has meant that Le Pen has been able to send powerful ripples flowing across the entire political spectrum.

Immigration seems likely to be the dominant election issue. Rather than simply berate the French for the appalling displays of racism and chauvinism this will undoubtedly produce, it is worth pointing out that historically France has been more welcoming to foreigners than any other European country. This is partly a matter of *force majeure*: the country has long land borders with five major foreign states (not counting Luxembourg, Monaco etc.) and immigration is intrinsically difficult to control. By 1900 one inhabitant of Marseilles in five was an Italian, while the 1920s saw a huge influx of Poles. By 1930 there were three million immigrants in France (one-third of whom were Italians). Indeed, if one goes back four generations one Frenchman in three has immigrant ancestors and demographers point out that without this continuous inward flow over the last century, France would today have a population of 40 million instead of 55. Britain, by contrast, has been a large and continuous net exporter of migrants.

Moreover, immigrants have gained acceptance in all walks of life in a way that the more chauvinist British might well not have allowed. Giscard's Interior Minister was a Polish Count, Michel Poniatowski: could someone with a name like that become Home Secretary? The head of the largest trade-union federation, Henri Krasucki, is a Polish Jew: could one imagine a Polish Jew heading the TUC? Among popular idols there are many of immigrant stock – Yves Montand (Italian), Johnny Hallyday (Belgian), Sylvie Vartan (Bulgarian), Constantin Costa-Gavras (Greek), Yannick Noak (Cameroonian), and so on. Even the French soccer team, the European Champions and the country's pride and joy, has an immigrant majority – three Spaniards, two Malians and one Italian, who is also the captain. Indeed, the more one reflects on the immigrant presence in French life, on the one hand, and the strength of French national culture, on the other, the more one is driven to the belief that a nation is simply a defined cultural space into which large numbers of originally quite different people can be almost interchangeably fitted.

According to the most recent figures, there were, in 1984, 4,485,715 foreign migrants in France (i.e. 7 per cent of the population – the same proportion as fifty years ago). To these one has to add a guesstimate for *clandestins*. When the Mitterrand Government offered to regularise the situation of all *clandestins* on a once-and-for-all basis in 1981, 130,000 stepped forward. It seems a little unlikely that a similar number of fresh *clandestins* has built up again in just four years, but this does not prevent the figure being conventionally put at 300,000 – or if you read *Figaro*, 500,000. (The discovery, last month, of a new source of *clandestins*, Chinese arriving from Zhenjiang province with bogus Cambodian passports, has received a great deal of attention, though to date the police have only found and deported 25 of these exotics – not quite the Asian tide of popular headlines.) A sensible maximum figure is probably 4.6 million, of which the largest single group (860,000) are Portuguese.

Politically, though, this is to miss the point. The heart of the matter is what *Figaro* refers to as the ENE – *Étrangers Non-Européens*. According to Gérard-François Dumont, President of the Institute of Political Demography and *Figaro*'s leading expert on the subject, there are 2.6 million ENE in France. This figure immediately gained wide popular acceptance, although M. Dumont's Institute itself turns out not to exist. When asked how he could justify his 2.6 million figure – far higher than anything the official figures will support – M. Dumont gave a glimpse of his somewhat unusual demographic techniques: 'Every Frenchman knows in his heart of hearts that there are more than 2.6 million non-Europeans in France.'

The interesting point here is the sudden and crafty omission of the word 'foreign': M. Dumont is clearly including those of non-European extraction who are full French citizens and are thus assumed to be right outside the debate. But there are a lot of them, starting with the 400,000 'Harkis' – Algerian Muslims who fought with the French Army and retreated *en masse* to France when Algeria became independent. There are also, no doubt, not inconsiderable numbers of French citizens from the old French empire, especially

Senegal, and from the French Overseas Departments, especially Martinique, Guadeloupe and Réunion. One certainly meets a lot of Antillais (West Indians) in Paris, but since they are and always have been French citizens, they do not get into official statistics about immigration. Undoubtedly though, for the man on the metro to Saint-Denis who finds (as one easily can) that his is the only white face left in his coach by the time the train gets to the terminus, the crucial fact is skin colour, not whether his fellow passengers are Harkis, Antillais or even tourists. (Out in Saint-Denis, by the by, one right-wing mayor is barring all immigrant children from the local schools, thereby implementing part of Le Pen's programme and doubtless hoping to provoke a confrontation with the Government just before the elections). It is now the official policy of the RPR – and thus of the next prime minister – to remove the right to citizenship of those born in France unless it is accompanied by a statement that the applicant will 'seek integration into French society' (by renouncing Islam?), but this is not going to get around the fact of the numerous Harkis and Antillais.

There are many ironies in the immigration imbroglio, starting with the fact that the tenacity of old French imperial assumptions has contributed a great deal to the present situation. It might, of course, have been even more difficult if the Right had got its way. Le Pen, after all, was the most extreme defender of Algérie Française: had he and the rest of the Right succeeded in keeping Algeria as a French department, another twenty million North Africans would now have entry rights to France. More mundanely, it was under de Gaulle, Pompidou and Giscard that the really massive influx of ENEs took place (the Mitterrand government has been more restrictive than any of its predecessors) – and yet the Right has now found in that influx the perfect stick with which to beat and destabilise the Left. Then again, we have the spectacle of Robert Hersant, who has struggled for so long to overcome his unfortunate beginnings on an anti-Semitic paper, reaching the culmination of his career by means of a fresh outpouring of racist panic-mongering. We have, too, the spectacle of Alain Peyrefitte, former Gaullist Minister and one of the forty 'immortals' of the Académie Française, solemnly warning that Colombey-les-Deux-Églises could soon become Colombey-les-Deux-Mosquées. (Peyrefitte, too, is now on the Hersant payroll.) Perhaps most ironic of all is the figure of Mourad Kaouah, an Algerian Deputy under the Fourth Republic and, like not a few Harkis, keen to prove that he is a sort of super-Frenchman through the strength of his hostility to Arab immigrants. A close friend of Le Pen, Kaouah was fourteenth on the FN list in the 1984 European elections (and thus not elected). It is assumed that several of the FN Euro-MPs will resign their seats when they get elected to the French parliament in March. Kaouah will then move up to take one of the vacant places and the Fifth Republic will have its first Arab Deputy at any level – under the colours of the Front National.

The election campaign is clearly going to be a nasty one. How permanent its effect will be is, however, quite another question. Once Chirac has control of the government, he will want to lose his rabble-rousing image and establish a calmer, more statesmanlike and, ultimately, more centrist appeal – essential if he is to appear as a Presidential winner in 1988. This could well militate against an attempt to fulfil some of his wilder anti-immigration commitments – which Mitterrand will anyway use the power of the Elysée to block. In any case, once the present racist mood has produced a right-wing government, it will have largely served its purpose. On the other hand, racism is not going to go away; the coexistence of 4.6 million immigrants and 2.37 million unemployed more or less guarantees that. Besides, the Le Pen phenomenon is well and truly established and while PR lasts Le Pen will remain powerful.

But will PR last? Quite possibly not. All polls show that a majority of Frenchmen want to go back to the old majoritarian system, which they associate with strong, coherent and stable government. Chirac is so determined to get rid of the system that every RPR candidate has been made to sign a contract engaging him to vote the old system back. The Communists and Le Pen will naturally fight for PR while they have breath in their bodies, but many Socialists, although they loyally voted the new system in, would privately prefer the old system back. The pivotal group is likely to be the Centre and Centre-Right. Publicly, they too are committed to going back to the majoritarian system, but the truth is that PR suits them in the same way that it suits the Alliance in Britain. There is already some sign of backsliding there. Chirac, naturally, wants the old system back right away but centrists are beginning to talk of such a change as something for 'after 1988' – the precious principle of unripe time thus making its familiar reappearance. The present betting has to be that Chirac will be strong enough to get his way and that PR will be a one-election wonder. All those who do not wish to see an escalating auction of racist rhetoric at every subsequent election will have to hope that Chirac *does* get his way.

It will be evident that the discussion of PR in practice in France does not have much in common with the *bien-pensant* discussion of PR in theory in Britain. No doubt Alliance spokemen will rush to assure us that it would all work quite differently in Britain because well, we're British. But how different are we? The French example suggests that if you introduce PR to a country which has two million-plus coloured immigrants, high unemployment and a muscular, nationalist Right, things can quite easily spin out of control.

Britain has, I have suggested, been less tolerant and welcoming of immigrants than France. In any case, we too have over two million coloured immigrants; we have at least a million more unemployed than the French; we certainly have a muscular, nationalist Right; and we have a right-wing popular press which is just as unscrupulous as its French counterpart and is run by our own passable imitations of Robert Hersant. Maybe it would be different in Britain. Maybe.

Chapter 8

Le Pen and his Legions

When Jean-Marie Le Pen, leader of the Front National, described his score in the first round of the 1988 French presidential election as a 'political earthquake' he was, for once, not exaggerating. Le Pen's 4.36 million voters – 14.6 per cent of the metropolitan French electorate – not only gave him more than twice as much support as the fading Communists, but also put him in a strong position to influence the result of the second round. In 1974 Le Pen got only 0.74 per cent, and in 1981 he could not even muster enough support to get on to the ballot.

Le Pen himself – a big, tall man with Breton good looks – was infuriated by suggestions earlier this year that his blond hair was not natural. He held a series of televised baths so that one and all could see that he was blond all over. The picture of Aryan manhood was no doubt reassuring to some, but to others it recalled memories of Mussolini speaking while stripped to the waist, or Doriot, the French Fascist leader of the 1930s, speaking with his chest clothed only in an undershirt – the authentic style of macho Fascism. Le Pen denies he is a Fascist or even a racist and claims to have been in the Resistance. (It turns out that as a 16-year-old he tried to join the Resistance on D-Day plus one and was told he was not required.) And he is quick to point out that though he owns a record company that sells disks of Hitler's speeches, the same company sells Churchill's speeches too. He is, he explains, simply a French nationalist and patriot. His election slogan this year was 'Let's defend our colours'. The fact that this was universally taken to imply hostility to the Arab and African immigrants Le Pen wants expelled *en masse* from France was, of course, merely coincidental. Le Pen is always able to point to (surprisingly) a handful of naturalised Jewish supporters to fend off accusations of anti-Semitism.

Le Pen is a veteran of far right politics – he was the youngest

Poujadist deputy swept into Parliament in 1956 by Pierre Poujade's proto-Fascist movement, but left Parliament to sign up with the French army in Algeria. Le Pen's career as a paratrooper in the bloody Algerian conflict has meant that he has been dogged ever since by repeated accusations of having carried out torture on Algerian prisoners, though as yet his accusers have not been successful in a French court. But today he has a strong following among the *pieds noirs* (returned settler) community in southern France, and counts a number of old OAS (Secret Army) Algérie Française fanatics in his entourage. Pierre Sergent, one of the FN deputies in Parliament, is the former head of the OAS who ordered the various assassination attempts on de Gaulle. (Sergent is completely unapologetic about his past and has spoken in Parliament on the need to commemorate as war dead those executed for their part in such attempts.)

After the Algerian war Le Pen devoted himself to the intense sectarian life of the far right fringe. He boasts a glass eye, having lost a real one in an election brawl in this period. Or at least that is what he says. His disaffected ex-wife, Pierrette, whose salty memoirs and bedroom secrets are regularly divulged to weekly magazines for high fees, insists that her former husband lost the eye through simple illness. The truth – whatever it is – is less interesting than the fact that Le Pen is keen to insist on the election brawl variant of the story.

Le Pen first emerged as a public figure in the 1983 municipal elections. Mitterrand's Socialist government had clearly lost its way and much of its popularity, while the opposition conservatives, in power for twenty-three years before 1981, were too tired and familiar to look like an interesting alternative. A political space thus opened up. At the same time Jacques Chirac, the Gaullist leader, opportunistically took up anti-immigrant and law-and-order themes for political effect against the Socialists. Le Pen found it easy to outflank Chirac on both fronts, and with that the movement was set on its way.

Chirac, appalled to find a destructive and charismatic rival on his right, has struggled desperately for five years to regain the political initiative, but to no avail. Indeed, in two years of Chirac government – during which authoritarian policies were initiated on law and order (the crime rate fell) and 130,000 immigrants were expelled or refused entry – Le Pen's support has grown from the ten per cent he achieved in the 1984 (European) and 1986 (parliamentary) elections to 14.6 per cent. In Marseilles, Le Pen took over 28 per cent of the vote.

There are two ways of understanding what Le Pen's Front National stands for. One is to go to the FN's annual Fête Bleu, Blanc, Rouge, typically held at the old Le Bourget airport outside Paris. The first difference from an ordinary political gathering is the tight security at the gate, with Le Pen's burly stewards much in evidence – and you have to pay ten francs to go in. An extraordinary sight then assaults the eyes: side by side on the grass stand a set of nuclear fall-out shelters, plastered with slogans about survivalism and how only Communist peaceniks are frightened of nuclear war, and, next to them, an 'original village of the Gauls,' replete with comic-strip Nordic characters strolling around in blond wigs and winged helmets. The idea seems to be that the village represents the idyllic racial source of the French nation. Inside the hall, every section of the FN has its own stand selling local produce, books, or – the most popular money-spinner – a cardboard cut-out of the Leader. For only forty francs you and your family can be photographed apparently talking to him: there are long queues at many of these stands. Other stands feature posters of John Wayne, highly stylised Wagnerian art – Siegfried in mortal battle with the Dragon and so forth, representations of Joan of Arc, soft-porn pictures of young things frolicking in strength-through-joy country walks, and collections of old right-wing newspapers from the 1920s and 1930s. Present in person when I last attended one of these affairs were Afghan guerrillas, Lebanese Christians and representatives of integrist Catholicism, the last frequently wearing traditional priestly garb. But the most popular thing to be is a para. In addition to the FN newspaper's own paratrooper team, groups of young men strolled around in battle fatigues looking tough while stands sell material defending the paras from charges of torture during the Algerian war (though the effect was rather spoiled by one pamphlet entitled 'Torture – Why Not?'). My favourite stand was a representation of the history of the French Right, with lengthy portrayals of 'the struggle over Dreyfus' right through to the present, but with a strange gap for the period 1940–45.

By evening all is ready for the appearance of the Leader. In the amphitheatre lights dim and thousands of hands hold lighter flames aloft in the dark (the FN symbol is a flame) as patriotic songs crash out. Finally the spotlight picks out Le Pen, and amid a surge of hysterical adulation he struggles through the crowd to the podium. Young couples hold their babies aloft to get a glimpse of the great man. Typically, Le Pen will warm up his audience by mentioning the names of journalists who have 'insulted' him (the names are heavily or exclusively Jewish), and the audience roars back its hatred after every name. Then he stops and reminds them that Jesus was angry when he saw the merchants in the temple and that when he, Le Pen, was insulted by such journalists 'I, like Jesus, knew the emotion of anger'. Euphoric cheers. The technique is simple: one minute the audience is baying like a mad dog in its hatred of Jewish journalists, the next it is up there in heaven, with the Leader and Jesus side by side. Le Pen maintains the same violent emotional swings for an hour or so – and often gets in a favourable reference to the old Vichy slogan of *'Travail, Famille, Patrie'*. As he speaks, he roams all over the stage like a rock star in concert.

The other way of understanding Le Pen is to look at who votes for him. Because the Communists have been losing strength at the same time that the FN has been gaining it, some observers have rushed to the conclusion that there simply has been a wholesale transfer of extremist votes from the Far Left to the Far Right. It is true that there are such cases, but they are the minority: only a quarter of Le Pen's vote comes from the Socialists and Communists put together, while fully three-quarters comes from those who previously supported orthodox conservatives.

Le Pen's support has changed, however. In the early days his voters had the classic profile of the old French Right – disproportionately upper-class, old, and Catholic. Over time this profile has changed radically, becoming ever younger, lower-class, more secular, and increasingly male. One is struck by this at FN meetings: the ageing Vichyites and *pieds noirs* are now often outnumbered by leather-jacketed – and frequently unemployed – working-class youths. Right across the age range men outnumber women by nearly two-to-one in FN ranks, but the further down the age range one goes, the more male Le Pen's support becomes: among teenagers the male disproportion is three-to-one.

It is also among the alienated young men – among whom the urge to *épater les bourgeois* is strong – that Le Pen finds his toughest and most radical militants. On my way home from one FN meeting I found that young FN militants had scrawled their own recipe for 'Jewish cooking' all over the Metro: 'first put your Jew in the oven', it began. But while FN voters seem to have a high tolerance of anti-Semitism, it is seldom what draws them to the movement. Typically, FN voters are disenchanted with the whole political establishment, furious that unemployment has risen (to twice the American and above the British level), and are highly susceptible to a simplistic superpatriotism. Hatred of Arab immigrants and an exaggerated sense of personal insecurity are the chief expressions of this frustration –

typically FN voters claim that they or those they know have been the victims of a crime rate far in excess of anything that actually exists.

But as Le Pen's movement grows it becomes a home for other discontented groups as well – small farmers threatened by farm amalgamations, small shopkeepers (31 per cent of whom have just voted for Le Pen), monarchists, the old Catholic Right and all manner of freaks and misfits. Special mention has to be made of the Moonies – the head of the Moonies in France (and nephew of the former head of the employers' federation) is an FN deputy. Moonie funds are said to flow plentifully into the movement.

But the FN coalition is still fragile. Many old conservatives have jumped aboard and are overrepresented among the FN's deputies in the French and European parliaments. They are resented by the more overtly Fascist wing – the *'purs et durs'* grouped behind Jean-Pierre Stirbois, the soft-spoken and methodical Secretary-General of the party. Disputes between Stirbois and more moderate elements (such as Le Pen's campaign manager, Bruno Mégret) have repeatedly erupted into violence. Shortly before the election only the intervention of Le Pen's personal bodyguards (led by the awesome Freddy the Catcher – the 'Butcher of Béthune') prevented Mégret from being beaten up by Stirbois heavies.

Stirbois is seen by many as the Himmler of the movement – he is a strong proponent of the view that the Holocaust never really occurred, and it is believed that Le Pen's description of the Nazi gas chambers as a mere 'detail of history' was an attempt to placate the Stirbois wing. And increasingly it needs placating, for Stirbois seethes at the possibility of a sell-out to the orthodox Right, and he has built up a formidable party apparatus over which he has personal and absolute control. Similarly, the party's newspaper, *Minute*, recurrently threatens to escape from Le Pen's control.

None the less, these tensions will likely be contained as long as the FN continues to prosper. One cannot but reflect that prior to 1940 the extreme Right was a permanent fixture in French politics and that each time it re-emerged after that – in the shape of Vichy, then of Poujadism, and then of the Algérie Française ultras – it was de Gaulle who smashed it, who beheaded the monster. Now, almost twenty years after de Gaulle's death, the monster has woken again.

The article above was written at what was almost certainly the moment of Le Pen's zenith. On the presidential second round Le Pen, while overtly

calling for a vote against Mitterrand, did all he could to help the sitting President – refusing to endorse Mitterrand's opponent, Chirac, and dropping broad hints about how tempting an option abstention was. The fact was that the FN had thrived in opposition to a Left government and it was Mitterrand who had brought in proportional representation in 1986, which had allowed the FN to elect thirty-five deputies. And, of course, since Le Pen has been competing for voters most directly with Chirac, relations between the Gaullists and the FN are particularly envenomed. Almost a quarter of Le Pen's voters took the hint and helped re-elect Mitterrand – who promptly disappointed Le Pen by dissolving parliament. Not only did the FN fall back towards the 10 per cent level but the return to a majoritarian voting system was quite fatal to the Front, who re-elected just one deputy. Ironically for such a macho party, their lone representative was a lady, Mme Yann Piat.

After this things rather fell apart for Le Pen. Deprived of a large parliamentary presence, he fought desperately to retain visibility and credibility – which in turn lured him into his notorious 'Durafour-crématoire' remark, that is to say, into another tasteless joke about the Holocaust. His support fell sharply this time – the polls suggested that many who had forgiven him his previous remark about the gas chambers being a mere 'detail' felt that twice was more than enough. Mme Piat certainly felt that way and parted company with Le Pen, who thus found himself with no deputies at all. This sudden fall from favour exacerbated tensions within the leadership – when the party Secretary-General, Stirbois, was killed in a road accident in late 1988 it was noticeable that Le Pen and most of the rest of the leadership boycotted the funeral. This combination of events has robbed the party not only of some of its credibility but, more important, perhaps, of its semi-respectability. Only a few years ago it was possible for someone like the film star Alain Delon to describe Le Pen as 'my good friend – a fine Frenchman'. One suspects that even the arch-conservative M. Delon would shrink from such a statement now.

All of which has led many to believe that Le Pen's success may have been merely an example of a 'flash' movement, enjoying a brief, if nightmarish, vogue. The best comparison may lie in the history of the FN's British analogue, the equally racist and extreme National Front, which enjoyed a striking surge of support in 1976, scoring well in a whole series of local elections and by-elections. This high tide of the British Far Right was achieved with much the same sociological mix we have seen in France – a largely young, male and working-class base of support drummed up in racist opposition to coloured immigration. The British NF never equalled the electoral heights gained by Le Pen: the summit of its achievement came in the city of Leicester in 1976 when the NF achieved almost 20 per cent of the local election vote – which, given that around a quarter of that city's population was non-white, must have meant that almost one white in four voted for the Front. The FN reached this peak in the midst of a strong conservative reaction against the Labour government elected two years earlier – just as Le Pen's movement thrived on a traumatised conservative reaction to the early years of Socialist rule in France. In Britain, the National Front collapsed almost as suddenly as it had emerged, riven by leadership squabbles and having shown the cloven hoof of pro-nazi sympathies once too often. For one of the conditions of success for a Fascist movement in the post-1945 world is that it does not too clearly reveal its kinship with the Fascist movements of the pre-1945 world.

At the time of writing, at least, Le Pen's Front National seemed to be experiencing exactly the same trajectory as the ill-fated British National Front. Despite that, a parallel collapse of the Front National in France seems unlikely. By 1988 Le Pen had already been a significant force for over five years, after all – rather a long time for a 'flash' movement. And the FN was better organised, had grown deeper popular roots, had a lot more money than the British NF ever had – and, of course, had a far more formidable leader. But you only had to listen to Le Pen's young militants selling Minute, the party paper, at a Le Pen rally, to notice a far more important difference – that the French movement had a far greater weight of tradition and history behind it than its British counterpart could ever have. Those shouts of 'A bas la République juive! A bas la démocratie juive!' might be emitted by the French equivalent of 1980s punk rockers and skinheads, but the cry comes echoing down to us from the era of the anti-Dreyfusards and before. There is the weight of a terrible tradition here, of an unhappy history whose sadness and poison have not been exhausted, much less expunged. Le Pen's legions are fewer now than once they were, but their march is not over yet.

Chapter 9

The Revolution is Over

When I was small I was marooned over several summers in the home of my grandfather, a retired engine-driver who had left school at the age of eleven. I was dreadfully bored and the only readable books in the house were the twelve volumes of The Wonderland of Knowledge, originally bought for my mother in the early 1930s. In those endless summer afternoons I read my way right through those volumes and had reason to feel grateful for the fact for many years afterwards. That is how I first learned the names of Marat, Danton and Robespierre. The Wonderland of Knowledge took a pretty stern line about them all: the latter was always referred to as 'the extremist, Robespierre', Louis XVI was pictured distributing alms to his peasants, and there was a lot about Marie-Antoinette's 'noble fortitude' and her (apparently deserving) beauty. None of this made much impression on me: I was pretty sure that the revolutionaries were goodies and that the king and queen had had it all coming to them. After all, The Wonderland of Knowledge clearly expected one to be enthused about the heroes of Marathon, Robin Hood, Spartacus and Hereward the Wake and I felt reasonably sure that they would all have helped sack the Bastille rather than defend it. This was enough. I have never really lost my enthusiasm for the Revolution, despite having had to read a lot about it and despite the 1989 celebrations, calculated as they clearly were to stamp out such enthusiasm for ever.

Eugen Weber, who contributes one of the essays to the interesting collection, edited by Best (1988), writes of the way the Revolution became a national obsession in nineteenth century France. The reason was, at least in part, that throughout the century the threat – or indeed the reality – of violent political change was never off the agenda. One can go further, however. Historical awareness of the Revolution may not run deep among the mass of Frenchmen, but it often does among the élite, for whom it constitutes an elaborate dramatic metaphor shadowing the practices and institutions of contemporary life. Thus at the height of the May Events of 1968, the French Communist Party, full of quasi-revolutionary rhetoric, announced that it would hold a large public demonstration through the streets of Paris. A route-map of the demonstration was published which showed that it would lead past the Hôtel de Ville (which houses the *mairie* of Paris); then, just before the march began, the route was altered so as to bypass the Hôtel de Ville. The point which the PCF was (rightly) sure would not be lost on the governing élite was, of course, that the seizure of the Hôtel de Ville has been the customary first step in any revolutionary seizure of power. In other words, the original announcement constituted an implicit threat that, unless concessions were made to it, the PCF might run up the red flag over City Hall; the revision absolved the PCF of all responsibility should, for example, any Trotskyites among the marchers try to take matters into their own hands. The authorities, in their turn, would have responded within this well-understood, if unstated, tradition, which is still sufficiently alive to allow such creative improvisation: indeed, stays alive through it. Many of the central traditions of British political life, by contrast, such as the state-encrusted flummery of Black Rod, the Mace and the Queen's Speech, are quite dead: the rows about the handling of the sacred Mace are really to do with the blasphemous disturbance of a corpse.

Eugen Weber amends Marx to say that when revolution repeats itself, it becomes not tragedy or farce but tradition. Looking at what is planned for the bicentennial of 1789, one can see that there is a further stage to this cycle, when everything deteriorates into a sort of Disneyland heritage theme-park replication of itself. And when it comes to sheer bad taste the French, on their day, have few equals. It's not just a matter of fireworks, tightrope-walkers and waiters in Phrygian caps, though we shall have all of these in abundance. Douglas Johnson, in a customarily masterful essay, mentions two rather finer examples. An immense tower will be built to desecrate the Place de la Bastille, and the entire population of Paris will then be invited to take a brick home with him/her (there will be a brick each) so that, this time, anyone can share in the dismantling of the Bastille. Better still is the proposal to commemorate the women's march from Versailles to Paris by building a trench the entire length of the route and filling it with six thousand urns containing urine. Floating irresistibly back come recollections of John Nance Garner, Vice-President of the United States, describing his own job as 'about as much use as a pitcher of warm piss'. John Nance Garner, where are you now that we need you? The *bizarrerie* that pleases me most is that in Nouméa, the capital of New Caledonia, 14 July will be marked by a pop concert by Johnny Clegg, 'le Zoulou blanc' (unknown in Britain, where, as a South African, he is banned from TV, but bigger than Springsteen or Michael Jackson in France). What would Danton have thought of the Revolution being commemorated by a left-wing South African singing Zulu rock in the South Pacific? Perhaps it's best we don't know. One longs, at times, for the more considered attitude of Mao Tse-tung, who, when asked what he thought the effects of 1789 had been, replied after some thought that it was still too soon to know.

It is perhaps worth remembering that the 150th anniversary in 1939 was a disaster. The Minister of Finance did not want to spend any money on the celebrations, while the President was frightened that the whole thing would turn into a giant left-wing demonstration. Bad weather and a complete absence of popular enthusiasm for the anniversary caused the celebrations to collapse into shambles and fiasco. At the end of the summer the whole thing was brought to a summary – and apocalyptic – conclusion by the outbreak of a new world war. The 1989 celebrations ought to avoid that fate, but their success should not be taken for granted. The bitter rivalry between Mitterrand's Elysée and Chirac's Hôtel de Ville has already caused the cancellation of Mitterrand's plan for an international exhibition. Chirac, speaking as 'M. le Maire', argued that Paris could not cope with all the visitors and attendant pressures such an event would entail: the President's plan, he said, simply took no account of the hassle and frayed nerves of his – Chirac's – municipal constituents. The argument was irresistible – the Exhibition clearly could not go ahead against the opposition of City Hall – but rang a little hollow given Chirac's simultaneous and Herculean attempts to attract the Olympics to Paris.

There are many good reasons why the Revolution should be popular. It is worth quoting Eugene Kamenka at length:

> Europe and Latin America by the end of the 19th century, and Asia, Africa and the Pacific by the last quarter of the 20th century, have come to stand in the shadow of the French Revolution, to live in . . . the new age inaugurated by that Revolution and symbolised by it. The appeal to reason, the elevation of the people as sovereign and of their welfare as constituting the point of government, the doctrine of progress, the acceptance of revolutionary ideologies and revolutionary transformations, are a basic part of the modern world. For two hundred years it has been impossible to speak of nationalism . . .

socialism and democracy, of self-determination for peoples and nations, of government by law and of the belief in human rights . . . of 'the people's' demands, of . . . 'secular' education, political propaganda and the state's role in promoting 'enlightenment', of popular participation, factional struggles and class conflicts, without thinking of or unconsciously echoing themes introduced by the French Revolution.

The Revolution produced more even than that. Among its fruits must also be counted religious emancipation, the notion of equality before the law, the abolition of slavery, the idea of the perfectibility of man, national unity, a common language, a rational and uniform system of administration, a common coinage and system of weights and measures (and with that the metric system), the guillotine, the provision of zoos and restaurants (and thus the generalisation of French cuisine), the concept of 'historical monuments', political banquets and the notions of 'Right' and 'Left'. At least, these were among the things that lasted: much else was invented that did not last, such as the worship of the Goddess of Reason, the new calendar of months (Thermidor, Brumaire, etc.) and the metric day, which left behind a sad little heritage of useless watches and clocks with ten-hour dials. Little wonder that Douglas Johnson quotes Chinese students coming to France in the early decades of this century because 'it is France which holds the three mainsprings of modernity: the doctrine of the rights of man, the theory of evolution and socialism'. (Englishmen who thought evolution was something to do with Darwin should take a stroll in the Jardin des Plantes, near Jussieu, where they may see the statue of Lamarck inscribed *Fondateur de la Doctrine d'Evolution.*)

As Johnson notes, however, the Revolution has never been really popular in France. This is so for a host of reasons, beginning with the tourist notion that kings and nobles left palaces and art galleries which the barbarous revolutionaries merely damaged. Moreover, historians have studied the Revolution almost to death, making it impossible for anyone to make any general statement about it with confidence. Finally, the Revolution was simply too radical for a cautiously bourgeois nation ever to feel quite comfortable with it. Take even so central an event as the execution of the King. As Conor Cruise O'Brien points out, for anyone committed to the notion of popular sovereignty the very existence of a king was an attack on all one held most dear, a crime against the nation – the King's indictment spoke of 'the nation blasphemed'. No British nonsense here about 'King and Country': if you were for the King, you were against country and put yourself outside the nation. When Stendhal heard of the King's execution he experienced 'one of the sharpest feelings of joy I have ever felt in my life'. This is all well and good, and not a few of us would wish that cutting off Charles I's head had had the same results as cutting off Louis XVI's; but the idea of feeling 'the sharpest feelings of joy' at the news of *any* execution is not a comfortable one. Similarly, one can understand why enthusiasts of the Revolution like Mathiez, Lefebvre and Jean Jaurès tended to glorify Robespierre: 'my place is among the Jacobins, alongside Robespierre', writes the liberal humanist Jaurès proudly. One can agree with Mignet that the Revolution saw 'transient excesses alongside lasting benefits'. But that is not enough: we have all seen how socialist enthusiam led to excusing Stalin, how ideological zealotry led to Pol Pot. Maybe we are too squeamish, but the idea of going along with 'transient excesses' has become pretty difficult these days, even for the left or liberal intellectual, let alone the comfortable bourgeois.

There is also the uncomfortable fact that the Counter-Revolution and the Right found it all too easy to turn the Revolution's innovations to its own account. The Revolution's early internationalism and republicanism were, of course, betrayed by Bonaparte, but O'Brien rightly points out how easily the early 'patriotism' was Prussianised into a racist, regimented nationalism. Similarly the conscription on which the Revolution's armies were based came to serve more reactionary causes, to the point where, instead of building the army in the image of the nation, we have all too often seen the building of nations in the image of their armies. And one reason why revolution so often gives way to counter-revolution is precisely that it has squandered its moral advantage, made it seem that the only choice is between equally murderous opponents. The love of mankind leads to the necessity of abolishing inequality and the levelling of class differences; and when the privileged resist, this leads to what Burke called 'homicidal philanthropy'. If you love man and equality enough, you end up killing men for their own good.

This, at least in part, is the argument of counter-revolutionaries from Burke to Solzhenitsyn – and 1789 introduced not merely the romantic notion of revolution but the idea of counter-revolution too. Their case is ably surveyed here by George Steiner: 'The attempts to institute on earth "kingdoms of justice", to legislate the messianic in secular terms, go not only against the grain of human nature . . . they go against the grain of divine providence. It is in the first and last nature of the human condition, in the alpha and omega of politics and history, that those who plant "trees of liberty" shall, rapidly, make of them gate-posts to prisons and to death-camps.'

Which is all very wise and well, and rather unfair – for the practitioners of revolution are here being held up against the theorists of counter-revolution. But counter-revolution has its practitioners too, its Admiral Horthys, Francos and Pinochets, men who are so devoted to Christian civilisation that they are willing to kill, torture and crucify quite endlessly in its name. This reality, too, must be considered. Even Burke's still-powerful critique of the Revolution has to be set alongside the fact that what his fine phrases were actually defending was the corrupt oligarchy of pre-Reform Act England, a world of squire-ish arrogance and a quite casual denial of the rights and sufferings of the majority. Burke, after all, spoke for the class that had just provoked – and lost to – the American Revolution, without ever really understanding that either: in that sense, his strictures on the French Revolution are the sheerest cheek. Men like Burke are always wise after the event, never before: it is only after the Bastille has been stormed that such men discover that their disapproval of those who stormed it is now matched by a retrospective sympathy for those who had been locked up in it. Not surprisingly, Burke has always been largely ignored in France.

What do the French think of their Revolution? An opinion survey made by the IPSOS polling agency taken on 20–1 December 1988 found that a third of those interviewed were 'Don't knows' even when asked such open questions as what they thought had been the most important events of the Revolution. Not surprisingly, the taking of the Bastille came top (37 per cent), followed by the Declaration of the Rights of Man (16 per cent), the execution of the King and Queen (13 per cent) and the abolition of aristocratic and other privileges (10 per cent). Among the changes wrought by the Revolution, human rights (17 per cent) and greater freedom (16 per cent) topped the poll ahead of universal male suffrage (some, oddly, attributed female suffrage to the Revolution, though that did not come until 1945). This identification of the Revolution with liberty (which is no doubt strengthened in the popular mind by the fact that 14 July marks the beginning of the summer holiday season) remains powerful but vague – only 30 per cent could cite the first article of the Declaration of the Rights of Man, and when asked which three words symbolised the Revolution, 55 per cent got liberty, 48 per cent equality, while fraternity, as ever the poor relation, got 43 per cent. In the poll for the most important personalities of the Revolution, Robespierre (48 per cent) and Danton (40 per cent) came far ahead of all others – Marat came next with 12 per cent. Neither Robespierre nor Danton were unambiguous heroes, as became clear when IPSOS asked respondents their views on what one might almost literally term the crunch issue: who did they think ought to have been guillotined? Twenty-one per cent thought Robespierre deserved to be executed (11 per cent thought the same of Danton), and another 12 per cent (16 per cent in Danton's case) thought that his execution was inevitable, that he had simply been caught out at his own game. By comparison, Louis XVI's execution evoked a mere 19-per-cent-all tie in the approval ratings, though nobody had anything positive to say about the King. What these figures suggest is that the revolutionary Terror has made a far deeper impression on the popular imagination than the more humdrum, everyday cruelties of the Áncien Régime. The main reason for this is that nobody can imagine the monarchy ever coming back – it is a bogy-man that has long ceased to exist, but Robespierre seems a frighteningly contemporary figure.

This was evident when respondents were asked to situate the Revolution politically. It is still not seen as an event that belongs to everyone. 10 per cent associated it with the extreme Left, 41 per cent with the Left, 23 per cent with the Centre, 9 per cent with the Right and 2 per cent the extreme Right.

When asked which contemporary political figures seemed to be the chief inheritors of the Revolution, two Socialists came top, Mitterrand with 31 per cent and Rocard with 14 per cent. It seems clear, however, that this is simply because they are the immediate exemplifications of the Republic. And the Republic, crucially, is seen as the chief legacy of the Revolution: indeed, to be virtually identical with it. Thus when respondents were asked who had done most to continue the Revolution, de Gaulle (30 per cent) had no real competition: Jaurès (8 per cent), Pompidou (7 per cent) and Mitterrand (6 per cent) brought up the tail with a host of others. De Gaulle, a Catholic conservative who disliked all politicians, fought the Left, and did all he could to reduce the role of the National Assembly, could hardly be said to personify the spirit of '89. But, quite clearly, this concerned voters less than the fact that he had stood out for the republic against Vichy in 1940 and had refounded the Republic again in 1958. Similarly, it is difficult to explain why Pompidou, President for only five years and dead fifteen years ago, should rank ahead of Mitterrand, the once and future President, but for the fact that Pompidou is still seen by many as the man who saved the Republic from anarchy in 1968.

The simplistic identification of the Revolution with liberty, the Republic and not much else attests to the fact that, as François Furet puts it, 'the Revolution is over' – a fact the large number of 'Don't knows' in the IPSOS poll would seem to confirm. Two things kept the Revolution alive so long: the ever-present possibility of violent political change and the opposition to it of the intransigent Right. These factors are now no longer relevant. Despite the speed wobble of 1968, the Fifth Republic is now assumed to guarantee political stability as far ahead as anyone can see; and the sort of Right which wanted to get rid of Liberté, Egalité, Fraternité as the national motto went down to defeat and disgrace with Pétain. Since 1944, all conservative movements of note, however right-wing, have been avowedly republican. Indeed, the Algiers coup of 13 May 1958, without doubt the most serious right-wing threat France has known since the Liberation, bore poignant witness to the strength of the republican tradition, even as it overthrew the Fourth Republic. Even before they got down to the business of planning the paratroop drop which was to take Paris and install a military junta, the right-wing officers and *colons* who staged the coup formally constituted themselves into a Committee of Public Safety, a quite self-conscious echo of 1789.

The Revolution is over in other ways too. The most fundamental social change wrought by 1789 was the seizure of the great estates by millions of serfs. Henceforward the first law of French politics, respected by all regimes irrespective of political coloration, was that these millions of smallholders must be kept happy, or at least solvent, by a policy of agricultural protection. In time, this policy was extended to the rest of Europe and renamed the Common Agricultural Policy. The CAP persists, of course, but at long last product ceilings and quotas have begun to open up cracks in it, and now that it benefits Greek, Portuguese, Irish and Spanish peasants more than French ones, there is a serious possibility of fundamental reform. By the same token, 1992 and all that points clearly towards a reduction of the system of European national states inaugurated by 1789.

Perhaps the man who has done most to turn the page on 1789 is Robert Badinter, the quietly-spoken Jewish civil rights lawyer who was Mitterrand's Minister of Justice from 1981 to 1986. M. Badinter was not a member of the Socialist Party, but he stuck to his libertarian principles with such bravery than many within the PS came to feel he was the best socialist in the Government. For the Right, he was the hated symbol of the Left's permissiveness and 'laxity' with criminals – M. Badinter even had to endure anti-Semitic demonstrations against him by a section of the Paris Police. Through all this he persevered with the gigantic task of replacing the Code Napoléon, an objective which reformers have had in mind for almost two hundred years but whose achievement had eluded everyone. This monument of law reform was shelved when the Left lost power in 1986, but now it is again before the National Assembly and it seems certain that this Parliament will legislate through the Code Badinter (as it is already called). I once visited M. Badinter in his office at the Constitutional Council (whose President he has been since 1986) and was much impressed by his soft-spoken intelligence and quick practical grasp. During our conversation my eyes kept wandering to an artefact standing on the mantlepiece in front of a large gilded mirror. It was a framed copy of another reform with which M. Badinter had signalled the end of the Revolutionary era: the Bill to abolish Madame Guillotine, no less.

References

Best, Geoffrey (ed.) (1988) *The Permanent Revolution: The French Revolution and its Legacy 1789–1989* (London:Fontana).

Chapter 10
The Battle for the Mairies, 1989

At least since the turn of the year only one topic has really mattered to the French political élite: the municipal elections to be fought over two rounds on 12 and 19 March. For these are the basic elections in French political life, held only once every six years and deciding who is to control the local power and patronage which form the necessary springboard to all other forms of political power. It is still the case, as it has been ever since 1870, that the great majority of parliamentary deputies are also mayors, and now that Mitterrand has made it illegal to hold more than two elected offices one has seen even former Cabinet Ministers giving up their parliamentary seats in order to keep their Mairie and their regional council seats. A man who really digs himself in as mayor of a great city – Jacques Chaban-Delmas in Bordeaux or Dominique Baudis in Toulouse are contemporary examples – becomes a great regional baron with whom all governments, whether of Left or Right, must treat. Sometimes one finds family dynasties running cities – the Baudis of Toulouse or the Medecin family in Nice, for example, but one can also find cases of major national careers built round a family's grip on a smaller town – as with the Centrist leader, Pierre Méhaignerie, who has inherited the Mairie (and overwhelming majorities) at Vitre. And the French sense of localism is so strong that even in far smaller towns, where there is not much real power at stake, a keen desire to achieve local notability can produce struggles of Clochemerle-like intensity. The French take a lively interest in who is to represent their town to the world, and even in the 34,306 towns of fewer than 3,500 people turn-out is generally over 75 per cent. But most attention fastens on the 2,084 bigger towns and especially the 388 towns with populations over 20,000. Voting is on a mixed majority/proportional basis and competing party lists may be combined between rounds, often after a somewhat Rabelaisian bargaining process.

An American candidate who lost a presidential election as badly as Jacques Chirac did in May 1988 would no doubt be finished. But Chirac is the undislodgeable mayor of Paris, the greatest prize of all, and that alone guarantees him continuing front rank on the national scene. But Pierre Joxe, the Socialist who leads the challenge to Chirac this year, has a number of cards up his sleeve too, for M. Joxe is also the Minister of the Interior, with control over Paris's police and, to the extent that anyone controls it, the city's traffic. Joxe got off to a spanking start by using his Ministerial powers to annul the voters' rolls drawn up by Chirac's men at 806 of the 957 Paris polling stations. But Chirac won all twenty of the city's *arrondissements* in 1983 and Joxe has already made it clear that he will be happy if he can just prevent another RPR grand slam this time.

M. Joxe has also pioneered a technique followed by a number of other Socialists: having failed to reach agreement with the Communists (PCF) he will run against them on the first round, leaving the few places on his list he is willing to concede them blank and hoping to get them to accept them on the second. The Socialist Party (PS) has conducted long and difficult negotiations with the PCF with the aim of achieving united Left lists, but at the end there could still be PS versus PCF 'primaries' in about eighty of the big towns – including seventeen which the Left holds. It is extremely unlikely that the PCF can capture any PS town, but the risk exists that this intra-Left feuding could cost the PS towns such as Besançon, Lens, Pau and Créteil. The PCF will also be defending against the PS in such key Communist citadels as Amiens and Dieppe and desperately hoping at least to beat back the PS in order to stay the leading party of the Left in towns which the Party lost to the Right in 1983, such as Arles, Nîmes, Reims and Saint-Etienne. The PCF is fighting for survival – its municipal bastions are almost all it has left – and it will be a no-holds-barred struggle. But the PCF is taking a suicidally sectarian line – which has already cost it Le Mans, its second biggest town (after Le Havre): here a popular sitting Communist mayor, Robert Jarry, has been expelled from the PCF for reaching an agreement with the PS of which the Party disapproved. Opinion polls suggest that the official PCF list now being run against M. Jarry will be humiliated and Jarry hugely re-elected. An exactly similar situation exists in Orly, where the popular sitting PCF mayor, Gaston Viens, has just been expelled from the Party. No anti-Communist could conceivably do greater damage to the PCF than it is currently doing to itself.

The Gaullist RPR and centre-right UDF have been more successful at achieving unity on the Right, but they have the same difficulties as the PCF faced with Mitterrand's attempt to create a pro-Government Centre-Left. Mainly, the Centre is trying to run with Right support, but in some cases (at Auxerre, for example) Centrists now find themselves challenged by their old UDF supporters, while in Grenoble the sitting RPR mayor, Alain Carignon, has sown confusion within the Left by including several old Socialists as well as Centrists on his list. At Lille much bad feeling has been caused by the fierce competition within the Right – won by M. Alex Turk (RPR) – over who should lead the anti-Socialist challenge to the PS party leader, Pierre Mauroy – a storm over nothing since Mauroy is bound to hold Lille whatever happens. (In 1983 M. Mauroy's right-wing opponent came to grief in spectacular fashion after his house burnt down in a clear case of arson. Fighting a tough law and order campaign, he attempted to instance the fire as an example of the sort of vandalism Socialist permissiveness had encouraged. Complete denouement followed when it emerged that the arsonist – apparently suffering a sort of political mid-life crisis – was the number two man on his own right-wing list.) Not far away, at the aviation industry town of Beauvais, Olivier Dassault, the heir to the enormous Dassault empire, is trying to storm the Mairie, having last year captured the Beauvais parliamentary seat held for thirty years by his grandfather, the legendary Marcel Dassault. The sitting PS mayor, Walter Amsallem, seems confident of fending off his young RPR challenger, pointing out that Beauvais had a left-wing mayor all the time that the elder Dassault was its (Gaullist) deputy and that old Marcel never dared run for mayor.

A very different sort of contest is going on in Cannes, where the RPR mayor, Mme Anne-Marie Dupuy, is facing a stiff challenge from a young UDF hopeful, Michel Mouillot, a close friend of the Republican Party leader, François Léotard. Léotard, who has a reputation as something of a Flash Harry, all media image and no substance, first lit upon M. Mouillot (an ex-marketing director for Pernod) when he was Minister of Culture, putting him in charge of advertising for one of the State TV chains, and clearly feels that Cannes, as a film city, will warm to a media man. M. Mouillot has brought lots of showbiz friends in to campaign for him and his list includes the rugby international, Jean-Pierre Rives, and Evelyne Leclerc, a lady TV announcer (known in French as *une speakerine*). He has announced that it is his ambition to become 'the Kennedy of the Côte d'Azure' and is certainly spending money as if he were a Kennedy. In a town where 40 per cent of the population are, like the sitting mayor, over 60, this glitz-at-all-costs approach looks a shade unwise.

The two most critical contests, however, are in the towns that vie for the title of 'the second city', Lyons and Marseilles. Lyons, always a conservative city, is to the UDF what Paris is to the RPR – the jewel in the crown. It is also the base of last year's UDF presidential candidate, Raymond Barre, Lyons has had only four mayors this century – including Edouard Herriot, the old Radical leader who died in office after fifty years as mayor. His successor, Louis Pradel, also died in office in 1976, since when a local UDF businessmen, Francisque Collomb, has ruled the city with an iron hand, M. Collomb's most notable achievement is that he saw off Jacques Soustelle's bid for the Mairie when the former OAS leader, returning from exile, tried to relaunch his political career from Lyons. Collomb, who has worked in Lyons since 1927, is known as an opinionated, authoritarian fixer. His is an administration full of *vieux crabes* and arcane back-stage deals. 'If people knew a fifth of what was going on', comments one young UDF councillor, 'nobody would vote.'

In 1983 M. Collomb only just beat back a strong RPR challenge from the ambitious young Gaullist leader, Michel Noir. Now, in 1989, M. Collomb is running again – 'Despite my age of 78 I can still do the 100 metres with anyone', he claims. M. Noir offered M. Collomb a unity pact this time if he could have the number two list position, i.e. so that he would succeed as mayor if, once again, Lyons's mayor dies in office. But the UDF can read the actuarial tables too, and the present UDF deputy-mayor, André Soulier, refused to budge. When, accordingly, M. Noir announced that he would fight the UDF head-on again, Raymond Barre felt badly squeezed: he senses (as do the polls) that the city's future may well lie with Noir's younger team, and announced that he could only support the UDF list if it was comprehensively rejuvenated. But not only is M. Collomb heading the UDF list, but eight of the nine old UDF *arrondissement* leaders are just the same as before. Despite this M. Barre has agreed to run on the list himself, for he realises that, in the crunch, the UDF simply cannot afford to lose Lyons to the RPR. A victory for M. Noir, on the other hand, would go a long way to restoring morale in the RPR, which has looked somewhat lost since Chirac's resounding presidential defeat last May. The UDF, for its part, has complained bitterly at the RPR's breaking conservative unity by its bid for Lyons – and is getting its own back with a similar bid to topple the RPR mayor of Brest.

The contest which has captured the country's imagination is, however, in Marseilles. For over thirty years the city was all but synonymous with its endlessly cunning PS mayor, Gaston Defferre. In 1986, however, Defferre fought a furious and losing battle for control of the local PS federation with its new rising star, Michel Pezet. On 5 May 1986 the unthinkable occurred: Defferre was finally outvoted at a stormy meeting of the PS executive committee. He returned home, fell into a coma and died. From that day on the Defferre faction – led by Defferre's widow, the writer Mme Edmonde Charles-Roux, and Defferre's doctor, Robert Vigouroux – have treated Pezet as a virtual parricide. Dr Vigouroux, whom no one has accused of being politically sophisticated, and whom Defferre had put on the municipal council simply as a loyal makeweight, took over as mayor and quickly announced that he had no intention of giving way to M. Pezet whatever happened. But M. Pezet is one of the most skilful and serpentine infighters in French politics. Bit by bit he consolidated his hold over the local PS, captured its mayoral nomination and won over a majority of the PS municipal councillors, putting Dr Vigouroux into a humiliating and impotent minority position.

Marseilles is by far the biggest PS city and the prospect of its being lost to the Right has shocked the PS leadership, from Mitterrand down, into endless – though fruitless – attempts to effect a Vigouroux–Pezet reconciliation. The local PCF, led by Guy Hermier, have sided with M. Pezet, so Dr Vigouroux has brought dissident Communists on to his list – which will make reconciliation between the two camps that much harder.

The Right's challenger in Marseilles is the UDF's parliamentary leader, Jean-Claude Gaudin, who actually had the galling experience of winning more votes than Defferre in the 1983 contest only to see Defferre take a majority of council seats thanks to an ingenious electoral system for the city worked out by the then Minister of the Interior . . . Gaston Defferre. Chirac's cohabitation government of 1986-8 naturally altered the system, this time to favour the Right, but a more significant advantage for M. Gaudin is the virtual collapse of Jean-Marie Le Pen's Front National (FN) in the last six months. For Marseilles, an old, crumbling port deeply marked by urban decay, high unemployment and severe social problems, is also a centre not only of Arab immigration but of bitterly anti-Arab *pieds noirs* resettled from Algeria – a mix which made it the FN's key stamping ground. In last year's presidential election Le Pen took a full 25 per cent of the vote right across the city, and it was universally assumed that Le Pen would run for the Mairie of Marseilles. All else apart, M. Pezet, Gaudin and the local PCF leader,

M. Hermier, are all reputed to be gay – a fact which the FN were keen to exploit in this ultra-macho city by running Le Pen as 'a real man'. But the FN, badly damaged by the abolition of proportional representation at parliamentary level – which cost it all its seats last year – and by Le Pen's tasteless jokes about the Holocaust, has seen its support in by-elections fall by over half, and this has led Le Pen to stick with his purely symbolic campaign in the same Paris district that he fought last time. Thus the FN challenge in Marseilles will be far weaker than once seemed likely, particularly since the FN's most popular local leader, Pascal Arrighi, has now been expelled from the party and is running his own rival list against the official FN one.

This may seem a rich brew of factors, even for Marseilles – but there is more. M. Gaudin was the only major conservative leader in France to do a deal with Le Pen last year, whereby he called for support for FN candidates in some Marseilles seats – something the Liberal-Left will never forgive him. If M. Gaudin finds himself forced into deals with the FN or even M. Arrighi, this time it could be too much for many marginal voters to swallow. Nor is it clear that M. Gaudin's rather desperate ploy of putting the boxer, Richard Caramanolis, on his list will really be enough to woo the macho vote. On the other hand, M. Pezet surely cannot win – in addition to his other woes, M. Defferre's widow, Mme Charles-Roux, is using her control of the local paper, *Le Provençal*, to wage a bitterly revengeful campaign against him. Moreover, the boss of the construction firm SORMAE, M. Claude Popis, has been testifying in court that he corruptly paid M. Pezet one million francs, using false invoices. (M. Popis also says he made similar pay-offs to M. Jean-Pierre Roux, the RPR mayor of Avignon, which has emboldened the Centrists to make a late run against him.) M. Pezet indignantly blames this story on leaks from his enemies within the local police force, but he looks like a loser now. After months of careful fence-sitting, Bernard Tapie, the millionaire whiz-kid businessman who recently won a parliamentary by-election for the Socialists in Marseilles, has finally come out in favour of M. Vigouroux. M. Tapie's popular standing in Marseilles, deriving principally from his ownership of Marseilles's soccer club, has never overly impressed M. Pezet ('I hate football'), but M. Tapie is not a bad weather-vane. Most locals still find it hard to believe that M. Vigouroux can defeat M. Gaudin, Arrighi and the FN while simultaneously beating the local PCF and the legendary Defferre machine – but that does now look the most likely result.

In Marseilles, as elsewhere, the intransigent statements made on all sides do not mean that last-minute deals before the first ballot on

12 March can be ruled out – and it is likely, too, that we shall see some fairly odd deals before the second ballot on 19 March. What is not in doubt is that the results will set the pattern of French politics for years ahead. This year French politics is all about city bosses, country notables and the struggle for control of the parish pump, just as 1988 was all about the sound and fury of the presidential election. Cabbages and kings, in a word – and France is a country where cabbages can matter more.

Across France as a whole, the Left did well. Or more exactly, the Socialists did – they and their Radical allies lost fourteen of the larger (over 20,000 population) towns but gained thirty-six. The Communists managed to regain Saint-Quentin but lost fifteen towns, including Le Mans and Orly, to their dissident and now ex-Communist mayors, and one of their crown jewels, Amiens. Of the sixty-seven major towns which the Communists managed to cling on to, no fewer than forty-two were in the Paris suburbs, though in Paris itself the Party all but vanished: out of 163 council seats there it won just three. But the Socialists were less than thrilled. Not only did Chirac repeat his grand slam in Paris, but M. Vigouroux utterly trounced his rival, Michel Pezet, in Marseilles. Indeed, the official joint Communist–Socialist list not only ran behind Vigouroux and Gaudin's UDF–RPR list but actually tailed in fourth behind the FN list. M. Pezet was immediately attacked by his own lieutenant, Philippe Sanmarco, who, however, denied that this was merely a power struggle. 'You can't have a power struggle', he added bitterly, 'because there's no more power.' The Socialist leadership in Paris resignedly began to cultivate M. Vigouroux with the hope of drawing him back into the party fold.

Although no one on the Right said so, M. Gaudin's failure to take advantage of the Left's divisions in Marseilles was a major disappointment. Chirac had other causes for concern too. Olivier Dassault fell well short in Beauvais and, despite Chirac's strong support, Mme Dupuy was just edged out in Cannes by her young UDF challenger. And while Le Pen's low scores almost everywhere were a source of consolation, the fact was that by no means all of his votes had trickled back to the orthodox Right. Some had undoubtedly gone Left and others had retreated into abstention.

The most sensational result was undoubtedly Michel Noir's stunning victory in Lyons, where the sitting mayor, M. Collomb, was utterly humiliated. This left Raymond Barre in a difficult situation which he did not recover by quickly announcing that he had known from the beginning that Collomb was doomed; that it was all Collomb's fault; and that he,

Barre, had run on Collomb's list purely out of party loyalty. M. Barre has, of course, built his whole career on a studied disdain for party and it was no secret that he had toyed with the possibility of supporting Noir early on. Once again, his political judgement was found severely wanting even in his own back yard. Chirac made the most of Noir's victory and trumpeted it as a major gain for the RPR. But his rejoicing was public rather than private: Noir had repeatedly opposed Chirac within the RPR and was close to being expelled from the Party just before the election. Originally Chirac had tried to stop Noir running again against Collomb and immediately the Lyon result came through the pollsters began talking of Noir as a possible RPR presidential hopeful for 1995, an eventuality which could only be achieved by Chirac's complete political effacement.

Chirac's discomfort was not entirely matched by Mitterrand's pleasure. In order to advance his government's 'opening to the centre', Mitterrand had had to squeeze out some Socialists to find room for centrist ministers. Given the old enmity between Mitterrand and his Prime Minister, Michel Rocard, it was by no means surprising to find that it was often the Rocardians in the government who had to make this supreme sacrifice. One of the more notable victims was Mme Catherine Trautmann – who now carried off one of the Left's most sensational victories by winning Strasbourg. Not only did Mme Trautmann make it fairly clear that she knew whom she had to blame for her earlier humiliation, but the Centrists were deeply distressed. Strasbourg had been ruled unbrokenly by Centrists since 1945 and had been the only really fixed star in the Centrist firmament. If alliance with the Left meant losing that, the bargain no longer looked so good . . . . But, as in Lyons, the UDF had been represented by an ageing and relatively inactive mayor. And while the municipal results had varying effects on the balance of forces for future legislative and presidential elections, the common trend was a wish that a new, younger generation should take the helm.

One can see why Frenchmen should feel like this, for M. Collomb in Lyons has his analogues throughout French political life. Jacques Chirac was, after all, a Cabinet Minister more than twenty years ago. Le Pen was a Poujadist deputy back in 1956. Giscard d'Estaing was the youngest member of de Gaulle's first Fifth Republican government in 1958. And Mitterrand was the youngest member of de Gaulle's first government, in 1945 . . . . But Mitterrand can afford to smile at this minor fronde against the old. He has no more elections to win. Three years ago, in March 1986, he was on the ropes, and you could get better than even money on the proposition that he would be the first Fifth Republican president to be forced out of office. But he triumphantly survived the two years of cohabitation with a Chirac government; was then re-elected as President; dissolved parliament and got back a Left majority there too; and has now seen the Socialists strengthen their municipal grip as well. After the clangour and tumult dies away from the town hall and the crowds disperse from the square in front of the mairie many Frenchmen will find they are being governed by new and younger faces locally. But the same old man sits in the Elysée, smiling at this yet further success. The age of Mitterrand rolls on.

PART II
Intellectuals

Chapter 11

Paul Johnson

The prominence Paul Johnson achieved in the Britain of the 1980s was itself an interesting phenomenon. (And his fame spread wider – he was frequently invoked as an intellectual authority both in Reagan's America and P.W. Botha's South Africa.) His position illustrated the way in which the arrival in power of a new Establishment has the effect of throwing a penumbra of legitimacy over a variety of groups and individuals beyond that Establishment's real confines. This was very evident in Reagan's Washington where all manner of crazies, from Birchers to Moonies, suddenly achieved regard as respectable folk. It was not that they were ever within the consensus, strictly speaking, but it was known that those in power shared many ideas with them, liked talking to them, were willing to be seen at their parties and receptions and so on. This meant that they had to be treated seriously – often by people who would have regarded them as a dangerous joke not long before. Suddenly, newspapers would ask them to contribute leader-page articles, TV chat shows would want them on as guests, they would get the odd citation in the leaders' speeches, and would be treated as a legitimate 'side' of any debate.

Something similar happened with Thatcher's arrival in power in England, and Paul Johnson was one of its chief beneficiaries, along with such other right-wing ideologues as Lord Chalfont, Lord Alfred Sherman, Sir Laurens van der Post and so on. Two things stand out about these figures: the extremism of their views – perhaps best instanced by Sherman's links with Jean-Marie Le Pen; and the fact that they are not the stuff of which intellectual revolutions are made. Despite all the talk about the new conservatism, when intellectual authority is wanted it is sought in writers of a generation and more ago – Hayek, Von Mises and Popper. But on the whole, the Reagan–Thatcher conservatives have distrusted their intelligentsias too much to want to appeal to intellectual authority. There was, indeed, no real prospect of dislodging or converting the liberal-left intelligentsia from the commanding heights it occupied. Instead, the new conservatives simply abandoned the intellectual high ground to these, their ancient foes, and swept round them at a lower level, making use of a ragtag and bobtail collection of polemicists, popular journalists, ambitious young hopefuls, born-again economics professors and whatever came to hand – sometimes even ex-lefties, foaming at the mouth in their eagerness to purge their own past sins. This little army, thanks to the patronage of government, a following wind in the media and the sheer energy and aggression of their polemic, achieved not inconsiderable success. Intellectually they were not good enough to win a war of ideas – to change the way the Academy thought – but they were wise enough to know this (see Johnson's exaggerated regard for Crossman below – intellectually the real man to his straw man) and to avoid open debate. But their job was merely to throw the Academy off balance (just as it was besieged and sapped and mined in a host of other ways), to keep it at bay, to surprise it with abuse. This they did, few better than Paul Johnson.

Paul Johnson does not, as they say, need much introduction. Whatever one thinks of his opinions, one has to admire his frenetic energy. From 1955 to 1970 he poured forth strong left-wing views in the *New Statesmen*, and since then has moved to pouring forth strong right-wing views in a whole host of publications, books and speeches. His collection of 76 pieces (Johnson, 1985), culled from the Conservative press of 1976–84, shows him again in full spate on subjects as diverse as 'The Decline of the Hat' and 'The Family as an Emblem of Freedom'. The essential unity of the book is, however, political. It is not just that extreme Thatcherism breathes from every page: both the strength of Johnson's writing and its often dreadful thinness derive from its sheer polemicism. Here, at last, the continuity with his *New Statesman* days is clear, for there is the same fatal, though exciting, tendency to go over the rhetorical top, the same eye for what will make 'our side' hug themselves with glee and what will most infuriate the enemy. The whole effort is a form of literary baiting which works up the troops on both sides and generally creates a deal of heat, sound and fury. This style of writing was the sole (and rather measly) contribution to English letters made by Kingsley Martin, and has been imitated by successive *New Statesman* columnists – Richard Crossman, Paul Johnson, Gerald Kaufman, Matthew Coady et al. (One only has to listen to the Parliamentary speeches of Gerald Kaufman to see how this sub-genre, once picked up, is hard to drop.) The origins of the style lie, only too audibly, in the world of the public school and Oxbridge debating society: it is at once over-heated and unserious, and has a sort of neighing ring to it, as of a clash of young geldings.

At his best, Paul Johnson's writing rises above this – for example, his picture of how the 1983 Labour Manifesto came to be written: 'The absurd policy document . . . which reads as though it was written by a covey of demented social workers with Napoleonic delusions, was supposed to be cut, hacked about and generally sanitised before becoming the manifesto. The idea, I gather, was that Michael Foot himself was to do the job . . . .. But either he was caught short by Mrs Thatcher's abrupt decision, or had simply forgotten, or had found it all too much for him; at any event he arrived without anything to show, and the document simply became the manifesto unamended.' The artful juxtaposition of 'covey' with the bumbling Foot (a bumbling so nicely elongated by the long line of hopeless alternatives) has, at once, a literary and political punch. But although Johnson contributes a rather pompous but quite good essay on 'The Craft of Writing', much of what he himself writes stays with one only because it is so abusive ('the pointy-head Tam Dalyell'), and a lot more is eminently forgettable. Indeed, it is meant to be. Johnson's greatest admiration often seems reserved for Dick Crossman, whom he takes to be a far greater intellect than he really was. Of his reports for the *New Statesman* Johnson comments that they 'were always illuminating and exciting, though sometimes wrong-headed and quickly belied by events. This was not a disadvantage. The purpose of weekly journalism is to encapsulate seven days, and stir up the minds of its readers; not to achieve a reputation for prescience in twenty years' time.' This is a judgement to bear in mind as one reads Johnson's own weekly journalism. The fact that Crossman was frequently wrong and silly, and encouraged delusions among his readers, is far less important than that he stirred them up.

It is difficult not to feel that this verdict applies to much of Johnson's own writing. Great acres of it are monstrously wrong and silly. About half the book consists of pieces about the media – the world Johnson knows best – and one gets wearily used to the convention whereby Channel 4 is seldom mentioned without the epithet 'Marxist' in close attendance. Of the BBC we hear of 'its growing reputation for anti-British views', while we learn that James Reston and Ben Bradlee (of the *Washington Post*) are 'left-wing trendies'. Georgetown University, the haunt of so many Reaganite super-hawks (including Jeanne Kirkpatrick), is rubbished as having 'moved sharply to the Left'. This sort of thing is quite palpable nonsense and it is also very coarse: there is no room for nuance or teasing out of complex strands here. Those whom Johnson likes (Olga Maitland, George Gilder, Rupert Murdoch) are heroes; and all those he dislikes are abused, jesuitically, as devilish. This leaves one only two choices. Either Johnson really believes what he says – in which case he is almost clinically silly – or else he knows it is nonsense but likes saying it to annoy – which is, in the last analysis, just childish. About which of these alternatives is true he does, though, keep one guessing.

More striking still are those essays where he dons the mantle of serious historian. The perversions of anything resembling historical truth which several of these essays contain are so gross and extraordinary that one rubs one's eyes in sheer disbelief. Because Johnson hates the film *Gandhi* he attempts to convince us that Britain only ruled India 'by consent'; that most British administrators in India wanted only that Indians rule themselves; and that Churchill's chief concern was how the Untouchables would be treated if we got out. One suspects that even Churchill would have found all this pretty funny. That anyone who worked on the *New Statesman* through the era of decolonisation could fail to achieve any understanding at all of colonialism is surely quite remarkable. One should not forget, moreover, that Johnson is no historical relativist: he sees things in fiercely moral terms, and there is here, accordingly, an attempt at the moral exculpation of much that was morally horrible.

A similar blindness to social reality occurs when Johnson turns his gaze to Central America. 'The present wave of violence in Central America and the Caribbean', he informs us, 'has its origins on the campus of Havana University.' This is utterly fantastic. Or, rather, it is the old agitator theory of history. All these people living in fear and poverty under torturous dictatorships would actually be jolly happy but for these damned agitators who keep stirring them up by alluding to their fear and poverty. But for that, these simple peasant people would have been quite happy with Batista, Somoza and Papa Doc.

Or again, there is an astonishing essay on Marxism and anti-Semitism in which Johnson attempts to portray Marx as an anti-Semite and Marxism itself as a sort of anti-Semitic conspiracy theory. All this to show that anti-Semitism is really, nowadays, a left-wing phenomenon. Johnson returns again and again to the question of anti-Semitism. He is not only humanely revolted by it but, in some deeper personal sense, clearly troubled by it.

The clue lies, surely, in his extraordinary exculpatory statement that 'traditional anti-Semitic conspiracy theory had been kept alive by the ecclesiastical Inquisitions of Spain and Rome'. That tepid 'kept alive' is the nearest Johnson (himself a Catholic) comes to

acknowledging that it is the Catholic Church, together with its
Eastern Orthodox branch, which has been the principal cultural
agent of anti-Semitism over two millennia. Odd to say 'ecclesiastical'
when one means 'Catholic'. Odd, too, to talk of the Inquisitions
keeping alive a 'theory' when they were torturing people horribly
and killing them. This was done to Jews, mind, not because they
were dissidents, but just because they were Jews.

Johnson inveighs passionately against the Soviet, East European
and leftist anti-Semitisms. They are real and evil things, but how far
are even these phenomena not the legacy of the undisputed two-
thousand-year hegemony of the Church, rather than the always
disputed two-or three-generation hegemony of Marxism? Too
much, perhaps, is made of Pius XII's refusal to condemn Nazi
treatment of the Jews, not enough of the fact that he was simply
acting as Popes have always done. Which Popes or Patriarchs
attempted to hinder the persecutions and pogroms of all the
centuries before that? Which Popes spoke out against the ferocious
anti-Semitism of the French Catholic Right, against the rampant
anti-Semitism in Horthy's Catholic Hungary, against the ghetto-
isation of the Jews in Catholic Poland, against the frequent anti-
Semitism of rightist regimes in Catholic Latin America? The truth is
that such regimes have always known they could rely on the benign
equanimity of Rome. It was the French Catholic Right, not the Left,
which shouted 'better Hitler than Blum', just as practising Catholics
are notably overrepresented in Le Pen's racist electorate in France
today. It was not until well after the Holocaust that the Papacy,
under strong liberal pressure, finally conceded that the Jews were
not, after all, collectively guilty of Christ's murder, and the Church
is still very far from admitting past errors in its treatment of the
Jews. Even today the Vatican refuses to recognise the state of Israel.

Any thoughtful or sensitive Catholic cannot but have deep
qualms of guilt about this shameful history. To this, in Johnson's
case, must surely be added an uncomfortable awareness that his
migration to the extreme Right has made him a political bedfellow of
those among whom an easy, golf-club anti-Semitism still flourishes.
It is to Johnson's credit that the question of anti-Semitism troubles
him, and one can understand why. But one would respect him more
if he faced up to where the primary historic responsibility for anti-
Semitism lies. To attempt to pass off this burden on to the Left is
historically ludicrous and morally discreditable.

But there is a sense in which it is silly to take Johnson too
seriously. By his own admission, after all, his judgement is terrible.
Everything he said or wrote between 1955 and 1970 he now thinks

was utterly wrong. He recounts how Kingsley Martin long felt Crossman would make a disastrous editor of the *New Statesman*; how he, Johnson, was convinced of the contrary and got his way; and how Crossman was indeed so bad that he had to be sacked. Johnson then became a passionate admirer of Mrs Thatcher – but has recently announced that she is, after all, nothing special. Even he does not attempt to make any consistent sense out of all these twists and turns. One feels no confidence that, as the intellectual and political tide goes out on the Right, he will not recant all he has said here. He is a man who clearly feels intensely whatever he is feeling at the time, but the only real thread is a radical instability of view. He has not one but many return tickets for the ride to Damascus. The real interest of these wanderings emerges only if one places them in their broader social and historical context.

Paul Johnson belongs to one of the most influential generational groups in recent British history – the Oxford student cohort of the immediate post-war period who clambered aboard the great Labour surge of 1945–51. This cohort was the exact British analogue of the bright young New Dealers from the American Ivy League campuses so tellingly depicted by Mary McCarthy in *The Group*. For these young people, the best and brightest of their day, the path towards modernity, social justice and rationally-administered change led unequivocally towards the Left, whose sweeping rise to power meant that one could combine all these good things with excellent career prospects and a certain chic. The combination was overwhelming. Through the long, locust years of the 1950s this Oxford generation was sustained not only by the memories of 1945–51, and a sense that history was still on their side, but by their own steady advance towards the summit of the Labour movement. Their day would come. In 1964–70, it did: never has a government been so overflowingly endowed with Oxford graduates – not just its ministers but its great flock of advisers and propagandists all came from the same stable.

The Wilson Administration of those years was, though, an unparalleled disaster and disappointment. Quite quickly, signs of acute intellectual confusion and disorientation were apparent: perhaps as striking as any was Paul Johnson's famous 'Blundering into Socialism' editorial which greeted the draconian July measures of 1966. Rather than accepting this event as the staggering blow it was to all hopes of planned growth, the editorial infuriated wide sections of the Labour movement by arguing that it somehow heralded a great socialist advance. Within a year or two, however, Johnson had swung the *New Statesman* round to demanding that the dreadful Wilson must go. As the trauma of 1964-70 sank in, the key Oxford cohort began to scatter in confusion. Deprived of all confidence in the intellectual compass-points they had clung to for twenty years or more, they resembled a broken cavalry charge: with *ésprit de corps*, discipline and forward momentum all gone, it was *sauve qui peut*. A large group began their move towards a new political Centre; others looked around and decided in the end to stay put; quite a few left politics. The most bizarre and radical directions were taken by the smaller subset within the cohort who had not only Oxford but public school backgrounds and who had travelled furthest to come into the Labour movement. Their faith had had to be sustained by a special intensity of commitment. Their post-1970 disorientation – and their reaction to it – was correspondingly sharper than those of others. Lord Longford (Eton and Christ Church) peeled off into a peculiar variety of religious activities. Tony Benn (Westminster and New College) decamped for the wild and intransigent Left. Paul Johnson (Stonyhurst and Magdalen) bolted to the radical Right. It would not be unfair to say that for most people what these diverse movements had in common was their sheer dottiness. In part, no doubt, such a judgement simply reflects the old English horror of 'enthusiasm' of any sort, but it is certainly true that these are all men who need intensity of feeling as others need strong drink.

Paul Johnson's own way of putting this is to say that the 1960s were the decade of illusion, the 1970s of disillusion and the 1980s of realism. Ah, we should have known. As one wanders through these pages, one learns that the reason for the rising rate of family breakdown among America's black and Hispanic poor is the welfare hand-outs they get; that Women's Lib has 'done no good to anyone at all, apart perhaps from hard-core lesbians, the Soviet ruling class – which finds the Greenham Women a useful propaganda tool, in a small way – and of course the self-publicists and media operators'; that telephone-tapping is essentially harmless unless used against tax-evaders ('some of the worse Gestapo-type searches at dawn have involved small businesses'); that the aims of the peace movement are 'objectively evil'; that the World Council of Churches has a 'contempt for faith, or worship, or what most of us understand by the Ten Commandments'; and that the *Daily Mail* has 'the best editor in Fleet Street'. Anyone who believes that such views are realistic or even reasonable will no doubt enjoy *The Pick of Paul Johnson*. Others will simply wonder at the new 'realism' of such a strong self-avowed Christian. The gospel according to Paul Johnson appears to be not only that camels *can* get through the eye of a needle, but that *only* camels can. A puzzle remains: if the camels not only have all the money and power but also this exclusive access to heaven as well, why should Mr Johnson – now such a fervent camels' man – be so angry about everything?

References

Johnson, Paul (1985) *The Pick of Paul Johnson: An Anthology* (London: Harrap).

Chapter 12

Conor Cruise O'Brien

One of the many delights in *Passion and Cunning* (O'Brien 1988a) is the description of the author's attendance at a National Party election rally in Springs (Transvaal) where P. W. Botha makes his appeal to English-speaking South Africans via a programme featuring 1. 'She'll be coming round the mountain when she comes'; 2. 'My bonnie lies over the ocean'; 3. 'Daizy, Daizy [sic], give me your anser [sic] do'. Such Afrikaner wooing of English-speakers, reflects O'Brien, has fortuitously coincided with the need to rephrase apartheid. Once it was Bantu Administration. Then it was separate development. Then it was community development, then co-operation and development. Perhaps, muses O'Brien, Afrikaner Nationalists simply had need of 'the richer rhetorical resources of Anglo-Saxon hypocrisy'.

Let us pause at that phrase, which is, in several different ways, vintage O'Brien. The whole passage is witty, beautifully observed, and in the Orwellian tradition – corruption of the soul is preceded by corruption of the language. But the fastening on hypocrisy says something of the author too. Long ago, in a book of essays (*Writers and Politics*, 1965) quite as good as this splendid new volume, O'Brien wrote of how intellectuals vented their lack of power in satire, their sole real weapon in the only form of struggle allowed to them, the exposure of hypocrisy. As if this did not sound autobiographical enough, O'Brien went on to note that Irishmen were particularly prone to this temptation, for the gap between ruling-class pretence and brutal reality had been wider for longer in Ireland than anywhere else, and this had affected even those who (like himself) were sufficiently privileged to be spared the worst of that reality.

> For some Irishmen, including some who were not themselves directly oppressed, the masks of power and the paradoxes of oppression were lessons in drama and in wit. Easily, too easily, irony became a way of life and the witty Irishman was born.

Conor Cruise O'Brien has been that sort of witty Irishman for many decades now, and the present book of essays displays once again his wonderful range of talents: a beautiful command of the language, gentle wit and coruscating satire, shrewd political judgement and a raking critical power. O'Brien is, moreover, a critic against all-comers, his spiky guns pointing in all directions: woe betide anyone incautious enough to presume that O'Brien is on their 'side'. The Irish Establishment made that mistake when they made him their delegate to the UN. The UN then made the same mistake by sending him to the Congo, a mission which produced a raking O'Brien critique of the UN. Nkrumah then made Dr O'Brien Vice-Chancellor of the University of Ghana, but this too ended in a great public resignation. As a minister in the Irish government, O'Brien was a similarly provoking presence. The Left had by then come to assume that this thorn in the flesh of the Nato culture was one of their own, but when E.P. Thompson attempted to presume O'Brien on to his side in the matter of CND there was a predictable and pyrotechnic response, with great carnage in the Thompson ranks. O'Brien is not a man to accept that presumptive arm around his shoulder: friendship is all well and fine, but the assumption of solidarity is intolerable: O'Brien believes in all manner of good causes, but his own independence is finally what he cares about most. His opponents, noting that such an attitude bespeaks a certain good opinion of oneself, hope to catch him in a posture of arrogance or self-importance, but O'Brien is far too fly for that. So he appears to one and all as a sort of pirate battleship, mounting heavy guns but belonging to no Navy and dangerously liable to sink anything he comes across. He attracted the nickname 'The Cruiser', not only because others have never been quite sure what to do with the Cruise bit of his name, but because of a definite marauding quality all his own. This aspect of his writing can seem so strong that for many he is simply and only a critic. But it is doubtful if O'Brien sees it that way, so the question remains: leaving aside all the things O'Brien is so gloriously against, what does he stand for?

The place to start is undoubtedly O'Brien's attitude to religion and, more specifically, to Catholicism. He is, he tells us, the only professed agnostic ever to be elected to the Irish Dail. But he makes that statement in a slim volume of lectures, *God Land: Reflections on Religion and Nationalism* (1988b), which betrays not only a thorough knowledge of the highways and byways of Christian theology but a positive fascination with it. Over and over again he returns to the fact that the religious impulse will out, regaling us with stories of the good Communists of the Lake Baikal region who worship the lake's otters on the understanding that they are the metamorphosed heroes of the 1871 Paris Commune: sacrifices to the otters are supposed to help with the fulfilment of the Plan. Better still, there is the Ethiopian dictator, Mengistu Haile Meriam, who enjoys the dual status of leading Marxist-Leninist and, as the Amharic anointed, the Servant of Mary. Moreover, as O'Brien points out,

> he is also the Lion of Judah. To prove it he has a full grown lion chained outside his office door. When I talked with Mengistu a few years ago, we could hear the lion coughing just outside the office; not roaring, just coughing, a dry melancholy cough that goes well with the tone and tenor of Colonel Mengistu's conversation . . . .. The lion's message is strictly for Ethiopians, to let them know where the sovereignty is: something they need to know.

The treatment is often so delightful that it seems churlish to object, but as one moves from one essay to the next one does find that somehow references to God, the Pope and Catholicism seep into almost everything. O'Brien rejects the cultural nationalism of Catholic Ireland but the fact is that he is also immersed in it. He once defined Irishness as merely the condition of being involved in the Irish situation, and usually of being mauled by it. What comes across all too clearly in these essays is how heavily and irretrievably he himself has been mauled by Catholicism. He always writes about the Church as if its views on any subject are a natural starting-point for any discussion, as if he would like to believe its claims and is disappointed when he finds he can't. O'Brien refuses to accept the thesis that Catholicism is intrinsic to Irish identity – but he writes as if it were true in his own case.

One of the most interesting essays in *Passion and Cunning* is a long and fascinating account of Nicaragua – seen (of course) through the prism of the Pope's visit there in March 1983. O'Brien insists, convincingly enough, that Sandinismo, with its great stress on the martyrs of the revolution – indeed, its virtual cult of the revolutionary dead – has strongly Catholic roots. But the main point of the essay is simply that John Paul II entirely deserved the historic comeuppance he received in Managua. The Pope, characteristically enough, went out of his way to declare his special affection for Cardinal Obando, who has been tougher in his opposition to the Sandinistas than he ever was towards Somoza; to denounce those priests who have taken office in the Sandinista Government; and to refuse to pray for those revolutionary dead, even when their mothers invaded the stage on which the Pope was saying mass, demanding prayers for their dead sons. The visit ended with unparalleled scenes

– a furious Pope shouting *Silencio!* at a crowd which jeered back with comments such as 'He's not a Pope of the poor!' and 'Look at his dress!' It was typical of the challenge to Papal authority engendered by the visit that all that gold and silver braid, paraded so endlessly before the hungry poor of the Third World, should at last have excited comment. An odd inversion of the old story, if one thinks about it: this king pretends to humility but goes forth in grandeur. So the revolutionary cry is not that the King has no clothes but that indeed he has clothes – wondrous, priceless clothes, and that he is indeed a sort of king, not a humble man at all.

O'Brien sides unhesitatingly with the revolutionary Catholics of Latin America: 'put not your trust in pontiffs', he counsels. Sandino, he notes, 'refused to call himself a Christian because all the most eminent Nicaraguan "Christians" of his day – like the Bishop of Granada who blessed the US Marines – were in the service of the enemy'. Today, however, Sandinistas insist that their leader would be a Christian Revolutionary – a judgement in which O'Brien concurs. And the wonderful thing about these Christian Revolutionaries is that their Reformation has no need to break with Rome. It keeps all 'the Roman symbols – and the Roman sacraments, which is more important', but just ignores Rome's authority. This cheers O'Brien greatly, just as, elsewhere, he signals his delight that Catholics across the world are happily practising contraception and treating the Pope's homilies on the matter with the contempt they deserve. In another essay O'Brien provides a careful but devastating dissection of the character of the present Pope, whose determined ability to hear without listening and whose stonily reactionary attitudes merit, in O'Brien's eyes, Orwell's equation of the Roman Church with Stalinism. O'Brien concludes that 'as I studied the writings of John Paul II, I found my faith revive: my faith, that is, in the 18th-century Enlightenment; in Voltaire and Diderot, as liberators of the human mind from an oppressive and obfuscating dogmatism'.

O'Brien, that is, while remaining a cultural Catholic, accepts the essence of the Protestant critique of the Church; sympathises with insurgents against Rome; denounces the Pope; and happily announces that the best sort of Catholics can now simply ignore Papal authority. I must say that I think this is both having it all ways and rather unnecessary. The Catholic Church is virtually defined by obedience to its indispensable, indeed infallible, Papal core, and Papal authority has ridden out many revolts before now. The Pope's extraordinary claims to moral authority may have received some challenge in Managua, but that hardly constitutes three falls and a submission. What beats me is that O'Brien should ever have expected the Pope to behave differently: the man gets a weekly briefing from the CIA's Rome chief-of-station, after all, and Cardinal Montini (later Paul VI) even handed over to the CIA files on the Italian episcopate and parish priests to help them discredit clerics thought to be soft on Communism.

Frankly, as someone born and brought up a Catholic, I cannot really sympathise with these elaborate attempts to treat the Church as if it were morally serious. In my teens, it was gradually borne in upon me that the Church in which I had been an altar boy had first been responsible for pinning the yellow star on Jews, had made torture a matter of Church policy, had blessed massacres, had supported Pétain and Franco, and so on and so on. I, too, came to accept the essence of the Protestant and humanist critique of the Church. And so, after several anguishing years, I left it. Maybe it is not my business to say, but I can heartily recommend thoroughgoing apostasy. One thing it does do for you is that when you read that Sandino repeatedly denied that he was a Christian, you tend to believe that this meant that he was not a Christian. If, like O'Brien, you somehow turn this into meaning that Sandino would today be a revolutionary Christian, actually something very Orwellian is happening: war is peace, peace is war, we have always been at war with East Asia and Sandino is, maybe even was, a Christian. Well, that's a relief. Thank the Lord for Newspeak. So why not thank the Pope for Lordspeak?

It is a bit the same when we come to Ireland, about which O'Brien writes with deep knowledge and passion. At the end of the day he seems to have swallowed the whole of the Ulster Protestant case. He is resolutely against a united Ireland, even against the Anglo-Irish Agreement, and champions the cause of internment without trial on both sides of the border. I happily bow to his vastly superior knowledge of Ireland, but I cannot agree with him.

If I were Irish, I don't think I could accept that the best to be hoped for was internment without trial throughout the land and the maintenance of the status quo, with the steady killings it brings. As an Englishman, I find these things unacceptable merely for what they do to England, let alone Ireland. If even the best of the Irish, among whom O'Brien can undoubtedly be placed, want to go round locking one another up without trial, it just makes me feel all the more that we Englishmen would be better off out of it all. English lives are being wasted in Ireland to no purpose and our involvement there corrupts England, just as it always has. Personally, I do not want to live in countries which go in for death squads or internment without trial. So I am in favour of the unification of Ireland, for the sake of the English.

The third theme of this book is South Africa (which, though O'Brien does not remark upon it, provides a pretty good example of what happens when you go in for internment without trial over a long period). In particular, he is exercised about the fact that his recent visit there had to be cut short in the face of vehement protests against him by black and radical students. I can well understand how upsetting this must have been, particularly since O'Brien's adopted son, Patrick, is black, and O'Brien has a quite faultless record on all questions of race and apartheid. But the fact is that, though he writes a pretty good general summary of the situation in South Africa, he is a little out of his depth there. In particular, he does not seem to realise quite why his tour was such a remarkable disaster.

It all started early in his tour with a question about what he thought about the academic boycott. Now the fact is that the academic boycott is not wholly observed. Hundreds of academics – some of them well to the Left of O'Brien – visit South Africa all the time, and have no trouble at all because they are sensitive to the fact that there might be trouble. O'Brien however, boldly told his questioners that in his view the boycott was 'a Mickey Mouse affair'. This was a red rag to a bull. South African radicals are used to that tone of contemptuous dismissal: they hear it from their government all the time. From then on the figure of Mickey Mouse featured quite largely in the growing student protests against O'Brien. His local hosts, who could and should have guided him away from these avoidable pitfalls, were, by all accounts, invisible once the trouble began. What really seems to have undone O'Brien is that the radicals wanted some unmistakable sign from him that he was on their side, while he could not refrain from bridling at any such presumption. With that, the fat was in the fire. All very unreasonable, perhaps, but South Africa is in a state of pre-revolutionary ferment: it is not reasonable and it is not an ideal stage for insouciant displays of personal independence.

This, at least, is what I have picked up about the visit from various South African friends. There is, oddly, no mention of the crucial 'Mickey Mouse' reference in O'Brien's account. He argues that the South African Government is actively in favour of the academic boycott and, indeed, that a police spy acted as an *agent provocateur* in the disruption of his visit. The police spy part of the story is probable enough: the South African Government would have been delighted to see a contretemps between its local radicals and an overseas liberal, and well aware what a propaganda coup was being dropped in its lap. But the notion that Pretoria could ever be favourably disposed to an academic boycott is utterly fantastical. It is not that Pretoria cares all that much about whether academics as such do or do not visit the Republic – the sports boycott is a hundred times more important. But the Government lives in constant fear of trade sanctions and economic boycotts, and also wants to reassure itself and its voters that South Africa's enemies have not wholly succeeded in isolating her: for all these reasons Pretoria is passionately opposed in principle to boycotts of any kind. It would, of course, be more convenient to O'Brien's argument if Pretoria was in favour of the academic boycott, for then he could be, if not on the side of the angels, at least on the opposite side to the devil. Unfortunately, it is just not true and O'Brien knows too much about South Africa not to know that is is not true.

This (otherwise small) point illustrates, I think, one of the dangers of his position. The way he secures his independence is through contrarianism: he is an Irish Catholic who denounces the Pope and accepts the Protestant case; an Irish patriot who wants to keep Ireland divided; a liberal who demands the extension of internment without trial; a UN head of mission who denounces the UN; a man who writes the definitive demolition of *Encounter* as cultural Cold War journalism – and then ends up writing for *Encounter* himself; who resigns from the *Observer* to escape the clutches of Tiny Rowlands – only to find a home with Rupert Murdoch's *The Times*. The list could go on and on. And contrarianism does have its problems. It means, over time, that the dangers of inconsistency and self-contradiction loom large. Heaven knows, honestly admitted inconsistency is no crime, but it would be nice if O'Brien could explain some of his volte-faces.

More important, though, the continual assertion of intellectual independence against all-comers (which is what contrarianism means) is necessarily a highly ego-centred exercise. In effect, you are always saying, 'I am right against the conventional view, whatever it is', and the most important word in that sentence is, or becomes, the 'I'. The danger is that one's treatment of subjects can become a little self-serving. There is a tinge of this in many of O'Brien's essays. Thus there is a wonderfully funny demolition of Norman Podhoretz – occasioned by Podhoretz's criticism of O'Brien's book on Camus. An essay on the press has a long, rambling attack on an editorial from the *Observer* – without ever mentioning that O'Brien was editor-in-chief of that paper. Or again, O'Brien finds Julius Nyerere delightful company, so he decides that if Ujamaa villages were a bit of a joke, they were a harmless joke.

Unfortunately, that too was very far from true.

But these are, in a way, weasel words to use of someone who writes with such consistent wit and intelligence: I would place him as an essayist second only to Gore Vidal among those now writing. And perhaps he has given us the key to his own evolution in the title-essay on Yeats:

> The politics of the left – any left, even a popular 'National Movement' – impose by their emphasis on collective effort and on sacrifice, a constraint on the artist . . . .. Right-wing politics, with their emphasis on the freedoms of the elite, impose less constraint, require less pretence, allow style to become more personal and direct.

Bad politics tend to make for good style, concludes O'Brien. And if you have to choose one or the other? It is a tribute of a sort to his contrariness – his passion and cunning, if you like – that even when one has read these essays one still cannot be quite sure which way he would jump.

Not long after writing this piece I had the experience of following closely in Dr O'Brien's footsteps around several South African univesity campuses, where the aftermath of his aborted tour still hung like a pall.

The part of the story about the police spy on the Cape Town campus proved to be a red herring. That is, there are always a good number of police spies operating on the English-speaking university campuses in South Africa (and a few even on the Afrikaans-speaking campuses too), and every now and again one of them gets exposed. The most notable thing about the young man Dr O'Brien refers to is the extent to which he had gone to maintain his cover – hurling stones at the police and so on. He had helped disrupt the O'Brien visit for the same reasons – to maintain credibility with the campus Left. To move from that to the suggestion that the Government is behind the academic boycott is to jump right out of gear.

The whole event shed little credit on anyone. Even those most sympathetic to Dr O'Brien felt he had courted trouble unnecessarily and that his visit had done a lot of harm to already threatened liberal institutions. There were, incidentally, a number of other foreign academics simultaneously visiting the campuses where Dr O'Brien met with such disaster – they kept their heads down and encountered no difficulty. What was different about the O'Brien visit was not only its higher profile but that he had launched it by writing an article for The Times in London before setting off, in which he had denounced the academic boycott and proclaimed his intention of breaking it. This seems to have been taken by the ANC, or its London branch anyway, as an open challenge. The university authorities I spoke to said they had learnt after the visit that explicit instructions to disrupt the visit had been sent out from London to the student Left within South Africa. One version had it that the ANC was 'punishing' O'Brien as a favour to the IRA, but this seems an unnecessary sophistication.

Moving round in South Africa in the O'Brien wake (as it were), I got the strong impression that no one at all was very proud or happy with what had happened. Anti-apartheid groups on the liberal English-speaking campuses were left feeling a little dazed by the whole affair. Accustomed to protesting endlessly about the suppression of the freedom of speech, the Left had set out to prove that a principle was bigger than an individual – and then seemed almost confused by the realisation that they had successfully suppressed freedom of speech themselves. The sheer ugliness of what had happened to Dr O'Brien appeared to have weakened support for the academic boycott quite considerably. So, given that Dr O'Brien had taken dead aim at the boycott, it must be said that in part he achieved what he set out to do.

One is left reflecting that in the West someone like Dr O'Brien (or myself) can express their contrarianism in the cut and thrust of columns for newspapers and magazines, with the debates and polemics thus engendered remaining comfortably with a metropolitan intellectual world. The worst that can happen to you, after all, is that someone worsts you in public debate, or that you look ridiculous, or just that you are not invited to write in a journal again. Contrarianism may goad your opponents but it is at least interesting in a world that hates to be bored. It is, indeed, a world that thrives on contrarianism, that can even spontaneously generate it after a while. Part of the lesson of the ill-fated O'Brien trip is just that in the real world beyond that shadow-boxing world, contrarianism is a far more dangerous quantity.

References

O'Brien, Conor Cruise (1965) *Writers and Politics* (London: Chatto & Windus).

O'Brien, Conor Cruise (1988a) *Passion and Cunning, and Other Essays* (London: Weidenfeld & Nicholson).

O'Brien, Conor Cruise (1988b) *God Land: Reflections on Religion and Nationalism* (London: Harvard UP).

Chapter 13

Raymond Williams and E.P. Thompson

The piece below may give the impression that I reject the world view expounded by E.P. Thompson and Raymond Williams. Actually, I would find myself in agreement with both of them on many, perhaps most, of the big political issues. They would only have to come under attack from the Right for me to rally behind them. But I have come to feel that all of us, on both Left and Right, are far too much affected by the politics of solidarity – that we feel we must protect our 'side' by telling little lies or observing some pregnant silences about it. I think this is wrong not only because it inevitably encourages one's side to blunder into avoidable errors, but because, dammit, there must be no higher loyalty than the truth. The trouble is that if one keeps insisting 'I must tell the truth against all', the really important words can become 'I' or just 'against all'. In case it needs saying, I feel myself guilty of many of the errors I criticise.

For the past forty years one of the most imposing groups in British life has been a profoundly talented generation of left-wing intellectuals. It is now an ageing group – sadly, some of the most illustrious of this generation, such as Thomas Hodgkin and Raymond Williams, have died. A large majority of others have retired or are on the verge of retirement – Christopher Hill, Eric Hobsbawm, E.P. Thompson and Basil Davidson, for example. To fill out the picture of this generation one should add such names as V.G. Kiernan, John Rex, A.H. Halsey, Ralph Miliband and Tom Bottomore, though this still leaves the list incomplete. Several things stand out about this group. It is all-male; they were and are marvellously talented and productive; almost all of them would have described themselves as Marxists at one time or another, indeed most were Communist Party members at some point; and all kept the faith – there are no right-wing renegades here. As one examines their collective *oeuvre* one realises how prodigious their contribution to British culture and letters has been, and also how improbable it is that they will have successors who are very much like them. Indeed, that much is already clear: there is not, in the generation behind them, any comparable group either intellectually or politically speaking. But one cannot but be struck too by the fact that although these men wrote books that fired many an undergraduate, their overall political influence was small. They grew up through the locust years of the 1930s, came to powerful maturity during the long Tory dominance of 1951–64, flourished mightily in the 1960s – when at last the Left felt no longer threatened within the university environment – only to spend their later years under the malign reign of Thatcherism. At all points in their lives they comprehensively outgunned the rather paltry conservative intelligentsia who were their natural foes, but having watched their tide come in during the 1960s they had the dispiriting (and to many of them, mystifying) experience of watching that tide go out on them again in the 1970s and 1980s.

Without much doubt the major political influence of this group will be found in their cumulative cultural effect. Young men and women as yet unborn will have their lives changed by reading Hill, Hobsbawm and Kiernan. But it is instructive to ask why the immediate political influence of this generation was so slight. The problem comes to a head in the work of the two figures among them who attempted to play an active political role, E.P. Thompson and Raymond Williams. Both men were mightily productive, but having written their major works – Williams's *Culture and Society* and *The Long Revolution*, Thompson's *The Making of the English Working Class* – they devoted themselves to a more direct style of political intervention. Williams was the major link-man between old and New Left and was indefatigably active in socialist societies, symposia and conferences. For his part, Thompson played a major role in the resurgent CND of the early 1980s and also in its European extension, END. In all this, it is fair to say, they met with very limited success. Mainly, of course, the tide was simply set against them. But they had their symptomatic weaknesses too. As usual, one glimpses the two men best through their essays; Thompson has produced several books of these while a fair selection of Williams's are to be found in his *Resources of Hope*, posthumously published in 1989.

It is fair to say that many of the essays in Williams's book blend into one another in an almost seamless way. This is, though, not altogether a compliment, for many of the essays have a dreamy sameness, a sort of lilting Welsh lamentation over Labour's shattered hopes in the 1980s, though ending always with the same note of dogged and defiant hope. Not surprisingly, one sees that most of them were first given as talks: one recognises a certain measured, rhetorical tread. The style is quite clearly that of the Welsh Nonconformist chapel and there is a quality of cadence and incantation, of necessary mentions and equally necessary silences, to many of these essays. It is a lofty, literary style, full of feeling, rich in reference but largely empty of fact. It involves a sort of stroking of the audience – the faithful only, for these essays are not written to convince outsiders or even neutrals. Many of the tributes to Williams after his death struck the same sort of note. Listen to Terry Eagleton, a William disciple, reviewing *Resources of Hope* for *The Observer*. Eagleton strokes his audience with certain ritual keywords, just as Williams always did:

> One of Williams' most striking qualities as a writer is a rare combination of reason and feeling. Throughout his work, a toughly analytic mind is fuelled by the rich emotional resources of the creative writer; and the political expression of this is a remarkable blending of vision and realism. These essays unite a steady humanistic faith in the possibility of socialism with a steely refusal of sentimental illusion . . . . Williams is more emotionally candid than many a political commentator, he is also more sober and sardonic.

And so on and so on. If you analyse this, it is actually just guff. All of us are, if you think about it, combinations of reason and feeling, just as all political perspectives are blendings of vision and realism, however conceived. And it is elitist nonsense to suppose that creative writers have special or especially rich emotional resources. As for that steady faith – here the chapel lights flicker in mute witness – well, Williams never actually spells out what socialism is for him. It seems, in the great tradition of British wooziness, to be all about values and community and wholeness; in a word, Christian socialism and brown bread.

Now listen to Williams on 'Problems of the Coming Period', originally a talk given just before the 1983 election. Thatcher, he argues, has not really achieved an intellectual hegemony. If you take the percentage of people who are going to vote Tory, 'from that figure, somewhere in the middle forties, you have to deduct another figure. It's difficult to put it in exact quantity, but it would be well over 30 per cent, it might be higher, which would vote Conservative if the Conservative party were led by Prior, Pym, Gilmour, Heath or whoever.' So Thatcherism has no majority; it exists 'at the level of 10 or 15 per cent, whatever it may really be.'

Now, if one is going to launch oneself forth as a speaker and writer in political analysis, this just will not do. The polls provide exact figures about the Tory vote and about what percentages favour this or that policy option, and one needs to be able to cite those figures. Secondly, this idea of deducting a dreamt-up 30 per cent is pure play, in this case a literary gent playing with political sociology, rather like Alec Douglas-Home doing his economics with matches. And finally, of course, Williams ought to know well enough that cultural, intellectual and political change are indeed effected by minorities – often by minorities so small as to make his imaginary 10 or 15 per cent a very big number indeed. There is, in a word, not much sign here of a 'remarkable blending of vision and realism', let alone a 'steely refusal of sentimental illusion'.

Literary gent amateurishness is one thing, but a far more important hollowness in the Williams perspective becomes apparent if one examines his 'Mining the Meaning: Key Words in the Miners' Strike' (1985), republished in *Resources of Hope*. The key words he chooses are 'the right to manage', 'economic', 'community', and 'law and order' – with fairly predictable polemical result. Williams stands passionately behind the then striking NUM. For him the strike is about a quite sacred issue, 'an issue which should be at the centre of the whole socialist project. This is the claim of workers to control not only the wages and conditions, but also the very nature of their work. The human substance of this claim is absolute.' There is then a lot of similarly heated discussion of community and how the strike, far from being the last kick of an old order, 'is one of the first steps towards a new order'. Law and order are, of course, all about requiring a simple obedience to authority from the miners, and this is contrasted with the better sort of order preferred by the strikers – 'a way of life chosen by a substantial majority of its citizens'. There is not the slightest hint, anywhere, that the NUM leadership had not allowed a vote on the strike; that it had required obedience to its authority; that there was not here something 'chosen by a substantial majority', that the 'community' of miners had not been allowed to decide; and that far from having control over their wages, conditions and work, the miners were not being allowed democratic control over the activities of their own union. There is no mention, no breath of the fact that a substantial minority of miners had refused the strike, had broken away over the issue of the denial of democracy, and that some had suffered intimidation and even violence as a result.

Most of the real meat gets compressed into a final elliptical statement:

> As the strike ends, there will be many other things to discuss and argue about: tactics, timing and doubtless personalities. But it is of the greatest possible importance to move very quickly and sharply beyond these.

Williams's complete failure, indeed refusal, to confront the cardinal facts of the strike is achieved here by several little keywords all his own. Note, particularly, the word 'ends'. This means 'the strike has been a complete and crushing failure, Scargill has spurned all chance of a negotiated settlement and the union is now in smithereens'. 'Tactics' means 'the complete denial of intra-union democracy; the decision of the NUM leadership simply to order a strike and then try to bully into line those who wanted a vote'. 'Timing' is a reference to the suicidal decision to launch the strike when winter was ending and coal stocks were high. 'Personalities' denotes the fact that the NUM was led by a blustering, autocratic bully who sacrificed the union on the altar of his own ego. These are indeed cardinal facts: without them the strike cannot be understood or even fairly described. But Williams not only refuses altogether to mention these facts but tells us that even later on we will not be allowed to talk about them much either – we will have to move on from them 'very quickly and sharply'. No sign here of the 'toughly analytic' critic we have been promised. The one word one cannot use of this performance is 'candid'.

It may be objected that the miners' strike was a special case, that a Welsh radical like Williams could not bear to give other than full-hearted support to Welsh miners on strike. Very well, but then that is just cheer-leading, not truth-telling – for which Williams was supposedly renowned. Anthony Barnett, for example, writes that 'Raymond Williams stands for a kind of *truthfulness*'. To read Williams on the miners' strike is to wonder about such a judgement. And it was not just the miners' strike. Listen to Williams reviewing Eric Hobsbawm's *The Forward March of Labour Halted*. The Left, he says, has endured a terrible defeat and 'ritual reassurance' (surely his stock in trade) is no longer enough. The question is, why has it happened? There follows a confused and meandering metaphor about the wings and body of the movement and an aside or two about 'militant particularism', which is Williams's greatly daring way of referring obliquely – no names, no pack-drill – to the trade union sectionalism which ripped the Left apart in the 1960s and 1970s. He then imagines a horrible future: that the British trade union movement might accommodate to a right-wing Labour or Lib-Lab government. This will produce 'the American, the recent German, the Japanese solution' and would thus, horror of horrors, 'be the end of the historical labour movement'. If it were so easy, of course, it would have happened. After all, German workers enjoy strong trade unions, relative industrial peace, immeasurably better training and apprenticeship programmes and a standard of living twice as high as their British counterparts. But the fact is that 'the historical labour movement' – sectionalism, demarcation disputes and all – is a truly sacred cow to Williams. He parochially assumes that the very idea of this beast no longer getting milked is a complete argument-stopper.

So what, according to Williams, is the way ahead for the labour movement amidst the Thatcherite onslaught? 'So get ready for militant defence? Agreed.' (Which means siding with every old craft union in turn in its fight to maintain restrictive practices). Then we also have to 'rethink our ideas of work' (which means that we are guiltily aware that those ancient restrictive practices are quite indefensible). In particular we have to dream up a new and 'workable settlement' between 'particular interests and the general interest', which means that we think that the old problem of trade union sectionalism can somehow be overcome by introducing sectional trade union leaders to the idea that they ought to be, well, less sectionalist. And above all we must remedy 'one of the labour movement's central failings . . . its quite insufficient attention to, and support of, research, education and popular argument' – the keening cry of the old WEA tutor.

To appreciate the final peroration one has to have a sense of theatre as well as of political ornithology:

> Wings? We have to put back the body. But the only body that will get anywhere will need a very clear head. So now, urgently, research, information, argument, publication: the conditions of any adequate militancy for a new kind of working class, a new and renewed labour movement.

To hear this properly one should inwardly listen to it in its original Welsh accent. Note the sheer staginess of beginning one's final rallying cry with the one-word question, 'Wings?' Then, at the end of a meandering essay which has delicately skirted some major problems with a sort of deliberate muzziness, we are paradoxically enjoined to have a 'very clear head'. Note then the deliberate terseness of 'urgently', a busy, polo-necked and directorial word. But all this exhortation to rethink, though carefully vacuous – no new thoughts are actually produced – may none the less be a little unsettling, so the audience is quickly given its dose of ritual reassurance. Thus, once more, with feeling, such favourite keywords as 'militancy', 'working class' and the 'new and renewed labour *movement*'. Note the careful balance, both political and theatrical, of 'new and renewed', and, especially, that long lugubrious Welsh stress on *movement*. *Mooooovement*. This sound, when emitted in a certain sort of left-wing gathering, is half way between cooing and lowing, and denotes the strong, nay unshakeable, feelings of the speaker, his deep commitment to the struggle, and much else besides. The word 'movement' is itself precious since it is the only term to include not just the trade unions and the Labour party but the CP, the Trots and the whole wide family of the Left. And it has that nice dynamic, progressive feel to it: the whole family of the Left in action, moving, going forward. In fact, what it means is nothing less than the essay's whole title, 'the forward march of socialism'. The fact that *movement* (Williams's italics) is the last word of his essay means that whatever uncomfortable questions have earlier been raised – well, if not exactly raised then hinted at – it is all alright in the end, the family is together and the forward march goes on. So, *moooovement*. Over the years this sound has brought down the house – and the curtain – at Labour and trade union movement meetings from Dolgellau to Tonypandy, from Bangor to Barry, and even beyond. To make fun of it is to risk the accusation of sacrilege, for it is a sacral sound.

There was, though a large hole where the middle of Williams's essay should have been. He refers, though apologetically, to 'militant particularism' ('an awkward phrase, but I wanted to get past my simple equation of militancy with *socialism*') but again, there are no names, no pack-drill – he does not even make it explicit that he means sectionalist trade unions. The leaders of such unions were routinely used to brushing off the outraged indignation of majority public opinion: one may imagine how seriously they treated criticism from someone too timid to come out and mention them by name. But Williams feels awkward about having gone even as far as he has and so hastens to assure his readers that as soon as these particularisms are challenged, he will rise in their 'militant defence'.

Williams's one positive recommendation is for more research, information, argument and publication. Now anyone writing about publication at that time (1981) could not but be aware of a militant particularism very close to hand – the print unions. They were, indeed, where all Williams's concerns intersected and it is quite difficult to see how he could avoid mentioning them. But manage he does. Yet no one can doubt that these unions were desperately abusive. They asserted and obtained the right to say who could work as printers and then doled out the jobs to their members' relatives. Indeed, jobs were inherited more strictly even than in the peerage. Wages were often extraordinarily high, and often for little work. Strikes and go-slows were endemic and the costs of publication were raised so high that ownership of the press was reserved for multi-millionaires. The printing of books was driven massively overseas. The whole weight and strength of the unions were concentrated on retaining in operation nineteenth-century printing presses and practices and in outlawing all the modern innovations which make publication cheap, easy and more democratically accessible. Not infrequently union chapels actually used their industrial muscle to censor the contents of newspapers they worked on. This is part of what militant particularism actually did, but to read Williams you would never know. In the end, the Left's failure of heart and nerve over criticising abuses within its own camp merely made a present of the issue to its political enemies. One must ask what good is a critical intellectual if he will not criticise his own side? Can one really justify making the truth subordinate to partisanship?

Robin Blackburn, introducing *Resources of Hope*, writes that Raymond Williams 'was the most authoritative, consistent and original socialist thinker in the English-speaking world'. One cannot but be struck by the warmth and number of similar tributes – and it seems clear enough that Williams was a kindly, generous man who provided inspiration and support for many less fortunate or younger than himself. But I must confess – I can offer only a personal view – that I simply do not understand the claims made for his political writings, which seem to me repetitive, ritualised, empty and downright evasive. No doubt the fault is mine.

It is famously known that when Williams authored the New Left's *May Day Manifesto 1968* the only practical proposal to emerge from its many thousands of words was for 1 May to be declared a public holiday. A later Labour government found this an easy demand to satisy without leaving Williams in the least satisfied. The fact is that Williams was far too deeply habituated to oppositionism to be at all comfortable about imagining what the Left should do if it ever had power. And being habituated to opposition means that one assumes defeat, makes no plans for winning, that deep down one is more comfortable with losing.

There is an altogether tougher quality about E.P. Thompson. Not that he hasn't almost invariably been on the losing side too, but he has fought on hard even in defeat. It was entirely typical that Williams should make friends of the new and younger guard who had taken over *New Left Review*, while Thompson found it impossible ever to forgive them for his eviction from the editorial board. Similarly, when Thompson resigned his chair at Warwick University over the student files affair he did so with a long, bitter and acute blast against the university authorities. There was a nakedly adversarial quality to his polemics which Williams would instinctively shrink from. And also a greater self-consciousness – Thompson could write with some irony about how people like him had always been against the Establishment, how appeals for 'responsibility' and 'order' were never likely to win his heart for no other reason than that he was emotionally with the ragged-trouser philanthropists as soon as the chips were down. Moreover, not only was Thompson's *The Making of the English Working Class* a greater work than anything Williams achieved, but the historian Thompson always had a far more powerful and pointed literary style than Williams, the literary critic. And Thompson's essays in *Writing By Candlelight* showed a lighter, defter and funnier touch than anything Williams ever wrote – Williams was earnest, sometimes ironic, but never funny. Indeed, the comparison goes in favour of Thompson on every count.

Something seemed to go wrong with Thompson with *The Poverty of Theory*, his immense blast against Althusser and his English interpreters, Paul Hirst and Barry Hindess. Thompson undoubtedly won the joust but he went on and on, achieving overkill after overkill. It was overheated and it was altogether too much. His prose became increasingly personal, more and more self-justificatory, more and more self-*involved*. It became clear that he would only write, self-indulgently, at greater and greater length – indeed, he became a famous despair of publishing editors. His own ego became more and more embarrassingly present, obstrusively so.

Anyone who writes a lot needs a strong ego. You cannot push on alone through all those midnight hours unless you believe in yourself. But the problem of having an over-developed ego is that one tends to feel too much the slings and arrows of enemies, rivals and critics, as well as those of outrageous fortune. In Thompson's case this led him into combat and polemic, often marvellously so. But he wanted praise, acclaim, to win, to be right, to be loved. An ego like this should not enter the world of mass politics, as Thompson then did with CND/END. True, the possibilities of praise, acclaim and love are greater that way, but one's enemies and critics multiply into forests. An ego which finds it difficult to bear criticism at all then finds it has critics all round the clock and begins to shoot away at them like a firecracker.

The results of this were seen in Thompson's collection, *The Heavy Dancers* (1985), the title coming from an exceptionally leaden-footed piece of verse which is so bad as poetry that it is difficult to believe anyone could quote it without satiric purpose. Sadly, no such purpose is present and the essays are mainly passionate, wandering monologues against all the generals, politicians and media commentators ('the heavy dancers') that Thompson the peace campaigner has taken on as enemies. It is an unwise term, for the reader of these essays may be inclined to feel, not altogether unreasonably, that 'heavy dancing' is a passable description of many passages here.

As one reads on, one wonders what has gone wrong. It is impossible not to agree with Thompson about nuclear weapons being so hideous and dangerous that their very existence in ever-mounting stockpiles is an affront to our sheer humanity. Similarly, the targets he aims at, both East and West, generally deserve all he can throw at them. But, rather as with the nuclear weapons he is concerned about, there is a tremendous problem of overkill. If we could have just one bomb and that acted as defence, deterrent and safeguard, that would be one thing. But the possession, even in one's own hands, of a great pile of planet-killers is not only alarming but actually undermines the credibility of the whole project. It is a bit the same with Thompson's prose.

Essentially, Thompson has developed a galloping case of the Michael Foot syndrome, or *dementia Footica*. This is a malady with a saddening impact on older men of intelligence who spend too much time haranguing large crowds from windswept podiums. The wind gets into their prose, levelling it down but also inflating it, so that their speeches get longer and longer (the hair is similarly affected). The garb of the rambler is increasingly matched by real intellectual rambling, each speech trying to touch on ten or twenty subjects and everything becoming just a debating point. Just how far this has gone may be judged by Thompson's confession that he had 'thought it would help readers' if he wrote a 'brief introduction' to this collection, 'in which I replied to my critics (and traducers) on both sides of the world', but that after two months this had 'grown to the length of a short book', at which he hit upon 'a unique solution'.

Yes, it will be a separate book, coming out later but to read as an introduction to this one. All this, one understands, to 'help readers'.

To these clear signs of the latter stages of *dementia Footica* must be added the increasing use of the Hectoring Dissenter mood, in which all subjunctive subtlety is lost. Thus Thompson: 'I'll be tougher. You perhaps suppose that during the Falklands war you weighed up the pros and cons for yourself and formed your own opinions. But many of you did *not*. You sucked in your opinion at the pap of an authoritarian state.' This is sometimes also known as the False Consciousness (F.C.) mood due to its implications that (a) others may have F.C., but never the speaker; and (b) that not only the sin (F.C.) is wrong but so is the sinner too (the innocent imbiber of F.C.). In the days before *dementia Footica* had been properly diagnosed, its symptoms – often seen in ageing Methodist preachers – were more vulgarily referred to in the phrase that the sufferer had become 'sermon-happy'.

Those who become sermon-happy are often unaware of their condition and regard attempts at treatment as simple persecution. When, spasmodically, doubt creeps in, this is seen as an effect of martyrdom. Thus Thompson: 'So I must for a little longer – either until the forces of peace win some little victory . . . or until the sky becomes so dark that it is too late for anything to matter – continue as a prisoner of the peace movement.' (This Last Day image is the rationale adopted by those who have to explain to themselves why they tramp round, week after week, carrying placards telling us to prepare to meet our doom.)

The correct treatment for *dementia Footica* is a long period of rest, reflection and reading in the subjects in which the sufferer claims expertise, with some practice in the writing of short, taut pieces. But the condition has its own momentum and the sufferer already believes himself an expert. (Yet in Thompson's case there is a vast literature in international relations and strategic studies of which he seems innocent.) The sufferer's diagnosis is quite opposite: he must go on 'for a little longer' – the prescription for sermon-happiness is . . . more sermons.

The end of this syndrome is best seen in the case of Foot himself. The sufferer goes banging on to ever-diminishing audiences (with even the faithful beginning to giggle, discreetly) until every subject the sufferer takes up loses credibility by the mere fact of his touch. Thus do good causes lose to worse ones: not through the lack of better arguments, or energy, or good intentions, but through simple self-indulgence.

Chapter 14
Tom Nairn and the Monarchy

The reason why any self-respecting Scot has to want independence for his country is simply that the Scottish relationship with England is like that of a wife who endlessly nags at a husband who endlessly beats her. Such women, faced with the possibility of freeedom, often clutch, insecurely, for the devil they know – but it never makes them more than continuingly miserable. It is just better to be done with such relationships. But there would be benefits for the rest of us, too, from an independent Scotland, for we would then see a flowering of Scottish letters and culture such as has not been witnessed for several centuries. Without doubt there would be a special place in that new pantheon for Tom Nairn, whose writing could only be Scots, in its humour and literacy, its Protestant sharpness and its sheer knobbly refusal – refusal not only of monarchy, but of the world of the Sunday supplements, of the smart Left (as part of smart London), of southern ease and southern comfort.

Tom Nairn has, for many years, been pondering the peculiarities of the British state with impressive intelligence and originality. His earlier work, *The Break-Up of Britain*, remains a landmark – but had the curious deficiency of devoting relatively little space to England, which is, even from Nairn's Marxist and Scots nationalist vantage-point, the heart of the matter. He has now repaired this lacuna with a long and brilliant meditation (Nairn, 1988) on the nature of the British or, as he calls it, the Ukanian or Anglo-British state, its identity and national culture. For we are not, he feels, a nation state – not only because there is not one nation but four, but also because we are a state-nation in which the antique ruling structure unites and defines the nation rather than the other way round. Nairn thus finds, somewhat angrily and almost reluctantly, that the monarchy must stand at the centre of his picture, and parts of his book are a form of polemic against those of his friends on the Left who feel the subject to be unimportant alongside the issues of class. Nairn derides not merely the 'Royal Socialism' of the Labour Party but the whole Ukanian notion of 'class', which here denotes a sort of lumpish, self-encapsulating and self-perpetuating corporatism: knowing-one's-place erected into social theory and a servile national identity. Less a nation of shopkeepers than of butlers – the most that can be said of a true patriot in Ukania is that he is 'a loyal servant of the Crown'. The ideal, it seems, is the Admirable Crichton. We even have a labour movement so denatured and corrupted by instinctive Ukanian authoritarianism that it takes a reactionary government to impose elementary democratic procedures on it, while in the party of Royal Socialism itself the democratically obvious idea of one-member-one-vote is bitterly resisted even by self-described 'democrats'. Nairn despairs utterly of this royal Left and is reduced to feeling grateful for Mrs Thatcher's transparent dislike of the Queen and the right-wing republicanism it implies.

For Nairn is a republican in a way that many, even on the Left, have forgotten to be. The matter is simply not much discussed in Ukania, for even the greatest devotees of the Family Windsor are aware that a theoretical discussion of monarchism will be bound to lead many to discover that they are republicans at heart. So royalists do not make a cause out of royalism and would be embarrassed by anyone who did. Even the most full-throated monarchical warblers – the purest example in Nairn's book is William Rees-Mogg – do not wish to argue that the Americans or, say, the Swiss ought to have a king. And many would probably be embarrassed to have the Windsors bracketed with the House of Saud or the Sultan of Brunei – although these are the only two monarchies to compare with them in wealth: the Japanese royal family, though presiding over a far richer country and actually being divine, are paupers by comparison.

One of Nairn's early chapters is entitled 'Are we all mad?' (occasioned by the sight of three middle-aged ladies bursting into tears of joy as they read the news of the Andy-Fergie engagement in the paper), and he has two chapters on 'The Sociology of Grovelling'. Nairn writes with a bitterness that is truly wonderful and has a line in highly literate, offhand abuse which is frequently extremely funny, especially when he espies what he calls 'the stuffed badger side of royalty'. The sort of thing which drives him wild is 'the warm smirk' of the TV announcer as, at the end of each BBC newscast, his tone abruptly alters to introduce the obligatory royal story; or the official biographer's treatment of Edward VII's gluttony. Edward loved huge amounts of rich food and pigged himself all day, every day, eating quickly and eagerly: even his coronation had to be postponed due to appendicitis brought on by overeating. His biographer, Sidney Lee, faced with this utter grossness, wrote only that the King-Emperor 'never toyed with his food'. This is, in a very strict sense, false consciousness: faced with the reality of monarchy, people simply lie.

Similarly, Nairn catches Kinnock at the Andy–Fergie wedding delightedly telling the media about how Fergie had smiled and 'that smile was worth all the rest of it!' Or Ken Livingstone, after a brief handshake with the Queen: 'I have always thought that the Queen is a very nice person indeed. Today confirmed that view.' As Nairn points out, our Ken 'had no basis whatever for this observation *in the normal sense* of the words'. We see this phenomenon all the time, even from the leaders of the Left. People are so overcome with pleasure at meeting a royal personage that they seek to rationalise this ecstasy by investing the said royal with impressive human qualities, often appearing to claim knowledge of the royal which they cannot possibly have. Again, monarchy makes them lie. And hence the phenomenon of the Royal Joke during which people fall about in near-hysteria when Philip or Charles say something like: 'If it rains today we could all get wet!' People then queue up to tell the TV camera about 'the Prince's wonderful sense of humour'. More lies, always more lies. The cultural compulsion is truly strong. I was once at a garden party attended by the Queen and Philip and saw many people I actually knew behave like this. They all lied like cabinet secretaries, the Americans just as much as the Brits.

Monarchy is, in a secular age, Britain's own curious form of religion – it is publicly far easier to say one does not believe in God than to say one does not believe in monarchy, as, in their own way, the quotations from Kinnock and Livingstone both attest. In other societies emperor-worship waned as Christianity waxed: in Britain it has been the other way round. Fewer people go to church here than anywhere else in the world, but that is because we have a monarchy which is not only a religion but a popular cult: it is Michael Jackson as well as Runcie. The younger royals instinctively understand that they are a sort of super pop star, and, while they may occasionally complain about it, the fact is that, as any pop star must, they court tabloid attention, are indeed largely tabloid inventions. Their lives seem to be constructions of sheer kitsch, in the approved tabloid style of thunderous bad taste. No wonder the *Sun's* journalists are so intrusive with Princess Di – it is they who created her and they who propagate what Nairn terms 'the expanding mass illusion of intimacy'. Monarchy is, too, our Cult of Personality: it is always a terribly bad sign when people's birthdays get to be celebrated, whether it be Nero, Joseph Stalin, Nelson Mandela or the Queen. But it is, above all, the Great Lie at the Centre. It demeans and corrupts our culture by commanding the worship of rank, not merit, of inheritance, not achievement.

It makes people accept that sheer humbug is normal, it makes people grovel and it makes people lie. Politicians long ago realised the uses of royal circuses: Lloyd George devised a wholly bogus Investiture Ceremony for the Prince of Wales at a time when the Irish were getting out of hand, and Harold Wilson did the same in the late 1960s when Welsh and Celtic nationalism was again on the rise. Despite an enormous media build-up, the latter occasion was a considerable flop – policemen outnumbered spectators, the crowd-control barriers had no crowds behind them, and houses trying to rent seats with views of the Procession found no takers. Even at the Castle itself the crowds were only 'Third Division football size'. But the press sells too many papers with royal guff to allow a Royal Flop. The media described it as a resounding popular triumph and crowed about 'investiture fever'. Lord Snowdon devised special 'tasteful' souvenirs for the Event – Investiture pie-funnels and Investiture doilies. In a word, more lies, more kitsch.

Nairn is, though, more interested in how the Crown has denatured Ukanian nationalism and national identity. The ideology of Great Britain (= Greater England) dates, he argues, from the mobilisation of popular opinion accompanying the titanic twenty-year struggle against Napoleon. But the problem has been that nationalism must ultimately be a populist phenomenon, must depend on a strong sense of 'we the people' – and this Ukanian nationalism cannot manage. Instead, a peculiar royal-conservative, not-above-one's-station national identity was imposed on the people from the top down. This has simply destroyed, or even prevented from birth, any genuinely popular national culture, and in its place we have a carefully nurtured folklore-from-above. Thus the question of nationalism and of its place as a constitutive part of modernity has never been properly solved or even raised in Britain, and 'the elements of infantilism so plainly present in the Royal infatuation derive from this history.' Instead, what we have is a true *ancien régime*, our own version of the Habsburgs, presiding over a country which is really just a super-Venice, a city state writ large. Typically, the educated classes of Ukania view things as if from the palace and talk, from the 'Home Counties', of 'the provinces' – thus triggering a typical Nairn soliloquy on the subject:

Those unversed in the Queen's tongue may not appreciate the full sodden misery of the concept. With medicine-pill intensity it evokes all that Crown and Court are not: a *terrain vague* of indeterminate rusticity and toil which chaps enjoy (on holiday) and quite definitely have a duty to help and encourage. This far-flung waste of garden-gnomes and factory-chimneys is in effect an image of nation-state prostration before the City's hegemony.

Much of Nairn's book is taken up with an exploration of the ways in which Ukanian culture is denatured by the monarchy: how our intellectuals have been corrupted by the cult of 'greatness' (a swipe at E.P. Thompson here), how, in a thousand ways, the culture tries to see things from the royals' view down – but, since we cannot be in their position, how the thing becomes contorted and crippled, decked out with a bogus 'pageantry', itself a key, ritualised part of the 'glamour of backwardness'. Other peoples' leaders retire back to ordinary citizenship, but, under our monarchical religion, ours do the equivalent of going to heaven, ascending into the peerage and presenting us with 'Druidic waxworks like the Gartered Callaghan'. Again, sheer kitsch reigns: when you get your knighthood the Marine band plays 'If I were a rich man'. Those who pay such large sums of money to Tory Party funds are really buying this. But they are buying something else too – a sort of trickle-down of deference. As Gustave Le Bon observed almost a hundred years ago, a title also brings a minor version of the ecstasy people feel when meeting the royals. There was, he said, a 'peculiar sort of intoxication produced in the most reasonable Englishman by the contact or sight of an English Peer . . . .. They may be seen to redden at his approach, and if he speaks to them their suppressed joy increases their redness, and causes their eyes to gleam with an unusual brilliance.' So you get a bit of redness for your money too. Many of our great men and captains of industry fight and scrabble for these honours like so many pigs after acorns. It is difficult to see how any word other than 'infantilism' can fit.

Nairn trudges through the various defensive justifications and cop-outs occasioned by any public mention of the themes above. Perhaps the most interesting is the Ukanian tendency to decry nationalism as if it always led to Nazism or other terrible (but, in fact, rather rare) deformations. Hence Kingsley Martin's famous dictum that 'if we drop the trappings of Monarchy in the gutter, Germany has taught us that some guttersnipe (or house-painter with a mission) may pick them up'. So there you have it, chaps. It may be a bit embarassing to be ruled over by 'Europe's greatest living fossil' but if you don't have the gluttonous King-Emperor, you get Hitler. What is left out here is the obvious comparison with French nationalism – indeed, our royal conservative identity was forged in resistance to it and its American cousin. And yet how much poorer we are in patriotic terms than the French. I well remember, in the *balle populaire* which followed the Mitterrand victory in 1981, seeing young Frenchman of the Left brandishing the Tricolore aloft in triumph: in Britain, if we see a Union Jack in a demonstration we assume it is the National Front. We do not even have a truly common flag. Similarly, the French President, when he addresses the nation on TV, begins: *Françaises, Français* . . . . But we cannot imagine the Queen, in her Christmas broadcast, addressing us as 'Fellow Brits'. Or 'fellow' anything, because the whole point is that she is not. My dear subjects? My loyal subjects? *De pire en pire*. Better leave an embarrassed silence. And who really calls himself a Briton? The word tends to get used only in newspaper headlines such as 'Rabid Hamster Runs Amok: Three Britons Bit'. We cannot even agree on a name for Ukania. Do I come from England, Britain, Great Britain, the British Isles or the UK? More feet-shuffling and embarrassed silences. No other country has this nonsense. And, of course, we cannot manage a national day.

Nairn, without much doubt, would like to celebrate that frozen January morning of 1649 when Charles I was beheaded, a scene he recounts with relish, together with the debate which followed in which it was voted 'that the House of Peers was useless and dangerous, and ought to be abolished'. It would certainly be nice to have our own Bastille Day, but the whole point of Nairn's book is that our Bastille has not fallen. In today's Ukania, which has not so much a Constitutional Monarchy as a Monarchic Constitution, the Bastille is full of Japanese and American tourists who have, for this privilege, paid large sums to the National Trust. The owners have long since removed to pleasanter seats; receive enormous tribute from their subjects (in addition to their huge private wealth, on which they pay no tax); and appear daily on stamps and coins, in the *Mirror* and the *Sun*.

Nairn's meditation on English nationalism is one of the most powerful and original pieces of writing I have ever read on the subject. Shakespeare, he feels, has played a critical role in the construction of the royal-conservative ideology: his depiction of an antique Kingship, already out of date when he wrote, has been taken to express eternal truths. But, Nairn argues, the key period in the development of English/Ukanian nationalism lay in the long counter-revolutionary struggle against France: like Shaw, Nairn feels we lost a great deal by not being defeated by Napoleon.

This is, though a contestable account. One of the key ingredients in the growth of national consciousness is the pressure of other nations upon one's own. Typically, the imagery which seems to inspire this consciousness is sexual: the foreigner is seen as someone bent upon taking and ravishing one's women or oneself. Far more than is often noticed, the language of nationalism is the language of violent sex. The foreigner will *invade* one's country, *penetrating* its defences; Germany will *rape* Belgium; coloured immigrants will *overwhelm* us; we are concerned about our nation's racial *purity*, and so on. Many other key words in the nationalist vocabulary – 'surrender', 'humiliation', 'oppression' and so forth – have at least an equal sexual meaning. In a country like France, with multiple and porous frontiers, this pressure was permanently and insistently felt: French boys would grow up knowing that, sooner or later, the Boches would come again, as they so often had in the past, and then one would have to fight for France. And there is, of course, nothing like living with the permanent expectation of fighting for one's country to generate an utterly profound nationalism: indeed, in a sense, that expectation *is* nationalism. Britain, being an island, has lacked this insistent pressure on its borders. For us, making war meant going abroad – we never fought on our own soil, and we were usually able to get away with employing mercenary armies.

So English nationalism was more often implicit than explicit, domestically presumed rather than externally theorised – and it really came into its own only when the fear of invasion became strong. In that sense, the Armada scare of four hundred years ago may indeed have been a fundamental moment in the birth of an English national consciousness – which Shakespeare was merely reflecting. Hence the immediate importance, too, of 1940 in the national psyche: at the moment of its happening the event became instant mythology. English nationalists have always known that they had to conjure up a really good invasion scare if they were to be listened to – hence the way in which many years before 1914 were lived as one long invasion scare. And hence the way English nationalists like Enoch Powell, seeking to excite a national reaction against the 'threat' of coloured immigration, instinctively couched their message in terms of an invasion: the immigrants would come in 'hordes', 'pouring in' in a 'flood' to 'take over' whole areas, 'robbing' the natives of their 'birthright' and so on. The French have had many actual invasions to endure – Frenchmen are used to fighting on French soil: our national consciousness has grown, more weakly, from mere invasion scares. In other words, the long-drawn-out threat from Napoleon may be seen as merely a chapter in a sporadic series and not, as Nairn would have it, the one key moment in the birth of Ukanian nationalism.

Nairn argues that for the oppressed peoples of the Habsburg Empire social emancipation could only be achieved through the national struggle, and that the same will be true in Ukania too. At least since 1923, when the Labour Party Conference turned down its last republican motion, no hope has lain in that direction. Instead, Ukania's various countries will simply have to go their own way in the end, he hopes, as republics. He argues strongly throughout that Ukania is suffering from irreversible decline, an 'unarrestable de-industrialisation' which may precipitate such a crisis. The concept of this 'decline' is vital to his thesis, for he believes that Ukania's economic failure stems from its antique political system, and that there can be no way forward without the completion of the democratic revolution. The question is whether this is more than revolutionary pessimism. It is not that Thatcherism has produced sustainable prosperity – once the oil and nationalised asset sales cease, all too many chickens will come home to roost. But a great deal of our 'decline' has simply been a matter of losing imperial markets as a deferred consequence of decolonisation, a process which has begun to bottom out. And many countries have achieved economic miracles under shambolic political regimes. Our antique social order, unique in the world, has already survived so much that I would not like to bet that it will not be able to survive 'decline', or indeed European integration.

In fact, something more interesting may be taking place. It has for sometime been clear that we are moving towards world standardisation in many things. We have the world car, the world soft drink (Coke/Pepsi), the world meal (steak and chips). Visibly, the Pope in recent years has won the competition for world holy man (world holy woman is Sister Theresa). As the integration of the global village moves on apace, the one thing that is dead is cultural parochialism. And it seems possible that there may be a slot for world royal family. In which case the Windsors have got it all locked up: there's no real Pepsi to their Coke. That is to say, elements of the British infantilist religion of monarchy may become universalised. Already, if one travels in the States or France, let alone the Commonwealth, one sees this happening: tabloid newspapers *everywhere* now feature the Windsor royals. Moreover Hollywood has realised that there is a market for a whole new genre about the fabulously rich – people so rich that every manner of sexual fantasy, power urge and designer-consumption can be paraded on screen.

That way, all the women can be beautiful; they can all have wonderful clothes, hair-do's, cars, houses, jewellery. And they can have scandals and sagas on the same heroic scale. The result – *Dallas, Dynasty* and various non-American imitations – have broken all audience records: the market exists all right. And all that is being sold is pseudo-royalty. The Windsors are, unbeatably, the real thing.

We should not then be surprised by the super-kitsch of the Windsors, nor by the way they jostle side by side with J.R. and Sue-Ellen and Joan Collins in the tabloids of the globe. For while Hollywood may have produced pseudo-royals, the royals in turn are too much the creatures of the media not to produce pseudo-Hollywood. The Windsors have all the right qualifications: fabulous wealth, estates, castles, servants, complicated sex-lives, horses, yachts, pretty women with the best jewellery, clothes and hair-do's – the lot. True, the royals have been held out to their Ukanian subjects as exemplars of niceness, decency and 'family values', and this is something of a problem if Balmoral is to rival the Ewing Ranch. But this fabled decency is, as Nairn puts is, only a 'taboo-supported niceness'. That is, it is not necessarily real: it's just that to sound a critical note is taken to be an attack on what Rees-Mogg, flushed with royalist passion, calls 'the inner spiritual essence of our national life'. These taboos are what really make all the lying possible, but the lying may only be necessary at, so to speak, the Rees-Mogg stratospheric level. For the rest of Ukania – and, increasingly, the world – the Windsors have become a sort of super-Dynasty.

Already they have done things for family life which might seem over the top even in an Aaron Spelling mini-series. Princess Margaret we have become accustomed to see as the Bad Sister of the family – with the spoilt behaviour and the boyfriends: the royal Joan Collins. Philip is clearly an ageing variant of J.R., with the Queen as Miss Ellie. The climactic episode will have, inevitably, to centre upon Princess Michael, with her driving social ambition. What she is after is nothing less than the Crown Jewels, and once she gets them she's off to Berchtesgarten in a stolen Gestapo helicopter (the famous Bavarian heli-chase scene). She can be confronted by a heroic Andy (in Falklands pilot-hero gear), who will snatch the purloined pearls from her quivering bosom. To be sure, the family badly needs someone called Bobby (there *has* to be a Bobby for the US market), and it would be a nice gesture towards the Australian serialisation if at least one Bruce or Barry could be found among the ever-proliferating royal brood, as also a Charlene or Betty-Lou. It's very promising that the royals have begun to visit America so much more: they have obviously got the point about marketing strategy. But these are details. The point is that, even if Nairn does turn out to be right about Ukanian 'decline', the Windsors can become world tabloid figures and thus escape Ukania's fate. We have long had monarchical soap and it has not stopped the Rees-Moggs worshipping at the Monarchical altar. Why should full-blown Soap Monarchy be different?

References

Nairn, Tom (1988) *The Enchanted Glass: Britain and its Monarchy* (London: Radius).

Chapter 15
A.J.P. Taylor

Not long after I wrote this piece Alan wrote a 'final' article for The London Review of Books in which he announced that he had decided to stop writing all such articles and reviews. In fact he wrote a number more. But then one noticed that his by-line had disappeared, that he had indeed fallen silent. I wandered about this and asked one of Alan's friends about it. 'Well', he said, 'he did try to carry on, despite having Parkinson's disease so badly. But it was no good. He'd lost the words.' My God, I thought; lost the words. Where would Alan be without words? For Alan has always been a naughty schoolboy at heart, wanting to shock the Headmaster and the parents and be given all the prizes – and his weapons in all this were words, words and more words. As he got older he minded more and more about the things he had not got, especially the Regius Chair, and would sometimes talk obsessively about it. You could not blame him, but you did marvel at the sheer power of that giant ego in that tiny frame. Once or twice he indicated that he saw me, if not as his successor, at least as a sort of poor man's pale reflection of himself, for our reviews and articles often appeared in the same places. I remember once complaining to Alan about the unfairness of a very jaundiced review of a book I had just published. Alan waved it aside, grinning, 'Remember,' he said, 'it doesn't matter a damn what they say as long as they spell your name right.' In practice Alan himself was incapable of taking such advice: his ego was like the princess's skin in the story of the princess and the pea. That is what powered him. It would be nice to say that he wrote because of his passionate love of the truth, or to give expression to his political radicalism, and so on. But it would not be true. That immense, schoolboy ego drove him on. And there was no harm in that.

Charles Taylor, who was for some years the Chichele Professor of Social and Political Theory at All Souls College, Oxford, told me once of how he had been phoned up from Tokyo by a Japanese journalist who asked if he could come and interview him in Cambridge about what he, as an intellectual, thought about the future of the world in the twenty-first century. His magazine was doing a series on the subject. One of his colleagues was flying off to interview American intellectuals on the subject, others were going to Africa and the Middle East and so forth: he was coming to cover European intellectuals. Charles, well used to being pestered for such manifestly silly projects, told the man that he had nothing of interest so say but would give him lunch if he would like, pointing out that he was in Oxford, not Cambridge. The journalist's gratitude knew no bounds and two days later he arrived for lunch at All Souls, heavily jet-lagged and with an extremely tight timetable – he had to interview de Beauvoir over tea in Paris and Salvador Dali over dinner in Madrid.

At lunch Charles gave the man his views about the twenty-first century, for what they were worth. The journalist wrote it all down, covering Charles with oriental praise at every juncture. Finally, Charles could not forbear to ask, 'Why are you interested in me? I'm amazed to think I'm known in Japan.' 'No, no, you velly famous man in Japan, Plofessor Taylor, velly famous, number one.' 'How come?', asked Charles. 'No, no, you velly famous man, your book is translated into Japanese, sell many copies, is number one.' Charles was at first delighted to hear that he had been translated, then smelt a rat: which book? 'Oh, velly famous. Number one famous is Olligins of Second World War.' Charles explained that he had the wrong Taylor, that that book was written by A.J.P. Taylor, who was indeed very famous, that he could try to phone A.J.P. in London for him, he knew he had a tight timetable but . . . he tailed off as he realised that the Japanese gentleman was utterly mortified at the loss of face he had inflicted on Charles and thus on himself. It was obvious that the journalist, from the first moment of situating him in Cambridge, had had a very slight grasp on his identity and that Charles Taylor was quite unknown both to him and in Japan in general. The more the case of mistaken identity settled on them both, the more frantic the journalist became. 'No, no, you velly famous, Plofessor Taylor, all Japanese velly interested. You do fine, you velly famous plofessor, not want other Mr Taylor. You velly fine, velly famous, number one.' And so on. Lunch at All Souls is always served as a serve-yourself carvery where you hack away at various joints with long, old knives. Charles found himself glancing anxiously from the agonised face of the journalist to those knives a few feet away. Stories of Japanese ritual suicide, of ghastly self-disembowelling, came drifting back. The altogether horrible notion occurred that All Souls was to have its first lunch guest to deliberately fall on his sword, or at least, his carving knife . . ..

I was careful to tell Alan this story. He absolutely loved it, of course. I am glad of that. I have spent enough evenings and nights pounding away at typewriters and computers to know a little of the fatigue and solitariness that Alan must often have known. How many times must Alan have pulled himself along through paragraphs and pages at hours when his *colleagues were long since in bed – and then made himself go on, and then on again? That is how it is. No worse thing could happen than that he should 'lose the words'. In those long, solitary midnight hours I shall think of him.*

When I became a fellow of Magdalen College, Oxford, the fact that my vote at college meetings counted the same as that of A.J.P. Taylor seemed to me, as it still does, a glorious democratic quirk of the Oxford collegiate system. I was just 26 and the youngest fellow; he was probably the most famous historian in the world. I was not long to think of him by his initials, for Alan was the least stand-offish of the senior fellows, the least likely to stand on his dignity. He loved talking – and being listened to. One could safely bring any guest to dinner and place them near him. They would be bound to come away delighted with a stream of funny stories, historical anecdotes and sly shafts of perspicacity. Some of this was due to his courtesy and gregariousness, but he also simply loved performing for an audience. If you provided the audience, he provided the performance.

Partly because of this love of an audience, he has lived a far more public life than most Oxford dons do. So successful was he in this respect that, no doubt to his own pleasure, he was probably not often popularly thought of as an Oxford don. The media have their own not very likeable stereotype of the Oxford don, and Alan clearly did not fit that (though, to be fair, Oxford is full of people who do). So he was not 'an Oxford don'; he was AJPT. But the fact is that he has been a fellow of Magdalen for half a century, and a fifty-year membership of a closed little world like an Oxford college is likely to leave its mark on any man – and on any college.

There was, for a new young fellow like myself, no shortage of AJP stories, by no means all apocryphal. How, at one college meeting, Alan had proposed that the chapel be turned into a swimming-pool. How Alan had loathed the loathsome Dylan Thomas. How Alan had crossed swords with C.S. Lewis, Magdalen's Fellow in English, on this or that occasion. How, on being asked as a young man at interview whether it was true that he had strongly-held left-wing views, he had replied: 'No I have extreme views, weakly held.' How Alan had been invited to give the main address at the speech day of one of Magdalen's schools and had regaled the boys with a history of the major benefactors of the college (and thus of the school), showing that all of them had acquired their wealth by foul means and had had enough left over to buy themselves indulgences through their benefaction: the moral being that if you hear that 'crime never pays', do not believe it.

Such stories blended all too easily with the myriad anecdotes of which Magdalen is full – more so, perhaps, than any other Oxford college. How C.S. Lewis had insisted on starting his lectures punctually on the hour but had seldom managed to get to the lecture room in time, so that he would begin his lecture while strolling up the High Street and enter the hall already well into his third paragraph. The Dean of Divinity who was alleged to have committed the only Magdalen murder, and how it had been decided not to call the police in for fear of scandal. How Harry Weldon, leader of the more progressive fellows, turned down every single Etonian applicant for entry on meritocratic grounds and how the Etonians already up at the college demonstrated in the quad against Weldon, 'the Red Dean'. How Weldon had worsted Lewis, who was generally on the reactionary side, and how Lewis had retaliated by using Weldon as his model for the Devil in some of his writings.

At the same time, one was conscious of the towering intellectual distinction of that earlier generation of fellows: not just AJPT and Lewis, but Bruce McFarlane, John Morris, Rupert Cross, Cyril Darlington, J.Z. Young, Sir Peter Medawar, Gilbert Ryle . . . the line stretched on. No doubt it was all more humdrum in reality, but one was left with the impression of great intellectual giants inhabiting a world of mad English eccentricity: an older world of indulgence, scandal, fun and wit. It was quite intimidating.

But there were echoes, too, of an older Magdalen of the 1920s and before, stretching back to the time when Oscar Wilde was an undergraduate, a world of rowing hearties, intellectual mediocrity and foppish wealth. The most ancient scouts muttered darkly about buckled shoes, Masonic links, a Young Octobrist cell, and the college having once been full of beautiful, aristocratic young men who wore make-up, walked hand in hand, and would not be seen dead with a woman. Old members, now great bankers or industrial magnates, confirmed this picture, swore that *Brideshead Revisited's* Oxford scenes had been based on Magdalen, and spoke of a law tutor who used to hide in his rooms to avoid his pupils, pretending not to be there when they knocked. Those had been the days when the later Duke of Windsor had been an undergraduate, as also Prince Chichibu, the son of the Japanese Emperor. On his first day in the college Chichibu, following custom, had called on President Warren – well-known as an incorrigible lover of blue blood. What, asked Warren, did the name Chichibu actually mean? 'The Son of

God' came the reply. 'Oh well,' said Warren, 'you'll find we have the sons of many famous men here.'

Against this shadowy myth-laden background, Alan stood out as representing the modern college. He had not merely written books, but was equally at home in the worlds of journalism and television, was a prominent supporter of the Labour Party and CND, had a wide range of outside contacts, was *mondain* to a degree. But he had also borne the normal, crushing load of the Oxford tutor, served in college offices and on college committees, lectured to huge audiences, supervised dozens of graduates, and got divorced from and married to a smaller, though still considerable number of wives. Marvelling at this heroic – and sustained – energy, I once asked one of Alan's closest colleagues what, then, had Alan stinted on? 'Nothing, really', he said. 'He simply had a wonderful economy of effort. He never wasted a minute.' The proof of this was clear for all to see in the Finals results gained by his pupils, for in the decade after the war he, McFarlane, Leyser and Stoye took the Magdalen History school to the very top of the Oxford league table. He stood out, too, as almost the last of a powerful group of fellows who, marshalled behind Harry Weldon, had been responsible for transforming Magdalen from a snobbish, reactionary and intellectually undistinguished backwater into a progressive – though still agreeably eccentric – institution. It was, by all accounts, a long, hard struggle, but bit by bit a more open, egalitarian and meritocratic dispensation was achieved – to such effect, indeed, that after the war Magdalen became the first college in over a century to surpass Balliol's academic results. By the time I arrived Weldon and most of his followers had disappeared – indeed the conservative Old Guard had made a somewhat surprising (though temporary) comeback. But Alan fought on. His great cry at college meetings was for the admission of women. Year after year he put the motion until at last it was passed. But it was not quite the same: Alan missed that old vanguard. Once, talking to me over coffee, he glanced at the Smoking Room door and said: 'You know, I'd give more than anything else in the world if only Harry Weldon could walk through that door right now.' Alan's other causes seldom won: I can't remember him finding a single taker for his doughty defence of Beaverbrook's reputation, or for the proposition that Michael Foot would make a great Prime Minister.

For many people mention of Alan's name immediately brings to mind the great *brouhaha* over the Regius Chair in History. His friends, perhaps not entirely discouraged by Alan, have tended to treat this as a sort of crime of the century: in the latest of the Taylor

Festschrifts (1986), Michael Foot goes banging on about it in much the same way that he banged on about even more distant events during the 1983 Election. This is all quite disproportionate. Of course Alan was the better candidate for the Chair, and of course the grounds – his popular journalism – given for his disqualification were scandalous: but the fact is that this sort of thing happens all the time in Oxford and is always liable to occur in the case of a chair which specifically lies within the political patronage of a Prime Minister. It is the existence of such a thing as a Regius Chair which is the real monstrosity. But in any case Oxford is still, in general, a somewhat inbred and reactionary place (especially in a subject like History), and decisisions like the slight to Alan reproduce themselves fairly regularly. It would indeed be possible to draw up a long list of distinguished historians turned down for jobs in Oxford – Namier, E.H. Carr, and a number still living whom it would be unfair to name.

The real point is surely rather different. In terms of the prevailing Oxford norms, Alan was a maverick. At any one time the reputation of the university rests quite heavily on such mavericks, so that outside it they are even taken to be representative. The truth is the opposite: they are hugely outnumbered by the tutorial drones, the committee bores, the self-consciously Great and Good, and the peculiar tribe of Oxford man-boys. This more mediocre majority is alarmed by the sheer ability of some of the mavericks and, even more, by their habit of truth-telling. This means that they are 'not sound', that their names will be greeted with knowing chuckles and that whatever their merits they will not get their deserts. This in turn makes the description of 'maverick' self-fulfilling, for those thus treated are torn between righteous indignation at not being allowed their deserts and a predictable contempt for such baubles: all of which leads them to live up to their maverick image. It is not an uncommon story and it applies beyond the mere confines of Oxford, to a great deal of English life.

There was, though, one considerable extra injustice about the Regius Professorship affair. Given Alan's public prominence it was inevitable that the case should attract enormous newspaper attention. Given, too, Alan's wide range of journalistic contacts, his perfectly reasonable consciousness of his own worth and his justified sense of slight, it was also quite inevitable that Alan should have been widely thought to have helped foment the press campaign on his own behalf. Alan has always denied this. One part of that campaign was, however, monstrously unfair. The suggestion was repeatedly made (and has lingered in many minds ever since) that

Magdalen was somehow conspiring to add insult to the university's injury by ejecting Alan from his fellowship there. Such stories generally began with 'A.J.P. Taylor's Magdalen colleagues, jealous of his public success . . .'. The truth was quite the opposite. Indeed, the college rallied round its own in quite spectacular fashion. Not only was Alan's tutorial fellowship never in question, but when Alan decided to resign it the college elected him, uniquely, to a Senior Research Fellowship. Fellows of Magdalen have since felt a little exasperated that they have mysteriously managed to come out of this affair with a bad press.

There were strange echoes of the affair when, ten years ago, Alan retired from his Research Fellowship. The college was, in effect, bound to elect him to an Emeritus Fellowship, but it quickly became clear that there was overwhelming support for his election to an Honorary Fellowship – the highest honour in the college's gift. Shortly before the election there was a sudden spate of stories in the popular press that A.J.P. Taylor's Magdalen colleagues, jealous of his popular success, were once again conspiring against him – this time to deprive him of the Honorary Fellowship which was his by virtual right. Once again, Alan denied that he had fomented such stories, even the ones in the Beaverbrook press. The college thus found itself in an unenviable position, so that even if it went ahead with the election as it had always planned, it would look as if it was cravenly bowing to a press campaign, perhaps even tacitly accepting the characterisation of itself which was a part of that campaign. It was decided to regard the Beaverbrook press as beneath contempt and to elect Alan to the Honorary Fellowship he so richly deserved.

The publication of his Festschrift has been accompanied by press reviews in the *Observer* and the *Guardian*, written by Alan's former pupils in both cases, which have taken up the joint refrain that it is something of a scandal that Alan has not received at least a knighthood, though one of the reviews hurriedly added that, of course, as a radical socialist, he would have refused any such bauble. Telepathy, no doubt, accounts for the similarity in these reviews. Personally, having heard Alan doughtily defend the public schools, I was a little surprised by the 'radical socialist' epithet. Talk of a knighthood seems a little odd too, for to the best of my knowledge Alan long since took a wager with Harry Weldon that neither of them would accept any title less than a hereditary earldom. Perhaps, if Michael Foot had become Prime Minister, even this might have come to pass: Foot has been nothing if not a determined defender of the unreformed House of Lords, after all. And Alan certainly deserved recognition ahead of such other ennobled historians as

Lords Blake, Dacre and Briggs. But again, that is to miss the point. In England men who offend against taboos do not get offered knighthoods, let alone peerages. This rule was sufficient to ensure that the greatest Englishman of the nineteenth century, Charles Darwin, ended his days as plain 'Mr'. It is not a scandal, it is quite the opposite of a disgrace, to fall within the same tradition as Darwin. Probably none of our other leading historians – Christopher Hill, E.P. Thompson, Eric Hobsbawn, Keith Thomas – will gain such dubious recognition either.

Alan's style of narrative history has drawn criticism in recent years from young historians seeking a more 'fundamental' history in social, economic, familial and demographic factors. I well remember Alan questioning one fellowship candidate after another as to who they regarded as the greatest living historian. This persistent question, which brought amused mutters about egomania from some colleagues, elicited one or two mentions of Fernand Braudel and more general protestations that there was no one then alive to whom such a title belonged. Both of the criticisms implied here are, I think, misdirected. First, writing is a solitary, hard and lonely business. To pour out a succession of books, lectures and articles over more than half a century one has to be driven by some muse or devil. There is, in a word, such a thing as a creative and necessary egomania. Secondly, I have no doubt that Alan, with his energy and omnivorous grasp, could well have written superbly in social, demographic or economic history if he had wanted to. He simply chose not to, was happier with what amused and interested him more. As one surveys his achievement, it is difficult to believe that anyone has anything to complain about or that anyone could have wished him to have written otherwise.

It is fitting that this new Festschrift, his third, is principally concerned with diplomatic and international history, for it is in this field that his mastery of the narrative style has worked best. His greatest work, *The Struggle for Mastery in Europe, 1848–1914*, will surely be read well into the next century. It is no small tribute that this book, though containing many judgements with which the Russians must surely disagree, is still used as a basic text in Soviet colleges. Alan's histories have been best-sellers not only throughout the English-speaking world but in Japan, Germany and innumerable other countries besides the USSR. Alan is, indeed, probably our only historian with a truly world reputation. In that respect he has simply left his peers standing, made them seem parochial figures by comparison. The fact that both the educational and political arms of the British Establishment have chosen to recognise Alan's peers ahead of him is merely a sign of its own parochialism and should be no great surprise. If our Establishment was in the habit of recognising merit rather than 'soundness', England would be a very different place.

References

Wrigley, Chris (ed.) (1986) *Welfare, Diplomacy and Politics: Essays in Honour of A.J.P. Taylor* (London : Hamish Hamilton).

Chapter 16

French Intellectuals, May '68 / & All That

The French intelligentsia has for many years been the envy of intellectuals in the Anglo-Saxon world. Partly this was because there was a tendency to look at the respect accorded to a small élite of Parisian writers and to assume that all French intellectuals shared that fortunate status. But there was also the fact that they were so terribly clever. The New Left Review of the 1960s and 1970s had a lot to do with this. For Anglophones the NLR was itself always by some distance the intellectually toughest journal around – and yet it was clear that the NLR itself stood in awe of continental intellectuals and saw as a major part of its mission the introduction and propagation of their thoughts to a philistine and empirical Anglo-Saxon audience. And while this meant quite a few Germans, notably Korsch, Habermas and the Frankfurt School, and a few Italians, especially Gramsci, it mainly meant an unending supply of French names – Althusser, Gorz, Garaudy, Lévi-Strauss, Nallet, Robbe-Grillet, Poulantzas, Lacan, Foucault, Derrida, and so on and on. With them such figures generally seemed to bring their own private languages which one had to learn in order to understand them. It was all very intimidating.

The NLR was not wrong: while one may lampoon the self-importance and somewhat overblown theoreticism of many French intellectuals, the fact remains that in the post-war world there has been no other intellectual milieu to rival Paris in the richness and profusion of its intellectual creavity. But the French intelligentsia is changing. These changes had begun before 1968 but the romantic, Utopian illusions of May 1968 cast their spell over many of the years which followed the Events, obscuring the fact that much of the change was in an altogether opposite direction. Now that 1968 has receded into an increasingly unimaginable, unrepeatable past, it begins to seem – sadly perhaps – as if French intellectuals are simply going to become more like intellectuals everywhere else.

It is a well-established law of social history and publishing alike, that a large surge of publication about a 'topical' social phenomenon is a clear sign that the phenomenon has fallen into irreversible decline. This is not quite the paradox it seems: often it is only as a phenomenon declines that it is possible to get a sufficiently external view of it to sum it up. There is no doubt that this maxim applies to the outpouring of books about the French intelligentsia, which in recent years has reached almost flood proportions.

The present crisis of the French intelligentsia has three major facets. The decline of the French Communist Party (PCF) and the waning of Marxism have deprived intellectuals of the ideological loadstone which has guided them since the war. The commitment to Marxism or Communism satisfied many needs: a taste for the absolute, a powerful world view, a chic radicalism, the possibility of alliance with a formidable political and trade union movement and an altruistic concern for the wretched of the earth. No replacement for Marxism is in sight and, looking at that list of attributes, it is difficult to imagine that any alternative can offer half as much.

The recession of this ideological tide has, moreover, coincided with the demise of many leading figures. Sartre, Aron and Foucault have died; Roland Barthes, on leaving a lunch with Mitterrand and the Minister of Culture, Jack Lang, was knocked over and killed by a laundry-van; Paulantzas committed suicide by jumping out of a fifth-floor window; and Althusser seems unlikely to re-emerge into public view after confessing to having strangled his wife. (Althusser's fate says something of the peculiar status of French intellectuals. Roger Garaudy, in Le Monde, wrote a highly sympathetic account of the tragedy, suggesting that Althusser had been so haunted by the idea of death that he had merely wanted 'to free those closest to him from the torment of life' and that it was really a case of 'altruistic suicide'. The rest of the press observed a respectful silence despite the fact that Althusser has never been brought to trial.) Garaudy himself is still with us. Having progressed from Politburo membership of the PCF to dissident Marxism, he became first a Green and now a Muslim, extolling the 'enormous debt' we all owe to Ayatollah Khomeini.

But the greatest threat to the traditional intelligentsia derives not from political sources but its own social behaviour. The sociologist

Pierre Bourdieu has written at great length of how intellectuals sought to consolidate their 'aristocratic' position in French society by the development of an ideology of 'distinction', the chief signs of which were an exaggerated taste for arcane and inaccessible language and theories. This is undoubtedly true, as anyone knows who has attempted to plough through theses developed in this specialized argot (in which words whose meaning one thought one had grasped now appear, bafflingly, in inverted commas, suggesting a new and always elusive refinement of meaning – one never does quite catch up). Even so intelligent and readable an interpreter of the French scene as Keith Reader falls into this trap occasionally, as when he observes that *Tel Quel's* politics of the signifier provided a sophisticated theoretical justification . . . for the radical liberating possibilities of the texts it exalted' (Reader, 1987), and goes on to suggest that the magazine's theorising may also be seen as 'a phallocratic enterprise of totalization'. Faced with prose like that, one could indeed do with a signifier or two. One hastens to add that Dr Reader is one of the surer guides through the subtleties of the French intellectual jungle of recent time; it is just that those jungle drums and that jungle talk gets to you after a while.

But there is another way of understanding Bourdieu, that he is in effect rationalising the way in which French intellectuals have latterly deserted the world of learned journals and arcane debates in order to go pop. The surest guide to this process is Régis Debray's *Teachers, Writers, Celebrities: The Intellectuals of Modern France* (1981). Reading Debray is a sort of delightful struggle through a sea of *bons mots*. There are so many of these that one can afford only a selection: 'Balzac observed all the things that Marx did not see'; 'The power of an elite is in inverse proportion to its numerical strength'; 'It is a general law, basic to the economy of institutions, that as those below reach a certain level of equality, the old inequality is displaced onto a higher level'; 'When there is nothing left but the *Academie Française* and satellite TV, and they are hand in glove, how can there be anything but dishonour?'; 'A review is pre-recorded and therefore forward-looking; a magazine goes out live and is therefore backward-looking. A good review is always twenty years ahead of its time, a good magazine is never a week late'; 'Periods of social crisis bring out the truth, stark naked'; 'The golden mean is where extremes meet'; 'The news goes to whoever is new, just as fame goes to the famous and money to the rich'; 'It is the same for ideas as for the manufacturers of ideas: there is no salvation outside Paris'; 'A million listeners or viewers can only receive: mass communication is a one-way process'; 'Europe today is suffering symbolic famine and cultural force-feeding'; 'Glossy paper feeds on young blood'.

And so on and so on. Sometimes the effect is sustained across a whole passage, leaving one dazzled and a bit confused. Thus Debray on the apathy-inducing instancy of the media: 'Our ability to see the world from our living-rooms condemns us to inaction and the eternity of the moment, a privilege reserved for rogues, children and poets. There are few poets among us, and we have grown up. Camus's prophecy is coming true before our very eyes: 'If nothing lasts, nothing is justifiable'. And if nothing is justifiable, everything is 'permissible.'

There is, though, the central thesis. This goes roughly as follows: Once upon a time the Church wholly encompassed and dominated French intellectual life. From the time of the Revolution onwards, intellectuals fought to escape its smothering censorship and obscurantism. Its hegemony was, however, only permanently and decisively challenged with the coming of the Third Republic, which not merely elevated a new secular ethos beyond the claims of the Church, but established a material institutional base for an independent intellectual life in its lay schools and universities. Hence the passionate anti-clericalism and heroic republicanism of many passionate anti-clericalism and heroic republicanism of many intellectuals during the Dreyfus Affair; in Debray's eyes still by far their Finest Hour: intellectuals were virtually compelled to fight the good fight if they were to secure, once and for all, the secular bases of their independence against the repeated revanchist attacks of the Church.

Even before this all-important battle had been won, the institutional basis of intellectual life had, however, begun to shift towards the great publishing houses and the mighty reviews (the *Nouvelle Revue Française*, *Annales*, etc.), whose cultural power was perhaps the chiefest glory of modern French intellectual life. (They have had many foreign imitators but no real rivals.) Having won their great battle, moreover, intellectuals were by no means a continuingly progressive force. The intellectual milieu of the 1930s, balancing happily between the universities, the publishing houses and the reviews, was snug, smug and often frankly reactionary. Despite later myths of the intellectuals' role in the Resistance, the fact was that most accommodated themselves happily with Vichy and the Third Reich. The Germans, after all, controlled the publishing houses, the reviews, the supply of paper. For intellectuals, who need outlets merely to exist, that was more than just something – it was everything. When the Liberation brought a massive reorientation towards the Left, intellectuals accommodated themselves just as enthusiastically to the changed conditions imposed by Gallimard, the Goncourt Prize, and *Les Temps Modernes*.

Gradually at first, and then decisively since 1968, the weeklies and the electronic media have displaced the publishers and reviews. And the new media are like the Church – they allow of no real rivals, only subordinates. True, the really successful modern intellectual entrepreneur will be like a pluralist medieval bishop: he will have his university chair, will also pass theses, advise publishers, edit reviews, have his colum in *L'Express* and serve on TV cultural chat shows. All of which involves, argues Debray, the most terrible degradation of intellectual life: the cults of immediacy, personality and the best-seller flourish, while thought dies.

There are several points to be made about all this. First, Debray is a fascinating and often an utterly brilliant writer and he has a strong case. His book has to be read, despite, as well as because of, all its pyrotechnics. The introduction of Francis Mulhern is a less happy affair: Mulhern tells one quite breathlessly that Debray is not only a profound and radical intellectual, but that *this book was a best-seller in France*. Given the fun Debray rightly pokes at the stupid awe and puffery involved in the cult of the best-seller, this is pretty rich. And the English reader is in danger of being over-convinced of Debray's case unless he also realises that one result of the present situation is a flourishing weekly and daily press in France which intellectually puts its British rivals far into the shade. *Le Monde, Le Nouvel Observateur. Libération, Combat, Le Point, Nouvelles Littéraires*, even *Le Quotidien de Paris*, may not be *Annales*, but they dwarf their British counterparts in sophistication and intellectual quality, as well as quantity.

The phenomenon which best illustrates Debray's thesis is that of the so-called *nouveaux philosophes* – a group of young, implicitly conservative intellectuals who received much media attention and political patronage from the Right in the early 1980s, mainly because of the sheer novelty effect of having intellectuals who were not on the Left. The *nouveaux philosophes* were packaged and marketed rather like pop stars – but often seemed singularly devoid of real intellectual substance. Debray's verdict on one of them, Bernard-Henri Lévy, is perfectly just:

> People like Bernard-Henri Lévy are stars. First, because they have an ego which needs satisfying . . . and the job of the intellectual is to exercise an influence on the way other people think. So the actual vector of influence is in the media, nowadays. All the intellectuals are in the media. A few centuries ago you would have found these same people as preachers at Notre Dame, because that was where the action was. Tomorrow, if being in the circus is where the action is, they'll learn how to do a flying trapeze act. These are not people who produce a body of serious work. They are people who want power. Stendhal did not exert any influence on his contemporaries. He wrote books.

Luc Ferry and Alain Renaut's 68–86 (1987) is an undisguised piece of book-making, based on the false analogy between the Events of May 1968 and the student demonstrations of December 1986 which forced Chirac to climb down on university reform. The latter event was, after all, the very model of conservative, respectable pressure-group politics, aimed at preserving the status quo which guarantees university entrance to any student with the *bac* and which does not allow of a national pecking order among universities. The Ferry-Renaut volume is simply one example of a wave of books trying to make a quick killing out of the twentieth anniversary of the May Events. Their book is full of empty philosophising, the tone of which may be gathered from the happy familiarity with which they refer to such intellectual giants as Abby Hoffman and Jerry Rubin as 'Abby and Jerry'.

Alain Finkielkraut's *La Défaite de la pensée (1987)* is not much better. It argues, plausibly enough, that the crisis of the French intelligentsia derived in part from the internationalisation of culture and the fact that all societies are becoming multicultural, losing much of their old national specificity. Finkielkraut then attempts to touch base with the entire pantheon of cultural influences, ranging from Stalin to Shakespeare, before somehow reducing it all to the Band Aid slogan (taken as the motto of the new universal culture) of 'We are the world, we are the childen'. Ho hum. Or rather, *bof*.

Bernard-Henri Lévy's *Eloge des intellectuels* (1987) is so profoundly silly and pompous as to be almost a self-parody. The main sign of the intellectual crisis for Lévy is the superior attention being showered by TV on pop stairs, comedians and charismatic entrepreneurs. Not, he hastens to add, that there is anything wrong with TV – 'I find myself very much at home there'. He then goes on to predict the emergence of a new kind of intellectual which, typically, he refers to as 'the Intellectual of the Third Kind'. This turns out to be a self-portrait, with the most important characteristic apparently being hostility to the Left. This is a book by a man with almost nothing to say but who cannot bear not to be in print.

Despite all of this the glamour of the French intelligentsia continues to exercise a strong magnetic power upon Anglo-American neophytes. At almost any time of year you can see hordes of English-speaking tourists paying fancy prices to sit and gawp and drink coffee at La Coupole or the Deux Magots, apparently in the belief that someone like Simone de Beauvoir might come and sit next to them at any moment. An almost self-parodying example of this genre is Melinda Camber Porter's *Through Parisian Eyes* (1987), a breathless rush through the contemporary French cultural scene in which Ms Porter is, quite audibly, so *excited* to be *really talking* to all these famous people that one has heard so *much* about. The sharpest observation in her book comes from that *grand journaliste*, Olivier Todd. One reason for the national prestige of French intellectuals, he points out, is that they gave France a world reputation for intelligence and sophistication, while the brutal truth is that the French read fewer books than most and can muster only one quality newspaper. (One cannot, for all the fashionable hype, count *Libération* – which carries far less news than, say, the *Guardian*, sells only 100,000 copies and carries soft porn.) Todd describes French intellectuals as 'drunk on words'. 'Sentences have a poetical beauty. But the verification principle just doesn't apply.'

There is an important point here. French high culture, even more than its British counterpart, has been essentially literary and philosophical. It has also had a boldness, *élan* and brilliance which one can only admire. But this literary bias – even the predominant Marxist current was always singularly lacking in any knowledge of economics – has meant that the intelligentsia has, in its political judgements, always been extremely open to the winds of fashion. In the 1960s this led to a largely uncritical acceptance of Third Worldism – Mao's claims for the Cultural Revolution found more believers in Paris than in any other European capital. Similarly, in the past few years many French intellectuals went overboard on Reaganism to a degree unequalled anywhere else in Europe. If one pointed out that the Reagan economic boom was based on unsustainable budget and trade deficits which spelt terrible trouble around the corner, one was met by blank incomprehension: it was all a matter of style and ideas, wasn't it?

Or again, the critique of communism mounted by French intellectuals in the last decade has centred, above all, on the gulag, a discovery always treated as new, shocking and explosive. But the historical facts about Soviet labour camps had been widely available for years – it was only the previously blinkered attitude of the French intelligentsia that made the phenomenon seem new. In general, the lack of any real roots in the more hard-nosed social sciences has meant that this has been an intelligentsia largely free to believe what it wanted to believe.

This is one reason why May 1968 still occupies such a central place in all these accounts of Parisian intellectual life. Hervé Hamon and Patrick Rotman, who made their name with a muck-raking exposé of Parisian intellectual life, *Les Intellocrates*, have launched out on a two-volume account of the generation which made the Events. The first volume, *Les Années de rêve* (1987), traces their story from the mid 1950s through to 1968; a second volume, *Les Années de poudre*, will follow the former *enragés* through to today. The authors have done their research well and the results are fascinating, especially since they intersperse their account of events with snippets in which the main actors look back with hindsight on what they said, did or felt at the time. The strength of the book lies in the careful reconstruction of the political and intellectual environment of the late 1950s and early 1960s – the world of the Union des Étudiants Communistes, Mendèsisme, the PSU, UNEF, the Servin–Casanova affair (Marcel Servin and Laurent Casanova, the young Turk reformers of the PCF, were expelled from the party in 1961); the impact on the likes of Debray, Daniel Cohn-Bendit, Alain Geismar, Serge July, Pierre Goldman, Alain Krivine and Bernard Kouchner of Hungary, the Algerian War, the building of the Berlin Wall, and of such cultural bombshells as rock-and-roll, *Jules et Jim*, *À Bout de souffle* and *Les Quatre cents coups*.

Hamon and Rotman are, I think, doubly right to insist on the importance of cinematic influence. In 1950 Paris had 140,000 students; in 1960 215,000; in 1963 308,000 and by 1968 600,000. While the ever-growing class could drift around the Boul' Mich and sit in the Deux Magots, La Rhumerie, the Old Navy and Le Buci, marvelling that the *cafés de papa* were all still playing their central role, the more humdrum truth was that the Sorbonne was still also *l'université de papa*: almost nothing had changed to accommodate the burgeoning student body. The reality was inaccessible professors, an ever-more desperate search for lodgings and, often, profound loneliness. Then, as now, the only real refuge lay in the huge number of cinemas which dot the Left Bank: there students can escape into a world of fantasy and surrealism which is often as real to them as anything else in their lives. It is impossible to understand the slogans of May '68 – 'Je suis marxiste – tendance Groucho', 'L'imagination au pouvoir', 'Sous le pavé – la plage', and so on – unless one takes this surreal, cinematic influence into account.

The cinema also probably played its part in the growing belief in voluntarist action. The students of the 1960s had seen the Algerian FLN take on half-a-million French soldiers – impossible odds – and win. Che Guevara, first in Cuba and then in Latin America at large, also seemed to preach the message that who dares wins. Mao's Cultural Revolution suggested much the same message – even the most massive social and economic obstacles could be overcome by determined acts of will. Most of all, of course, the continuing struggle of the Vietnamese suggested that sheer determination might overcome even the might of American imperialism. And given de

174 Intellectuals

Gaulle's crusade against that same imperialism, it seemed easy enough to conclude that 'Vietnam fights for us!' Without doubt the Tet offensive of February 1968 had a major, perhaps even a decisive, impact on the events that were to erupt in Paris three months later. The Vietnamese had taken everything the Americans could throw at them, had been napalmed, targeted with smart bombs, hunted down by fleets of gunships, carpet-bombed with B-52s- and yet here they were, by a gigantic and heroic assertion of will, carrying the war right into Saigon, fighting from the very basement of the US Embassy, running up the NLF flag in Hué. What could the will not achieve? It was indeed like the films where the western heroes triumphed against impossible odds . . ..

It is conventional to celebrate May '68 as the source of the new ideological directions of the 1970s – feminism, participation, ecology and so on; a new beginning. But May was also an end, a defeat. The retrospective comments of participants leave no doubt about that:

> My years as a militant did nothing for me. I deplore the fact that all that knowledge, all that savoir-faire, was not recognised by society. In that career I met people who were more intelligent than my present superiors in the hierarchy. None of them holds real responsibility today. Of that whole adventure, nothing remains. Nothing. [A junior official in the Education Ministry]
>
> To find yourself a star from one day to the next, that goes to your head. You couldn't go into a bistro without people expecting you to utter historic words. The patron of your usual restaurant in the Rue Cujas would offer you a gun in case it might be useful. People quite unknown to you would kiss your hands and call you a son of the people. It was strange, worrying, but of course enjoyable. And it was hard, aggressive and frightening. I didn't know who I was any longer. [Alain Geismar, today a Vice-President of the Informatics Development Agency]
>
> I lived from day to day. Like everybody else I was surprised at the scale of the events. I had no idea as to the outcome. I didn't know what the limit was, or if there was a limit. I felt isolated and cut off. Politically I was rootless, incapable of debating with the Left militants with their certainties. I started off because I'd been left behind. It was a flight. [Daniel Cohn-Bendit].

Poor Cohn-Bendit. The press lit upon him during the '68 Events in a somewhat fluky way, and one gets the impression that it thereby gave him an identity which he has never been able to shake off. In his *Sixty-Eight: Year of the Barricades* (1988), David Caute has an account of a rather puzzled Cohn-Bendit interviewing Jerry Rubin, as if trying to understand the origins of his own *enragé* status. It is difficult to believe that Rubin, now a Wall Street broker, was much help. He burbles on about how 'the way to fight the state is to become the state. We – the doctors, dentists, managers – are the state'. A healthy reminder, this, that the era of student revolt should not be too solemnly regarded – it had more than its share of jokers and hucksters. Rubin claims to have now found the answers to many of the questions he posed in those years. Actually, he sounds as if he is well equipped for his present job ('business networking' social events for yuppies) but not for anything remotely useful. Cohn-Bendit himself sounds more straightforwardly lost. 'Today I am a militant of the Green Party,' he says, 'but I hate the countryside.'

So one should resist the temptation just to celebrate May '68. It may have been a sort of birth, but it was a defeat. And while it showed that even de Gaulle's regime could be shaken to its foundations by a spontaneous, voluntarist revolt, it also showed that voluntarism was not enough.

The Fifth Republic regime might well be authoritarian and unresponsive, but it had given France a decade of stability and unexampled prosperity. In the crunch, that was not to be lightly cast aside. A voluntarist student revolt, even when accompanied by the greatest strike wave the country had ever seen, produced, in the end, a crushing right-wing parliamentary majority. It may be possible, once in a while, under the exactly right conditions, and with a simple trumpet blast, to bring the walls of Jericho tumbling down, but brick walls do not usually behave like that. And it is naïve and parochial not to have understood that before. For the truth was that the Paris intelligentsia had, as ever, been indulgently selective in the images of voluntarist triumph it sought to emphasise. The students had, notably, paid almost no attention to those other and even more moving events of Spring 1968, in Prague. Eastern European Communism in crisis? So what else was new? Dubček promising reform? Who on earth could be interested in reformism? The Russians as oppressors? Well, of course.

Nothing is more telling than the image with which Hamon and Rotman end their book. Two of May's leading figures, Serge July and Alain Geismar, set off in August 1968 for a cultural conference in Havana, to be presided over by their hero, Fidel. When their plane made its obligatory stop in Prague the two men walked the streets without much interest – though events there were on the brink of their tragic climax. Arriving in Havana, they heard the news of the Soviet invasion, and were vaguely shocked when Fidel made no mention at all of the Paris Events but supported the invasion of

Czechoslovakia. The *realpolitik* of this seemed wholly to escape them: that as a small, threatened Communist outpost, Cuba had no wish to give gratuitous offence to the French government but every reason to acclaim energetic Soviet action to protect Communist regimes elsewhere. July and Geismar, feeling distressed and uneasy, decided to cut their visit short and return home. Meanwhile, Régis Debray sent an indignant letter of protest to Castro. No mean feat – the letter had to be smuggled out – for Debray had heard the news on his transistor while sweating out time in a far-away Bolivian jail, where he had been landed by his own pilgrimage after Che Guevara.

References

Caute, David (1988) *Sixty Eight: Year of the Barricades* (London: Hamish Hamilton).
Debray, Régis (1981) *Teachers, Writers, Celebrities: The Intellectuals of Modern France* (London: New Left Books).
Ferry, Luc, and Renaut Alain, (1987) *68–86: Itinéraires de l'individu* (Paris: Gallimard).
Finkielkraut, Alain (1987) *La Défaite de la Pensee* (Paris: Gallimard).
Hamon, Hervé and Rotman, Patrick (1987) *Génération. Tome l: Les Années de rêve* (Paris: Seuill).
Levy, Bernard-Henri (1987) *Eloge des Intellectuels* (Paris: Grasset).
Porter, Melinda Camber (1987) *Through Parisian Eyes: Reflections on contemporary French arts and culture* (London: OUP).
Reader, Keith (1987) *Intellectuals and the Left in France since 1968* (London: Macmillan).

PART III
Spies, Merchants of Death and Other Monsters

PART III

Chapter 17

Edgar Hoover: Public Enemy

Edgar Hoover was one of the greater villains of this century. Anti-Semite, anti-black, the man who murdered Ethel Rosenberg and Jean Seberg, who persecuted America's greatest policeman, Melvin Purvis, into suicide, the man who unleashed Joe McCarthy, the man who . . . .. The list goes on. But villainy is banale; the fascination of his career lies elsewhere. He was a remarkable bureaucratic warrior and a shrewd sniffer of the political wind: the way he resisted launching a Red Hunt in the 1930s and risked dismissal rather than get too involved in Nixon's dirty tricks displays a man of greater subtlety and a longer view than any mere cardboard cut-out baddie.

But he was also a man peculiarly outside his own history. That is, it is today's commonplace that politicians' private lives are now subject to a degree of public scrutiny which was unthinkable in the old days when all public figures were presumed to live lives of Gladstonian probity. (Given what we now know of Gladstone and his ladies of the night, even the simile will not work properly any more.) But for Edgar Hoover, all alone, this was not true. He could – and did – listen to tapes of Eleanor Roosevelt, John Kennedy and Martin Luther King making adulterous love. He knew what an immense crook and bully Lyndon Johnson was. He had documentary evidence on the many-sided villainies of Richard Nixon. He knew all about the childhood secrets, student indiscretions, business misdemeanours, homosexual liaisons and adulterous attachments of America's politicians, trade union and business leaders, journalists, film stars and even of some of its criminals. He knew all this while clinging to a strict, parochial and bigoted morality which must have made all this seem even worse than it was. He knew that the public morality was a fraud, that most of American public life was a fraud. He must have felt that he was sailing his ship on a sea of excrement, that he alone knew just how seamy and steamy American life was – and that part of his mission was to protect America even from knowledge of itself. What we still do not know is what compromises with the Devil he himself made. It is amazing enough that he managed to deny the very existence of the Mafia for decades, that he refused to fight the drug traffic, that he even conspired to keep mention of the Cosa Nostra out of the press. It would be even more surprising if these wonderful favours to the Mafia happened by accident, if there was not some deal between Hoover and the Godfathers . . . .

'Dick, you will come to depend on Edgar. He is a pillar of strength in a city of weak men. You will rely on him time and time again to maintain security. He's the only one you can put your complete trust in': thus Lyndon Johnson to Richard Nixon, 1968. It is not often that a book casts fresh light on American history throughout this century, but this biography of Edgar Hoover does just that. Not only was Hoover, as head of the FBI, America's leading policeman: he enjoyed an extraordinary political longevity – his career, which ended under Richard Nixon, began under Woodrow Wilson. That Hoover persecuted Martin Luther King is notorious, but Hoover was also the man who drove Marcus Garvey out of America. Similarly, the Hoover who turned his malign attention upon the anti-Vietnam War movement was the same man who had, half a century before, hounded Emma Goldman and John Reed and, later, put Leon Trotsky under surveillance in Mexico. This longevity makes Hoover's biography a wonderful subject. Powers's book (1987) is painfully neutral and somewhat pedestrian at times, but his authoritative command of his sources makes it unlikely that it will be surpassed.

Hoover was virtually born into the Federal bureaucracy – his middle-class Wasp family lived in Washington and almost all its members worked for the Government. As Powers stresses – at somewhat inordinate length – Hoover thus inhabited an extremely narrow, self-satisfied and self-righteous little world. Even as a young man, he was conservative, respectable, a Freemason and a keen, church-going, racial bigot, disliking all non-Wasps. Born in Washington, he went to school there, attended university there, worked there all his life: he left America's shores just once, for Central America, and that only when business forced him. Apart from vacations, all spent in America, he was a home-town boy who spent his whole life in that town. He never married and lived at home with his mother, whom he worshipped, until he was 43 (when she died). As he got older, he got narrower. Apart from his dogs (who had names like Spee Dee Bozo), he had, in all his life, only one close friend, Clyde Tolson, whom he promoted from raw FBI recruit to

Assistant Director in two years flat. Hoover and Tolson were, for over forty years, inseparable – they breakfasted, lunched and dined together every day, socialised together, invariably went on holiday with one another. Although Hoover was always loud in his denunciation of 'sexual deviates', his relationship with Tolson was at least implicitly homosexual – though woe betide anybody who hinted so.

Hoover began his career in the Justice Department's Alien Enemy Bureau at a point when Woodrow Wilson had already begun to whip up what became the great Red Scare. Since aliens (i.e. those who had not yet got their citizenship papers) did not enjoy the protection of the Constitution, Hoover found himself, in his early twenties, able to consign suspects to prison at the stroke of a pen. He took avidly to this work and in 1919 Attorney-General Mitchell Palmer made him head of the Radical Division – at the age of 24. Palmer, a strongly religious man given to public moralising, was deeply corrupt – he had used the Alien Property Bureau to transfer large amounts of confiscated German wealth both to himself and to the cronies on whom he was relying to secure him the Democratic Presidential nomination. His road to power, he decided, lay via a great crusade to crush the Bolshevik revolution in America which he had regularly predicted – and the young Hoover was to be the herd-driver of the Reds. Hoover enthusiastically carried out vast night swoops, rounding up as many as six thousand suspected radicals in January 1920 alone. The violations of civil rights – and sheer illegalities – involved in these raids were, however, so gross as to lead to a major public backlash, leaving Palmer's Presidential bid in ruins and Hoover running scared in front of angry Congressional investigators.

The Palmer raids marked Hoover for life. He had had a terrible fright: his career had almost been ruined before it had properly begun. He was, for ever after, extremely conscious of how quickly political moods could change, determined never to be caught on the wrong side of such a change again – and deeply cautious about taking risks for any politician. But Communism had also become Hoover's lasting monomania. Eager to know his enemy, he had set himself to study the slender literature then extant about Bolshevism. This admirable thoroughness he combined with a poor education, somewhat absurd philosophical pretensions and an entire confidence in his own views. Thanks to this crash course he acquired, in his own eyes, the lifetime status of leading American expert on Communism. What it more truly made him was the founding father of American anti-Communism. It is in his long, rambling homilies that one first sees elaborated many of the themes which have since become so familiar, including such notions as the antithetical duality between Communism and 'Americanism'. Hoover's primal passion was greatly assisted by the fact that the suspected radicals were aliens – Poles, Russians, Jews and other non-Wasp degenerates. You could, he told Congressmen, recognise 'revolutionists' just from their photographs: 'Out of the sly and crafty eyes of many of them leap cupidity, cruelty, insanity and crime; from their lopsided faces, sloping brows and misshapen features may be recognised the unmistakable criminal type.'

But this sort of rhetoric had to be put into cold storage after the denouement of the Palmer raids. Hoover now spoke the language of liberal reform; asked, on becoming FBI Director in 1924, for the Bureau to be cut back; insisted, above all, that the FBI must stay out of politics. It was, he now averred, not against the law just to be a radical, and he refused to give further speeches on the 'Red menace' because FBI agents would naturally 'take the cue and begin looking for radicals all over the place'. Indeed, while US Military Intelligence maintained a large domestic espionage network in the 1920s (especially in the unions), Hoover had been so badly burned that he wanted nothing to do with it. When he came under strong Congressional and White House pressure to start a new Red hunt in 1930, he argued that such a thing was strictly illegal – and since the agitators were mainly in the unions, would it not be better to hand the whole thing over to the Department of Labor? The project quietly died.

Herbert Hoover's Administration staggered to its end amidst a growing climate of outrage against the 'crime wave', and particularly against the breed of sensational, violent gangsters who were apparently challenging the very authority of the state. To many, the fact that the Government had in the end only got Al Capone for evading income tax symbolised the complete inadequacy of the law-enforcement structure. The Lindbergh kidnapping of 1932 became so huge a national melodrama – it was, said H.L. Mencken, 'the greatest story since the Resurrection' – that Edgar Hoover (who co-ordinated the kidnap hunt) became for the first time, a national figure. None the less, once FDR won the election it seemed clear that Edgar Hoover was finished: the new Attorney-General, Tom Walsh, had loathed Hoover ever since the Palmer raids and was determined to sack him. But on the way to FDR's inauguration, Walsh had a heart attack and died. The new Attorney-General, Homer Cummings, was a very different man: like Mencken, he realised that in the US, the crime business was, above all else, a branch of show business.

Americans were divided by ethnicity, religion, colour and language – but when the good lawman overcame the wrongdoer, a wider sense of community was, for once, triumphantly affirmed. When the sheriff brought the baddies to book, the meaning of America was demonstrated: no group was above the law; everyone was equal before the law; a community of the law-abiding was re-created. Thus the drama of crime and punishment was a unifying ritual of community solidarity and law enforcement was intensely politicised – and publicised. While English crime writing revolved round fictional characters like Sherlock Holmes and Moriarty, in America centre-stage in the criminal drama was held by real people – by Billy the Kid or Jesse James, Wild Bill Hickok or Wyatt Earp. The American public expected its lawmen to be colourful popular heroes and the boundary between crime fiction and non-fiction was tenuous indeed. Allen Pinkerton, the most famous detective of the nineteenth century, was also an enormous best-seller, publishing eighteen volumes of 'true crime stories'. The first head of the FBI, William Flynn, edited a popular crime magazine, *Flynn's Weekly*. His successor, William Burns, was a national celebrity and the subject of countless feature articles. Like Flynn, Burns was an affable, extrovert Irish cop – a major figure in New York night-life as well as a popular lecturer, and the author of two crime novels as well as the compiler of a collection of 'true crime stories'.

Hoover, the super-bureaucrat, could not easily compete with this. But while the respectable America of the 1920s had been shocked by the opportunities Prohibition had given men like Capone, with the Great Crash came the panic-stricken presumption that the whole structure of civilised society was tumbling – and that the gangster, not the lawman, was winning. The result was an all-out media crime craze. From 1930 on came a great rash of prison movies and a new genre of gangster movies such as *Little Caesar* (1930, with Edward G. Robinson) and *Public Enemy* (1931, with James Cagney), in which the Capone-like celebrity gangster was the star and the Police were depicted as impotent or simply absent: Hollywood morality insisted that the gangster got killed, but usually this was accomplished by rival gangsters, not the Police. The new genre was so popular that fifty such films were rushed off in 1931 alone. Such films drew upon, and further fed, a genuine folk panic. There were incessant calls for martial law, for public hangings and floggings, for a network of American Scotland Yards, for the setting-up of an American Devil's Island. Monster anti-crime rallies were held, many States passed 'public enemy' laws making it a crime merely to consort with known criminals, and the

American Legion armed its members to act as police auxiliaries against the terrifying crime wave. (Actually, such statistics as exist suggest that crime fell steadily in the decade following the Great War.) What the public wanted, said Chester Gould, was 'a symbol of law and order who could dish it out to the underworld exactly as they dished it out – only better. An individual who could toss the hot iron right back at them along with a smack on the jaw thrown in for good measure'. Gould was describing his new comic-strip character, Dick Tracy, launched in 1931, but FDR's Attorney-General, Homer Cummings, was not slow to grasp that immense political advantage was to be gained if real law enforcement could somehow be brought into line with what the movies promised and the comic-strips demanded.

This was where Edgar Hoover and his G-Men came in. In a blaze of publicity Cummings presented Hoover to the public as the world's greatest detective and the FBI as the great scientific organisation which he, Cummings, would now unleash upon the gangsters. Where ordinary policemen had failed, they would not. In another great public relations coup Cummings set up a new maximum security prison for celebrity gangsters – Alcatraz, sited, predictably, on Hollywood's doorstep. To the accompaniment of saturation media coverage the FBI was launched on one feverish crusade after another against 'number one public enemies': Pretty Boy Floyd, Machine-Gun Kelly, the Ma Barker Gang, Baby Face Nelson and, above all, John Dillinger. Hoover and his agents were so caught up in the media excitement that they frequently acted like comic-strip actors themselves. When Baby Face Nelson killed FBI agent Sam Cowley, FBI Special Agent Melvin Purvis rushed to Cowley's deathbed where, he told reporters, he had taken 'an oath in Cowley's blood' to avenge him, helpfully providing the press with the headline quote they wanted: IF IT'S THE LAST THING I DO, I'LL GET BABY FACE NELSON. Hoover behaved in similar fashion, charging about the country pistol in hand as if he himself was personally leading the man-hunt. He luxuriated in a tough-guy image, and was frequently photographed holding machine-guns or at ringside seats at big fights along with sundry Hollywood stars. In public speeches he excoriated 'namby-pamby' penal reformers and the 'cream-puff school of criminology'. He was, he said, 'proud to be termed a member of the so-called machine-gun school of criminology'.

The hysteria reached its height during the hunt for Dillinger, who had repeatedly escaped from jails, the Police and the FBI, leaving a trail of carnage behind him. Cummings made the hunting-down of

Dillinger a major Federal objective and told the press that his orders were 'shoot to kill. Then count to ten.' *Time* put Dillinger on its cover, he was sighted everywhere: the whole country had simply gone 'Dillinger happy' – he was the most famous outlaw since Jesse James. Success came in the lucky and squalid way it usually does in such matters: Special Agent Melvin Purvis got a tip that Anna Sage, a Chicago brothel-keeper, knew something. Sage was facing deportation and agreed to shop Dillinger in return for the reward money plus help with the Immigration Bureau. Thanks to Sage's tip, Purvis found Dillinger and killed him. Across the country excited radio announcers broke into programmes to announce that the 'archcriminal of the age' was dead.

Inevitably, Cummings was lost sight of in the media hurricane: the press wanted only Purvis. Hoover, however, elbowed everyone else aside in his determination to monopolise the publicity. He refused to accept Purvis's deal with Sage and Sage was deported. The Dillinger story was then sanitised so as to be a triumph of scientific investigation for the Bureau, not a personal triumph for Purvis (Sage disappeared altogether from this version). Purvis, the FBI's greatest agent (he had also bagged Pretty Boy Floyd), was forced out, and Hoover then systematically worked to prevent him getting a job elsewhere. When, in the end, Purvis committed suicide with the same machine-gun with which he had shot Dillinger, Hoover refused even to attend the funeral.

Meanwhile, Hoover sponsored comic-strips, pulp magazines, films, books and radio serials about the FBI – in which, inevitably, he emerged as the central figure. All else apart, Hoover kept such a tight, personal grip on the Bureau that it was impossible for agents to have the freedom of action the crime-writers wanted: the only person in the FBI with that sort of freedom was Hoover. From the mid 1930s on, Hoover was stamped indelibly on the popular American consciousness. A host of books, speeches and interviews made his name synonymous not only with law and order but with a broader set of conservative verities, for Hoover took himself extremely seriously as a moralist, tirelessly lecturing audiences on the need for a return to religion and the centrality of the family. Unhindered by the fact that he had never managed to leave home, marry or have children, and that his knowledge of women was pretty much restricted to his large private collection of nude pin-ups, he saw himself as having a special mission to the nation's youth, and developed strong opinions about the proper forms of child-rearing and, in particular, the father–son relationship. Increasingly, conservatives came to accept Hoover's depiction of himself as a moral guardian of the nation's values and institutions. In time, like his predecessors, he became a best-selling author himself.

Hoover and the FBI thrived under the New Deal as never before, and Hoover saw in FDR a President worthy of his entire devotion. The domestic political espionage service that Hoover had begun to run for earlier Presidents was now greatly expanded for FDR, providing him with regular intelligence on everything his enemies, rivals and even his friends were up to. At FDR's request, Hoover had by 1936 also placed the American Nazi and Communist Parties under surveillance and the net was rapidly extended to the whole panoply of labour and liberal groups, which meant, ironically, that many of FDR's own keenest supporters were under illegal surveillance. When Hoover learnt that Eleanor Roosevelt had complained to FDR that the FBI was being developed into a veritable Gestapo, he opened a secret file on her, but was canny enough to leave it at that. The Army Counter-Intelligence Corps (CIC) was bolder and, by bugging Eleanor's hotel bedroom, got tapes of the President's wife having intercourse. These tapes were then played to FDR, producing a bitter row with Eleanor and also the complete disbanding of the CIC, whose members were ordered to the Pacific by a furious Roosevelt 'for action against the Japs until they were killed'. The tapes ended up in Hoover's files, ammunition against a rainy day.

By the end, even FDR saw that Hoover had become too powerful to control: in 1943 a proposal for OSS–NKVD co-operation which had the backing of the Army, the State Department, the OSS – the CIA's predecessor – and the President had to be abandoned when it was realised that Hoover would work up a gale of opposition by strategic press leaks. This was precisely the weapon Hoover was to use repeatedly and to deadly effect against Truman, whom he hated from the word go, for he had learnt that Truman, not unreasonably, believed Hoover should never have kept his job after the terrible failure of US counter-espionage over Pearl Harbour. Hoover tightened his links with the Right and began to make sweeping allegations of Communist infiltration of the Government, insisting that even major figures like Dean Acheson were pro-Soviet. Hoover, indeed, more than any other man, was responsible for the post-war anti-Communist hysteria from which the American political system has never fully recovered: ambitious politicians like Nixon or Joe McCarthy were largely made by Hoover, who leaked titbits to them at will. When Truman refused to sack all those fingered by Hoover, Hoover took his anti-Truman case to Congress and thus to the people, to rapturous conservative applause.

If, as seems likely, the motive behind Hoover's launching of the great Communist witch-hunt had been to destabilise Truman and make it impossible for him to sack Hoover, it must be adjudged a success, but the lack of scruple Hoover demonstrated takes one's breath away even today. Thus Whitaker Chambers had for three years previously sought to interest Hoover in the notion that the State Department functionary, Alger Hiss, was a Communist spy. Hoover reviewed the evidence, found it lacking in substance, and dismissed Chambers as a crackpot. As soon as Truman became President, Hoover hauled out the Chambers charges and, with Nixon's help, crucified the hapless Hiss. In the famous Medina trial of 1949, where the leaders of the American CP were all found guilty and sentenced to jail, effectively for being Communists, Judge Medina rounded off the proceedings by sentencing the defence lawyers to jail as well. Given that the latter had not been on trial in the first place, and that his precedent made it all but impossible for those later accused of leftism to find defence lawyers at all, this was no small breach in the rule of law – but Hoover publicly congratulated Judge Medina. The worst of all came with the trial of Julius Rosenberg for passing atom secrets to the Russians. Hoover encouraged the notion that Rosenberg had committed the 'crime of the century' by giving the Russians the A-bomb – when in fact he knew that it was Klaus Fuchs who had done this. When Rosenberg failed to provide the FBI with the information Hoover wanted, he persuaded the Attorney-General to indict Rosenberg's wife Ethel as well, though purely as 'a lever' to make Julius crack. Hoover, who had always placed motherhood on a pedestal, was shocked when the ploy failed and Ethel, the mother of two young children, was electrocuted along with her husband. Hoover reconciled himself to this by convincing himself that Ethel had been a bad mother.

Eisenhower, having seen Hoover stand up to Truman and win, was quite openly deferential to him. Henceforth FBI loyalty reports on Administration recruits would have the virtual force of law, and ex-FBI agents generally headed the security sections all government departments now set up. Together these measures meant that Hoover had complete veto power over all government appointments. Hoover, in return, got on famously with Ike. Both men tended to be anti-black and to see civil rights agitation as, at best, a nuisance. Hoover had had the NAACP under surveillance since 1941 and kept Ike supplied with a steady flow of reports stating that this or that NAACP initiative was 'in line with Communist plans'. For the FBI remained obsessed with the Communist 'menace', despite plentiful evidence that the American CP was a tiny, dying and impotent force. It was, fatefully, against the CP that Hoover first deployed a COINTELPRO (Counter Intelligence Program) in 1956. COINTELPRO was a new, aggressive technique of destroying organisations by 'dirty tricks' – the use of disruptive rumours, disinformation, framing loyalists as FBI informants, sexual blackmail, anonymous phone and letter campaigns' etc. It was a roaring success: in a year CP membership collapsed from 22,000 to under 4,000 (and many even of them were FBI informers). But COINTELPRO was also entirely illegal and represented a new police intrusion into American politics. From obsession with the 'Communist conspiracy' the FBI had itself become a conspiracy. In the years to come, COINTELPROs were launched against a whole series of domestic 'enemies' – the Socialist Workers Party, the KKK, Black Nationalists and the New Left.

Hoover was, by the 1960s, a man further and further out of touch with his times. Having destroyed the CP it was harder for him to persuade others that the top domestic priority should still be the struggle against what he called 'the Trojan snake of Communism'. His homilies no longer went down well with the young, whose long hair and liberal attitudes scandalised him. And the new Attorney-General, Bobby Kennedy, was – with Martin Luther King – one of the men Hoover hated most in all the world, especially since Bobby soon began pressing Hoover to integrate the lily-white ranks of the FBI. Hoover's spies also told him that Bobby was looking for a chance to ease him out. But, of course, Hoover had voluminous files on Bobby's brother Jack, going all the way back to tape-recordings of Jack in bed with Inga Arvad (Miss Denmark) in 1942. (Indeed it seems possible that Jack was hurriedly shipped off to war on PT-109 largely to avert a scandal, for Inga had visited Hitler and Goering in Nazi Germany and was then under suspicion of being a German spy. On the tapes Jack could be heard, *inter alia*, discussing military matters with her.) Hoover's files bulged with the evidence of many more recent Kennedy indiscretions, as well as the health problem Jack had so carefully concealed from the electorate. So Bobby never got round to firing Hoover and LBJ was delighted to have an FBI chief who shared his own passionate hatred of Bobby. Hoover and LBJ had, in any case, been close friends and neighbours for decades and LBJ was delighted with the vast stream of domestic political espionage Hoover sent him, so much so that he kept Hoover in office indefinitely after his statutory retirement age. In return, LBJ achieved one of his true miracles: levering the FBI into tracking down white extremists who murdered civil rights workers.

While Hoover was not averse to launching a COINTELPRO

against the Klan, he never ceased to see civil rights agitators as tools of Communism. His hatred of Martin Luther King was greatly strengthened by the tapes acquired by bugging which revealed King's rich and varied sex life and proved, to Hoover's satisfaction, that King was a hypocrite. When he heard that King had been awarded the Nobel Peace prize, he sent King a copy of the tapes with a long letter of denunciation ending with the words: 'There is but one way out for you. You better take it before your filthy fraudulent self is bared to the nation.' King – who ignored the threat – was never sure whether the object was to get his wife to divorce him, to get him to turn down the Nobel prize, or to get him to commit suicide.

Hoover had more success with the actress Jean Seberg. When he learned that Seberg was pregnant by a Black Panther, Hoover inspired cruel press stories about her 'black baby' which led Seberg to try to commit suicide, causing the baby to be born prematurely. It died almost immediately. Seberg never recovered from her baby's death and when, several years later, she learnt that she had been the object of a COINTELPRO, she committed suicide as also, not long after, did her ex-husband.

Nixon's accession to power was the final apotheosis, for no one doubted that by handing him the Alger Hiss case Hoover had given the crucial push to Nixon's career. At last Hoover had a President of his own making. But the hard-edged young men staffing the Nixon White House saw Hoover as a Neanderthal old bore and tension grew when Nixon, determined to stop leaks, ordered the FBI to carry out widespread bugging of Administration officials. Knowing the risks of such operations, Hoover dragged his feet. As Nixon's appetite for bugging, wiretaps, mail-opening and black-bag jobs increased, so did Hoover's nervousness: he thought word of such gross illegalities was bound to get out in the end and that the resulting explosion might badly damage the FBI.

Then in March 1971 the FBI's history changed for ever. A group of radical Catholics burgled the FBI's Pennsylvania office and stole a large number of files – which soon began to appear in print in New Left journals. The files revealed widespread FBI domestic surveillance, a network of campus informers and the penetration and secret surveillance of such inoffensive movements as the Jewish Defense League and the National Black Economic Development Conference. All this material covered just one State and it took no genius to realise that similar illegal FBI operations were bound to exist in the other forty-nine States. Worse still, one of the documents used the dread word COINTELPRO, and before long an

NBC journalist had used the Freedom of Information Act to start opening that can of worms. Hoover hurriedly wound up the still current COINTELPROs and tried hard to batten down the hatches, but the FBI's image had been irreversibly damaged. Nixon continued to press Hoover to carry out various black-bag jobs but Hoover, now badly burnt, refused to do anything without a signed Presidential order – and Nixon was far too shrewd to sign anything like that. Later, the White House came to feel that Hoover had 'caused' Watergate by his refusal to allow the FBI to do the President's dirty work, since this had 'forced' the White House to recruit its own special set of 'plumbers', who were not only amateur enough to get caught but could then be traced right back to the White House. Nixon was furious at being baulked and Hoover was probably closer to being fired than at any other point in his career when, on 1 May 1972, he died.

Hoover's overriding aim was always to preserve the FBI as an organisation under his exclusive personal control. Despite the fact that the Bureau was supposed to be subject to the Justice Department and, through it, to the President as chief executive, trainee agents were taught that 'the Director has learnt from the bitter experiences of the Roosevelt and Truman administrations when the Justice and State Departments were infiltrated with Communists that the Bureau must be free of the control of any Department or executive in the Government.' Recruits were left in no doubt that their real loyalty had to be to Hoover personally. They were told that 'if the Director does not receive adulatory letters from the agents he takes this as an indication of apathy towards the Bureau and a sign of disloyalty and lack of dedication'. Trainees were treated by Bureau lecturers to an idealised version of Hoover's life and told that

> the Director chose the path of sacrifice . . . he remains the guiding light of the FBI – in spite of liberal-leftist moves for his ouster. He still works longer hours than any of us, every day of the year . . . yes, boys, J. Edgar Hoover is an inspiration to us all. Indeed, it has been said, and truly – the sunshine of his presence lights our lives.'

Trainees were also instructed that 'they have more Communists in the Harvard Yard than you can shake a stick at'; that Adlai Stevenson supporters were 'Communists, Communist-sympathisers and pseudo-intellectual radicals'; that the NAACP was 'a Communist front group that has been instigating fictitious complaints against police officers in Civil Rights cases'; that the Director was keen to see 'Communist sympathisers' removed from the Supreme Court; and that he favoured the impeachment of Chief Justice Earl Warren. Trainees would also hear that the American Civil Liberties Union was a Communist front, that New Left activists had a liking for 'Jewish ass' and that the Justice Department was an enemy never to be trusted. Finally, at the end of their induction, new recruits would be given a short interview with Hoover. They were rigidly drilled in what to say and warned that to show signs of weakness – to fail to meet his eye, to have a quiver in their voice, wipe their mouth or pick their noses – would result in instant dismissal. Also,

> our Director enjoys standing on a little box when he greets people in his office. Of course, it's just a small one, only six inches high. Pretend you never even notice it! Not long ago we had a new agent who for some reason just couldn't keep his eyes off it. He was fired.

Loyalty was backed up by the fact that FBI pay was high (better than the CIA's), that its pension scheme was the best in government, and that Hoover kept agents on contracts which enabled him to fire them on the turn. Usually, the mere threat of transfer was enough to ensure total obedience. Thus in 1963 the head of the FBI's Domestic Intelligence Division, William Sullivan, wrote Hoover a long and careful memo arguing that Communist attempts to infiltrate and control the civil rights movement had been a complete failure. Hoover's anger was such that Sullivan found his whole Division in uproar. Its employees, hearing of the Director's displeasure, 'thought they would all be transferred out of Washington; selling their homes and uprooting their families would ruin them financially. They wanted another memo written to the director to "get us out of the trouble we were in"'. Sullivan quickly wrote a craven new memo explaining that 'the Director is correct. We were completely wrong', that the Communist danger in the civil rights movement was indeed very great, and that Martin Luther King was 'the most dangerous Negro of the future in this nation from the standpoint of communism'.

The truth is that Hoover was a lousy policeman. The daily stream of intelligence he sent to the White House was often useless because no attempt was made to sift and organise the material. He was heavily to blame for US unpreparedness at Pearl Harbour: for weeks beforehand he accumulated evidence of Japanese diplomats being shipped out of America *en masse* and the burning of vast numbers of documents in Japanese consulates, but he failed to warn FDR and specifically forecast that the Japanese would not attack at Pearl

Harbour. Similarly, the Kennedy assassination was another gross FBI failure and earned the Bureau the censure of the Warren Commission. But it was worse than that: Hoover was determined to keep the FBI small enough to allow him to maintain a completely personal control over it. So it became an article of faith with him that there was no such thing as organised crime, requiring a large-scale national police organisation. It was only in 1957 when a New York police sergeant stumbled on a meeting of sixty Mafia dons that Hoover was finally forced to admit that such a thing as the Mafia did exist, though the FBI kept the term Cosa Nostra out of the press until 1963. Similarly, Hoover always refused to have anything to do with combating drug trafficking on the grounds that the problem was so vast that, to fight it, the FBI would have to grow unmanageably larger. Instead of attending to these genuine threats to American society, Hoover concentrated his energies on chasing often imaginary Communists, on building his beloved Bureau into a Frankenstein's monster which broke the law as often as it upheld it, and, in the extreme case, on destabilising an Administration he did not like.

Nixon gave a rather different picture in his funeral oration.

> The good J. Edgar Hoover has done will not die. The profound principles of respect for law, order and justice will come to govern our national life more completely than ever before . . . . The American people today are tired of disorder, disruption, and disrespect for the law. America wants to come back to the law as a way of life, and as we do come back to the law, the memory of this great man . . . will be accorded even more honour than it commands today.

To be fair, Nixon cannot have believed a word of what he was saying. The Watergate burglary took place just a month later.

References

Powers, Richard G. P. (1987) *Secrecy and Power: The Life of J. Edgar Hoover* (London: Hutchinson).

Chapter 18
Rising Moon

The success enjoyed by the Moonies is in one sense a replication on the religious level of the challenge mounted on an economic level by the newly industrialised countries of East Asia. That is, Taiwan, South Korea and the rest have become rich by leap-frogging up the technology scale, mass-producing state-of-the-art technologies in demand in the West: Asian peasants have been recruited to make not just steel, shoes and textiles but transistor radios, TVs and computers. The equivalent model for the Moonies seems to have been the glitzy high-tech fundamentalism of Billy Graham and his successors, the televangelists. There is, after all, no doubt that the sects spawned by such men are the market leaders – in an increasingly secular world they have the keenest followings and the fastest growth rates. Religion, in their hands, is all about fund-raising, marketing, anti-Communism, over-the-top emotionalism and the personification of the sect in a single, charismatic preacher-leader.

Having honed their product up to scratch in the home market, the Moonies, like any other ambitious South Korean industry, have invaded the American market. And here they are outperforming the American competitors they modelled themselves on just as successfully as Samsung, Hyundai and Lucky GoldStar are outperforming theirs. In a world peopled solely by Protestant groups, their marketing edge is devastatingly simple: they have grafted on the one trait where Roman Catholicism is superior, the ability to get large numbers of people to work for you for no salary at all and to practise celibacy so that they do not develop competing emotional (and expenditure) loyalties. The result is a vast engine of credulity and devotion, of hysteria, deception and money: a formidable juggernaut indeed.

Jean-François Boyer's book on the Moonies (1986), is one of the most striking pieces of investigative writing that I have read for a long time. It tells the story of how Sun Myung Moon (his American name – real name, Young Myung Mun), from his origins as a North Korean peasant, has built a politico-religious empire with an annual revenue of over half a billion dollars (making it one of the world's fifty largest private corporations). The young Moon seems to have been an ordinary enough peasant child until, at least, the age of 14, when his father, shaken by a series of family disasters which saw several of his children fall mentally ill, had the family converted to Christianity. But this domestic crisis was overshadowed by the terrible national disaster of Japanese occupation and annexation. The context was ripe for messianism. The Buddhists, among whom Moon had grown up, hoped desperately for a new Buddha to lead them, Moses-like, out of their cruel new subjugation, while Korean Christians believed Armageddon was nigh and looked likewise for a Redeemer. Sure enough, Jesus appeared to the 16-year-old Moon and informed him that he was the chosen man, thus making him one of the hundred-plus Messiahs Korea had spawned in only a century.

According to Moon's official biography he then gained a degree as an electrical engineer at Waseda University in Japan (though the university has no record that he was ever a student). What is certain is that he had become a strong Korean nationalist. In 1944 he was arrested by the Japanese Police and imprisoned and tortured for anti-Japanese activities, but the outbreak of peace allowed him to return to Pyongyang, marry and, for the first time, proclaim himself the new Messiah. According to his official biography, it was his initial success in gathering followers that led jealous Christian rivals to denounce him to the new Communist authorities, leading to further imprisonment and torture in a 're-education' camp. Moon was certainly interned for a year but Korean Christian researchers claim to have established that actually he had contracted a bigamous marriage, asserting that God had authorised him to do so. History, once again, violently intervened: the Korean War broke out, the camp was overrun by the US Army, and Moon ended up a free man in Seoul, his aggrieved nationalism now directed against the Communists, whom he held responsible for the division of Korea. In May 1954 Moon finally founded his Unification Church.

Moon has always made extreme demands on his followers: they are enjoined to give up everything on becoming members of his flock, and have to work long hours for no pay – engaging in a plethora of activities to raise funds for the Church. They are celibate, eat little and take part in long monotonous hours of praying, chanting and singing. Inevitably, this quickly led to accusations that Moon was applying the same brainwashing techniques to which he had been subjected in his North Korean re-education camp. In 1955 the Syngman Rhee regime arrested several Moonie leaders (including Moon, as a draft-dodger), alleging 'the illegal detention of persons'. Somewhat mysteriously – for there was no doubt about the draft-dodging – Moon was released all smiles and uncharged. The case was a turning-point all the same: Moon seems to have concluded that he needed to make powerful friends and now began to direct his attentions towards the real power in South Korea, the military.

Moon's recruits among the young Turks of the South Korean Army were to play a decisive role. Most notable of all was a younger major, Bo Hi Pak, who has almost become Moon's co-equal in the movement. Pak, with several other young officers, was the intermediary between the Moonies and Kim Jong Pil, the architect of the 1961 *coup d'état* which replaced Syngman Rhee with President Park Chung Hee – and made Kim Jong Pil Prime Minister. Straight after the coup Kim Jong Pil, with the help of the CIA, set up the KCIA, which, from that day to this, has remained the real power centre of the Korean regime. One key Moonie sympathiser, Steve Kim, left the Army immediately to join the KCIA and became Kim Jong Pil's indispensable aide, acting as the intermediary between the KCIA and CIA. Another young Moonie officer, Aka Bud Han, also became an assistant to the premier/KCIA chief, acting, for example, as his interpreter with President Kennedy, before launching on a successful ambassadorial career. A third important KCIA Moonie was Sang Kil Han, who became military attaché at the Washington Embassy.

All these young officers were fluent Anglophones, and major links in the tight CIA-KCIA nexus. All four are today to be found at the very summit of the Moonie movement. Bo Hi Pak heads the movement's American press operation, News World Communication Inc., where he is seconded by Steve Kim. Bud Han helps run the Moonies' most important newspaper, the *Washington Times*, while Sang Kil Han is Moon's private secretary, supervises the education of his children, and helps organise the mass wedding ceremonies (where Moon marries up to six thousand couples at once) for which the Moonies are famous. (One of the biggest of these took place in 1982 in Madison Square Garden.) In effect, Moon's strategy was to attempt to make himself indispensable to the Seoul regime, the KCIA, the CIA and the American Right, apparently on the assumption that with patrons as powerful as these he would be safe from further harassment. Certainly, the fanatical anti-Communism of the Moonies ('some say Communism is soluble in Coca-Cola, but it is only soluble in napalm') dates from this dramatic move into the world of politics and the intelligence services.

Thereafter, the Moonies grew fast in both numbers and respectability. When Bo Hi Pak set up the Korean Cultural Foundation for Freedom (one of innumerable Moonie front organisations), he was able to get ex-Presidents Truman and Eisenhower to accept its honorary presidency. Naturally, this opened doors for the Moonie fronts throughout the US, and they were soon sending out fund-raising appeals signed by numerous respectable citizens and Hollywood stars. Back in Korea, the Moonies set up the Seoul Freedom Centre to host the Asian Peoples' Anti-Communist League (using money gathered from the American Right) and founded Radio Free Asia, whose programming was controlled by the KCIA's psychological warfare section. Soon it became hard to know where the Moonies began and where the South Korean Government ended. Thus Bo Hi Pak continued to travel on a diplomatic passport long after he had ceased to hold an official post; the Moonies were given free use of the state-owned radio transmitters and the franchise to sell official commemorative coins in the US; Moon himself was treated by the Seoul authorities as of equal status with a visiting head of state, and Korean leaders from the Prime Minister down were to be seen as guests of honour at mass Moonie ceremonies. Mickey Kim, a leading KCIA executive and former counsellor at the Washington Embassy 'worked simultaneously as one of President Park's bodyguards and director of the Moonies' own internal law-and-order force. The Moonie children's ballet group, the Little Angels (patron, Dwight D. Eisenhower), travelled the world as a quasi-diplomatic operation – dancing at the 1968 Mexico Olympics, for example, and at the celebrations to mark the fiftieth anniversary of Turkey's independence.

The money necessary to the Moonies' growing political and cultural activities was generated, not only from the unpaid labour of thousands of brainwashed militants, but from a spreading ring of Moonie enterprises. Symbolically enough, the first such operation was a gun factory, and soon the Moonie Tong Il group gained a key role in the Korean defence industry. In 1966 Tong Il obtained the official American franchise to make M16 assault rifles in Korea, though on the strict condition that the weapons not be exported. Moon's own cousin ran this enterprise and somehow by the mid 1970s these Moonie-made M16s were being exported all over the world. Tong Il was soon making car and truck components, M60 machine-guns, M79 grenade-launchers, the Vulcan anti-aircraft gun, and much else besides. (Boyer records the claim of the

British military attaché in Seoul in 1985 that he had a two-page list of Moonie companies working in the Korean defence industry.) But soon the Moonies had branched out into agricultural machinery, machine tools (by 1985 they had taken over two West German machine-tool manufacturers), the titanium industry, pharmaceuticals, fishing, the import-export business, printing, steel, agricultural products and banking. These interests are organised under a plethora of labels (including such typical Moonie appellations as One Up Inc., Uniworld and Happy World Inc.), and Boyer does a heroic job in trying to enumerate them – by 1985 there were 118 such companies in the US alone. There have been large and repeated tax scandals relating to many of these enterprises, for the Moonie leadership seems to feel that it is wrong that their operations should have to pay tax at all. In addition to the enormous volume of funds generated in this way, Moon is also able to rely on the formidable efforts of his Mobile Fund-Raising Teams. Moon long maintained that his mission was to rebuild the Kingdom of God in Korea: but the world opened up first by access to the money-bags of the American Far Right, and then by the growing weight of the Moonie commercial empire, led to a strategic resiting of this divine intention. In 1970 Moon formally transferred his base to the United States and henceforth the main fruits of his financial empire have been poured into Moonie activities there.

Moon immediately set out to win the hearts and minds of the Washington Establishment. Friendly links were rapidly established with the various components of the Moral Majority – especially the Mormons: when Moon was jailed for tax evasion his most energetic defenders were Senator Orrin Hatch (Utah) and Congressman George Hansen (Idaho), both Mormons. Jerry Falwell, the Moral Majority leader, joined in the Moonie chorus that Moon's imprisonment was a violation of religious liberty. Congressmen and Senators were bombarded with offers of free hospitality at the Washington Hilton. Moonies were soon to be found lobbying away and offering their services in the corridors of power: some of the Moonie 'sisters' even gained permanent jobs on Capitol Hill, notably Susan Bergman, who became an assistant to the House Speaker, Carl Albert. Before long various Moonie front organisations had won the willing patronage of numerous conservative Congressmen and Senators – including Robert Michel, the Republican Minority Leader, Barber Conable (now head of the World Bank) and Jesse Helms. The real high-point came, however, when President Nixon, warmed by the Moonies' unconditional support for him during Watergate, invited Moon to the White House, where the two men prayed together.

Nixon's fall was a grievous blow to Moon, who immediately set out on a campaign of extreme right-wing agitation to reverse what he saw as the decline into leftism inaugurated by Watergate. The Moonie newspaper, *Rising Tide*, played a key role in these years in rallying the disparate elements of the American Right into the great crusade which was to culminate in Reagan's election in 1980. *Rising Tide* was warmly greeted by Barry Goldwater and its columns featured articles by such luminaries of the conservative movement as Congressman Larry McDonald (head of the John Birch Society), Fred and Phyllis Schafly, Ray Cline (former Deputy-Director of the CIA), General Daniel Graham (now leader of the High Frontier – i.e. Star Wars – lobby) and Reed Irvine. Irvine brought a fresh raft of influential supporters into the Moonie milieu with his Accuracy in Media movement: among AIM's patrons were William Simon, the former Treasury Secretary, Joseph Coors, the beer magnate and Reagan confidant, Claire Booth Luce, Jimmy Goldsmith and Richard Mellon-Scaife. Moon now felt confident enough to take on the hated *New York Times* by launching the New York *News World* and, in 1982, to take similar aim at the *Washington Post* by launching the Moonie *Washington Times*. The *Washington Times* alone loses $50 million a year and is the final destination of a large chunk of Moonie funds.

At this point disaster struck, in the shape of the Congressional Sub-Committee on Korean-American Relations, chaired by the liberal Minnesota Congressman Donald Fraser. The Moonies have never fully recovered from the 'Koreagate' revelations that followed. Day after day the media regaled the public with the details of KCIA attempts to bribe Congressmen, intimidate Koreans living in the United States, and use the Moonies' cover for a wide range of interference in US political life. Two former KCIA directors were named as unindicted conspirators and the fall-out suddenly robbed Moon of much of the respectability he had so expensively achieved. The fact that the Moonies were able to help secure Fraser's speedy exit from elective office was small compensation for the fact that even in Seoul the Moonies were now becoming something of an embarrassment. Suddenly the Little Angels could no longer get visas and large tax bills were presented to Moonie companies. Within the United States, Moon's own tax problems grew, culminating in a jail sentence for tax evasion. Meanwhile a great clamour grew from anguished parents who accused the Moonies of 'stealing' their children, brainwashing them and turning them against their families. Several Moonies defected and told blood-curdling tales of the sect's inner life. Perhaps most important of all, the Moonies' cover was well and truly broken: the full list of front organisations (Causa, CARP, the KCFF, etc.) was exposed. Henceforth anyone who collaborated with the Moonies would have to do so knowingly.

But the machine held. The vast majority of Moonie activists remained fanatically loyal to 'The New Messiah'. Some parents mounted dramatic missions to recapture their children; more did not, or failed. The Seoul regime slapped Moon's wrist – but no more. Moon's commercial empire remained intact and continued to churn out huge profits. These in turn guaranteed that Moon was able to remain a valuable asset to those whom he had befriended. The result has been a remarkable come-back. The key was Reagan's election in 1980. Moon threw his immense resources into an all-out effort behind Reagan – who appeared on election night proudly brandishing the Moonie *News World* headlining his victory. Moon was invited as a VIP to Reagan's inauguration. At last he had what he wanted: no mere Nixon in the crippled death-throes of his Presidency, but a strong, new and grateful friend in the White House with eight years ahead of him.

The *Washington Times*, under Bo Hi Pak's guiding hand, rapidly became the focus of this new and unparalleled Moonie influence. William Simon, who had been one of Reagan's chief fund-raisers in 1980, Jim Watts, Reagan's Interior Secretary, and the Presidential counsellor, Claire Booth Luce, all agreed to accept honorific positions with the *Times*, which rapidly became the preferred house magazine of the Reagan Administration. The President himself has frequently counselled campaign audiences to read the Moonie paper and on being re-elected in 1984 accorded the first exclusive interview of his second term to it. Bo Hi Pak has been entertained in the White House by the President and in 1984 was awarded honorific 'Eagle' status by the Republican Party for his large donations to its cause. The paper itself took the hardest of hard-line positions on every issue: it is anti-*détente*, anti-arms control, pro-Contra, pro-South Africa. At the end of 1984 Reagan recruited one of the paper's chief editorialists, Pat Buchanan, to become his main speech-writer. Buchanan was responsible for such egregious Reagan dicta as the assertion that the SS men buried at Bitburg were as much victims of Nazism as the Jews. Soon Buchanan ranked second only to Don Regan among the White House staff: even Moon could hardly have dreamt that he would achieve so much so soon.

The announced ambition of Bo Hi Pak is to make the *Washington Times* one of the ten great newspapers of the world, with editions in every major language. This ambition suffered a setback when the paper's editor, James Whelan, parted on bitter terms, alleging that all power on the paper was still concentrated among a handful of ex-KCIA Moonies. His replacement as editor was Arnaud de Borchgrave, a journalist long known for his extreme right-wing views and his sympathetic relationship with several Western intelligence services. De Borchgrave (who claims to be sixteenth in line of descent to the Belgian throne) had been named by the *New York Times* as one of the group of Western journalists to have received large cash sums from the Shah of Iran, and had had to leave his job on *Newsweek* when it was discovered that he was keeping files on his fellow journalists. (Like his close associate, Robert Moss, a former Thatcher speech-writer, de Borchgrave is obsessed with the infiltration of the Western press by alleged Soviet moles and has personally briefed President Reagan on the subject.) As early as 1982 de Borchgrave and the French conservative journalist, Jean-François Revel, now an *Encounter* columnist, had been star invitees at Moonie media conferences. Even at the salary he demanded ($300,000 a year) de Borchgrave was a natural choice.

One of de Borchgrave's major coups was to launch the Nicaragua Freedom Fund in 1985 when Congress turned down funding for the Contras. Accusing Congress of treason to America, the *Washington Times* launched a large-scale private funding operation for the Contras, with dramatic ads signed by Jeane Kirkpatrick, Midge Decter, Michael Novak, Charlton Heston (who raised funds in Europe for the cause) and the usual right-wing backers. Bo Hi Pak led off the campaign – backed by Reagan 'with all my heart' – with a $100,000 contribution. Such gestures win the Moonies hearts and minds in Washington, as well as in the Central American jungles: few sights could better symbolise the extent to which Koreagate had been glossed over than that of Bo Hi Pak, Moon's faithful number two, dining at the table of honour with the White House Chief of Staff, Don Regan, or welcoming Ronald and Nancy Reagan as guests of honour at Moonie-sponsored pro-Contra receptions – at a time when Moon himself was still in jail for tax evasion. De Borchgrave, for his part, is a familiar of such key Reaganauts as Ed Meese and the former National Security Adviser, Robert McFarlane, while McFarlane's predecessor-but-one, Richard Allen – another star invitee at Moonie conferences – took a $100,000 fee to prospect the possibilities of an Asian edition of the *Washington Times*. Above all, de Borchgrave has privileged access to Reagan himself: he is, after all, the editor of the President's favourite newspaper. Thus, immediately prior to his first summit with Gorbachev, it was de Borchgrave whom Reagan sought out for his advice on how best to confront the Soviets. His advice: 'Don't give an inch on SDI.'

Moon's ambitions are not confined to America: 'If we can manipulate at least seven nations, we'll control the whole world.... In the camp of God, Korea, Japan, America, England, France, Germany and Italy are the nations on which I count in order to conquer the world.' In fact, the bulk of the sect's followers are in Korea, Japan and the United States, but it is active in Africa and Europe, and especially in Latin America. To list the Moonies' favoured contacts is to compile a sort of international *Who's Who* of the Right. Bo Hi Pak has links with the Paraguayan dictator, General Stroessner (whom he has pronounced 'a special man, elected by God to rule his country' – which is just as well, for no one else has had the chance of electing him). The Moonies have strong links with the Bolivian military, too – indeed, Boyer cites material to suggest that the Moonies collaborated there with Klaus Barbie to organise the 1980 *coup d'état*. In Chile, the links are with Pinochet, accorded the signal honour of being compared with Moon himself as a 'pillar of the struggle against international Communism'; in Argentina, with ultra-conservative Catholic bishops concerned to combat liberation theology and 'the Marxist Alfonsin' (the Moonies have bought up several Argentinian newspapers to further this cause); in Central America with a host of right-wing dictators, and the Contras. Boyer reports that Moonie insignia, T-shirts and even converts are now a familiar sight in Contra and Miskito refugee camps.

Boyer is naturally fascinated with Moonie activities in France and details at length the long list of contacts with extreme French conservatives – the names of Jean-François Revel and Olivier Giscard d'Estaing (the ex-President's brother) occur over and over again. But the Moonies' closest and most intriguing links are with Le Pen's Front National. Pierre Ceyrac, nephew of the former head of the French employers' organisation and one of the most prominent Moonies in France, was accorded a leading place on the FN list in the 1986 elections. But, according to Boyer, the most striking example of a Moonie in politics is Gustave Pordéa, the ex-Romanian diplomat who sits for the FN in the European Parliament. Boyer pours scorn on *The Sunday Times* allegations that Pordéa is a Romanian Communist agent and suggests that, in effect, *The Sunday Times* reporter was an innocent taken for a ride by dissident elements within the FN. Certainly, Boyer is able to produce lengthy chapter and verse for Pordéa's membership of the Moonies over a period of seven years. And there is no doubt that links between Le Pen and the Moonies go back a long way and that relations are close: in November 1986 Le Pen made a special trip to visit the Moonie leader in Japan.

Herman and Brodhead's *The Rise and Fall of the Bulgarian Connection* (1986) has more to do with this strange and luxuriant world of right-wing extremism than one might at first suspect. It is at once the best and most careful analysis of the 'Bulgarian plot to kill the Pope' yet to appear, and a quite stunning account of how this ludicrous fiction was dreamt up and then amplified throughout the world's press. As Herman and Brodhead show, independent evidence that the Pope's would-be assassin, Ali Agca, with his long career in the neo-Fascist Turkish Grey Wolves, had anything to do with the Bulgarians was virtually non-existent from the start. Ultimately, the case collapsed amidst a welter of embarrassment in the Italian court-room where Agca, sole witness for the Bulgarian Connection, repeatedly denied and contradicted his own evidence, and continually asserted that he was Jesus Christ. The immense media ramp mounted around the case collapsed virtually overnight and the story that had garnered so many acres of newsprint for three years simply vanished from view – to the sound of a good deal of red-faced throat-clearing on editorial desks around the world.

The story originated with three writers: Claire Sterling, Paul Henze and Michael Ledeen. None could exactly be termed reliable sources. Sterling has long been known for her somewhat wild rightwing views and her heavy reliance on anonymous 'intelligence sources'. Henze was a long-time CIA station chief in Turkey with a history of good connections with the Turkish Far Right, Ledeen, the 'Italy expert' in Reagan's 1980–81 transition team, has a history of association with both the Italian and US Far Right and was a close collaborator of Francesco Pazienza, the Italian secret service agent sentenced in 1985 for a variety of crimes including corruption, involvement with the Mafia, the P-2 Lodge scandal and the Ambrosiano Bank affair. None the less, the Sterling–Henze–Ledeen story was picked up and amplified first by such familiar names as Arnaud de Borchgrave and Robert Moss and then by a whole panoply of conservative columnists (William Safire, George Will, William Buckley, etc.), then by conservative 'experts' at Georgetown University and elsewhere. Ultimately this wild concatenation of non-facts was running regularly in *Time*, the *New York Times*, the *Washington Post*, *The Times* and almost everywhere else one turned. It was, quite simply, one of the largest and most successful disinformation campaigns ever mounted. The curious thing is that journalists like Moss, Sterling and de Borchgrave advertise themselves as experts on Soviet disinformation as purveyed by the Western press. Soviet disinformation does, of course, exist. It is to be found in large, indigestible chunks in Tass statements to the effect that South Africa killed Samora Machel, or that Jewish dissidents in the USSR are virtually all CIA agents. It is not hard to recognise. And it is very foolish indeed not to recognise that, for all sorts of obvious reasons, the Western press is a far, far more fruitful field for disinformation stemming from the Right than from the Left.

How much does all of this matter? Moon is fairly clearly mad, after all; the number of his followers is stagnant; and journalists like de Borchgrave seem unlikely ever to gain the full-hearted respect of their profession. If there is a villain of the piece it is surely those Western conservatives who seem so determined on a 'no enemies on the Right' policy that they are willing to provide access and lend legitimacy to all manner of freaks, charlatans and hot heads. This is not a matter of the Reagan Administration alone: Mrs Thatcher too has, notoriously, her 'poisonous acolytes', including not a few figures whose psychological balance is seriously in question. Nor is it just a matter of politicians. The records of Claire Sterling, Ledeen, Henze, Moss, de Borchgrave *et al.* are sufficiently known: what on earth are newspaper editors and proprietors thinking of to lend credence to them? Similarly, the record of Moon, Bo Hi Pak and the Moonies in general is familiar enough: what on earth was the Pope playing at when he accorded an audience to Bo Hi Pak and other Moonie leaders (even being photographed with them) in December 1985? Our new rulers seem to have in common a penchant for being stroked by counsellors more extreme than themselves. Perhaps it is pleasant to be thus put 'on side', to be made to feel moderate for a change? One worries more that there is a deep insecurity at the heart of the New Right, explaining at once its visceral character and its willingness to give house room to those who would have been simply shunted aside by a Macmillan, a Taft, a de Gaulle or a Churchill. Why else should regimes that boast, above all, of being liberal (in a free-market sense) choose such illiberal associates? Why else should those who boast of a new democratic majority for the Right countenance such profoundly undemocratic friends?

References

Boyer, Jean-François (1986) *L'Empire Moon* (Paris: La Découverte).
Herman, Edward and Brodhead, Frank (1986) *The Rise and Fall of the Bulgarian Connection* (New York: Sheridan Square).

Chapter 19

Living with Terrorism

Most people – and most governments – try to dispose of the subject of terrorism with a simple, sweeping dismissal. But it is not that easy. Most of us have, at one time or another, sympathised with movements – the Resistance movements in Occupied Europe, for example – which have used terroristic means. Similarly, many people will tell you that terrorism is a modern phenomenon when what they really mean is that the placing of bombs on jet airliners has only happened in the last twenty years. Well, of course. But the giving and taking of hostages used to be a normal part of warfare, as did the large-scale massacre of innocents simply to prove how much one was to be feared. Indeed, it may be that one reason why terrorism so shocks us is that it is a primitive survival, not a modern phenomenon. What is not new but newer is that these primitive means are now almost exclusively deployed in the name of some abstract cause, rather than being an unideological part of the normal tactics of kings or tribal leaders. This typically involves a form of moral arrogance whereby the practitioners of terrorism claim that they are the privileged guardians of the sacred flame and therefore exempt from normal rules of conduct. Sometimes, as with Andreas Baader, that arrogance will be part of a purely personal pathology; at other times, more difficult to judge, a whole social pathology is involved.

In the first few pages of Walter Laqueur's *The Age of Terrorism* (1987) (largely a reworking and updating of his 1977 work, *Terrorism*), the author attempts to confront the old adage that 'one man's terrorist is another man's freedom fighter.' Laqueur will have none of it:

> Of all the observations on terrorism this is surely one of the tritest. There is no unanimity on any subject under the sun, and it is perfectly

true that terrorists have well-wishers. But such support does not tell us anything about the justice of their cause; in 1941 Hitler and Mussolini had many fanatical followers. Does it follow that they fought for a just cause?

A moment's reflection suggests that this is a most unsatisfactory dismissal: as anyone with even high-school debating experience knows, the sudden, irrelevant jump within a few sentences from 'freedom-fighters' to 'Hitler and Mussolini' is simply an attempt to foreclose an argument before it gets started. After all, even the supporters of the Axis leaders did not regard them as 'freedom fighters', and few regimes have been louder in their condemnation of terrorism – that is, the Resistance movements – than the Nazis and other Fascists. The fact is that neither Hitler nor Mussolini belongs in the argument at all.

There are two points about this. One is that Laqueur's work, for all its thoroughness and the largely justified praise that has been heaped on it, is undeniably biased. He suggests, for example, that the USSR is somehow responsible for Abu Nidal, Carlos, the Red Brigades and the Red Army Faction – although evidence for such a proposition is lacking, even in his own work. The ANC is several times mentioned as a terrorist organisation, but there is no mention of the numerous terrorist incidents and assassinations to which ANC exiles have been subjected over the years. The murder of several members of the South Korean Government in Burma in 1983 is flatly attributed to North Korea, but there is, as far as I know, no evidence for this. Of the attempted assassination of Pope John Paul II Laqueur can only comment that 'the extent of Bulgarian involvement cannot be proven in a court of law', as if only an excess of legal fastidiousness – rather than a complete lack of evidence – stands in the way of our believing this story. Similarly, Laqueur has far more to say about left-wing terrorists in the United States than about the historically far more important right-wing variety; we hear about the Vietcong as terrorists but nothing about the parallel US programmes for the assassination of 'hostiles' in the Vietnamese countryside; we are told that the Cubans now sponsor terrorism but not that the CIA repeatedly attempted to assassinate Castro. All of which is a pity, for terrorism is a murky subject, on which it is difficult to get an adequate moral or intellectual purchase. If, in addition to that, one begins to distrust what an author writes about it, the murkiness can become impenetrable. This is regrettable, for Laqueur writes well and intelligently and knows a good deal about his subject.

The second, more important point is that we *do* all carry around with us some version of the freedom fighter/terrorism dichotomy: that is precisely why it is difficult to get a proper moral purchase on the subject; why so many morally sensitive people have been thrown into varying states of confusion about whether they should support the FLN/NLF/Tupamaros/Afghan guerrillas/Unita/ANC/PLO, etc.; and it is the very difficulty of that dichotomy that terrorists trade on, not only in their attempt to enlist external support but in the way they rationalise their own activity to themselves.

The reason for this dichotomy is also quite simple: historically, we can see movements which undeniably used terrorist means; which seemed to have little option but to do so; which succeeded in the end; and the reversal of whose success now seems unimaginable and, perhaps, undesirable. With only minor variations such a case could be made for Irgun, the Stern Gang, the Vietnamese NLF, the Patriotic Front in Zimbabwe, the FLN in Algeria, and so on.

Let us take the last two cases. It was, surely, both historically inevitable and morally just in some fundamental sense that Algeria should be ruled by the Algerians and that Rhodesia should be ruled by its black majority. To imagine, let alone to wish, to return to the *status quo ante* requires a moral as well as a historical Canute-ism. But neither in Rhodesia nor in Algeria was there the slightest sign that the minority white regimes would give way to anything less than overwhelming violence: indeed, all means short of that were tried – and failed. But neither the FLN nor ZANLA could hope to take on the conventional military force of their opponents on anything like equal terms. And while they began by attacking arguably strategic targets such as civilian policemen, it was not long before they were placing bombs in supermarkets, massacring the families of outlying farmers, shooting down civilian planes, mowing down crowds of shoppers or holiday-makers. In addition, they had no scruples about turning their guns on their own side when 'necessary'. Again, they may have begun with rough-and-ready courts martial of informers and traitors, but fairly soon it was a matter of large-scale murder and intimidation to ensure that peasant communities gave them the supportive welcome that all the textbooks on guerrilla warfare suggested they ought to. (Since the opponents' army will be deploying a similar terror to persuade the peasants not to give the guerrillas this kind of support, a cycle of terror and counter-terror may be inevitable.) These struggles, of course, have no shortage of sympathisers willing to accept, even to project, a more heroic, romantic and hagiographical picture: but the fact is that what took place both in Algeria and in Zimbabwe were successful terrorist revolutions – or, if one prefers, successful national revolutions carried through by terrorist means.

Typically, while such struggles are in full gory flood, a revulsion against all such means is the dominant reaction among 'men of good will'. But it takes only a few years for this to be forgotten; the means that were used to bring about the change are quickly ratified by success and by history and nobody has any qualms about embracing erstwhile terrorist leaders as valuable political partners. The present British Government may condemn ANC terrorism now, but if such means bring the ANC to power in South Africa who can doubt that its leaders will speedily be greeted as honoured guests in Downing Street and Buckingham Palace? And would it not be ludicrous to act otherwise?

What this seems to imply is that we do, in effect, recognise terrorism as a legitimate political tactic on certain conditions: first, that our recognition should not be contemporary and explicit, but retrospective and implicit; second, that the movement which uses terrorist means lacked any real alternative; and third – and most important – that the movement has succeeded. Stripping this of simple hypocrisy, what one is left with is that we are willing to accept terrorism as legitimate provided it is harnessed to realisable political ends. Our lasting condemnation is thus reserved for those movements whose terrorism is futile because their political ends are impossible of achievement: nobody loves a loser. Many will feel unhappy at the thought of a merely conditional condemnation of terrorism – especially since what is realisable or not is inevitably a somewhat subjective judgement and there are bound to be border-line cases – but the above would seem to be the logic of what we believe.

Most of us can see why the FLN or Irgun took the road they did – and probably cannot find it in ourselves to wish that the French had continued to rule Algeria or the British Palestine. The true puzzle lies with those numerous terrorist groups whose ends are not remotely realisable. Stefan Aust (1987) has provided a remarkable picture of one such, the Baader-Meinhof – he does not explain why he calls his account an 'inside story', though clearly he was close to many of the principal actors – but at the end the puzzle remains.

Andreas Baader, the undisputed leader of the group, was, from his earliest years, a self-willed, highly talented nonconformist. Insolent, humorous and rebellious, he seems never to have obeyed any rules and had to change schools repeatedly. His last headmaster spoke of him as 'a particularly gifted young man', but noted that he got into so many fights that 'a second Baader would be more than my school could stand'. While at school he conceived a lasting passion for motorbikes, and thereafter his record was liberally sprinkled with every possible offence connected with them – driving without a licence, speeding, endless thefts of bikes. The decision to call the gang the Red Army Faction was a typical Baader joke: a deliberate reference to the RAF whose bombs had hit German cities so hard a generation before.

Ulrike Meinhof was an altogether more attractive personality, an intelligent girl with a passionate Christian commitment and once one of the white hopes of the SPD. A talented journalist with what seemed to be a fulfilling life in front of her, her motives for joining the RAF by springing Baader from jail in 1970 remain obscure. It is unclear why her name was given equal prominence with Baader's, for the real number two was always the ferocious Gudrun Ensslin, the daughter of a Protestant pastor, who brought to the group a zeal and cruelty of almost witch-like intensity. What Meinhof and Ensslin did have in common, both with one another and with most of the several score young people who drifted in and around the group in the 1970s, was an involvement in the world of the SDS, the anti-Vietnam War movement, of anti-nuclear protest and of Third World good causes. The watershed was the great demonstration against the Shah's visit to Berlin in June 1967. The Berlin Police, assisted by an irregular corps of pro-Shah Iranians organised by Savak, ran amok, brutally beating up hundreds of demonstrators and shooting one of them dead. (The Shah was unbothered, telling the Mayor of Berlin that he must not think too much about it – 'these things happen every day in Iran.') Gudrun Ensslin's verdict on these events was both typical of what many young radicals felt and a manifesto for what was to come:

> This fascist state means to kill us all. We must organise resistance. Violence is the only way to answer violence. This is the Auschwitz generation and there's no arguing with them.

Andreas Baader had, till then, shown no interest in politics. He had gravitated into the lively bohemian society of West Berlin (where his acquaintance included the young Werner Fassbinder). He was quickly sacked from the newspaper he worked on after he had, while drunk, kicked the senior editor in the face and swung Tarzan-fashion from the office chandeliers. He moved in with a painter couple – the two men shared the woman and Baader fathered at least one of the children – and amused himself by dressing up in drag, replete with false eyelashes and perfume, in order to hang around gay bars and make fun of gays who tried to pick him up. He was deeply enthused by every form of sexual excess and deviation, sado-masochism, Black Masses and whatever other sorts of mystic nonsense were on offer. Most of his time was spent boozing and brawling. Typically, he had missed the anti-Shah demo because he was doing time for yet further motorbike theft and driving offences, but he was immediately attracted to the vengeful mood of the battered demonstrators and by dint of making the most 'revolutionary' suggestions soon became their leader. When they thought of flying a protest banner from the tower of the Berlin Memorial Church, Baader suggested blowing the church up. He was, in effect, an anarchistic young thug who slipped into extreme political action because it was violent, exciting, and best expressed his mood of anti-bourgeois revolt. Ironically, it was the fact that he had never shared the strong humanitarian feelings which originally motivated Ensslin, Meinhof and the others which freed him from the constraints they felt and made him their natural leader.

The group's career began with an amateurish attempt at arson in a department store by Baader and Gudrun Ensslin (the bombs came from an undercover agent in West German Counter-Intelligence, a prodigious supplier of Molotov cocktails to student revolutionaires). After fourteen months in jail the two skipped bail and went underground, staying in Régis Debray's flat in Paris while Debray was detained at the pleasure of the Bolivian authorities. After a good deal of stealing and smashing up of cars in Italy and Austria, Baader ended up in jail again before being sprung by Ulrike Meinhof (one policeman was shot in the process). The group then set off for training in Jordan, dispensed by the Al Fatah leader, Abu Hassan.

The period in the Al Fatah camp was pure black comedy. Baader's request that his group be trained for bank robberies was easily met, but real trouble arose over their insistence that men and women should be allowed to sleep together. Baader won this round, but the tendency of the women members of the group to sunbathe naked in full view of the young fedayeen guerrillas training nearby, none of whom had seen a naked woman in his life, created a showdown he could not win despite heated attempts to prove to the Palestinians that 'the anti-imperialist struggle and sexual emancipation go hand in hand' or, as Baader put it, that 'fucking and shooting are the same thing'. Baader demanded equal status with Abu Hassan, as one partisan leader to another, and when he did not get this, led his group on strike. But Abu Hassan was more than a match for him and the group's training was summarily called off. The Germans had become a severe embarrassment to Al Fatah, which shipped them back to Germany as fast as it could. This probably saved their lives, for the camp was wiped out almost to the last man by the Israelis only a few weeks later. Abu Hassan himself survived to organise the Black September atrocity at the 1972 Munich Olympics, and for the next seven years, until Mossad finally blew him up with a car-bomb in 1979, was probably the most wanted terrorist in the world.

Back in Germany, the group remained decidedly ineffectual for a good while as they learnt on the job. After a time, however, their expertise was signalled by a series of successful bank robberies which had the effect of making them the nation's most wanted criminals. Their avowedly political stance against 'the West German fascist state' gave them a certain romantic appeal and they began to attract sympathisers among the remnants of the radical student movement and actual adherents among a radical psychology group, the Socialist Patients Collective. (Their slogan, 'Madmen to Arms!', had the merit of literal truth.) The Police became increasingly jumpy and began to arrest all manner of false suspects, though they did manage to shoot dead one of the gang, Petra Schelm. This tragedy, together with the group's early Robin Hood image, gave them a certain counter-culture chic. Their penchant for stealing BMWs led to the car being dubbed the Baader–Meinhof–Waggon and a poll in mid 1971 found one in ten North Germans saying they would be willing to shelter wanted underground fighters overnight, while one in four of all West Germans under thirty professed 'a certain sympathy' with the gang. Some of those who joined became disgruntled when they found that the group's increasing professionalism meant that the reality was now less romantic than the image. One recruit, Klaus Jünschke, complained that 'you join the urban guerrillas and then you find yourself spending a month fixing up an apartment, and there's always shopping to be done, things that are needed. That's 99 per cent of what goes on.' But a network of secure (and often ingeniously disguised) apartments was the key to the group's ability to stay on the loose, and the hysteria of the German public mounted as the group began to kill the odd policeman and still evade capture.

Inevitably, the group's activities began to call into existence many of the things they claimed to be fighting against. The Police became more willing to cut corners – to shoot first and ask questions afterwards, for example. During one hostage crisis Franz-Josef Strauss argued that the best counter would be to respond by shooting captured terrorists one by one. Most striking of all was the way the traditional boundaries between the various Federal Police Forces were broken down, welding the Criminal Investigation Office

(BKA) into a vast computerised machine with the almost exclusive aim of hunting the group down. The remarkable Horst Herold, head of the BKA, devoted his entire energies to studying the group, developed a love-hate relationship with it, wrote papers on it which became required reading inside the group, and, above all, worked endless hours building an electronic storehouse of Orwellian proportions. The BKA's staff was doubled to 3,536, its budget quintupled, and it assembled computer files on 4.7 million people and 3,100 organisations. Its fingerprint section had 2.1 million people on file.

After a series of particularly bloody raids on US bases in Germany, the group were finally rounded up in 1972. There followed a long and ludicrous trial in which Baader and Ensslin defiantly foul-mouthed the judges, lawyers and everyone else in sight. Placed in jail under maximum security conditions, the group managed to smuggle in all manner of devices, to set up an intercom system linking their cells, and finally to acquire a number of firearms with which they committed collective suicide in 1977. There were still enough misguided sympathisers for demonstrations to take place against the 'murder' of Baader, Meinhof, Ensslin and the rest.

Once the group's members were caught up in the maelstrom created by their own activities, there was no looking back. Politically, they were from start to finish ridiculous. The notion that they could seriously undermine the West German state was as far-fetched as their analysis of it as Fascist. One is used to a certain sort of Far Left rhetoric which angrily proclaims that 'nothing could be worse' than this or that blandly democratic leader, party or government, but their sort of intellectual crudity is seldom accompanied by a willingness to kill and be killed in its name.

When one looks at the childhood of several of the group's leaders, one is struck by certain similarities. Baader's father had been an anti-Nazi whose wife dissuaded him from joining the Resistance. He disappeared on the Eastern Front in 1945 and the young Andreas was brought up exclusively by women – his mother, aunt and grandmother, who all spoilt him totally. Many of his antics in prison – refusing to wash, for example – were things he had first got away with in the nursery. Ulrike Meinhof also came from an anti-Nazi family and her father died when she was six. She, too, was then brought up by three women, to one of whom she was fiercely and lastingly attached. The young Ulrike seems to have compensated for this exclusively feminine environment by the adoption of a deliberate mannishness: she spoke out against unpopular teachers with unexampled boldness, was often the only woman in gatherings dominated by men, smoked a pipe, and so on. Gudrun Ensslin came from another anti-Nazi family, immersed herself in the all-feminine environment of the Protestant Girls' Club, went to a single-sex girl's school and, as one of seven children, had an inevitably limited relationship with her father even before she quarrelled fiercely with him over her choice of boyfriend. Jan-Carl Raspe, who committed suicide along with the rest in 1977, lost his father before he was born and was brought up by a mother, two sisters and two aunts. The Baader–Meinhof group itself was, of course, a fairly feminine affair – at one time or another a good half of its members were women. One can see what a psychiatrist might make of this, but it is not enough. Many Germans were anti-Nazi and, given the huge losses of German men in the war, many were brought up in all-female environments: very few became terrorists.

Perhaps the most puzzling thing about many of the group's leaders was the way they abandoned their children to take part in the 'struggle'. Only Ulrike Meinhof seems to have been seriously concerned about this and at one point kidnapped her children and deposited them with some Italian comrades. (Stefan Aust, the author of this book, then teamed up with a wanted terrorist, Peter Homann, to snatch them back and hand them over to their father.) In general, the longing to see one's children was condemned as so much bourgeois nonsense: when one woman, Edelgard G., decided she had to quit the group to go back to her child, she had a bucket of tar poured over her head and was denounced as an informer. In prison at the end, Ulrike Meinhof rediscovered her wish to see her daughters and had a considerable correspondence with them as well as several visits from them – before suddenly deciding that she did not want to see them any more.

One has the feeling reading this book that Ulrike Meinhof was the truly tragic figure of the group, that she might have led a useful, decent, possibly even happy life had she not fallen under the bullying spell of Baader and Ensslin. Early on, before Ulrike Meinhof joined the group, she put up Baader and Ensslin in her flat. Her little girls felt that Baader did not like children – when they fell over and hurt themselves he would not pick them up, but merely laughed at their tears. In one of their books there was a man so unscrupulous and cowardly that the Red Indians in sheer contempt decide not to execute him but simply throw him in the river: this, the little girls decided, was a picture of Andreas Baader.

References
Aust, Stefan, trans. Anthea Bell (1987) *The Baader-Meinhof Group: The Inside Story of a Phenomenon* (London: Bodley Head).
Laqueur, Walter (1987) *The Age of Terrorism* (London: Weidenfeld).

Chapter 20
Collaborators and the Purge

One of the dangers of writing for newspapers and magazines is that you do not choose your own titles and headlines. For the piece below my editors chose the headline 'Why Barbie may never be tried', which was not what I would have chosen. In fact Barbie was tried, partly, perhaps, because of mounting speculation that the Government was dragging its feet: Mitterrand, when informed by the Ministry of Justice that the lawyers wanted several more years to prepare the case, allegedly told them that this would never do. Just as the original intention seems to have been to stage a show trial to the Left's advantage just before the 1986 elections, so the actual trial was staged well in time for the 1988 elections. It was a damp squib. No embarrassing secrets emerged. In fact nothing much of anything emerged. After only a brief appearance in the dock, Barbie refused to acknowledge the court's jurisdiction or appear before it again. Arguably, too much attention is focused on the ageing figures of Nazi war criminals, who still surface at the occasional trial like doddering monsters from the deep. More interesting, surely, is the way such groups as judges, bishops and other key members of the Establishment behaved, and how differentially society dealt with those who had offended the national amour propre.

Modern states very seldom acknowledge their own crimes. In 1944, however, France had to assume responsibility for the fact – unlike Germany or Italy, there was no army of occupation to do it for her – that in almost every field her élites had been compromised. The resulting purge was not only a comprehensive attempt to found a new moral order: it had undeniable echoes of the Revolutionary Terror. Indeed, prosecutors and ministers alike frequently compared themselves to Danton and Robespierre, often with a note of genuine admiration for the latter. Robespierre, they said, had always had the guts to take public responsibility for his actions: Liberation justice, too, should have no truck with anonymity. Teitgen, the Christian Democrat Minister of Justice, for instance, boasted that he had purged more people than the sea-green incorruptible himself.

The analogy with the Terror was, of course, seized on by critics of the purge. 'The criminal courtroom', one critic wrote, 'was filled to bursting. People were smoking, eating, shouting, exchanging comments in the pure tradition of the French Revolution . . . .. The spectators were agitated; the tumult never died down.' This way of talking, together with allegations of sweeping acts of private vengeance amounting to a virtual massacre, created the powerful right-wing myth, still sedulously propagated by the Hersant press, that the purge was really a Communist-led attack on the privileged classes. According to *Le Monde*, the news of Mitterrand's victory in 1981 was greeted with horror by at least one woman in Giscard's campaign headquarters: the Left's victory, she said, would inaugurate a new purge, recalling 'the terrible years of the Liberation'. Examples like this are not without their own historical irony. Hersant himself was made to suffer for his early career on an anti-Semitic paper under Vichy; while just before the 1981 Election Giscard's Budget Minister, Maurice Papon, had had to resign when *Le Canard Enchaîné* reprinted Vichy edicts in which, *inter alia*, Papon described certain buildings as subject to 'Jewish infestation'.

Criticism of the purge is easy. 'Treason', as Talleyrand remarked, 'is a matter of dates.' And the sight of so many *résistants de la dernière heure* naturally encouraged cynicism. 'Wasn't the secret of the purge', Roger Peyrefitte wrote, 'that there had to be victims so that there could be heroes?' In a sense, it is difficult to take the opposite view: advocates of the purge were in much the same position as pro-abortion lobbyists today. No matter how just the cause, the hounding of terrified victims, like the termination of a foetus, is an irretrievably sad and ugly business: no one can feel any enthusiasm for it. It is much to Herbert Lottman's credit that he weighs the evidence judiciously and avoids the easy emotional let-outs his subject affords (Lottmam, 1986). He is also likely to be right in his overall judgement that the purge was remarkably light and that all too many of the guilty got away.

Judges led the most charmed life of all, but the Catholic hierarchy – which had included many of Vichy's keenest supporters – was not far behind. Even the Foreign Minister Georges Bidault, a leading Catholic layman, was moved to write indignantly of 'the silence of the bishops of France' as Vichy and the occupation authorities went about their business. Pius XII, as Bidault learned to his horror, was calmly assuming that Valeri, the Papal Nuncio and former Dean of the Vichy Diplomatic Corps, would remain in place under the new regime: he would merely be extending the ritual New Year greetings to de Gaulle rather than Pétain. Valeri was blackballed and had to be replaced by an angry Vatican with Mgr Roncalli (later John XXIII). In return Pius XII insisted that the French Catholic hierarchy remain unchallenged. This was clearly impossible: opinion polls showed that a better than eight-to-one majority wanted the collaborationist bishops punished. (Some of them had already had to flee their dioceses at the Liberation; and Cardinal Suhard of Paris, who had received Pétain at the gates of Notre Dame in April 1944, was warned by the Gaullists that his presence at the thanksgiving mass at Notre Dame in August 1944 would be not only inopportune but dangerous.) De Gaulle took personal charge of the Church purge and seven bishops were quietly removed. But Roncalli bargained hard. De Gaulle told him, for example, that the presence of Archbishop Feltin in Bordeaux was 'not desirable' and that he should on no account be made a cardinal. Roncalli compromised: he kept Feltin in place, but promised that he would never receive his cardinal's hat. In the event Feltin was promoted to the Archbishopric of Paris in 1949 and became a cardinal in 1953. As for the seven ousted bishops, no public reference was ever made to their forced retirement.

The case of that other pillar of the French Establishment, the Académie Française, was equally scandalous. The Academy had long been a notoriously reactionary body: in the 1930s it had elected Maurras a member just after his release from prison for having called for the murder of members of the Popular Front legislature. Under Vichy it came into its own, joyfully electing Pétain and other members of the Vichy Government to the ranks of the 'Immortals'. Despite direct pressure from de Gaulle himself, the Academy refused outright to expel Pétain and Maurras, and when a decree was issued banning them from all public functions and official bodies their seats were left vacant as a mark of respect. The most that could be wrung from the Academy was a grudging discretion. Ten years was deemed a decent enough interval in the case of Paul Morand, for example, whose 'role during the last war' led to the defeat of his candidacy in 1958: in 1968 he was duly elected to the Academy. The Academy's refusal of all attempts at reform and renewal had not done it much good: today it is seen by most people as the epitome of reactionary mediocrity.

Many of those 'collabos' who were punished were given remarkably light sentences. Xavier Vallat, the notorious Vichy Commissioner for Jewish Affairs (who at his trial objected that one of the judges was a 'son of Isaac') received only a ten-year sentence, and served far less than that. René Bonnefoy, sentenced to death *in absentia* in 1946 for crimes under the Occupation, emerged from hiding in 1955 and got off scot-free. This was all too frequently the pattern: the Vichy high-ups, quicker than their minions to grasp the likelihood of an Allied victory, fled abroad leaving the small fry to face the purge. In 1953 a general amnesty was declared and they returned to France. Franco's Spain was, of course, a favoured refuge, and a number of those found guilty of torture and anti-Jewish atrocities lived out their days there in peace and tranquillity. But successive amnesties gradually made even exile unnecessary. Lottman cites the case of the last three collaborators to serve in French prisons. All three (whom the law, incredibly, prevents him from naming) were at one time or another sentenced to death for large-scale murder and torture: their sentences were commuted and by 1983 all had been released.

The brunt of the purge fell on those whose collaboration had been most visible. The political parties did their own purging – none more thoroughly than the Socialists, who found it necessary to exclude from their ranks as many as half of the Socialist Deputies who won seats in the Popular Front election of 1936, as well as twelve of the seventeen Socialist cabinet ministers still alive at the Liberation. The purge also cut deep among the press: nine hundred newspapers and periodicals were banned and 115 press companies confiscated. Journalist collabos were weeded out to a man, in a purge more thorough than that suffered by any other profession – they had, after all, provided indisputable evidence of their sympathies by signing their articles. Among book publishers the purge was far less sweeping – most had carefully played both sides of the street. The most striking case was that of Gallimard, who had published the pro-Nazi *Nouvelle Revue Française* and accepted the Occupation ban on Jewish authors. Claude Gallimard's trial produced predictable fireworks from such Gallimard authors as Sartre, Camus and Malraux, the heart of the intellectual Resistance, as they saw themselves, who argued that they would be tainted with dishonour if their publisher were punished. Had Sartre not put on 'Resistance' plays under the Occupation? (Critics could not resist pointing out that the 'message' of Sartre's plays was so routinely obscure that it had not been difficult to do this while wholly escaping the attention of the Vichy authorities.) Even the Communist poet Eluard rallied to his publisher's support and Gallimard was exonerated. The case of Grasset was more difficult, given that Bernard Grasset himself had written a book in praise of 'the creative power of the Führer'. Grasset was found guilty and the judge ordered that his publishing house be confiscated: but there was an outcry at the closure of the house which had published Proust, Malraux and Mauriac. The confiscation order was replaced by a fine and then by a pardon. Grasset remains a major imprint.

In the entertainment world hostility fastened on actors and singers who had worked for Radio Paris or for Continental Films, both Nazi propaganda organs, as well as on those who had toured Nazi Germany. This brought a number of household names to trial – Sacha Guitry, Maurice Chevalier, Fernandel and Edith Piaf. It turned out – surprise, surprise – that the show-business community stood solidly behind its stars: all of whom, it emerged, had only toured Germany to give comfort to French prisoners of war. Chevalier, who had been granted special privileges under the Occupation, had a particularly difficult time: indeed, there were reports just after the Liberation that he had been stoned to death by angry Parisians. Chevalier said that the Germans had done him 'a bad turn': 'they announced that I sang and acted for them . . . .. But all that is false.' Luckily for him – and embarrassingly for the authorities – he was already much in demand as a performer with the British and American troops. Fernandel and Chevalier were exonerated; Guitry was indicted for collusion with the enemy – *L'Humanité* spoke of him 'banqueting with the torturers' – but the prosecutor 'lost' his file. Guitry thus escaped. On a tour of Lyon in 1948 he and his troupe were met by a contingent of local Résistants who forced them out of their car and marched them to the Resistance memorial, where they were made to observe a minute's silence.

Only Piaf emerged with real credit. It turned out that she had posed for photographs with French prisoners in Germany so that they could have fake identify papers rigged up for them by the Resistance when she got back to France. On subsequent trips she would then smuggle the papers back to them in a false-bottomed suitcase. She had thus, at great risk to herself, furnished 147 prisoners with bogus papers. She was also able to prove that she had secretly distributed her earnings to Jewish friends and had hidden Jews in her apartment. Piaf was not only pardoned but congratulated. She became something of a folk-heroine, and when she died she was buried in Père-Lachaise among the heroes of the French Left.

The most heavily used sanction – especially in the case of artists and intellectuals – was that of *indignité nationale*. This was, in effect, a simple reversing of the traditional French notion of *citoyenneté*: a collabo was judged to have excluded himself from the community of French citizens. He was not allowed to hold a position in the professions or in public life, to stand for elective office or even be a company director: in the public world of the citizen he was henceforth a non-person. A large number of such sentences were handed out, only to be revoked a few years later, just as thousands of civil servants were dismissed without pension only to have their pensions restored in 1953.

Critics of the purge were later to claim – as they still do today – that 105,000 people were murdered in private acts of Resistance vengeance, and that one way or another up to a million people were affected by the purge. These figures are nonsense. De Gaulle's own office, after a careful accounting in 1959, gave a figure of 10,842 summary executions, of which two-thirds had occurred in the weeks leading up to the Liberation. The figure of a 'million' allegedly affected by the purge is equally fictitious: cases were only brought against a hundred and twenty-five thousand people. Of these, forty-five thousand never went to a trial and a further twenty-eight thousand were acquitted. This left some fifty-one thousand guilty – almost exactly the number the Vichy Minister, Marcel Déat, had had in mind in 1943 when he complained bitterly that there were only fifty thousand true collaborators in France. Of the 6,763 death sentences handed down, only 767 were actually carried out. On a per caput basis, four times as many collaborators were punished in Denmark and the Netherlands, while in Belgium and Norway the proportion was six times as high.

Beyond the narrow legal framework of the purge, a national convulsion was taking place. As in every other occupied country, this convulsion went through several stages: an initial burst of self-righteous fury at the Liberation; then, a year later, a deeper, less manic fury as the advance into Germany revealed the awful truth about the fate of those who had vanished into the camps. Throughout Europe the realisation that so many friends and relatives were not coming home at all but had been horribly tortured and butchered led to a great wave of vengeful anger. It was at this time that local Prefects, fearing that embittered families would take justice into their own hands rather than stomach the long delays of the official courts, effectively defied de Gaulle's ruling that only official courts be allowed to try the collabos: the choice was summary justice or virtual insurrection. Then, with some justice achieved, passions began to cool. This in part explains why swingeing sentences were at first handed out so liberally, only to be revoked with equal liberality a few years later. As with any great burst of anger, there were elements of pantomine in all this.

Liberation justice was far less heavy-handed in Paris than it was in the provinces, particularly in the South. This for two reasons. In the North, where the Resistance had started, the Germans had largely crushed it by 1944; in the South, where real resistance only got going after 1942, the movement was still at the height of its strength at the Liberation and in 1944-5 it provided a well-organised and vengeful army eager to fall upon collabo necks. It was also the case that collaborators found it far easier to retain their anonymity in the metropolis than in closed rural communities where everyone knew what his neighbour was doing. And while the Sartres and Mauriacs could play on sophisticated (and guilty) Parisian consciences to obtain mercy for a famous intellectual or someone who had lost a leg in the Great War, in the provinces such arguments cut little ice: a more atavistic and typically peasant view of justice – an eye for an eye, a tooth for a tooth – prevailed. Some collabos ended up in court-rooms looking badly bruised and beaten up, but there was, to be fair, no evidence of recourse to the barbarous methods of the Gestapo and the Vichy Milice, even in the most benighted rural areas. It is easy to talk about 'typical peasant' behaviour, but the Milice had pulled out their victims' eyes and put live cockroaches in the eye-sockets before sewing the eyelids shut again.

There was a political dimension too. The Communists had shouldered most of the burden of the Resistance and were naturally keener than any other group for retribution. In calling for justice, they sought to rally a general patriotic fervour behind what they saw as the anti-Fascist cause. But once the Communists were expelled from the Government in 1947 and the Cold War set in, anti-Communism came into its own – and who could lay a better claim to anti-Communism than the old collabos? It was in this period of reaction – so well portrayed by de Beauvoir in *The Mandarins* – that the myth of the purge as a sort of Communist terror first took root.

On the other hand, there was an awkward realisation that many people had had to live double or treble lives under the Occupation, that too much delving into the crimes of the past might turn up some embarrassing facts. Even dead Resistance heroes might turn out to have betrayed their comrades under torture, to have traded the life of their best friend for that of their child. These dark doubts live on. Take the interesting case of Klaus Barbie, who has now been held without trial since February 1983. Just before the 1986 elections an indictment was drawn up listing all the crimes he had committed against the Jews. This was thrown out on the reasonable grounds that Barbie had tortured and murdered many Résistants too and that their deaths could hardly be ignored. The problem is that laying charges under that head would give Barbie an opportunity to disclose the information that he alone has about who betrayed whom. A lot of people, as the saying goes, don't know that. And a lot of people don't want to know that. Barbie is now 73: it is quite likely that he will die without ever coming to trial. And if he does, his death is likely to be met with a growl of frustration – and a sigh of relief. The French are waiting for a ghost to die, but the ghost lives on as part of the national consciousness: the shame and humiliation of the Occupation is seldom talked about, but it will not go away. Just as the Americans have still to come to terms with Vietnam, the French have still, collectively, to come to terms with Vichy. Mere trials – lawyers' rituals – will not help.

References

Lottman, Herbert (1986) *The People's Anger: Justice and Revenge in Post-Liberation France* (London: Hutchinson).

Chapter 21

The Price of Indépendance

If you go to the fine Musée de l'Air et de l'Espace built out at the old Orly airport and wander through the halls of ancient biplanes, Ariane rockets and Soviet space capsules, you will come upon a wall chart depicting the history of the Armée de l'Air. The pre-war era, one notes, ends in 1940 – when Vichy took over what was left of the Air Force, apart from the Free French émigrés who were integrated into the RAF. The next chart, entitled 'The Reconstruction of the Armée de l'Air', runs from 1945 to 1966, but is then followed by a further chart which runs from 1966 to the present day and is entitled 'The Era of National Independence'. What happened in 1966? Well, that is when France left the integrated command of NATO, when the USAF bases were kicked out of France and the Armée de l'Air thus reverted to wholly national control . . . .

After I wrote the article below I discussed the Rafale project with a leading Gaullist member of the National Assembly's defence committee. He agreed both that his leader, Chirac, was wholly committed to the Rafale – and that the project was quite mad. But, he gloomily cautioned, the project might well go ahead even if Chirac lost power, owing to the overwhelming enmity between Dassault and British Aerospace (BAe). BAe were already heavily involved in the EAF programme – and this was enough to make any thought of joining that programme anathema to Dassault, whose representatives could hardly bear to be in the same room with their opposite numbers from BAe (a feeling heartily reciprocated by BAe). It would, he warned, take a strong Minister of Defence in Paris to stand up to this.

The Socialists won the 1988 elections and the leader of the party's left wing, M. Jean-Pierre Chevènement, became Minister of Defence. He immediately became an all-out champion of the Rafale project and soon established himself as one of the most conservative defence ministers the Fifth Republic had seen. Plus ça change . . . .

The Price of Indépendance 223

A good Trivial Pursuit question is to ask which country was the world's biggest car manufacturer in 1900: not many people correctly guess France. In similar vein, not many would guess that in 1936 France was the world's biggest arms exporter (displacing the 1935 champion, Czechoslovakia) – though to be fair, Britain was normally top of the merchants-of-death league by a fair mile. In fact, French arms played a very minor part in the Second World War and few would have predicted that within a generation France would have become the world's third leading supplier of arms and military technology. Up until 1958 this renaissance was based simply on the fact that France drew greater benefit from Nato in terms of economic and military aid than any other State, more even than Britain. The turning-point probably lay in the military nuclear programme which a whole succession of Fourth Republic governments gingerly pushed along. The United States was anything but keen on this development and refused France access to nuclear know-how and material, thus enraging de Gaulle – under whom the French arms industry then took off, becoming not only a major structural feature of the French economy but a dangerously destabilising influence within the whole international system. Everybody knows about the Super Mystère and the Exocet reaching Argentinian hands and the equipping of the South African Air Force with Mirage IIIs and Alouettes: fewer would guess that Alouettes also go to China or that the most advanced Mirage types, the 5 and the 50, go to Libya. More recently and famously, France has emerged as a major arms supplier to both Iraq and Iran, just as it had earlier armed the Israelis and their enemies, Nicaragua and its opponents, and so on. In the end one arrives at a situation in which oil supplies to France and her European allies have to run the gauntlet of Iraqi forces armed with Mirage F-1s and Exocets.

Edward Kolodziej has produced what will surely stand as the definitive work on this remarkable phenomenon, his study centring on the Fifth Republic and running right through to the early 1980s. His book (Kolodziej, 1987) is a wonderfully thorough account, well up to the highest standards of American scholarship. He insists powerfully that although private arms manufacturers like Matra and Dassault grew rich on the back of Gaullist weapons policy, the key impulsion has always come from the State. De Gaulle's insistence on a defence policy of national independence brought a wave of highly directed State investment, but the French armed forces could never be big enough customers to make an independent French defence industry economically viable: large-scale arms exports were a necessity from the outset. And as buoyant arms exports put AMX armoured vehicles on to the sands of Yemen and the streets of Chile, or French planes into the skies of South Africa and Saudi Arabia, the whole effort was borne up on a wave of patriotic enthusiasm for these triumphs of French technology – particularly since such sales greatly added to the general never-had-it-so-good tide of 1960s Gaullism. Every succeeding administration has taken the same view: not surprisingly, the Socialists soon forgot their promise to 'moralise' arms shipments and began to beat the export drum as loudly and indiscriminately as anyone else.

The nerve-centre of the French military industrial complex is the Délégation Générale pour l'Armement, a virtually autonomous agency within the Ministry of Defence. In typical French fashion, the DGA has its own specialized élite recruitment of *énarques* and *polytechniciens*, particularly the engineers who graduate through a whole series of special armament and technical colleges. The DGA not only reports direct to the Minister and President but is a sort of runaway corporate monster for whose creation French *dirigisme* has always displayed a special genius. Powered by corporate *élan*, penetrated through and through with all manner of old-boy and peer-group friendships and rivalries, bound hand and foot by bureaucratic controls, the whole cemented by the heady mix of patriotism and multi-billion-franc deals, the DGA is, suggests Kolodziej, pretty much beyond anyone's control – Giscard d'Estaing, he says, was never much more than an 'interested observer' of its doings. Personally, I wonder if Kolodziej has not underestimated the significance of the complex and multiple pay-offs which exist between the defence industries and political parties, but he does seem to be correct when he asserts that no one actually feels they are in control. Not even those who run the DGA:

> Do I feel myself to be the director general of the DGA? Frankly, no .... I have no power in social matters. The public sector is inserted in such a network of general rules that I can decide nothing alone .... This absence of power stems directly from the state of quasi-financial irresponsibility in which I find myself. The rules of public accountability leave me no latitude, either in buying or, what is worse, in selling .... I do not have the right to draw on profits to use for ... investments. I cannot even, as any boss, support my operations from the treasury.... I characterize myself often as a Gulliver in Lilliput, rendered financially and socially inert by an immense network of tight ties which prohibit the least movement.

Thus the military-industrial complex – although highly regulated by the State, whose creation it is – is neither under the control of private arms manufacturers, nor of politicians, nor even of the people who man the State machine. It is an immensely impressive, highly bureaucratised runaway train. The only final laws it obeys are those of economics, and here the squeeze has become increasingly tight. Part of the problem is the huge investment made by the State in the French nuclear deterrent. The British have taken the cheap option of buying American nuclear weapons but France insists, expensively, on developing and making its own. And since France is unwilling to devote so crazily high a fraction of its GDP to defence as Britain routinely does, her resources available for conventional arms are inevitably squeezed. Moreover, costs are escalating out of sight. The Mirage F-1 cost five times as much as the first French jet fighter, the Ouragan; the Mirage 2000 cost twice as much as the F-1 and the Mirage 4000 twice as much again. Faced with cost pressures such as these, governments tended to slow down investment programmes, with the risk that the new weapons would be obsolete even before they went into service. Moreover, the French arms export effort was too dependent on ex-French African countries and the Third World in general. Even the astonishing appetite of Third World leaders for fancy weaponry has been somewhat dulled by the debt crisis. And just as Toyotas and Nissans nose Renaults and Citroëns out of Third World markets, so the willingness of Morocco or the Ivory Coast to buy French arms cannot be expected to last for ever.

Unfortunately, Kolodziej leaves the matter at that point, with things hanging delicately in the balance – the book hardly progresses beyond 1983 and some of the statistical series stop in 1980. Since then things have changed fairly dramatically. Looking back, many French industrialists feel that the arms manufacturers suffered from the sin of pride and failed to realise what aggressive competition the British and Americans were determined to provide; the Americans even marketed weapons like the F-20 Tigershark, a fighter specifically designed and built for export. The rot began to set in when the Saudis preferred first the F-15 and later the Tornado to the Mirage 2000. Other disappointments crowded in – Matra's Mistral missile found the American Stinger tough competition, for example – and from 1983 there was a virtual sales panic in France. As the Contrôleur Général des Armées, M. Barba, pointed out in his recent report on the Luchaire affair (involving illicit arms shipments to Iran), Emile Blanc, then heading the DGA, found himself facing the prospect of a two-thirds drop in arms exports in a single year. Blanc recommended urgent action in a number of areas, including the acceleration of arms exports to the Maghreb and the Gulf. It was perhaps not surprising that the Luchaire company should have taken this as an encouragement to sell sensitive equipment to Iran, even if certain documents did have to be forged. The then Minister of Defence, Charles Hernu of Rainbow Warrior fame, indignantly denies that the collaboration of Defence Ministry officials in these forgeries resulted in the payment of sizeable sums to Socialist Party funds, but it would be fair to say that not everybody believes Hernu – particularly since he has now, after several years of denial, admitted responsibility in the Rainbow Warrior affair.

Even with this helping hand, French arms exports fell by 30 per cent in 1983 and the trend has continued downwards since. The result has been a stampede to get out of the arms business – Matra reduced the military share of its business from 48 per cent in 1982 to 36 per cent in 1986 and plans to reduce that to 26 per cent by 1991. But, as one might have expected, at the heart of the storm was Dassault-Bréguet, which saw exports fall, as a share of its orders, from a remarkable 90 per cent in 1982 to 51 per cent in 1986. The unhappy Serge Dassault, who succeeded his father, the legendary Marcel, in 1986, now finds himself facing such derisive headlines as 'Is There Still a Pilot at Dassault?' Already four Dassault factories have been shut and 13 per cent of its labour force laid off, but while the French armed forces order thirty-five Mirage 2000s and five Atlantique-2 Navy surveillance planes every year from Dassault, the company needs at least that volume again of exports to stay viable – and this it simply lacks. In the past two years only nine Mirage 2000s have been exported (to India).

Everything suggests that Dassault, and with it the French arms industry as a whole, could well meet its Waterloo with the Rafale, Dassault's new fighter unveiled by Marcel Dassault in December 1985, shortly before his death. Simultaneously, France withdrew from the European Advanced Technology Fighter (EAF) programme, in which Britain, Germany, Spain and Italy collaborate – for, of course, Rafale is to be the independent French rival to the EAF. Rafale's cost is officially put at 44 per cent higher than the Mirage 2000, but the Defence Ministry is already routinely assuming that it will cost at least 70 per cent more, with 160 per cent a more realistic all-in figure. The whole of Dassault's future is mortgaged to this plane: construction is due to start in 1993 and the plane is to enter service with the Navy and Air Force in 1996. Jacques Chirac has virtually made it a matter of Gaullist honour that the plane will indeed be built (Dassault has always been a large contributor to Gaullist party funds and Chirac is a friend of Serge Dassault), but others are sceptical – costs seem certain to over-run; Dassault have got to get through to 1993 in one piece first; and who, besides France, is going to buy the Rafale? Exports are essential if the plane is to survive, and with it France's 'national independence' in defence.

Currently, we are still in the fantasy stage: the Rafale gets lot of media attention and the cameras love its super-sleek, almost erotically lovely lines. (They made such a fuss about them during the 1985 presentation that announcers quite forgot to say that the plane had, as yet, no engine.) Belgium, we are told, might buy it, and a special presentation of the plane is to be made to the West Germans. And perhaps Spain might be tempted away from the EAF to buy it. This is all pretty certain nonsense, so speculation then wanders to getting the Americans in on the act – McDonnell Douglas, perhaps, or Northrop. (We forget, for convenience's sake, that the Americans have an advanced technology fighter project of their own to sell.) But already such speculation provokes a deep Gaullian groan. The Americans will want their pound of flesh, and what they want is to kill off all rival fighter projects. They have already managed to bully the Israeli Lavi and Japanese FX out of existence, and under the pretext of 'co-operation' they will work to kill the Rafale too.

If Chirac wins the forthcoming presidential election it is possible that the Rafale will indeed be built and that we will have to wait for the whole cycle to go round one final time before the inevitable nemesis. For the absurdity of the present doctrine is that Dassault is just as hostile to Airbus Industrie as the Americans, and for similar reasons. And yet the Airbus is a triumph of European co-operative technology, the first real challenge to the American airliner monopoly since the days of the Comet and the Caravelle. Similarly, the insistence that France must, to retain independence, build the Rafale, implies that France is the only independent country in Europe. It would not matter so much if only Frenchmen had to pay for this folly, but as Kolodziej so eloquently shows, the price has been far more widely shared, with the arms exports France needs to stay 'independent' helping to make the world as a whole a more dangerous and less stable place.

References

Kolodziej, Edward A. (1987) *Making and Marketing Arms: The French Experience and its Implications for the International System* (Guildford: Princeton University Press).

Chapter 22

Making Things Happen

It is extraordinarily difficult to find authors who write about the intelligence services of East and West with anything like professional detachment. On the whole, those who write about the CIA have little, if anything, to say about the KGB, while those who write about the KGB tend to assume that the CIA's virtue is universally acknowledged. To be fair, there is a large and fairly good literature about the CIA, while the literature that exists about the KGB is both sparse and rubbishy. So it is hard to achieve balance.

I had a hard lesson in what results from this after writing a book about the Soviet shooting down of the South Korean airliner, KAL 007, in 1983. The evidence which I presented for the involvement of US intelligence in the tragic affair was, I felt, overwhelming – and a US judge has since ruled that the plane could hardly have been off course by accident. At the time of writing, the victims' relatives' suit against the airline continues. When my book, Shootdown: The Verdict on KAL 007, appeared, I was startled to find how reluctant many were even to look at the evidence. Some newspapers and magazines refused, as a matter of policy, to review the book, while some of the reviews were really just wild fulminations. To my surprise, one of the most remarkable of these reviews appeared in The Times under the signature of Christopher Andrew (whose own book I favourably review below). Dr Andrew thought my book was utter rubbish and summed it up by declaring that one could judge what to make of the book from the fact that while the Index contained many references to the CIA, it contained none at all to the KGB. This was odd enough as an objection: no one had ever thought the KGB had had anything to do with KAL 007 flying so far off course, after all. But, as I hastened to point out, the Index did include an entry for the KGB, together with a number of references to it: the grounds for Dr Andrew's dismissal of the case were simply fictitious. Quite where this left Dr Andrew I never discovered. . . .

> As for his secret *Spials*, which he did employ both at home and abroad, by them to discover what *Practices* and Conspiracies were against him, surely his Case required it: He had such *Moles* perpetually working and casting to undermine him. Neither can it be reprehended. For if *Spials* be lawful against lawful *Enemies*, much more against *Conspirators* and *Traytors*.
>
> Francis Bacon,
> *The History of the Reign of Henry VII*

One of the benefits of the contemporary fascination with the world of intelligence operations is the growing perception that this 'missing dimension' which lies behind so many newspaper headlines lies behind a good deal of history too. Unfortunately, and sometimes scandalously, a good deal remains hidden. Despite the Thirty-Year Rule it is only now that evidence is beginning to dribble out about the police spies and informers among the unemployed workers' movements of the 1920s and 1930s; even their activity among nineteenth century Fenians and anarchists remains a closed book. The only possible reason for such continuing secrecy is that any government which reveals how its predecessors spied upon their own populace may also face some embarrassing queries as to what comparable actions it is getting up to itself today.

It is, at first sight, odd that we know a great deal more about the more necessarily secret world of military and foreign intelligence. The reasons for this are actually quite simple. Not only will one's foreign opponents seek to publicise one's activities, but the continuing bureaucratic war for scarce resources not infrequently leads intelligence services to boast of their past coups. Moreover, when military intelligence becomes really important – that is, when there is a war on – large numbers of outside 'amateurs' have to be recruited into the machine – and in the long term such people leak.

Without doubt, the richness of the Andrew and Dilks collection (1984) owes much to such factors. Most of the essays are concerned with the 1900–45 period, and one learns of such fascinating byways as Japanese covert support for Russian socialist revolutionaries against the Tsar, and the intelligence gained by these from such Finnish dissidents as Konni Zilliacus. (Interestingly, *Who Was Who* reveals that the Labour MP of the same name, whom I take to be the former's son, began his career as an officer in the British Intelligence Mission to Siberia in 1917–19.) Similarly, one reads of Woodrow Wilson's laborious and amateur efforts to encode his own messages to Colonel House: his code for the Secretary of War and The Secretary of the Navy was 'Mars' and 'Neptune'. As Andrew drily adds: 'European codebreakers doubtless found the few hours required to decrypt Wilson's most secret communications unusually diverting. The great champion of open diplomacy was splendidly unaware of the degree to which he was practising it himself.'

Inevitably, 'the Cambridge Comintern' comes in for further treatment, this time in a long autobiographical essay by Robert Cecil. Perhaps the chief novelty is the persistent implication that the writer, academic and MP, Goronwy Rees, may have been active in the Soviet cause over a considerable period of years. If so, it certainly lends a new twist to one's reading of the vitriolically right-wing pieces Rees (under the pseudonym 'R') later contributed to *Encounter*, especially when one considers that journal's funding by the CIA. Moles within moles?

Otherwise one's main conclusion in respect of the Maclean, Burgess, Blunt and Philby cases has to be less about the current television image of privileged young Bolsheviks conspiring to the sound of choirboys in the ancient quad than about the sheer blithering incompetence of the mandarins who let them get away. But one could usually survive one's blunders in the British Foreign Service if one came from the right class. Thus Sir H. Knatchbull-Hugessen, our Ambassador in Ankara, not merely survived his laxity in the 'Cicero' case, which led to the leak of the D-Day plans to the Germans, but was actually promoted to be Ambassador in Brussels. Similarly, Kim Philby's career would have come to a summary end in 1945 but for the absurd amateurishness and procrastination of Sir Maurice Peterson, the British Ambassador to Istanbul. If Peterson had acted more quickly or had even addressed his letter to the right man, Philby would never have had time to destroy the Russian defector, Volkov, who was about to shop him. As Cecil adds, with bitter restraint: 'It is painful to record that in 1946 Peterson was promoted to be Ambassador at Moscow.' But it was really the same with Burgess and Maclean: in any normal organisation they would have been sacked for their wild and drunken behaviour long before they had done much damage. And Blunt too: Rees had promised not to betray Burgess or Maclean, but when Burgess fled Rees decided to own up and shopped Burgess, Maclean and Blunt. None the less, it took another twelve years for MI5 to accept fully that Blunt was a traitor too.

The British media have an insatiable and utterly disproportionate appetite for ever further titbits about the 'Cambridge Comintern'. No sooner was the long hunt for the 'third man' settled (with the defection of Philby) than a further breathless search for the 'fourth man' began. Finally Blunt was run down. Almost immediately we are off on the chase for the fifth man (Rees?) and perhaps even a sixth (Sir Roger Hollis?). It may make good copy, but all these men save Philby have been dead for some time and we cannot continue hunting the moles of the 1930s and 1940s for ever without a complete loss of perspective about today's vastly different intelligence world. The whole affair is now principally a media excuse to opine wisely (and gossip endlessly) about treachery and homosexuality among the Oxbridge elite of fifty years ago. In espionage terms, the fixation with the Burgess and Maclean period leaves one trapped in the out-of-date world of the le Carré novels. For a quarter of a century now the basic artefact of intelligence-gathering has been the reconnaissance satellite. For over a decade the chief concern of British Intelligence has been to turn inwards, to penetrate the domestic worlds of Ireland and the Far Left. Simultaneously, intelligence services have begun to spend more of their efforts on internally-directed propaganda campaigns and the spreading of disinformation and misinformation. None of this makes any appearance in the le Carré novels or in the endless Sunday journalism about third, fourth and fifth men. It is a false focus, and our concerns today are, rightly, different.

The service which led the way into the new world of intelligence was undoubtedly the CIA. During the war-scare of 1948-9 the Agency was endowed with a Charter which, as H.H. Ransom puts it, was designed 'for conducting what was, in effect, a secret Third World War'.[1] Not only was the CIA exempted from all Congressional supervision, but its Director was endowed with large funds for secret operations which he could spend at his personal discretion. Moreover, the Agency's remit covered not only espionage and counter-espionage but provision 'to carry out covert actions designed to weaken Soviet control over its own population and the peoples of Eastern Europe'. It seems likely that the implicit model for this radical departure was that of the European Resistance movements. Just as the OSS had sought to create and assist movements of the Maquis in Occupied Europe with the aim of destabilising Nazi rule ahead of the advancing Allied forces, so now the CIA would seek to promote similar destabilisation behind Soviet lines – perhaps as a preliminary to a more general armed movement to 'roll back' the new Communist frontiers.

There was no doubting the extreme dangers of this radical new doctrine. Small-scale covert action was nothing new, particularly in time of war, but no power had ever formally espoused such means as an arm of peacetime policy before. Forsaking the traditional intelligence role of attempting to discover what was really happening, the

CIA from the outset saw one of its main tasks as making things happen. By 1953 it had already grown to six times its 1947 size; by 1952 covert action accounted for three-quarters of its budget. The restriction of such actions to Eastern Europe was almost immediately jettisoned, and it was not long before the CIA was boasting of its successes in arranging coups in Iran (1953) and Guatemala (1954). As Ransom puts it, it was effectively 'an independent organisation, a huge bureaucracy in its own right, with its own foreign policy, it own bureaucratic turf to protect, its own secret communications channels, its own airlines and secret armies, and vast sums of unvouchered funds'. The CIA, moreover, went in for news management on the grand scale. Not only were journalistic activities extensively used for cover, but the Agency soon had its man – or several of them – on almost every major US paper and journal and not a few abroad. Where such handy conduits did not exist, the Agency just went out and created them. It was the sheerest form of America can-do-ism.

Throughout its ups and downs of the 1960s and 1970s, the CIA never really lost this central thrust. In the Nixon period the Agency attracted into its ranks some quite remarkable 'cowboys' gung-ho for even the riskiest and most illegal operations. Stansfield Turner, Carter's CIA chief, quickly discovered that his instructions to rein in on covert operations were simply being ignored. This led to a sweeping purge which was, however, put into full reverse within months of Reagan's election. The old Nixon 'cowboys' came flocking back in greater numbers than ever. Under Reagan the CIA budget has increased by between 17 per cent and 25 per cent every year, and by 1983 its new chief, William Casey, was able to boast of a new record in the scale of covert operations – the putting into the field of a 'secret army' of 10,000 Somozista 'contras' against Nicaragua. One former CIA employee estimates that there has been a fivefold expansion of world-wide covert operations under Casey in only three years: currently, in Africa alone, some twenty such operations are apparently under way.[2] This is 'making things happen' with a vengeance. Moreover Reagan has, for the first time, given such activities explicit Presidential blessing: 'I do believe in the right of a country, when it believes that its interests are best served, to practise covert activity.[3] Two days before making this statement the President awarded the National Security medal to Richard Helms, the former CIA Director who had been fined $2,000 and given a two-year suspended jail sentence for lying to Congress.[4] Casey himself has been awarded the CIA's highest medal for bringing 'imagination to our operation'.[5]

Reagan's open justification of covert activity was quickly qualified by his press secretary: the President had meant the statement to apply 'only to the US'. How far, though, have others copies the CIA model? The record is somewhat patchy. Under the redoubtable Jacques Foccart, de Gaulle's *barbouzes* had a well-documented record of intervention in a number of African states, with several *coups d'état* to their credit. But there is scant evidence of such activity outside Africa, and not much of comparable actions in more recent time. The Shah's SAVAK was quite willing to commit kidnapping and murder in other countries besides Iran, but generally such activities centred only on Iranian exiles. South Africa's BOSS seems to have been capable of rather milder forms of 'dirty tricks' both in the United States and the United Kingdom. Perhaps the most adventurous of the others has been the Israeli MOSSAD. Some of its members cut their teeth in the early terrorist campaigns against the British, and later MOSSAD was quite open about its expertise in kidnapping Eichmann or assassinating Palestinian terrorists. Thereafter the Israelies have sometimes attempted to gain diplomatic advantage by hiring out MOSSAD's expertise to third parties. Apart from co-operation with BOSS in Namibia-Angola, the Israelis have emerged as a factor of some importance in the current Central American turmoil, while at the time of writing three of the four men charged with the Nigerian kidnapping in London are Israelis. A priori it looks as if the Israelis may have been seeking to curry favour with the new Nigerian military regime by carrying out some of their cloak-and-dagger work for them. One's major reservation about such a conclusion has simply to be that MOSSAD's operations do not normally end in such a mess as the Dikko kidnapping did. One up to MI5?

How far Britain's external intelligence arm, MI6, followed the CIA into the world of major covert activity is harder to say. According to Philby's account, there was concerted co-operation with the CIA to launch armed raids into Georgia and the Ukraine in 1949–50 – and he claims that there was a fairly major 'Bay of Pigs' type of operation mounted against Albania in 1950.[6] If so, it seems unlikely that such co-operation outlasted the breakdown in US – UK intelligence co-operation which followed the Burgess and Maclean scandal. Bloch and Fitzgerald's book,[7] despite the claims made for it and the Home Secretary's furious reaction to it, does not actually instance anything much more sinister than attempts to fund and assist colonial political groups favourable to Britain. No doubt covert action 'dirty tricks' have been employed in Ireland over the last fifteen years: but this is, after all, no more than one would expect in a war situation and does not necessarily prove a point about normal modes of peacetime operation.

The really big question-mark is that over the KGB. Most of what one can read in the press about this legendarily tough organisation is of poor quality, and no good book exists on it at all. It is clear that it maintains a vast internal apparat, that it is involved in all the normal forms of espionage, and that it has a considerable appetite for Western high technology. Beyond that, it is clear that the Russians make extensive use of the (rather obvious) cover of Embassy officials and of Tass, Novosti, Aeroflot and other employees. But of KGB covert action there is almost no hard evidence at all. Not a single major KGB covert action – comparable, say, to the Bay of Pigs or the Chile destabilisation – has been uncovered. No intelligence service is that good or that lucky for forty years on the trot, so one is forced to the conclusion that the KGB employs covert action sparingly, if at all.

The CIA answer to this – indeed, the major justification for the CIA's covert activities in the first place – is that the presence of Communist Parties around the world gives the Russians a large group of willing agents almost everywhere. No doubt Russian advice and support has frequently been proffered to such parties (and to Third World nationalists), but by the 1960s and 1970s even the CIA was forced to acknowledge that this was not really an equivalent phenomenon. There has been no shortage, of course, of local Communists willing to act as individual agents in the ordinary way, but there is no record of CPs or Third World nationalist parties as such getting involved in covert activities on the Russians' behalf. In any case, when such parties matter at all, it is because they are genuine social movements – and thus legitimate political actors – in their own countries. Even in Eastern Europe, the Soviet style has been different. When confronted by a rebellious client state, of the sort the United States faced in Chile or Nicaragua, they have either intervened overtly and militarily (Hungary, Czechoslovakia) or have simply let them get on with it (Yugoslavia, Romania, Albania). The novel exception seems to be Poland: the way the Jaruzelski coup was managed – with the declaration of martial law being actually preprinted in the USSR – far more closely resembles the classic CIA-style coup. The Russians, like the Israelis, may have been learning from American can-do-ism. Still, it is worth pointing out that the evidence for Soviet covert action is patchy even within its 'empire', and beyond that it is even thinner.

As if bothered by this relative lack of evidence for KGB covert activity, many Western Cold Warriors have fallen back in recent years on attempts to prove a connection between the KGB and international terrorist groups. Recently, prompted by the strong following wind of Reaganism, this has culminated in an enormous international media campaign to prove that the Russians were behind the assassination attempt against the Pope. There is, actually, no evidence for this at all. The would-be assassin, Mehmet Ali Agca, was a long-time member of the Turkish fascist group, the Grey Wolves, and also of the extreme right National Action Party. He had been sentenced for the murder of a leading Turkish newspaper editor in 1979, was rescued from prison with Grey Wolf assistance and had a formidable career of Grey Wolf terrorism to his credit. In 1979 he openly boasted of his intention of killing the Pope. Captured by the Italian Police, he was threatened with release into the general prison population (among whose strongly Catholic ranks he would not have survived for long) unless he 'confessed'. Under such pressures he came up with a story involving meetings with Bulgarian diplomats. One of these he described as bearded (though he was in fact clean-shaven) and also spoke of meetings with his family (who were in fact out of the country).[8] On this slender tissue the whole 'KGB plot against the Pope' rests. The Pope is a highly vulnerable target, and, one suspects, had the KGB really decided to kill him, he would be dead, and there would be no convenient suspect to point a finger at the Soviet bloc. The unpalatable truth is that it is far easier to give chapter and verse for CIA involvement with terrrorist groups in, say, Nicaragua or El Salvador than it is to do the same for the KGB.

Mention of 'the plot against the Pope' brings one, finally, to the question of intelligence-sponsored disinformation. Comparisons are difficult. In the Soviet bloc (and in most underdeveloped countries) the media are subject to rigid and institutionalised censorship and control. Practices vary, but the most common form of censorship is the simple omission of inconvenient truths (misinformation). This creates something of a problem when positive disinformation is added to the stew, for in such countries the media are so generally realised to be untruthful that not too much is believed either way. Within the Soviet bloc the quite normal result is that very large numbers of people rely on the BBC, the Voice of America or Radio Free Europe for their news. It is an ironic result, for, under Reagan, at least, not only RFE but the VOA have become synonymous with strong news-slanting from an opposite direction. All that one can say is that if the Soviet bloc Intelligence Services have anything to do with this, they have scored the most spectacular of own goals, creating the objective conditions under which the other side's propaganda is more readily believed than their own, even by their captive, home audience.

The freedom enjoyed by the Western media, however imperfect, makes them qualitatively different. To be sure, a good deal of 'news' does filter into our media from the intelligence community. Indeed, there is a whole category of journalists quite routinely described as 'close to Western intelligence sources' – Robert Moss, Brian Crozier, Claire Sterling, Arnaud de Borchgrave and so on. In the end, however, there is still a decision to be made by editors and proprietors as to whether they will give house-room to such sources.

There is, in any case, nothing necessarily sinister about information being derived from intelligence sources. More often problems arise through journalists who are intelligence camp-followers picking up disinformation from the wilder and more disgruntled fringes of the intelligence community. Thus, for example, the recently touted theory that the Sino-Soviet split is a sham, designed to lull the West into a false sense of security – a 'story' given mass coverage recently by *The Sunday Times* for two consecutive weeks. It seems possible that the ultimate source for this nonsense lies in bureaucratic conflicts within the CIA. The former CIA agent, Ralph McGehee, describes in some detail how the CIA's China desk, deeply threatened by Nixon's opening towards China, sought desperately to propagate such a theory: 'Case officers developed a very personal interest in keeping China as one of the primary enemies of the United States. Promotions, foreign travel and assignments abroad all depended on maintaining that concept.' McGehee goes on to relate how one of the staff of the CIA's East Asia Division 'tried to convince me that the Chinese and the Soviets had secretly agreed to split in order to lull and conquer the rest of the world'.[9]

In the end, real intelligence information (though not covert action) is a benign thing. It would be worrying if those running MI5, MI6 or the CIA really believed the nonsense about the 'Pope plot' or the 'Sino-Soviet sham split', but one may be fairly sure that they do not. It would, no doubt, be safer and pleasanter to live in a world where there was no need for intelligence services. In the world as it is, we are all much safer if both Cold War 'sides' know as much as possible about one another. In that sense, the more agents, double agents and electronic reconnaissance we have deployed among the Russians, *and* the more they have deployed among us, the better: and the more their genuine findings are available to the media, the better that is too. Perhaps, indeed, we have gone on too long discussing intelligence activities in the hushed, treason-and-plot terms applied to Guy Fawkes. Neither of the Establishments of East and West can be expected to show much appreciation for their Penkovskys or Philbys, but in the interests of a more open world perhaps the rest of us should be glad that they exist.

Notes

1. H.H. Ransom, 'Secret Intelligence in the USA, 1947–82', in Andrew and Dilks, *op.cit.*
2. *The Sunday Times*, 15 April 1984; *Guardian*, 12 June 1984.
3. *New York Times*, 23 October 1983.
4. *New York Times*, 21 October 1983.
5. *Washington Post*, 7 October 1983.
6. Kim Philby, *My Silent War* (1973), pp. 138–46.
7. J. Bloch and P. Fitzgerald, *British Intelligence and Covert Action* (Junction Books, London 1983). Bloch, a South African, has effectively been sentenced to expulsion from the United Kingdom – a curious action given that no charge under the Official Secrets Act has been made against his (British) co-author.
8. See F. Brodhead and E.S. Herman, 'The KGB Plot to Assassinate the Pope: A Case Study in Free World Disinformation', *Covert Action Information Bulletin* (Washington), No. 19, Spring – Summer 1983.
9. R.W. McGehee, *Deadly Deceits. My 25 Years in the CIA* (Sheridan Square Publications, New York 1983).

References

Andrew, Christopher and Dilks, David (eds.) (1984) *The Missing Dimension: Governments and Intelligence Communities in the Twentieth Century* (London: Macmillan).

Chapter 23

Subversions: The Shadowy History of MI5

The article below surmises what there is to be surmised about MI5's activities in recent years: we are no nearer knowing the full facts now than when it was written. The situation has, indeed, got worse since then, with the passage of a new Official Secrets Act which will make publication of what the State does not like even harder. At the time of writing the Thatcher Government is acting to prevent the publication in the United Kingdom of a book about British interception of Japanese intelligence in the 1930s on the grounds that this could damage national security. Simultaneously, the Government has been pushing its nominees into the broadcasting media with the clear aim of reducing investigative reporting. The appointment of Lord Chalfont ('what we need is more secrecy, not less') to a leading position in the Independent Broadcasting Authority is merely a well-publicised example of a more general phenomenon. More sinister still has been the revelation, in relation to the celebrated ITN documentary, Death on the Rock, that the government-inspired section of the press not only willingly collaborated to smear witnesses whose testimony in the affair was embarrassing to the Government but even, in the case of The Sunday Times, deliberately falsified reports on the matter submitted by one of its own journalists. In Thatcher's Britain behaviour of this sort by newspaper editors has frequently won them favours and honours, but there will one day, if only in the history books, be a reckoning for all this which is likely to be altogether less kind.

British attitudes to the intelligence services are governed by two separate obsessions. The discovery of Maclean, Burgess, Philby and Blunt as Soviet agents has produced a long-lasting preoccupation with hunting down moles, 'agents of influence' and the like. Newspapers love it, the public are interested, and the whole business is endlessly stoked by the more enfevered spirits of the Right. There is no doubt that this is a compulsion which goes beyond reason: Blunt, after all, had given up his allegiance to Communism by 1951, yet the whole business is still breathlessly featured by the quality Sunday press several times a year. The second obsession is that of all British governments to prevent their voters knowing even the most elementary facts about the intelligence services their taxes pay for. The Peter Wright trial in Australia has recently brought out the full absurdity of this, with Sir Robert Armstrong attempting at one point to suggest that the very existence of MI5 and MI6 (let alone the identity of their directors) was a secret which could neither be confirmed nor denied. There is no other state in the world which behaves like this and national security cannot be the reason for it. The Russians, after all, are fully cognisant of the existence of MI5 and MI6 and of their directors' identity – and even the Soviet state tells it citizens that the KGB exists and who the head of it is.

It is on this crazy situation that Chapman Pincher has built his entire career. Since he is extremely right-wing, and willing to swallow even the most ridiculous claptrap in the furtherance of the anti-Communist cause, Pincher at least has some access to the officers of MI5 – for in practice the one small hole in the veil of secrecy is the one through which titbits of information are fed to a privileged coterie of writers or journalists on the Far Right. In Pincher's work the two obsessions chase each other's tails: the alleged need to protect national security legitimates the compulsive secrecy, while the need to expose Communist infiltration legitimates attempts to pierce that secrecy. Pincher has been going round and round this mulberry bush for forty years now, with considerable commercial success.

Pincher's latest (1987) offering is at least as awful as the rest. As a literary construction it is a mess, rambling endlessly and repetitively around the same warmed-over material which he has already recycled in *Too Secret Too Long*, *Their Trade in Treachery* and other melodramas. Needless to say, Pincher accepts as gospel virtually every allegation ever made by the extreme Right in either Britain or the United States. Thus Joe McCarthy's allegation that Alger Hiss was a Communist spy is treated as a simple fact, as is his claim that FDR's most trusted adviser, Harry Dexter White, the founder of the IMF and the World Bank, was also working for the Kremlin. The intellectual level of the book is perhaps best illustrated by Pincher's laborious attempt to construct a mathematical equation to explain treason. The equation, in case readers would like to use it in their Christmas party games, is: $A + m + r + b + f + s + i \rightarrow T$, where

A is access, m is money, r is resentment, b is blackmailability (sic), s is self-satisfaction, i is ideology and T is Treason. Ha, thought I'd forgotten f? No, it's just that f is the pièce de résistance: it stands, would you believe it, for flawed character.

It is with some relief that one turns to Anthony Glees's *Secrets of the Service* (1987). Glees is a professional historian and rightly attempts to place British intelligence operations in the context of the twists and turns of British foreign policy. In so far as it is possible, Glees has been meticulous in his examination of the available sources and is almost painfully judicious in sorting the wheat from the chaff. The basis of the story he has to tell lies in the two enormous changes the war brought to MI5 and MI6. The sheer necessity of national survival and the huge expansion of the services had the effect of bringing a whole new wave of highly talented intellectuals into the services, which, until then, had been the exclusive fief of 'anti-Bolshevik old buffers'. These recruits were so markedly superior that they rapidly rose to positions of power and influence. Given the nature of the 1930s intelligentsia, it was pretty well inevitable that these recruits should have included at least a few who were to turn out to be Soviet moles. The second change followed from the fact that, from June 1941, as Glees puts it, 'the Soviet Union was England's only chance of defeating Hitler.' An immediate decision was taken to stop reading Soviet radio traffic and a large measure of intelligence collaboration with the USSR was instigated. There were always strict limits to this: a team of people was specially charged with drawing up bundles of intelligence marked 'OK for Russia', but given that everything gained from the most important source of all, Enigma, was held back, the Russians were always getting far less than half of what we could have told them. (No doubt the same was true in reverse.)

This was, of course, a combination of circumstances in which the likes of Kim Philby were likely to thrive. For the two changes worked together: the young intellectual recruits as a class tended to feel contemptuous, even angry, at their elders' continuing obsession with the Bolshevik menace to the virtual exclusion of the threat posed by the Nazis. One of the most interesting passages in Glees's book is his report of an interview with a former MI6 officer who worked with Philby through that period:

> 'Philby', the officer said, 'seemed so bright and dynamic . . . .. The "old buffers", the pre-war ex-Indian police officers who formed the core of MI6, were simply not a match for him: he was able to ridicule the "Indian Policemen", obsessed with Communists and drinking

cups of tea . . . .. Like Blunt, too, Philby was simply a very clever man, far above the level of most of the other officers.'

Among the new recruits, he recalled, there was a strong feeling that people 'like the deposed King and Mrs Simpson' had deceived the public about Nazism, encouraging them to see it as a bulwark against Bolshevism and depicting the greatest evil as another war with Germany. This naturally led to a counter, pro-Russian feeling, which has since been misunderstood.

> Chapman Pincher is quite wrong to see Oxbridge intellectuals as responsible for this sort of view. The *Daily Mirror* and **Cassandra** were far more significant: it was an anti-upper-class populism that made us so pro-Russian . . . .. People had different illusions about Russia and its future . . . .. They knew that one day Russia might be our main target, but for the moment it was the Germans who were the bad ones.

Glees rather tut-tuts about all this, suggesting that it shows a terrible naïvety about Soviet intentions and that perhaps British Intelligence would have been better-off without all these bright recruits, given that a number of them were Soviet moles. This seems to me wrong-headed in several different ways. The key judgement is surely that of William Strang, the Under-Secretary of State at the Foreign Office, in a paper of May 1943:

> We need Russian collaboration. The conclusion of the Anglo-Soviet Treaty marks our decision that this must be our policy . . . even if fears that Russia lay a 'heavy hand' on eastern, central and south-eastern Europe are realised . . . I should not like to say that this would be to our disadvantage . . . .. It is better that Russia should dominate Eastern Europe than that Germany should dominate Western Europe.

Of this passage Glees asks, 'How could he have got things so wrong?' and suggests, darkly, the pernicious influence of Philby, Blunt and Burgess. Yet it is clear that Strang was absolutely right. German domination of Western Europe presented Britain with an immediate threat of invasion and of the butchery of many of its citizens: Soviet domination of Eastern Europe has never posed anything like the same danger to our national interests. And the task of defeating Nazism was so urgent that we could not afford to let our intelligence services remain in the hands of the 'old buffers'. If the price for that was the admission of a number of Soviet moles to the service, then, despite all the damage they did, it was a price worth paying. In fact, the reason MI5 got itself into such a disastrous mess with Kim Philby had nothing at all to do with any sort of opening up towards the liberal intelligentsia: quite the reverse. The point is not often enough made that Philby's cover was to join the pro-Nazi Anglo-German Fellowship and to become an active sympathiser with Franco (by whom he was decorated). The real scandal about Philby's recruitment was that we were fighting a war against Fascism and yet MI5 was quite happy to promote into a leading position someone with overtly pro-Fascist views. Nor can this have been a fluke: Philby's Soviet controllers were nothing if not pros. They had no doubt studied their target with care and reached the conclusion that the apparent possession of extreme right-wing views would make Philby all the more acceptable within MI5. In this they were proved triumphantly right.

It is worth emphasising, too, that the intelligence services had been securely in the hands of the political Right from 1909 to 1939 and that the period when the Right's hegemony was tempered to any degree lasted at most six years. Unfortunately, Glees's book, thoughtful, serious and well-researched though it is, does not really live up to its title, for it is almost wholly concerned with the war period, thereafter tending to wander off on long excursions. The fact that these excursions have their interest (was Hollis a spy? definitely not, says Glees) is only partial compensation. It would have been interesting to hear how the resumption of anti-Bolshevik normalcy after 1945 affected the service's culture and personnel, whether any of the 'old buffers' made a come back in the new climate of Cold War, and so on.

What is not in doubt is that the circumstances of the post-war period have progressively and dangerously shifted the intelligence services to the right. To be fair, it would have been hard for any institution to keep its sense of balance through more than forty years of Cold War. But to those pressures many others have been added, all pushing in the same direction. The era of decolonisation saw the services deployed against a whole panoply of left-wing Third World nationalists – in Nasser's case they were willing to go so far as to attempt his assassination. At home, even Labour politicians were willing to see Communists as the principal enemy – hence the scandalous attempt by a committee of right-wing Labour MPs headed by George Brown to get MI5 to spy on their left-wing opponents within the Party in 1961, and Wilson's use of MI5 against the seamen's strike in 1966. Meanwhile the successive defections of Maclean, Burgess and Philby not only created an atmosphere of hysterical anti-Communist mole-hunting within the service but led to American threats to withdraw co-operation on the grounds that the British were a security risk.

This threat of American non-co-operation was the final turn of the screw. British politicians, eager to see themselves as Greeks to the American Romans, were mortified at the thought that we might be dumped as untrustworthy. Moreover, MI6 had come to rely heavily on its links with the Americans: US Intelligence was vastly bigger and better-funded, and had the priceless asset of satellite intelligence, which we did not. To be cut off from all that would relegate the British to the level of the French or Italians, would finally bury our great power status, would ruin MI6. Successive British premiers, on visits to Washington, repeatedly attempted to assure one US President after another that we had put our house in order, that now we could really be trusted. But in order to be trusted the British would have to satisfy the demands of the all-powerful and long-serving head of CIA counter-intelligence, James Jesus Angleton, who has recently died.

The undeniably brilliant Angleton was also at least half-crazy. He saw moles everywhere and had paralysed the CIA for years on end with his frenetic witch-hunting. (One CIA officer wrote a bitter report suggesting that if there was a KGB mole inside the CIA, it had to be Angleton since no one else had done anything like so much damage to the Agency. The officer was forced to resign.) Angleton himself was so high-handed and paranoiac that he would refuse to attend briefing sessions with intelligence colleagues on the grounds that he did not wish to break his cover, for any of them might be moles. Within the United States he organised Operation Chaos, a vast, illegal mail-opening, phone-tapping surveillance of anti-war and dissident groups, and he was wont to interfere grossly and on the flimsiest suspicion in the affairs of other countries. He was finally sacked in 1974 when Operation Chaos broke surface – at which point it was also discovered that on the basis of no evidence at all he had told the head of Belgian Intelligence that the CIA chief of station in Brussels was a KGB mole. For many years, retaining US confidence in MI5 meant keeping James Angleton happy.

Angleton's pressures served greatly to reinforce the position of the extreme right-wing zealots within MI5. The most alarming feature in all this was the total credibility conferred by Angleton on the Soviet defector, Anatoly Golitsyn. Golitsyn had a theory which depicted virtually every international event since 1945 as a Soviet manipulation. Soviet moles were everywhere, said Golitsyn, and the

Soviets had duped the West at every turn. The bitter Soviet – Yugoslav conflict? A mere ruse to fool the West: Tito was a KGB tool. The Sino–Soviet conflict? Another vast KGB ruse to make the West think the Chinese and Russians were at loggerheads when in fact they had planned the whole thing together. And so on and so on. Despite the transparent craziness of such notions, the head of MI6 himself, Sir Maurice Oldfield, went along for some time with the idea that the Sino–Soviet split was a fake. The terrifying fact was that Angleton, when asked about co-operation with friendly intelligence services, would deny that there *was* such a thing as a friendly intelligence service. Keeping Angleton happy increasingly meant keeping Golitsyn happy, for Angleton believed everything he said.

Golitsyn had defected in Finland in 1961 and immediately asserted that almost every other Soviet defector was a double agent: that is, that he, Golitsyn, could alone be trusted. Virtually all Western governments had been penetrated at the highest level, he said. Jacques Foccart, de Gaulle's legendary spy chief, was actually the French Philby and there was a whole network of spies ('the Sapphire network') within the French Government. A huge and inconclusive hunt was conducted. Then Golitsyn announced the existence of the 'Sasha network' in German Intelligence. Another huge and inconclusive hunt. Occasionally, Golitsyn did provide useful leads, but mainly his accusations led to paralysing wild-goose chases. (Golitsyn believed that he himself should be given the directorship of a Nato security service, a sort of Western Cheka, and Angleton actually got him an interview with Bobby Kennedy so that he could put in his request for $30 million to set up such an organisation. He was bitterly disappointed when the ambition was not realised. In the end, Golitsyn did so much harm to Western intelligence services that an inquiry was held – to determine whether he might not have been a Soviet mole himself. As for England, Golitsyn said there had been a 'Ring of Five' big-time spies: Burgess, Maclean and Philby and two others who were at large. Thus began the endless search for the Fourth and Fifth Man. It is this story which is at the root of the accusations against Sir Roger Hollis, for when Blunt was turned up – not through Golitsyn's efforts – it was already gospel among MI5 mole-hunters that there must be a Fifth Man somewhere.

More alarming still was Golitsyn's allegation that the KGB had so penetrated the Labour Party that it was little better than a Soviet fifth column. This notion has provided the basis for a particular genre of right-wing thriller based on a Soviet take-over of Britain through its Labour moles – a genre inaugurated by Constantine Fitzgibbon's *When the Kissing Had to Stop*. Most shocking of all was Golitsyn's suggestion that Gaitskell had been murdered to make way for a Soviet plant. In no time Angleton had drawn the obvious conclusion that Harold Wilson was a mole – in typical Angleton fashion he held back the 'evidence' for this on the grounds that the British were not secure enough to be told – and MI5 were launched on a trail of investigation and anxiety about the Labour leadership. As far as one can see, the only points that could be made against Wilson were that he had a liking for seedy businessmen, some of whom, like Lord Kagan, he eventually ennobled, and that he had visited the USSR nineteen times. Leaving aside the extreme difficulty of believing, on the basis of Wilson's years in government, that he was a Communist, we have to remember that Wilson also befriended and distributed titles to men like Alun Chalfont, Eric Miller and Jimmy Goldsmith, and that he seems, indeed, to have been a very poor judge of character in those who flattered his ego. As for the nineteen trips to Moscow, Wilson was always prey to the hope that he could achieve an economic turn-around via a large increase in Soviet trade, that this would be his own personal trump card. It goes without saying that, had he indeed been a Soviet mole, the last thing his KGB controllers would have allowed would have been give-away trips to Moscow. One must bear the Philby example in mind: Philby, as far as we know, never went near Moscow till he defected. The Philby model suggests that the cover for a Soviet mole today would be extreme Thatcherite views, an admiration for Norman Tebbit and Roger Scruton, and a subscription to the *Salisbury Review*.

The moment of truth arrived in 1964 when Wilson became Prime Minister and attempted to impose his own appointee as head of MI5. The service resisted and Wilson backed off. Indeed, to prove his good will Wilson even acquiesced in the continuing surveillance of a large number of Labour ministers and MPs. This was enough to ruin the careers of several alleged security risks (one, Bernard Floud, committed suicide), but the only MP who was found taking money from the Eastern bloc was Will Owen. (This is quite surprising: so many MPs are on the take from one interest or another that one would have thought even a random sort-through might have thrown up half a dozen.) There was anxiety about the contacts of some of Wilson's personal friends – notably, Kagan. But again nothing was proved: the most that could be said was that anyone who conducted business with the Eastern bloc was bound to brush up against the ubiquitous KGB at some point or other. There was, in sum, remarkably little to show for the enormous investigative effort mounted over a period of years.

The important thing was that the security service was all but out of control: the British Prime Minister had in effect surrendered his power of appointment to Angleton's veto and allowed the service to live out its fantasies at the expense of his own party and government. Wilson was, of course, paranoiacally suspicious of plots against him within the Labour Party, particularly when he thought they emanated from James Callaghan, and he knew that George Brown, his old leadership rival, had attempted to enlist MI5 support against him and some of those who were close to him. Callaghan, who is sometimes said to have used the Labour Party treasurership to cosy up to the trade union paymasters, used his tenure of the Home Office in 1967-70 largely as a launching-pad for involvement in Northern Ireland, which inevitably brought him into close contact with the security services. Wilson seems to have feared that Callaghan had cultivated the same sort of special relationship with those services which he was supposed earlier to have gained with the unions. Putting two and two together, Wilson may well have decided that he must keep the intelligence service sweet in order to stop it ganging up with Callaghan against him. For Wilson, despite all his vainglorious talk about the 'smack of firm government', was not a man to reflect that appeasement simply encourages more bullying.

All of this came to a head in the wake of the 1973-4 miners' strike and Labour's surprise victory in February 1974. The shock of seeing a Tory government evicted by what appeared to be almost insurrectionary means (the mass picketing of the Saltley coke depot was the *locus classicus* of this image) produced hysteria in the Conservative Party. Some Tory MPs began openly to espouse institutional strategems – PR, a written constitution, etc. – to prevent any future 'imposition of socialism'. Lord Hailsham characteristically inveighed against what he called 'elective dictatorship', while more generally the refusal to accept the verdict of the electorate was justified with talk of 'adversarial politics'. It goes without saying that all these concerns were to vanish like chaff once a Tory government, bent on far more nakedly adversarial policies than anything favoured by Wilson-Callaghan, was itself elected on a minority vote. But in the feverish atmosphere of 1974-5 that seemed a distant, perhaps unrealisable prospect: after all, October 1974 saw Labour win its fourth election out of the previous five, thus severely weakening the Right's faith in the ballot box. In this climate all manner of schemes flourished for military intervention in case of a 'breakdown of the civil order'. Private armies like 'GB

1975' were publicly set afoot (no doubt other initiatives remained more discreet, more truly private) and the lessons of 'low-intensity warfare' learnt in Northern Ireland were pondered for their relevance to the mainland. There is an uncomfortably close parallel with the way the French Army attempted to extend to the French mainland, at the expense of the civilian power, the practices it had learnt in Algeria.

The significance of the miners' strike, in other words, was to extend the concerns which had long been the preoccupation of a mere cabal within MI5 to wide sections of the Tory Right. Meanwhile the pressure from Washington did not lessen until Angleton was finally sacked in December 1974, and the pot he had stirred so hard for so long continued to boil for some while after that. An indication of the prevailing climate within MI5 is given by the fact that it was in 1975 that Michael Bettaney (later jailed for trying, unsuccessfully, to sell secrets to the KGB) was recruited. What is usually forgotten in the Pincheresque version of events is that Bettaney was a deeply unstable young man, committed to the extreme Right. Having failed to become a Catholic priest, he fell in love with a German girl, announced that he would have preferred to have been born German, and was well known for his habit of giving the Nazi salute. The fact that someone with such an obviously volatile, extremist, perhaps even Fascist disposition should have seemed an acceptable recruit to MI5 says not a little about that organisation's state of mind in 1975.

Meanwhile, on returning to power in February 1974, Wilson seems to have capitulated even more abjectly than before to the pressure of the intelligence services. Callaghan, it should be remembered, had attempted to stage an intra-Cabinet coup against Wilson in 1969; there was no love lost between the two men; and Wilson was already worried about Callaghan's links with the intelligence world. Yet Wilson now made Callaghan Foreign Secretary, with direct responsibility for GCHQ, MI6 and, via the Joint Intelligence Committee (for which he provides the chairman), links with MI5. On the other hand, this was the time when the services for which Callaghan was responsible were running amok. How far was he really in charge? Was Wilson's sudden resignation as premier in 1976, and his deal to ensure the succession for Callaghan, related to concerns stemming from the intelligence world? Then again, the South African security service, BOSS, was heavily engaged in dirty tricks campaigns against Liberal and Labour politicians at about this time: was Callaghan aware of this?

Not the least interesting aspect of the current controversy over the Wright memoirs is the way in which both Wilson and Callaghan have kept the lowest possible profile, Callaghan only finally supporting the call for an inquiry when continuous pressure from the Labour Party and the press would have made it more embarrassing not to. (It is known that in the weeks before issuing his inquiry appeal Callaghan had been in frequent phone contact with Downing Street. Might he not already have known, when issuing his appeal, that Mrs Thatcher would turn it down?) Wilson, of course, did speak at the time of MI5 and BOSS plots against him, but age and ill-health seem to have reduced him to a state of bland benignity about everything. Callaghan is another matter. Harry Wharton, a former MI5 operative named by the Labour MP Dale Campbell-Savours as having played a part in the destabilisation campaign (though Mr Wharton fiercely denies this), has not unreasonably pointed out that he was given the CBE on Callaghan's recommendation and that if credence were lent to the allegations made by Mr Campbell-Savours, it would imply that Callaghan himself was conniving in such a campaign. Callaghan has now twice in succession picked a fight over Labour defence policy in an election run-up, acting for all the world as if he wishes to keep faith with the military establishment and actually prevent his own party returning to power. It is clear that there are a lot of burning questions to which Callaghan could give the answer if he cared to, and that he does not care to.

Callaghan, however, will never hold power again. Mrs Thatcher presumably will. The really tough questions relate to what her inner circle, and she herself, were up to in the mid 1970s. It is at this point that the picture achieves maximum murkiness. The Tory MP, Airey Neave, who had gained junior office under Macmillan but had been shunned by Heath, had decided in 1974 that Heath must go and begun to scheme for Thatcher's succession. Neave, who had an earlier career in MI9, maintained close links with the intelligence world, and it is difficult to believe that he was not, at the least, fully aware of its goings-on in this period, particularly since it now emerges that some members of MI5 had also come to the conclusion that Heath must be replaced by a tougher, harder Tory leader. We now know that this period saw large-scale law-breaking by the services: unauthorised phone-taps, mail-openings, burglaries and smear campaigns against both Heath and leading Labour and Liberal politicians. Some of the key questions to which we require answers are:

1. Mrs Thatcher's victory in the Tory leadership contest

represented an unprecedented triumph for the Tory Right and Thatcher herself was desperately conscious that she would not survive as leader if she did not win power at the first attempt. With Neave acting as her *éminence grise* she must surely have known of the MI5 destabilisation campaign against the Labour Government: but how far did she or Neave encourage it?

2. Those wild spirits who were dreaming of a military coup, or something very like it, would have had one question at the front of their minds: if they were able to dislodge the Labour Administration by unconstitutional means, would the Tory leadership accept power won in this way? The Thatcher inner circle of this period included such men as Robert Moss, who played a somewhat shadowy role in Chile, allegedly for the CIA, and was a leading apologist for the Pinochet coup. Was there any contact between the Thatcher entourage and such groups as Colonel David Stirling's GB 75? Did Mrs Thatcher know that Airey Neave had been involved in discussions about raising a 'resistance army' if Labour were returned in 1979?

3. Airey Neave was later killed by a car bomb outside the House of Commons. It has always been believed that this was the work of the IRA. However, Enoch Powell, normally one of the IRA's most implacable enemies, has suggested that the assassination was the work of the British and US intelligence services. (A former army intelligence officer, Captain Colin Wallace, has revealed that at one point the assassination of Ian Paisley was under active consideration by the services.) Mr Powell is unlikely to have made such an allegation without at least some circumstantial evidence. What is this evidence and has it been investigated?

4. The Thatcher period itself has seen an unprecedented politicisation both of patronage appointments and of the use to which theoretically non-political arms of the State have been put. It has also seen a considerable centralisation of police powers and, as we know from the Massiter revelations, a wide and continuing use of illegal phone-taps, etc. against those believed to be the Government's political opponents. We also know that Mrs Thatcher, when appointing Sir Maurice Oldfield to a senior intelligence post in Northern Ireland in 1979, was kept in ignorance of the fact that Sir Maurice was a homosexual, even though this had been known to senior figures in the intelligence community for many years. This suggests that, initially at least, the intelligence world was taking the same high-handed line with its political masters as before. The question is: has the Thatcher Government brought the intelligence service under control and, if so, to what uses is that control being put?

5. It is clear that our intelligence services have been far more closely controlled by their American counterparts than by any British authority: the great wave of 'bugging and burgling across London' seems, for example, to have taken place at the CIA's behest – to have replicated the Operation Chaos which Angleton had simultaneously launched in the US. How far is our intelligence service still primarily under foreign control?

6. Finally, what has happened to those intelligence operatives guilty of illegal actions: have they been sacked or retained? Or even promoted? (The news that the MI5 officer in charge of the 1970s smear campaign has just been re-engaged as an adviser to the service is hardly reassuring.) Are there still elements within MI5 and MI6 who retain their faith in Golitsyn's fantastic allegations? It is worth pointing out that in 1984, twenty-three years after Golitsyn's defection, a number of former intelligence officers thought it worth helping Golitsyn to publish his fantasies, declaring them to be of the greatest importance and relevance. Astonishingly, when the book, *New Lies for Old*, came out, *The Sunday Times* ran excerpts from it repeating the suggestion that the Sino–Soviet split was all a KGB fabrication and so on. When I mocked the book in a review, the editor of *The Sunday Times* Review Section wrote angrily that he had been assured by intelligence officers of the validity of Golitsyn's allegations. The idea that *The Sunday Times* would give preference to the views of extreme right-wing spooks over those put forward over the years by its own journalists was not the least remarkable feature of the affair. It seems clear that, in some circles at least, Golitsyn's fantasies are alive and kicking.

At the time of writing it seems unlikely, despite the heroic decision of *The Independent* to publish and be damned, that we are going to get any real answers to these questions. Mrs Thatcher has acted much as she did during the Westland Affair, denying absolutely what is quite generally known to be fact and suddenly announcing that an internal inquiry has taken place and found that everything is 100 per cent OK. Via their usual conduits within the Murdoch press and the *Telegraph* papers, both the security services and Sir Robert Armstrong have been declaring their willingness, even their enthusiasm, for an inquiry. How could they possibly have been ignorant of the fact that there had (according to Mrs Thatcher) just been an inquiry? Similarly, Mrs Thatcher tells us that MI5 did not mount a surveillance operation against the Labour Government in the mid 1970s, while CIA spokesmen have publicly confirmed CIA participation in just such an operation.

It would in any case be unwise to place much faith in the notion of an official inquiry into MI5. It is unlikely that an opponent of open government like Sir Robert Armstrong would favour such an exercise unless he were confident that it would be waste of time. An inquiry would mean that a committee of the great and good (Lord Franks yet again?), selected by Mrs Thatcher, would meet in camera and emerge with a bland report. Everything essentially fine. Rumours almost wholly unfounded. All responsible citizens will understand that national security precludes provision of any actual details. Some mistakes were made, but these were minor and no one is to blame. Valuable lessons learnt and long since put into practice. Rigorous discipline, fine tradition, record of responsibility, nation can take legitimate pride in service. Those who made the mistakes did so honestly and for patriotic motives. But in any case they are no longer with the service. In fact, most of them are dead. Indeed all of them are dead. Long ago. God save the Queen.

What we need is not a one-off inquiry but a permanent charter setting out exactly what the intelligence services are and are not allowed to do, and a permanent Parliamentary oversight committee on the American model. We also need to make a comprehensive move towards more open government.

Three newspapers are currently being sued and two others prohibited from carrying material that discusses allegations of treason on a grand scale. That is, the argument of national security is being used to prevent discussions of a gross threat to national security – and in that extraordinary cause the freedom of the press is taken to be expendable. How can we not feel bitter at the fact that this enormity is being practised on us at precisely the same time that the Irangate hearings in Washington are demonstrating the necessity of a free press and real Parliamentary scrutiny? Next year will see the 300th anniversary of the Glorious Revolution. It would be nice to think that we might celebrate this event by taking steps to control our irresponsible executive, and thereby emerge at last from our *ancien régime*.

References

Glees, Anthony (1987) *The Secrets of the Service: British Intelligence and Communist Subversion 1939–1951* (London: Cape).
Neuberger, Julia (ed.) (1987) *Freedom of Information . . . Freedom of the Individual?* (London: Macmillan).
Pincher, Chapman (1987) *Traitors: The Labyrinths of Treason* (London: Sidgwick).

Chapter 24

Spycatching

At most normal times the British believe that they have one of the best legal and judicial systems in the world. Then, from time to time, something happens which leads at least some of the public to believe that perhaps this is not so in the case of this or that particular judge. One of the benefits of the Spycatcher case was that it had the effect of showing, over a protracted period of time, that far more than this was wrong. The piece below was written in the wake of the Law Lords's decision that it was illegal to publish Peter Wright's book in England; illegal to quote excerpts from it (as The Independent had done); illegal to review the book; and illegal to report the proceedings of the trial concerning the book then going on in Australia.

Let us first dispose of *Spycatcher* – a well-written book which eschews a sensationalist style even when dealing with sensational matters (Wright, 1987). The widespread impression that the book is mainly about MI5 attempts to destabilise the Wilson Government is quite wrong – there are just a few pages about this. Most of the book is an account of the endless mole-hunting undertaken in the aftermath of the Burgess/Maclean/Philby affairs and the construction of Wright's case that the MI5 chief, Roger Hollis, was a Soviet spy. This latter question is, for Wright, very much the heart of the book, but I doubt whether readers will be universally convinced by his case or even that they will be chiefly interested in it. Most, one suspects, will savour more the chillingly casual way in which Wright details how even friendly embassies were bugged and assassination schemes plotted, and also the sheer le Carré-like richness of the bureaucratic and diplomatic intrigues, particularly when they involve characters as colourful as Edgar Hoover or James Angleton. Wright describes how Angleton ingeniously contrived to enjoy simultaneously his three main hobbies of drinking, smoking and fishing. Having brought a stretch of river, he buried bottles of Jack Daniels at regular intervals in the river bed, so that he could always fish with a whisky and a cigarette in hand.

Wright himself emerges as a believable source – though caution is perhaps advisable: he is a professional dissembler. He is that peculiarly English type, the man recruited from below into one of the Establishment's magic circles, who embraces the Establishment's (conservative) principles with enthusiasm, only to explode finally in rage when he finds that those principles are a fraud. Specifically, Wright feels he was cheated out of his pension by ungentlemanly gentlemen and seems to have written this book for revenge as well as for profit. From time to time a dramatic name or sensational detail is thrown in front of the reader with a sort of studied naïvety, as if Wright is unaware that it is a veritable hand grenade. But his own book shows how, over and over again, he was able to turn the merest smidgeon of a clue into deadly evidence of betrayal: he is decidedly not naïve, and if he drops names, it is for a purpose. He seems, though, to have made his own assessment of what he can and cannot responsibly say – and certainly the book gets much thinner in explosive detail as it advances toward the present. Wright is clearly still holding back a good deal. If I were the head of MI5 or the Prime Minister, I would be far more worried about grenades still in Wright's armoury than anything he has said here.

Readers of the *LRB* will need no reminder that the Law Lords have made the writing of a review of this book a matter of grave legal risk. For all I know, even what I have written above is illegal in their eyes. What they would certainly regard as heinous would be to write a proper, long review in which one quoted Wright directly or extensively described the contents of the book – the sort of thing I would normally do for the *LRB*. More wicked still, one could go to the Australian High Commission in London, obtain copies of the *Melbourne Age* or *Sydney Morning Herald* and then reproduce from them reports of the *Spycatcher* trial going on in Australia. One can without fear publish accounts of trials in the USSR or Albania, or anywhere else where, as here, the judges know their duty to the government, but you cannot report what is going on in that Australian court. The most severely unfunny side of things is the rapid and arbitrary way in which the legal goal-posts are being moved about, in which new rules and laws are being made without public discussion and outside the legislative process. Under our judge-invented law it has not only suddenly become illegal to publish a book review or cite Australian newspapers, but a vast new legal doctrine has been invented: that an injunction against X also binds Y. What if X has never heard of Y, does not even know about the injunction against him? Ignorance of the law is presumably no excuse: so that doing or writing anything is now dangerous.

And one must always remember that there is no legal aid to protect freedom of expression. If, for example, a rich and powerful corporation or individual decided, as a result of something I have written, to launch suit against either me or the *LRB*, we would be utterly at his mercy. Any attempt to resist his suit would undoubtedly bankrupt me and close the *LRB*, for neither I nor the *London Review* has the financial resources necessary to fight an opponent with a really deep purse. Even to get into the ring with such an opponent one needs to have many hundreds of thousands of pounds to spare: it is not a question of poverty, just a matter of not being exceedingly rich. Our lawyers, knowing the draconian libel law, which means that almost all libel suits are won, would advise that discretion was the better part of valour. So even if the *LRB* and I were innocent in law and in fact, we would, in effect, be found guilty on grounds of insufficient wealth. Indeed, our lawyers would hasten to advise us to make truly cringing apologies in order to minimise our damages. Lack of great wealth makes one so guilty that the only responsible thing to do would be to say we were wrong when we knew we were right – to commit a sort of private perjury. It would be unwise to protest. And one must remember that our judges are, by definition, rich men. A Law Lord earns £71,400 a year; our senior judges are recruited from the comfortable upper-middle classes and from among barristers earning hundreds of thousands a year.

The latest antics of the Law Lords have deservedly created a storm. But no one who has studied the process of the British law and the behaviour of the English judiciary as it touches questions of freedom of expression can be in the least surprised at this fresh monstrosity. It is worth setting out where we stand.

One starts with the fact that we have no constitution. Generations of English schoolchildren have had the vast mystification practised upon them that we *do* have a constitution (until recently you could do an A level called 'The British Constitution'). But this constitution was not written down, so you could not read it, use it, study it or be sure exactly what was in it. But you could feel very, very proud of it. One can imagine the general hilarity which would greet the claim by, say, the ruler of Uganda that his country had a constitution, but that it existed only in the mind. Those who wish to go parroting solemnly on about an unwritten constitution here might reflect that this is precisely the sort of claim that an Idi Amin might have made there.

The lack of a constitution or bill of rights means two things. First, nowhere does our law positively uphold freedom of expression – it is a freedom negatively defined as the things one can say or write through the chinks left in our draconian laws on official secrets and libel. This is quite bad enough, and quite routinely leads to the situation where one cannot reprint in Britain things that have appeared in reputable foreign newspapers. Secondly, it means that our judges clamber happily into the yawning gap thus left.

And our judges are a problem all of their own. They are exclusively political appointees; they are, as a group, notably illiberal – anti-black and anti-Semitic feeling is not uncommon and women are still often shamefully treated by many judges; and they are more executive-minded than any other judiciary this side of the Iron Curtain. They also tend to invent (or disregard) laws when they want to. The classic case here was *Shaw* v. *DPP*(1961), in which the Law Lords, wishing to ban a certain publication but finding no law allowing them to do so, simply invented a new offence of 'conspiracy to corrupt public morals'. When it was pointed out that the laws passed by Parliament knew no such offence, the Law Lords asserted that the courts were the ultimate guardians of 'the moral welfare of the State' and that this gave them 'residual power, where no statute has yet intervened'. Quite apart from this extraordinary act of self-arrogation, it is difficult to imagine any group further out of touch with contemporary morality than the Law Lords. Yet the years since 1961 have seen hundreds of convictions for offences against this impudently invented law. On the whole, it has been pornographers who have suffered, but this 'law' has also been used to harass *Oz* and the *International Times*.

This was followed in 1972 by the 'thalidomide trial' in which the Distillers company sought to prevent *The Sunday Times* from publishing articles about the plight of the thalidomide children. The Law Lords found, on contempt of court grounds, that the articles were indeed an unfair form of pressure on the company, upheld Distillers and gagged *The Sunday Times* – until the European Court of Human Rights overturned the judgement in the cause of freedom of expression. Parliament later attempted to reconcile the British and European notions on contempt of court in the Contempt of Court Act – but Lord Diplock speedily announced a new law of his own, making it clear that Parliament had not done this and that the new Act could even open up fresh ways of curtailing press freedom. Then in 1975 the Attorney-General sought to prevent *The Sunday*

Times from publishing the Crossman Diaries. The Lord Chief Justice, faced with the difficulty that there was no law forbidding indiscretions by (dead) Cabinet Ministers, announced a new 'law' under which the courts could decide what opinions Ministers might express about Cabinet discussions – but then allowed publication on the grounds that the Diaries dealt with events a decade old.

In all this, the chief concern of the judges is to try to see things the Government way. Lord Reid, in *Conway* v. *Rimmer* (1968), best summarised the attitude of the Law Lords. The premature disclosure of Cabinet Minutes was, he said, in no way allowable, for

> ... disclosure would create or fan ill-informed or captious public or political criticism. The business of government is difficult enough as it is, and no government could contemplate with equanimity the inner workings of the government machine being exposed to the gaze of those ready to criticise without adequate knowledge of the background.

Probably only an English judge could believe that the right way to cope with people who are ill-informed and who lack adequate knowledge is to prevent them having more information. In France, by the way, a list of the projects approved by the Cabinet is routinely issued to the press the day after each meeting – and such a practice is normal in many other countries too. Once again, the whole Army is out of step with our Johnny.

In 1981 the judges even discovered that censorship might extend to covering what went on in open court. In the case of *Home Office* v. *Harman* the Law Lords found Ms Harman guilty of contempt for having communicated to a journalist a copy of a document which had already been read out in open court. Had the journalist taped the trial or taken it down in shorthand, there would have been no case. But Lord Denning defended this manifest absurdity with further stern warnings: 'the danger of disclosure is that critics . . . will seize on this confidential information so as to seek changes in government policy, or to condemn it.' Who but an English judge would describe efforts to criticise or change government policy as 'the danger'?

English judges are so slavishly executive-minded that it is probably seldom necessary for them to be told precisely what the Government would like. But it would be folly to think this could never happen. As both the recent books on the Stephen Ward case have shown, his trial was rigged from beginning to end. The Police threatened and blackmailed witnesses into lying on a grand scale and

Lord Chief Justice Parker went through extraordinary antics in order to try to prejudice the result of the trial. According to Knightley and Kennedy's *An Affair of State*, the judge in the case, Mr Justice Marshall, was overheard in conversation with 'a person very high up in the judiciary', who asked: 'Are you certain that you'll be able to get him?' Marshall replied: 'Don't worry, I'll get him on the immoral earnings charge.' Similarly, Lord Denning appears to have been told that Ward was telling the truth when he asserted that he was an MI5 agent, but Denning omitted this vital information from his Report and asserted instead that Ward was a crypto-Communist. The fact that all this judicial bad behaviour should occur in connection with a trial which was of enormous importance to the government of the day is, to say the least, fishy. Judges are not merely appointed and promoted by politicians but come from the same class, frequently attended the same schools and universities, and belong to the same clubs and Masonic Lodges. A quiet word in the right ear from time to time is normal behaviour for members of the human race, and despite occasional appearances to the contrary, judges are members of the human race.

The *Spycatcher* ruling merely confirms that it will be no good bringing in a bill of rights (which will have to be interpreted by the judiciary) unless we also do something about our judges. Bluntly, a good number of them need to be sacked or forcibly retired. The judicial retirement age of 75 needs to be lowered by at least ten years. And if we are to have a politically-appointed judiciary, let them be recruited from outside the ranks of barristers and their appointment be made the exclusive prerogative of the Parliamentary Opposition. The British quality press is an institution in which we can take greater national pride than we can in our judges: the former is still the best in the world. We must not let the bad drive out the good.

The whole quality press is now under judicial attack: the only papers to behave the way the Law Lords want are the *Express*, *Mail* and *Sun*. Best of all is the *Sun*: at every stage of the Wright affair it has abused Wright, praised the Government and applauded the judges. Indeed, the *Sun* could be said to be *the* judges' paper. Unlike the qualities, it has never attracted the adverse attention of the Law Lords or Lord Denning or the Attorney-General. Sure, it invents news; that's OK. Sure, its election coverage consisted of Page Three girls wearing Tory rosettes on – well, you can guess where. True, it featured articles by Joseph Stalin ('Why I'm voting Labour') and Winston Churchill ('Why I'm voting for Maggie'). The actual authorship of these articles may be controversial but no complaint has been received from Messrs Stalin and Churchill, so the *Sun* is legally in the clear. In any case, the *Sun* is owned by Rupert Murdoch, who unswervingly supports Mrs Thatcher and is exceedingly rich. The Soaraway *Sun* Newspaper of the Year, say Lord Lords. I Could Really Drop My Knickers For Those Cuddly Judges, says Page Three Linda. Those Law Lords in Spanking Form *Again*, says Sam Fox, see Centre Pages.

Peter Wright is watching all this from far away. I hope he is enjoying it – and reflecting upon it. Throughout his career he chased down Communists and pinkos because they subverted the Establishment he held dear. He has now demonstrated that what they could do was as nothing compared to the subversive power of telling just some of the truth. Let us hope he tells us more.

References

Wright, Peter (1987) *Spycatcher: The Candid Autobiography of a Senior Intelligence Officer* (New York: Viking).

Chapter 25

Rainbow Warriors

'A hoodlum's job done by honest men. With us, you only kill for reasons of state.' This is the opinion of Maurice Robert, research director of the French secret service (and later Ambassador to Gabon), as recorded by Faligot and Krop (1986) in their excellent and well-researched book. It is difficult to accept such a verdict on the DGSE (originally the BCRA, then the DGER, then the SDECE). A more accurate summing-up would be that the service has proved both ruthless and frequently incompetent, that it has known its fine romantic hours and impressive coups, but that it has depended on a low-grade and poorly educated cadre prone to tough-guy tactics, and that many of its problems derive from the political purges to which it has been subject, and the chronic distrust it arouses in all its political masters. None of the purges and shake-ups has ever been quite complete: they have always left a *cave* within the organisation owing loyalty to the *ancien régime* and not above sabotaging their new political masters in the hope that this will help bring the old lot back. Politicians, knowing this, act accordingly: in the Greenpeace affair, the Elysée first heard of the disaster in New Zealand, not from the DGSE, which comes under the Defence Ministry, but from the Interior Ministry, whose internal secret police, the DST, routinely tap the phones of the DGSE. Similarly, the Government was furious to discover that in the frogman training school whose agents sank the *Rainbow Warrior*, a portrait of Giscard still hung where the obligatory portrait of Mitterrand should have been. The training school has since been closed down.

Mitterrand himself was involved with the secret service as early as 1944. The BCRA (as it then was) represented a simple outgrowth of the wartime Gaullist network, and Mitterrand, then in London, worked closely with Jacques Foccart – later de Gaulle's spy chief and *bête noire* of the Left – on the romantic but generally disastrous mission to parachute agents into occupied Europe ahead of the

Allied armies in order to liberate French deportees from the camps. So many agents were killed to no effect that the project was suspended – though not before one agent had made a quite wonderful haul at Niederdorf: among the detainees he found the former (and future) Socialist premier Léon Blum and his wife, the former Austrian Chancellor, Schuschnigg, a son of the Hungarian dictator Admiral Horthy, Mgr Piguet, Bishop of Clermont-Ferrand, Prince Xavier of Bourbon-Parma and Prince Frederick of Prussia, the entire Greek General Staff, a nephew of Molotov and a cousin of Churchill. This strange ensemble dined together in the camp that night (with champagne). Blum, though fresh out of Buchenwald, wanted, above all, to know about the latest French election results.

For a while the BCRA was mainly preoccupied with wartime sequels. Under the urgings of the Communist Minister of Industry, Ferdinand Porsche was grabbed and set to work at Renault (when the Communists left the Government Porsche was sent back to jail). A director of the Junkers aircraft firm was grabbed from Vienna, where he was staying with an Austrian actress and her little daughter, the future sex symbol Romy Schneider. He was set to work at Dassault and ultimately helped to devise the Mirage. The BCRA also found Klaus Barbie and interrogated him: finding he was already an American agent, they had to let him go. But the man the BCRA really wanted to get was Franco: plans were laid to destabilise his regime and assassinate him – until the British vetoed the idea.

In these early years, the British SIS and the American OSS effectively laid down the parameters within which the French were allowed to operate. Thanks to them, French agents got pulled into the crazy and murderous scheme to place anti-Communist guerrillas in Albania, the Ukraine and Russia. Worse, the French had to be passive partners while a similar operation was mounted by the British and Americans on French soil in 1946–7. Against all the evidence, the two Allied services had somehow convinced themselves that the Communists were plotting revolution in France: so an embryonic guerrilla movement was set afoot, with arms caches scattered throughout France (especially in Brittany, where the SAS and the British controller, Earl Jellicoe, appear to have been particularly active). Money was gathered from the Catholic Church and 'safe' conservative elements recruited – which, of course, frequently meant Vichyites and extreme right-wingers. To their horror and naïve surprise, the Allies then discovered that these elements were planning a Vichyite coup – the Blue Plan – which was to commence with the assassination of de Gaulle, the blame thrown on to the Communists, and the Right riding back to power on the inevitable wave of indignation, using the arms caches so helpfully supplied. The French secret service, born of the Resistance, had had to sit by as foreign secret services came close to restoring Vichy. By 1949, under similar pressures, the French were rounding up hundreds of refugee Spanish Republicans as suspect Soviet agents.

By this time the Socialists (SFIO) had taken over the SDECE (as it now was), sweeping most of the Gaullists away and installing loyal SFIO men at every level. One such was the remarkable Léon Kastenbaum, former secretary to the revolutionary socialist leader, Jules Guèsde, and later director of the Tour de France. Kastenbaum maintained close relations with all the parties of the Socialist International and not a little 'dirty money' got passed on to sometimes quite unlikely clients – the early career of Salvador Allende appears to have been a major beneficiary.

Even by the late 1940s, however, the focus of SDECE attention had shifted to the colonies. It was here, especially in Indo-China, Black Africa, the Middle East and North Africa, that the SDECE found its true focus and built up formidable networks. None the less, there were a fair number of Clouseau-like disasters. In 1949 it was learnt with horror that the Communist Vietminh radio was broadcasting verbatim the secret report of the French chief of staff on the Indo-China situation within weeks of its being written. The trail of leaks traced proved so embarrassing to both the military and the government that the only solution seemed to be to declassify the report, thereby obviating the necessity of bringing anyone to trial (though the chief of staff was quietly sacked).

Similarly, in 1952 an SDECE agent in Vietnam discovered simultaneously that the Director of the Franco-Chinese Bank was actually the Vietminh's treasurer, and that there was a secret arms ring supplying the Vietminh's needs via crooked French merchants and Haiphong port officials. When the agent reported, he was ignored; when he insisted, he was sacked and threatened. He fled to France and revealed all in a book. A commission of inquiry was set up by a scandalised parliament but the Ministry of Finance refused all co-operation with the inquiry. Even so, the commission was able to discover that large sums were flowing through the accounts in question to de Gaulle's RPF party. Like most French scandals, this one was never properly cleared up. No doubt it afforded Ho Chi Minh considerable amusement.

The beginning of the Algerian war in 1954, and the rise of Nasser, brought the SDECE into collaboration with Israel's MOSSAD as well as with MI6. At one point the SDECE and MOSSAD decided to assassinate the Algerian leader Ben Bella, and explosives were delivered to the French Embassy in Cairo by agents operating (presumably with British cognisance) out of Cyprus. At the same time Franco-British plans were afoot to assassinate Nasser. But Nasser acted too quickly, nationalising the Suez Canal: war ensued and diplomatic relations were broken off. It was not until 1963 that relations were restored and the SDECE was able to retrieve its explosives from the Embassy building in Cairo. Meanwhile the traditionally bad relations between the French and British services had not been improved by the discovery by Service 7 (the SDECE's section specialising in the opening of diplomatic mail) that Egyptian agents in Britain were opening all French diplomatic mail. No doubt the question of how Nasser always managed to be one step ahead was further discussed in the light of this discovery.

Meanwhile, thanks largely to the remarkable Jean Violet – an international lawyer with strong Swiss and Catholic connections and a close friend of Antoine Pinay – the SDECE had become heavily involved in the Vatican's own holy war against Communism. Embroiled with the OSS (later the CIA) during the war, in the immediate post-war period the Vatican had three separate institutes training agents for missions behind the Iron Curtain. At the Papal Russian College, the Russicum, for example, 'missionaries' were trained in Russian language and history, hand-to-hand combat, firearms, and various chemical and machine-based intelligence techniques, before being parachuted behind the lines. The SDECE, through Violet, had close links with the Vatican's services (and the support of a good number of cardinals in the know) and was able to use these connections for a variety of purposes: thus the Vatican delegation at the UN moved to divert Afro-Asian pressure over Algeria, and Church circles in Switzerland helped to secure the first foreign sales of the Mirage fighter. The trouble was that the French were not alone: when the French lost a helicopter order in Lebanon to the American Bell Company, they angrily pointed out that the Papal Nuncio in Beirut was on the Bell pay roll.

While the Vatican seems to have been happily promiscuous in its links, the Swiss were to get fed up with the way the SDECE used them as a sort of offshore dirty tricks facility, penetrating the Red Cross and the Government itself. Sometimes the French just had bad luck: when they decided to poison the Cameroonian nationalist Félix Moumié in Geneva, the idea was to slip him a slow-working poison so that he would be back in exile in Guinea before he died, and his death could be blamed on Sekou Touré. The agent slipped Moumié one poisoned drink, but Moumié neglected to drink it. He was slipped another – and then drank both together, dying almost immediately, and scandalously. The Swiss then discovered that their own secret service, the 'BUPO', had been deeply penetrated by the French, who had a whole network of phone-taps in Switzerland. When a BUPO double agent was arrested, it emerged that René Dubois, the Swiss Procurator-General, was also a French agent, and had furnished the SDECE with hundreds of documents and even expelled Algerian nationalists into France at the command of the SDECE. Hearing that the balloon had gone up, Dubois blew his own brains out. The Swiss were much vexed and, for a while, Switzerland ceased to be such friendly territory for the SDECE.

On coming to power, de Gaulle took a directly personal interest in the SDECE – and asked them what they could tell him about the Russians. He was 'ulcerated at the banality' of what followed, for the fact was that the service was far too embroiled in North African affairs to bother much about the USSR. True, the SDECE had combined with the Chinese intelligence service to frustrate a CIA coup against Prince Sihanouk of Cambodia in 1958, but this was more to do with neo-colonial instinct than, as de Gaulle saw it, a more commendable wish to face up to the great powers. De Gaulle preached the notion that France should have 'a great intelligence service – like the British'. None the less, though he placed his own men in the SDECE, he seems to have remained largely preoccupied with arranging coups and counter-coups in Black Africa, through the services of Jacques Foccart. (Foccart had a twenty-minute audience with de Gaulle every day – no mere cabinet minister ever dreamt of such access.) Michel Debré, de Gaulle's prime minister, played an equally active part in running the SDECE. For all Foccart's notoriety, the fact is that de Gaulle and Debré – like not a few politicians before and since – found the world of intelligence and secret *coups de main* too fascinating to leave alone. Great as Foccart's power was, he was also, in some sense, a fall-guy: de Gaulle and Debré's responsibility for the 'dirty tricks' of the period was quite equal to his.

Inevitably, North Africa continued to be of dominating importance, but the situation was now heavily complicated by de Gaulle's bitter resentment at the almost neo-colonial nature of the Anglo-American relationship with France during the war and in the immediate post-war period – and his determination that this should never recur. The result was a fierce if undeclared war between the CIA and SDECE throughout the Third World. The CIA, furious at the way the French had tipped Sihanouk off about their impending coup, reciprocated in 1959 (together with the West German BND) by tipping Bourguiba off about the extensive 'Magenta' network through which the French had sought to maintain control in Tunisia ever since independence. Not only had the French placed agents in the Red Cross throughout the Middle East but they were actually listening in to Bourguiba's private telephone. The Tunisian secret service pounced. A key French agent 'fell' from the fourth floor of the building where they were interrogating him; the whole network was rolled up; and French agents scattered in confusion and panic. One of those who fled was Armand Belvisi. Joining the OAS, he blew up the left-wing Maspero bookshop in Paris and then organised the 1961 assassination attempt on de Gaulle at Pont-sur-Seine. Belvisi was the real-life 'Jackal'.

The OAS could clearly count on the sympathies of some SDECE agents, so de Gaulle purged the organisation and then employed it pitilessly against the OAS. In 1966, however, came the Ben Barka affair, with the Moroccan nationalist leader kidnapped in Paris in broad daylight, never to be seen again. De Gaulle was livid, for it seemed clear that SDECE agents had been involved. Even de Gaulle, it was now clear, had failed to master the *piscine* (SDECE headquarters are next to a swimming pool). The General blamed Pompidou – for whereas Debré had enjoyed playing spies, Pompidou, his successor as Prime Minster, felt the revulsion of the true Enarque for the poorly-educated tough-guys, bagmen and *barbouzes* of the SDECE. Although the SDECE was the responsibility of his office, Pompidou wanted to know as little as possible about it all. Realising that the SDECE mice could give trouble even to a watchful cat, de Gaulle removed the SDECE from the premier's charge and handed it over to the Defence Ministry. Pompidou had been badly burnt, and on becoming President, appointed the formidable Alexandre de Marenches as his SDECE chief with firm instructions to take the organisation in hand – and clear it out of 'anti-American' ultra-Gaullists. Under de Marenches, the SDECE strengthened its already powerful position in the Middle East, to the point where it alone knew in advance of the precise date of the start of the 1973 Yom Kippur war – information which it carefully avoided passing on to the Israelis. The close relations with the intelligence services of South Africa, Japan, Spain, Greece, Turkey and Denmark, begun under de Gaulle, continued, so that some agents became a little uncomfortable about the reactionary company they were keeping. With Franco still in power in Spain, the Colonels in Greece and BOSS in the hands of Vorster and Van Den Berg (both of whom had been imprisoned for Nazi sympathies during the war), almost half their contacts seemed to be Fascists.

Under Giscard, this trend continued, especially after his top-secret 'Safari Club' was formed, linking the SDECE to the Egyptian, Moroccan and Saudi Arabian services, as also to the Shah's SAVAK, in a great crusade against left-wing regimes in Africa. But, as often happens, the greatest problems arose with friendly regimes, particularly those of Tombalbaye in Chad and Bokassa in the Central African 'Empire'. Tombalbaye owed his downfall to his confiding in two Parisian prostitutes. The SDECE maintains close links with the luxury brothels for which Paris is famous and not a few of the girls are on the payroll, for their clients include many visiting politicians and diplomats. While visiting one of these houses in early 1975, Tombalbaye let slip that he was planning a great coup in the gold market. The SDECE were much interested, and told the girls that they wanted to know where on earth the permanently bankrupt state of Chad was going to find the money for this. The answer, it emerged, was that Tombalbaye was on the point of selling off his country's oil and gas exploration rights to American oil companies. This was clearly out of order and a few months later the SDECE arranged a mutiny in Chad in which Tombalbaye was killed.

Bokassa became an embarrassment largely because of Giscard's close relations with him and his penchant for big-game hunting in Chad. Bokassa's Amin-like lunacies could be tolerated, but when he started massacring schoolchildren Giscard's own image began to suffer by association. In 1979, after a second massacre of schoolchildren, it was decided that Bokassa had to go – but Bokassa then let it be known that, if threatened, he would release documents concerning the lavish gifts he had made to French politicians, including Giscard. In the subsequent SDECE-organised coup a special team of paratroopers were sent in to cart off the Chad archives wholesale to Paris. But, France being France, SDECE agents grumbled that they were being used in the private service of an individual and incriminating papers were allowed to leak out.

The coming to power of the Left in 1981 represented a crisis in two senses. The SDECE feared the worst and there was a great deal of burning of documents relating to its spying activities on French political parties and trade unions. On the other hand, the Common Program signed by the Socialists and Communists in 1972 had committed them to the simple abolition of the SDECE. Appalled, a number of SDECE officials had made contact in the mid 1970s with the Socialists' Defence spokesman, Charles Hernu. Hernu became a strong advocate of the service (as he was of all the other military services), and prevailed on his old friend Mitterrand to come along to a series of regular meetings with SDECE officials, from which emerged a plan for a 'reformed' service. In 1981 Mitterrand carefully omitted the abolition pledge from his Presidential platform and even tried, after the election, to persuade de Marenches to stay on – without success.

Like de Gaulle before him, Mitterrand was appalled to find that the SDECE's intelligence about the Eastern bloc was abysmal to non-existent and ordered a sweeping reorientation of effort in that direction. The service was to be re-formed into the DGSE and strictly forbidden to operate inside France (as the SDECE had been – though that had never stopped it). There was to be a sweeping purge of 'unhealthy elements'; the service's office in South Africa was to be shut down; and, not least, the DGSE was to be computerised – a full twenty years and more after the CIA and MI6.

All of which sounded promising – but problems soon arose. The purge of 'unhealthy elements' was, inevitably, incomplete. Mitterrand's replacement for Foccart (as intelligence specialist for African affairs attached directly to the Elysée) was the shadowy Guy Penne – and he, like the new DGSE boss, Pierre Marion, Hernu himself, and a number of the other top military and intelligence officials, were all exceptionally devoted Freemasons. Hernu was anyway a soft touch for anything military and had no need of this extra Masonic loyalty to those whose boss he was supposed to be. When Mitterrand became discontented with Marion because of his utter failure over terrorism, and, perhaps even more, because of the long and boring lectures he was prone to inflict on the President, Hernu tried desperately to save his fellow Mason – though in vain. Meanwhile the DGSE had slipped back into its old ways, collaborating with the Moroccans and South Africans in support of UNITA in Angola, and, after Régis Debray's trip to Afghanistan, with the CIA in support of the Afghan guerrillas.

Against this background it is difficult to feel too surprised by the Greenpeace affair. The main facts are well enough known – of the books under review Dyson (1986) is by far the surer, better-written guide – and they suggest that little has really changed. The DGSE and its predecessors have never, after all, had principled objections to committing acts of violence in other people's countries. Once again, the Minister of Defence seemed to be under the control of the DGSE instead of the other way round. The ludicrous incompetence and braggadocio of Dominque Prieur, Alain Mafart (both of whom are still in a New Zealand jail) and the other French agents suggests that the era of the *barbouze* is far from over. Once again the service contained a sufficient *cave* of opponents of the Government to ensure that some highly embarrassing facts leaked out. But once again the collective hush-up has been good enough to leave many key questions unanswered.

One of these is what role, if any, the British played in the affair. Clearly, the suggestion in the ill-fated Tricot Report that the French DGSE might have been the helpless victim of a British frame-up is nonsense. And it also seems possible that the decision to buy the dinghy used in the expedition against the *Rainbow Warrior* in London was an attempt to lead a false trail back to Britain. Thereafter, one is less sure. The DGSE has always hated being unfavourably compared to MI6 and relations between the two services have long been such that either would be far happier striking a deal with the KGB than with the other. The British have always regarded the DGSE, perhaps not too unfairly, as exemplifying a peculiar combination of national and personal egoism and therefore not to be trusted with any secrets. This distrust, however well-merited, was deeply resented by the French even before Gaullism erected such *méfiance* into a national ideology. In a variety of Third World situations – such as the Biafran war – MI6 found itself in a virtual war with the French service.

This history has left both services with an almost overpowering wish to tweak the other's tail. Shortly after the Brighton bomb attempt on Mrs Thatcher, agents accompanying Mitterrand on a trip to the United Kingdom smuggled explosives in with them in order to jeer at the laxness of British security. The explosives were found and a DGSE agent expelled. The fact that MI5 had been so distrustful of the French as to check for explosives, let alone the decision to make the expulsion so humiliatingly public, greatly wounded French *amour propre* – and left the British feeling, once again, that the French were impossible. Then, according to Shears and Gidley (1986), a disaffected Gaullist DGSE agent leaked advance notice of the Greenpeace plan to a Western agent in Paris. As a result, the matter was brought up at the weekly UKUSA meeting (involving the US, UK, Australian, Canadian and New Zealand intelligence services) in Whitehall a whole two months before the fateful attack on the *Rainbow Warrior*. According to Shears and Gidley, the news failed, for essentially bureaucratic reasons, to reach the New Zealand Police. This may or may not be true. Either way, no doubt, MI6 enjoyed the discomfiture of the French, and the French, knowing they were being laughed at, hated it.

As a consequence of the Greenpeace affair, the DGSE now has its fourth different director since 1981 and yet another purge – no doubt, once again, incomplete – has been taking place. It seems certain that the new Chirac government will want to make yet more changes, putting in its own men, probably including yet another new director, and will then want to purge the Mitterrandistes. But with a Socialist President still in office and quite capable of winning the Presidential election in 1988, the situation will remain fluid.

In the end, though, the DGSE's best protection is a national public opinion which finds it normal that their government should display a ruthless egoism in the furthering of their interests abroad, that it should have a 'dirty tricks' department to assist in that, and that the exposure or punishment of such activities by indignant foreigners is an unforgivable wound to the national *amour propre*. During the recent election campaign, the Front National leader, Le Pen, offered a place on his FN list to Dominique Prieur. From her Auckland cell she politely declined: but the offer reflected the French mood. Prieur and Mafart are now seen as martyrs, as political prisoners for France in a foreign land, and Hernu, who sent them on their mission, has just achieved a major electoral triumph as his reward. He is undeniably popular and more than one Le Pen voter can be heard voicing admiration for this Socialist. New Zealand meat imports to France have hit a damaging but invisible brick wall and their wool imports are being examined bale by bale before being allowed in: all this to force New Zealand to act 'properly' by breaking its own laws and letting Prieur and Mafart go. Mere elections will not change this.

Indeed, as soon as the new parliament met in April a fresh hue and cry over the Greenpeace affair broke out, with Le Pen demanding the creation of 'a parliamentary inter-party group for the liberation of Prieur and Mafart' and Chirac's new Defence Minister asserting that he had seen the Greenpeace dossier and could only say that such missions were 'quite routinely' discussed with the President. Chirac himself has not forgotten that when he served as Giscard's Prime Minister in 1974–6 Giscard had had bugs planted in his premier's office. A grand sweep against bugs planted by Mitterrand's agents has been carried out in all the ministries, including Chirac's own office; and the head of the internal security service, the DST, has already been replaced by Chirac's own man. Even more tellingly, not only Maurice Robert but the legendary Foccart himself have been recalled to service. *Plus ça change . . .*

In 1981, on the eve of Mitterrand's presidential victory, I met M. Charles Hernu in his mairie at Villeurbanne, near Lyons. Mme Hernu swept in as we talked – a handsome middle-aged woman accompanied, after the

French manner, by a vast dog on a steel chain. M. Hernu had been one of Mitterrand's closest associates from the earliest days – he had run his presidential election campaign back in 1965 – and he clearly felt confident, not only of his friend's impending victory, but of high cabinet office in the government Mitterrand would then appoint. M. Hernu, a large, burly, bearded man, exuded a sense of great physical power and managerial competence. I gave him a copy of my book about the French Left and he autographed one of his own books for me. The book, entitled Nous les Grands, featured a nuclear submarine on its cover and was, I thought, an oddly chauvinist work for such a committed Socialist. The book, together with the huge dog, the steel chain and the burly, bearded man, left a composite image of power and muscularity in my mind.

I have often since recalled that scene in the light of what later befell M. Hernu. Forced to resign over the Rainbow Warrior affair, M. Hernu for long continued to deny all responsibility in the matter, but within the Socialist party he was increasingly shunned. When the affaire Luchaire broke, involving covert arms shipments to Iran, it was discovered that some of the Iranian proceeds had found their way into Socialist Party funds in Villeurbanne, prompting a virtual stampede away from M. Hernu by his erstwhile associates. M. Hernu held an angry press conference in the mairie. Abandoned now not only by his party but by his wife, M. Hernu had a new young wife (his former secretary) by his side, but amidst his denials of these new charges he now furiously admitted responsibility in the Rainbow Warrior affair. Happily, the voters of Villeurbanne have continued to regard M. Hernu as a local hero, badly treated by the Parisian press. One retains the impression of a man of great talents, tragically wasted. The story ended more happily for Prieur and Mafart, both outrageously spirited out of jail by Chirac prior to the 1988 elections. The Rainbow Warrior affair itself remains the single greatest stain on the record of the Mitterrand administration.

References

Dyson, John (1986) *Sink the 'Rainbow': An Inquiry into the Greenpeace Affair* (London: Gollancz).

Faligot, R. and Krop, P. (1986) *La Piscine: Les Services Secrets Français 1944–1984* (Paris: Seuil).

Shears, Richard and Gidley, Isobelle (1986) *The 'Rainbow Warrior' Affair* (London: Allen & Unwin).

Chapter 26
The Age of the Vampire

It is impossible to read about vampires without becoming fascinated by the figure of Montague Summers. I really had met someone who thought Summers believed himself to be a vampire, but the publication of the article below drew a letter of anguished protest from someone who had known Summers, denying that he had ever entertained such a belief. What really seems beyond question is that Summers did believe in vampires. 'Outside the districts we have specified', he writes, 'the appearances of the vampire are rare, whilst in his own domain even now he holds horrid sway, and people fear not so much the ghost as the return of the dead body floridly turgescent and foully swollen with blood, endued with some abominable and devilish life.' Summers tells us, by the way, that werewolves, who suffer from the same unquenchable thirst (sitis immodica) for blood, are close kin to the vampire and, not surprisingly, are particularly prevalent in Livonia, Bohemia and Hungary. But the good Summers has various stratagems against vampires that Hammer Films seem never to have heard of. Thus, if an animal of ill omen (especially a cat) should jump over a corpse, it is highly likely to become a vampire unless the corpse has two sack-needles driven into it, with mustard seed scattered on the roof and the doors barricaded with brambles and thorns against other vampires. If you do have to deal with a vampire, a number of things work besides those used by Peter Cushing against Christopher Lee. Whitethorn and buckthorn, as well as garlic, are good for keeping Dracula away and he can be decapitated with a gravedigger's shovel. He can also be killed by a silver bullet blessed by a priest, but if you do it that way you must be particularly careful not to lay out the dead (i.e. really dead) body of the vampire in the full moonlight or he will then revive 'with redoubled vigour and malevolence'.

In a cultural sense, the twentieth century has been the great age of debunking, of secularisation and demythologisation. It is not just that we believe less in Gods and superstitions: it is impossible now for racial mythologies about Jews, Aryans and blacks to get a respectable hearing; and in large areas of social and private life the old taboos have fallen like sand-castles before the advancing tide of rationalism. In a sense, we are all agnostics now.

There is one great exception to this: the vampire myth. To be sure, the myth is hardly a modern creation. But the audience and resonance this myth has achieved in the twentieth century is quite unparallelled.

In mid nineteenth-century England, a number of attempts were made to exploit the literary and theatrical possibilities of the myth, but apart from Thomas Prest's penny dreadful, *Varney the Vampire or the Feast of Blood* (1847), none of them made much impact. Theatrical attempts to depict vampirism, such as St John Dorset's *The Vampire* (1821), simply never reached the stage. The first stage production seems to have been Reece's *The Vampire* in 1872, but the subject was treated strictly as a joke, and Edward Terry, acting the vampire, was greeted with gales of laughter every time he walked on stage.

The breakthrough came only with Bram Stoker's *Dracula: A Tale*, which first appeared in 1897. Stoker was merely plagiarising from a long and unsuccessful literary tradition, but his success knew no bounds. By 1913 his book was in its tenth edition, and despite the interruption of the First World War, the myth only gathered pace thereafter.

In 1926 we hear of Eleonore Zügun, a 13-year-old Romanian peasant girl brought to London for study. The girl was apparently persecuted by some invisible force which continually left teeth-marks on her neck and limbs. Her persecutor was known to the girl only as 'Dracu, *anglice* the Devil'. Cases such as this caused widespread *frissons*, and in 1927 the first stage production of Stoker's *Dracula* was mounted. First in London, then in the provinces, and finally in New York the play was an awesome success, with women in the audience fainting in their dozens.

After this there was no looking back. Sales of Stoker's book doubled and redoubled, and by the 1930s the first vampire films were enjoying a runaway success. Again the interruption of a war made no difference, and in more recent times Hammer Films and a host of imitators have enjoyed extraordinary success with a long series of vampire films. Today, many hundreds of millions of people are thoroughly familiar with all the minutiae of the vampire myth. I do not think I knew who or what Dracula was supposed to be till I was 14 or so; my own children came home from primary school discussing Dracula at half that age.

Familiarity with the vampire myth tends, however, to mean familiarity with the Bram Stoker version. There is a tendency to see his work as the *locus classicus*, and even to view Dracula as the quintessential vampire, so that naïve but ghoulish tourists set forth every year to visit the castle of Count Vlad in Transylvania, believing they are visiting the true well-spring of vampirism. This is about as sensible as viewing old Tarzan films in order to learn about Africa. Anyone seriously interested in the vampire myth has to start elsewhere, with the extraordinary two volumes, *The Vampire: His Kith and Kin* and *The Vampire in Europe*, produced in 1929 by Montague Summers.

Care is needed in reading Summers's work. To some extent it lies within the learned tradition of amateur English anthropology of which Frazer's *The Golden Bough* represents the summit. But Summers was undoubtedly a very strange man – a long-vanished, though still legendary, Oxford 'character'. Although he always used the title 'Reverend', those who knew him aver that he was effectively defrocked by the church on suspicion of necromantic practices – black masses and the like. His biographer, Joseph Jerome (1965), freely admits that much of Summers' life remains cloaked in mystery. He seems to have been involved in a scandal over Satanic rites in 1913 and certainly those who took over the house in which he had lived felt impelled to have it exorcised by a priest first.

Summers is described as a man of exceptional pallor and extremely sinister bearing, always wearing a black cloak. His books make it clear that he more than half believed in the vampires he studied – 'the vampire tradition', he wrote (he always spoke of the tradition, never the myth), 'contains far more truth than the ordinary individual cares to appreciate and acknowledge.' I have, indeed, met those who were convinced that Summers believed himself to be a vampire.

If you believe in vampires, it follows that they must always have existed. Not surprisingly, then, Summers finds traces of them in all ages and places: as long ago as ancient Greece and as far away as Malaya. Even he, however, admits that 'the conception of the vampire proper is peculiar to Slavonic peoples', and that the root word is from the old Magyar *vampir*. And while Summers is keen to show that reports of vampirism are rife throughout eastern and central Europe, it seems quite clear that it is the area occupied by modern-day Hungary and Romania which provide the true epicentre of the myth.

The myth clearly has a rough date in the late seventeenth and early eighteenth centuries. There was a minor flood of scholarly works on vampirism (mainly by Germans) in the early 1730s, and in them the vampire myth appears for the first time in more or less its full modern form. For the first time the vampire is not a ghost or demon but is a real human who is 'un-dead', whose body will not decompose while it can feed itself on human blood, and whose victims quickly become listless and die soon thereafter, sometimes admitting on their death-bed how their fate befell them.

A further help in dating the myth derives from the fact that, in 1738, Cardinal Schratternbach, Bishop of Olmütz, wrote in some panic to the Pope that his diocese was afflicted by a terrifying outbreak of vampirism. The Pope sent a special legate, Archbishop Davanzati, to report. Davanzati's report – in many ways the real authority on the subject – reveals that though he was an exceptionally learned man, he had never heard of the myth before his mission.

The very first report of vampirism had actually occurred in the Hungary of the 1680s, spreading outwards towards the surrounding countries in the following decades. It was only when reports began to come from 'civilised' Germany that the Vatican really sat up. In the 1740s the myth had its first real impact on the west – there is then a great flood of scholarly work on the subject, together with earnest instructions as to the various ways of disposing of the fiend (a stake through the heart, burning, cutting off the head and tearing out its heart). The first allusion in English comes from *The Travels of Three English Gentlemen* (1745) and the term quickly passed into popular use.

Why should the myth have crystallised in the form it did in late seventeenth-century Hungary? One can suggest three possible strands of explanation.

First, in all Europe this was the area where the pattern of landholding was most unequal, and where the aristocracy was most notorious for the rapacity and ruthlessness with which it battened on its serf and peasant population. In very many of the myths the vampire appears as a Count (or Countess): it is possible that the Transylvanian peasantry were simply anticipating Marx's later metaphor of social exploiters sucking the very blood of the poor unfortunates beneath.

Second, this was a particularly troubled, violent and terrifying part of the world in which to live. Incidents of almost indescribable cruelty abound both domestically and in the continuous wars of the period. The whole area was haunted by the terrible fear of the Turk, the faceless, ruthless foe to whom (like the vampire) the Cross was in intolerable affront.

And finally, it is possible that by this time tales had begun to drift back of the vampire bats found in the New World.

This was certainly a potent brew in which popular picnics, witch-crazes and the like would have been quite understandable. But whatever its precise local origins, there is no doubting the amazing rapidity with which the myth spread. For Magyar folk-panics to travel right across Europe and produce a new word and new mythology even in England, in the space of sixty years, was no mean testament to the shocking power of that myth. Then, as now, the sexual and religious implications of the myth, as well as its sheer horror, meant that it struck a deep note everywhere.

Thereafter the myth seems to have become part of a barely-acknowledged literary underworld, cropping up mainly in penny dreadfuls and unrespectable Gothic novels. Dumas and Byron both wrote on the theme but, tellingly, such works did nothing for their reputations. It was as if the bottomless horror of vampirism also had to be nameless, not a topic which the polite world of respectable literary society could really acknowledge. The audience for literary works on vampirism was left very much to the plebs. It is notable that, even in the world of low-brow theatre, plays about vampirism were very often burlesques, as if this was the only 'safe' way to tackle a myth which was simply too horrible and terrifying to be treated seriously.

In a way, then, Bram Stoker was simply lucky. The first stage of demystification is to bring a subject out into the full serious light. Stoker wrote a 'serious' tragedy about vampires, and the twentieth century, which demythologises everything, was ready to begin the long process of accepting – and thus defusing – the most powerful subterranean myth of all. By the 1970s and 1980s we have actually got round to really funny films about vampires – not burlesques, which refuse to take the myth seriously, but comedies which accept the myth head on, and still laugh at it. Seen in that light, Stoker was simply the man who brought the myth to the surface of the real literary world and caught the wave, while Polanski's comic film treatment of vampirism should really be set next to *The Life of Brian*, a contemporaneous satire on an equally powerful myth, that of Christianity.

There may be another point, though. The twentieth century has simultaneously brought great crises of social and personal identity, of alienation and anomie on a quite new scale. It has pushed the exploration of the material world all the way into conceptions of negative particles, of antimatter, of black holes. The vampire fits well into such a world.

He is human antimatter. He lives only by killing. He does not eat and he hates garlic (taken with food). Water, crucial to human life, is anathema to him, as is the Cross, the symbol of life for Christian man. He has no identity – he cannot even be seen in a mirror. He cannot stand daylight, crucial to all life. He does not have sex, strictly speaking; or rather, for him the sexual act is always a violent rape which brings forth not another life but another death. He is immune to bullets, cannot stand Holy Water, and can pass through solid objects. He does not even die, as a man does: he is un-dead.

He is, in other words, a pure inversion. There is no anomie, no alienation, as great as the vampire's: he is *the* alienation of man, and that alienation is potentially immortal. He is ultimately exploitative – a spreading centre of alienation, despoiling others of their very lives and identities too.

There is no doubt that there is much here which echoes our peculiar age, with its strange mixture of scientific advance into the very boundaries of the surreal, its horrors of self-annihilation and super-exploitation, its terrible, lasting sadnesses. The late twentieth century is the true age of the vampire.

References

Jerome, Joseph (1965) *Montague Summers* (London: Cecil and Amelia Woolf).
Summers, Montague (1928) *The Vampire. His Kith and Kin* (London: Kegan Paul, Trench, Trubner).
Summers, Montague (1929) *The Vampire in Europe* (London: Kegan Paul, Trench, Trubner).

PART IV
Blacks and Whites

Chapter 27

South Africa 1980: The Last 'Good Year'?

Moving around South Africa in mid 1980 I could not but feel, amidst the tidal wave of affluence, a sense of impending doom. I tried to communicate this in a number of lectures I gave, suggesting that this might be the country's last best chance for bold reform, pointing to the way that White Rhodesian refusal to reform and deal with moderates in the 1960s had merely led to bloodshed and the victory of the radical Mugabe a few months before. I remember, in particular, giving a talk in the Afrikaner stronghold of Stellenbosch university. My (wholly white) audience reacted with a mixture of impatience and incomprehension. The economy was, it turned out, growing at a 9 per cent rate that year and the gold price hit $830 an ounce. Things could hardly have been better.

Soon thereafter the sky began to fall in. The gold price collapsed, internal discontent mounted to a quasi-revolutionary pitch, sanctions began in earnest, investment collapsed, capital fled, the currency collapsed, and white emigration soared. A ludicrous new constitution, wholly excluding blacks from the government of the country, was indeed introduced. And they began to frisk you at the entrance to supermarkets too. For White South Africa (and not a few non-whites too) less than ten years on, 1980 already looks like a lost golden age.

The beginning of wisdom about contemporary South Africa is that a single overall impression is no longer possible. In different parts of the country, and at different levels of the political structure, events seem to have developed an autonomous momentum. When you are there, even the (censored) news reports produce a bewildering staccato effect.

Confusion lies thickest, naturally enough, over the uncoordinated flarings of black protest politics. Sitting in Cape Town a few days ago, I spread out the previous fortnight's news-cuttings in front of me. The red meat boycott in the Western Cape (in support of striking meat workers) had been temporarily suspended. The bus boycott dragged on, with routine reports of police harrassment of boycotters and stonings of buses that did run.

The almost complete school and university boycott by Coloureds and blacks throughout the Western Cape remained in force more than a whole term after it had begun, with sympathetic boycott actions reported from widely scattered parts of the country. Only two schools in Soweto were affected, but the university at Fort Hare was completely closed down, and a rash of schools in the Eastern Cape and Zululand were also shut.

The Cape children's leaders were still being held in detention by the police, leaving the boycotters somewhat rudderless, but all the more bitter. Children were simply dropping out of school altogether, knowing they could not now catch up on all the work they had missed. Many Coloured head-teachers, caught between the wrath of the authorities on the one hand and their pupils on the other, had more or less gone into hiding. Those who remained on the job faced a steady stream of protest meetings and disturbances. There were sporadic reports of further children arrested for leafleting, for stoning school inspectors and school delivery vehicles, and for sundry other instances of 'deliquent' behaviour.

A pall of bitterness still hung over the Cape from the riots at Elsie's River and Lavender Hill six weeks before. The *Cape Times* was still pressing the police for an official casualty list; forty two bodies of dead 'rioters', including many women and children and a baby of 18 months, had been recorded in Cape hospitals. The police, who blame 'criminal elements' for the riots, simply said: 'If you want the names, you must get them from the families of the dead. We are not going to release them.'

A similar air of confusion surrounded the riot at the giant Sasol (coal-into-oil) plant in the Transvaal, recently the target of a successful guerrilla strike. Persistent rumours told of a second large explosion in the week after the guerrilla raid. Large detachments of soldiers and armed police had moved into the plant area, and, according to black workers there, three workers had been shot. Sasol officials simply reported that one man had died of unspecified injuries after being found drunk.

After several days of blank denial, the authorities acknowledged that two further men had suffered gunshot wounds. Meanwhile, black and Coloured workers had rioted against the security forces, stoning and burning vehicles. One white man was killed: burnt alive, the radio said; stoned to death, according to eye-witnesses.

Particularly confused accounts filtered through of trouble in the little Eastern Cape town of Grahamstown (a sort of South African Cheltenham). According to the first reports, a 57-year-old black woman had been 'found dead with head injuries' after the police had 'acted to disperse pupils boycotting schools'. Later it emerged that the particular sort of head injury she had suffered from was a bullet wound. But the police continued to disclaim responsibility on the grounds that they had only been using bird-shot. When, however, further disturbances broke out at the ensuing funeral a 16-year-old youth was reported as 'shot dead with bird-shot'.

Thereafter, a crowd of Grahamstown blacks 'attacking a hospital' were shot at 'by hospital staff'; and an 8-year-old boy was killed by shotgun fire from a passing truck. Bantu administration officials, the *Sunday Tribune* reported, 'are believed to carry shotguns'. They also drive trucks.

Sundry attacks on, and burnings of, official vehicles were then reported from Grahamstown, along with rioting and looting. The original victim's son was shot dead, and the house of a suspected police informer was burnt down.

The police moved in on the Grahamstown townships with hippo trucks, armoured vehicles, sneeze machines (shooting tear gas and pepper) and a helicopter. Even these vehicles, astonishingly, came under attack from the inhabitants. This act was so foolhardy as to convince the police that 'large-scale drunkenness' was chiefly to blame. All local liquor stores were closed down 'indefinitely'.

Other reports of violence and death came from further afield. At the Deelkraal gold mine near Johannesburg, fighting between (communally segregated) Basotho and Pondo miners left nineteen dead and thirty-six injured. Faction fights – often the rural carry-over from mine-compound quarrels – saw six blacks killed (mainly hacked to death) in two separate incidents in Natal. Similar fights a week earlier had produced at least ten deaths, forty injured, and a large number of hut-burnings.

The war in Namibia

And, of course, the war in Namibia dragged on. There were some heavy South African raids into Angola as the army sought to inflict massive retaliation for the rather high casualities it has suffered in recent months. These raids, the public were promised, would destroy SWAPO's offensive capability for a long time to come. SWAPO waited only a week before subjecting the border town of Ruacana to a heavy mortar bombardment. In the meantime, there was an outbreak of rioting, followed by the inevitable shooting, in Windhoek. The house of a member of the Namibian National Assembly (internal settlement version) was attacked. This did not prevent the police from describing the incident as 'non-political'.

Almost all of these incidents merited mere snippets in the press (which devoted far more space to the rumbling wave of industrial unrest, particularly the Johannesburg municipal strike). This lack of interest was, it is fair to say, shared by almost all the South African whites.

'Look,' said the old school friend with whom I was staying, 'I *expect* there to be trouble. We're going to have to live with school boycotts, the war on the border, terrorist incursions, township disturbances, and all the rest. And the strikes aren't going to go away, either. They're here to stay. I dare say the day will come when you've got to be frisked to go into a supermarket. There's no doubt urban terrorism is coming. But most of the damage they [blacks] are doing now is to themselves. A lot of criminal elements are mixed up in these riots. Things are changing here, anyway. Okay, not changing fast enough. But the government's got to keep control, and I'm glad that it can. The economy's come right again, and I like the life here.'

As we talked, his children and mine played happily in his swimming pool. I could see his point.

Two years ago, when I had visited the same friend, his conversation had returned obsessively to the subject of emigration. Now he laughed at the idea, and recited the names of several acquaintances who had left after Soweto but had come sheepishly back. Yet, since then, the country had progressed from that single great explosion to the slowly growing rumble of a what amounts to continuous, low-intensity civil war. The generalised acceptance of this as normal is frequently macabre in its effect, and it is often quite unconscious. Examples abound. On Cape Town's Main Street, a shop called Surburban Guns sits snugly next to a Woolworth's and the ads for Pepsi-Cola. The Pietermaritzburg city council, in a gesture of patriotic support for the army, has just announced that it will set aside a 'warriors' acre' for members of the security forces killed on the border. The area to be set aside, the council proudly announced, would be as big as that used for the dead of the two world wars.

The key to this easy accommodation to a high level of civil strife lies in the economy. Thanks largely to the higher gold price, this is now enjoying a wondrous boom. Economically, the real story in

South Africa this year has been that of Sherlock Holmes's dog that did not bark. The Johannesburg Stock Exchange has hitherto been the most politically sensitive of all the world's bourses. Both Sharpeville and Soweto produced major market crashes. This year, however, the market has just shrugged off the news of unrest. While the Stock Exchange's index stood at under 300 at the end of 1978, by early 1980 it merely consolidated around the 600 mark before soaring through the 650 level in the very midst of the bloody Cape riots. The new mood of business confidence is deep-rooted. In one year the number of small investors has increased by 25 per cent.

How strong the economy now is emerges clearly from a comparison of the first half of 1980 against the first half of 1979. With large and expensive purchases of oil and arms leading the way, South Africa's imports have soared by 48 per cent this year. But exports, with gold leading the way, have increased so hugely as to still leave a 50 per cent cash surplus. The country's reserves have, therefore, more than doubled.

But gold is not the whole story. Coal production is also booming. There is the increase in local coal usage: when Sasol 3 comes on stream, 32 million tons a year will be being turned into oil. But South Africa has now also become a major coal exporter. In 1974, coal exports were only £12 million: In 1979, they topped £283 million and South Africa overtook Poland, to become western Europe's major supplier. By 1985, coal exports are expected to top £1,100 million a year. And South Africa's coal reserves are estimated at 60 billion tons.

What is true of coal and gold is true of many other sectors besides. Despite all the political obstacles, exports to the rest of Africa (which buys neither gold nor coal) increased by 65 per cent last year. Figures like these are causing some embarrassment in states such as Zambia. The Zambian appetite for South African goods has *increased* since the new Zimbabwe government took over and Kaunda's boycott of that country ended. So strong is South Africa's position that the main inhibition to further increases of exports to Zambia is the nervousness of South African bankers about Zambia's reputation as a poor payer.

The result within South Africa is a galloping consumer boom. Overall economic growth is likely to reach 6 per cent this year. It could go higher still in 1981. The whole country is awash in money. A great deal of it is going into a frenzy of construction. After several slack years, the number of buildings completed in 1980 are already 34 per cent up on 1979, and planned construction has increased by a prodigious 84 per cent. Demand for bricks and cement has so far outrun supply that small fortunes are being made in black market building materials. All this has as yet made only small inroads into the high level of black unemployment. But already the government is talking of a shortage of nearly five million skilled and white-collar workers by 1988.

The fact that their protests, boycotts and strikes are, for the moment, lapping ineffectually in the wake of this economic juggernaut tends only to deepen black frustration. And now this frustration is experienced against the background of greatly heightened political expectations, roused by the heady sight of what is happening in Zimbabwe.

The stark enormity of the gap between these two emotions has caused many blacks to look with a renewed and searching dissatisfaction at all the 'leaders' they currently have. These leaders are of two sorts. There are the chief ministers of the homelands, imposed by the government; and there are the 'spokesman' leaders, who have emerged out of informal or extra-political organisations. Dr Motlana of the Soweto Committee of Ten and Bishop Tutu, the Anglican bishop of Johannesburg, are the leading examples of the second variety.

Whatever shaky legitimacy the homeland leaders have enjoyed is shrinking still further. In the Transkei, ruled by the brothers Matanzima, Kaiser and George, things have reached a point where not only is the opposition locked up, but even cabinet ministers refuse to talk in their offices for fear of phone-taps. The Transkei police are a byword for drunkenness and extortion. There are frequent armed clashes between police and tribesmen. The Government as a whole is tottering under a huge weight of corruption and debt. Pretoria has been forced to rescind such financial independence as the regime hitherto enjoyed, simply in order to prevent the whole structure from collapsing.

In the neighbouring homeland of the Ciskei – whose leader, Lennox Sebe, hovers on the brink of 'independence' – things are not much better. Nowhere have the black school boycotters been treated more ferociously than in the Ciskei. Pupils were driven back to their classrooms under massed baton charges by the police – ably commanded, as perhaps one might expect, by Colonel Charles Sebe, Lennox's brother.

Buthelezi moves Right

More striking has been the fact that similar treatment has been meted out to protesting black students by Mangosuthu Buthelezi, the powerful ruler of the Kwazulu homeland, who was until now clearly the most popular single black leader in South Africa. But Buthelezi was always hyper-sensitively intolerant of criticism. He has now allowed himself to be provoked by the youthful black radicals into a series of disastrous moves to the right. He has repeatedly inveighed against the students in terms even white politicians might avoid, publicly putting himself forward as being a centrist force against the black left. He is cultivating links with the far-right Afrikaans student organisation. He has even swallowed the ludicrous story, put out by BOSS, that the exiled African National Congress is trying to assassinate him.

There has been a very steep falling off in his popular support. His Inkatha movement is clearly stagnating. Even among his loyal core of Zulu followers, there are marked signs of disaffection. In the huge Zulu townships round Durban, Buthelezi is drawing crowds of 5,000 and 10,000, where a year ago he would have drawn 40,000 or 50,000.

Dr Motlana and Bishop Tutu had less of a following to lose than Buthelezi, and they have conserved it better. Their problem is more that they have become spokesmen on everything – including much about which they know little. Their interventions have developed a predictable, jack-in-the-box quality. In the wake of Zimbabwean events, the shadow of Bishop Muzorewa lies heavily over all such impeccably bourgeois leaders who are allowed to operate freely by the government. This is particularly true of Tutu, whose displays of excitable exaggeration and public lachrymosity stir unfortunate memories of other political clerics in Africa.

The result is a yawning leadership vacuum among the blacks. This does much to explain the wide – though often skin-deep – resurgence of support for Nelson Mandela, who has just celebrated his sixty-second birthday on Robben Island, after eighteen years of imprisonment there. The oddity is that while most blacks know little of Mandela, a majority now would probably vote for him in an election. He has a certain historic legitimacy. He has sacrificed himself to the cause. Unsullied by any whiff of compromise or opportunism, his name has a unifying, *deus ex machina* quality.

The holiday crowds who ascend Table Mountain by cable car can gaze easily down upon Robben Island basking in the bay, and wonder what dispensation they might expect from the island's most famous inhabitant. Away to their right there stands the (white) House of Assembly – and at the moment there is something of a mystery about what they can expect from there, too. The Prime Minister has promised that he will introduce a new constitution at the October session.

But at present the final details are unknown; and since all political meetings of ten or more people are currently banned, there is not much chance to discuss it either. Probably Botha will press ahead with the plan for a new President's Council from which blacks are excluded – and will try to sweeten the pill by offering major territorial additions to the existing black homelands. Such a plan will be dismissed out of hand by nearly all blacks, and by a good many whites.

If Botha has truly laboured all these months to bring forth a mouse such as this, then a great deal will have been lost. Against almost all the odds, the Government has suddenly found itself with the initiative again. It is successfully weathering yet another wave of discontent. The economy is strong. The black opposition is fragmented and is largely leaderless. Foreign pressure has eased: the threat of sanctions has receded, and a possible Reagan presidency lies ahead.

As blind as Rhodesia

The government has plenty of money to pay for reforms, and all the strength it needs to hold the ring while it makes them. The trouble is that strong conservative governments, feeling rich and secure even after thirty-two years in power, are not easily persuaded that the moment for radical change has come. It is far easier to believe (as, dangerously, most white South Africans are now coming to believe) that if you cannot prevent trouble, you can just about live with it.

It was in just such a mood that white Rhodesia steered blindly on towards its doom, gradually accepting ever higher degrees of civil strife as 'normal' – until the war came all the way home. The point of no return was there when whites stopped thinking in terms of 'solutions' and began talking instead only of a mortgage on 'fifteen good years'.

Perhaps more significant than the boycotts, the stonings, the shootings, and all the rest, is the stealthy way in which the psychology of 'fifteen good years' has begun to take firm root in South Africa, too.

Chapter 28

South Africa in the Era of 'Reform'

As South Africa lurched through the uprisings of 1983-6 it became a matter of faith in many circles to argue that the Botha government's 'reforms' were a fraud. This was absurd: the reforms may have been timid and incomplete but collectively they have changed the baseline from which future change must depart.

Looking back on this article (written in mid 1986) one would change several things now. The continuing vacuum in Black political leadership had, by 1989, given Tutu and Boesak a significance which seemed unlikely then. Then again, the example of Zimbabwe makes it clear how one resolves the conundrum of giving high quality education to Black nationalists without provoking White flight: under the cover of a superficial socialist rhetoric the old white private schools remain open and admit larger numbers of the children of the privileged black élite. All other children, black and white, go to very mediocre schools. White emigration occurs all the same but is highest among poorer whites with school-age children; the older and richer find it easier to stay. Finally, while I got the identity of Botha's successor right, the possibility of a National party split seems slight at the time of writing, the State President having contrived to unite the party against himself by first appearing to resign and then trying to stay on. Nothing could have more brutally reminded Nationalist MPs how much they had resented the autumn of the patriarch, Botha.

'South Africa', write Adam and Moodley (1986),

> evokes a morbid fascination. A vast literature of condemnation wallows in moral predicaments. Ambivalent friends of Pretoria respond with ever more sophisticated justifications of the unjustifiable. Foreigners cherish the easy accessibility to an English-speaking

police state, where the press is critical, intellectuals are tolerated, and the repression occurs out of sight. The apartheid issue allows even diehard conservatives to look radical in a unique laboratory for social engineers. A worthy cause attracts causeless entrepreneurs. Instant experts pontificate about ready options for a creeping revolution. Some claim to seek 'moral clarity' that derives from the 'scale of the land and its antagonisms'. Many more, one suspects, secretly enjoy what Gordimer calls 'the last colonial extravaganza'.

It is difficult for anyone who knows South Africa not to feel a twinge of this revulsion as the books on this unhappy country continue to pour from the press – the quotation about 'moral clarity' somehow deriving from the land's scale comes, incidentally, from Joseph Lelyveld's Pulitzer prize-winning *Move Your Shadow* (1986). Similarly, within South Africa itself one keeps stumbling across the half-cold trails of any number of Congressmen and retooled Vietnam experts who are confidently attempting to apply the lessons of the US civil rights struggle to a country where the black-white ratio is quite the reverse of what it is in the United States. (When Henry Ford, on last visiting his investments in South Africa, was questioned about his company's policy on black employment, he actually boasted of Ford's 'proud record towards minorities'.)

Despite Adam and Moodley's quotation, such strictures do not apply to Lelyveld's work, which deserves at least most of the extravagant praise already heaped upon it. This montage of interviews, reflections and rapportage conveys the texture of South African life at every level with a sensitivity and honesty not often found. And although many of the encounters with the politically prominent have a journalistic importance in their own right, it is often in passages dealing with the lives of the obscure that Lelyveld's virtues shine through most effectively. Moreover, he really does know what he is talking about: unlike all too many foreign observers, he has gained a deep acquaintance with South African history and with the vast country which exists outside the four great cities of Johannesburg, Pretoria, Cape Town and Durban – all that most visitors ever see.

This is not a Studs Terkel study of South Africa: the characters do not quite talk for themselves. They are the people Lelyveld has chosen to interview and we always get his sensitive, wry, humane asides about them. Since it is these which thread the book together, it is difficult in the end not to feel that Lelyveld, for all his self-effacement, emerges as the hero of his own book. Inevitably, his own liberal prejudices shine through, so that, for all his gentle humanity, most of the whites interviewed come across as bigots, fools or monsters. And indeed many of them are just that. But if one is going in for this sort of participant-observer montage, it is better to get right inside the mind of, say, a white policeman – or just let him speak for himself without the asides. The trouble is that if you do this, then everyone comes out as, in their own way, sympathetic – oppressors as well as oppressed.

Lelyveld's stylistic approach has, in fact, some important political implications. He is so righteously revolted by the South African realities he meets that he seriously underplays the significance of white-imposed reform, treating it mainly as a sort of sham covering a still triumphant apartheid system. The fact is that every single other white regime in Africa has become more reactionary and intransigent as the pressure on it from below has grown, while in South Africa the general drift, however slow and inadequate, has been in the opposite direction. The Botha Government, of course, wants credit for this. It is a matter of political choice whether one accords it or not. Really to understand what is going on means giving 'reform' its proper weight too, not just liberally inveighing against its insufficiencies. The boy I sat next to in class in Durban, a racist and white supremacist to the marrow, now sits in integrated cinemas, theatres, restaurants, and on integrated beaches. He wonders whether perhaps he can live with majority rule after all and tells me that he does not like being searched at the entrance before going into a shopping centre, that he is happy that his daughter sits next to an Indian in class. This is not as impressive as all that, but its is not meaningless either. I have a feeling that my old school friend would come out very badly in any interview with Lelyveld. Maybe he would deserve to. But he has changed and things have changed.

If one wants to understand what is really going on in South Africa and the likely direction that events may take, there is no doubt that the Adam and Moodley book is far superior to Lelyveld's. It is, indeed, the best book on South Africa that I have read for a very long time. As they point out, belief in reform, however slow, however defective, has already become 'an essential part of the psychological glue that holds this deeply divided society together'. To see how true this is one merely has to imagine what would happen if Pretoria announced that reform would now stop. There would be an explosion of black rage, a multiplication of foreign pressures, accelerating disinvestment, a white scramble to emigrate and an ever-deepening economic and financial crisis: that is, all the things which are happening despite reform would double and redouble if it stopped. Pretoria may posture, talk defiantly, or warn, but the truth is that the Government has already virtually lost control over the direction in which it is travelling.

Blacks know this, which is why such terrifying fissures have begun to show within their ranks: the race for power is on, and is being conducted under a peculiar set of rules and handicaps, for Pretoria has historically tolerated only very limited avenues for black political organisation and has amputated successive generations of black political leadership. Pretoria's tactic has been to create the black leadership it wanted and then to declare a broad-minded willingness to negotiate with its puppets. The result has been farcical: a series of pocket Trujillos, Duvaliers and Somozas in the Bantustans, and urban 'leaders' like the now-ousted mayor of Soweto, Ephraim Tshabalala, who demanded a ban on celebrations of the 1976 unrest, together with denial of Christian burial to victims of unrest, and declared that apartheid had been created by God. Even now, Pretoria still clings to the notion that it can somehow 'negotiate' with men whose natural constituents are anxious only to place burning tyres around their necks.

Under these circumstances the only way for even a half-authentic black leadership to emerge was for it to play as hard as possible to the gallery of an overseas Western liberal opinion anxious to discover a potential black leadership likely to guarantee long-term Western economic and strategic interests in South Africa. Buttressed by the support of these powerful and respectable overseas patrons, such leaders could then develop room for manoeuvre at home, using their relative immunity from the cruder forms of suppression to make gestures of liberal defiance against Pretoria. Since their externally guaranteed immunity made them the only blacks able to make such gestures on a continuing and highly visible basis, such figures could then, without serious competition, conjure up a black following at home – the ensuing crowd scenes being proudly exhibited to the overseas patrons as further evidence of how deserving they were of further support. The ideal forum was the Church: even Pretoria found the idea of imprisoning prominent Christians embarrassing, and a strong profession of Christian faith was the best guarantee of anti-Communism that the overseas patrons could wish for. Hence the careers of Desmond Tutu and Allan Boesak, the latest and best exponents of this crab-like upward leverage into power-broker status. The Western liberal dream was that black south Africans could somehow be gently led to liberation by living saints – Christian Gandhis – who would blessedly leave Western investments and strategic interests undamaged in the process.

The era of this type of black leadership is now drawing to a close. Perhaps the symbolic moment came with the visit to South Africa of Senator Edward Kennedy at the invitation of Tutu and Boesak. Had things gone as in the old days, the latter would have been able to enhance their local position by basking in the charismatic shadow of such a glamorous symbol of Western liberal opinion. But at this point local black militants parted company with Tutu and Boesak and the Kennedy visit ended in acrimonious disaster. In their survey of the black leadership groups that will contest the future, Adam and Moodley pointedly make no mention of either Tutu or Boesak.

Discerning the likely contours of intra-black political competition is still not easy, particularly since several of the major contenders deliberately avoid any sort of programmatic commitment: the ambition is to gain power by becoming a single great catch-all nationalist rally. The time for making one's policy clear will be after one has won power. Thus Inkatha, Chief Buthelezi's powerful Zulu-based mass movement – whose strength is probably sufficient to ensure Buthelezi at least a blocking role in any future dispensation – proudly declares that 'Inkatha has never adopted a view about the nature of the South African state in the medium or long term'. Similarly, the ANC exile leadership, despite the presence of a strong Communist element within its ranks, energetically denies that it is a socialist party at all. The UDF, which functions as a quasi-internal wing of the ANC but which contains many whose commitment to the ANC is dubious or conditional, achieves, if that is possible, an even greater programmatic vacuity. The larger part of the powerful black trade union movement, while subscribing generally to the aims of 'the liberation movement', eschews any sort of political or economic credo and is distinctly hostile to its manipulation by political parties or groups. All of which leaves the field clear for the one group not afraid of policy commitment: the Black Consciousness/AZAPO militants who criticise all the others from the radical left. But BC/AZAPO has a miniscule mass following and is playing a different game: its aim is to gain influence among the small but potentially pivotal black intelligentsia, and it has had considerable success.

This hardly exhausts the list of groups which may have to be counted in any final power equation. The young township militants are unlikely to constitute a political grouping in their own right, but the potentially volatile way in which they may force issues could well have a major impact on the serious contenders. None of the other 'homelands leaders' has a body of support which remotely resembles Buthelezi's, but some of them may still have useful pockets of traditionalist clients to throw into the balance. And what to make of a man like Bishop Lekganyane, whose Zionist Christian Church regularly assembles crowds of one and a half million blacks at its Easter rallies? President Botha was canny enough to attend the 1985 Easter Zionist rally and, in addressing the crowd, to defer respectfully to Lekganyane as 'Your Grace'. Lekganyane returned the compliment in his address to the enormous crowd: 'Lord, we pray that you keep our State President, Mrs Botha and us all, safe from harm.' He has shown no sign to date of developing Tutu-like political ambitions – and the quietist creed of the Zionists would appear to preclude such a notion. But well over a third of all blacks now belong to the independent African churches, and the number is still rapidly increasing. Compare this with the mere 4.7 per cent of blacks who belong to Tutu's Anglican flock: one is looking at a leviathan which, if it ever did decide to act politically, could well have decisive weight.

Most of these groups represent sections of the growing black middle class. In Buthelezi's case, the full pomp and ceremony of traditional chieftainship is added to the giant white Mercedes, the espousal of private enterprise and a rejection of economic sanctions against South Africa. With the UDF leadership a more straightforwardly middle-class set of assumptions is almost naïvely made. When, in August 1985, the UDF decided to send a message to Mandela on behalf of 'the people of South Africa', it gave a quite unconscious self-definition: 'We, the people of South Africa represented by the UDF, university students, school pupils, academics, teachers, lawyers, doctors, clerics and other concerned citizens . . .'. No nonsense here about a worker-peasant alliance, toiling masses, sons of the soil. Even the position of the allegedly radical socialists of the BC/AZAPO is ambivalent. Most of their constituency is undeniably middle-class and will be among the chief gainers from continued 'reform', let alone the wholesale displacement of white power. And while their anti-white rhetoric is principally targeted against the white Communists within the ANC, the fact is that it is also highly usable in campaigns for job Africanisation from which Black Consciousness militants will be among the main beneficiaries: a pattern we have seen in too many African states to be surprised by.

The real conundrum is the ANC. There is no doubt that Communists such as Joe Slovo do play a powerful role within the exile leadership. Nor is there any doubt that men like Slovo are old-style Leninist-Stalinists: Slovo, for example, has no time for trade union autonomy. 'It depends on us', he says, meaning the CP faction of the ANC, 'having the capacity of injecting the right kind of politics and thinking into the working class.' No Eurocommunist nonsense here. Understandably, many trade union leaders feel considerable revulsion at the notion of being thus 'injected', having had their fill of similarly paternalist attitudes from Verwoerd, Vorster, Botha and white employers. But the exile leadership also includes many quite old-style African nationalists: both Tambo and Mandela himself are somewhere on the Centre-Right of the movement and both come from the topmost layer of the black middle-class élite. There is also the fact that many of the top exiles have now been abroad for a quarter of a century or more and, not to put too fine a point on it, have been living quite high on the hog. This is not just a partisan point, as in Buthelezi's retort that he 'will not be dictated to by South African exiles who sit drinking whisky in safe places', or the frequent criticism of Tambo for having had his son educated at an English private school. It is simply a sociological fact that the exile leadership, Communists as much as nationalists, have been through a lengthy acculturation to metropolitan comforts which they do not seem very keen to give up.

The result is that to the geographical distance which separates the exiles from their militants on the ground there must be added a growing social and political distance. This distance is variously expressed – by the open contempt of some young township militants for 'Uncle Tom' Tambo, and by the continuous history of trouble in the ANC guerrilla camps. As one report on the decisions of the 1985 ANC conference at Kabwe in Zambia put it:

> ANC 'draft-dodgers' will not be allowed to opt for Moscow as an alternative to the more austere Angolan camps, where the ANC leadership has been increasingly concerned with a breakdown in discipline. A rebellion there was ruthlessly put down last year. Among ANC militants who have become accustomed to the comforts of Western life-in-exile, mention of Angola is comparable to the connotations Siberia has to the Soviets.

All of which may sound close to saying that whichever black party comes to power it will be middle-class and that the future of South African capitalism is thus ensured. There is, indeed, a good chance that this may be true. If so, it would be deeply ironic, for few more bitter intellectual battles have been fought over the last fifteen years than the liberal – Marxist debate as to whether apartheid was intrinsic to South African capitalism or a hindrance to it which would be destroyed by the onward march of the market. Merle

Lipton, long one of the doughtiest proponents of the liberal thesis, has summed up her work in *Capitalism and Apartheid South Africa 1910–84* (1986) a valuable and succinct historical account, packed with useful data. But the fact is that the whole debate has begun to look somewhat *passé*. Those who backed themselves into a corner by arguing that apartheid was essential to capitalism have cause for some embarrassment as the apartheid system is steadily dismantled with capitalism still firmly entrenched – though this would be as nothing to their embarrassment if capitalism were to prosper under black majority rule. However, apartheid is being dismantled not because it has been eroded by the market but because, on the one hand, the need for cheap labour is now less as South African industry becomes more capital-intensive and as farming becomes more mechanised, and, on the other hand, because growing black pressure threatens the stability of the system as a whole unless sweeping concessions are made. At a certain point the argument about what economic conditions are most satisfactory to industrial, mining or agricultural capital becomes otiose, for the white capitalist is now more concerned about the larger question as to whether he and his family can continue to live safely in the country at all. In a country where every white is liable to military conscription up to the age of 60, such thoughts are never far away.

There are, however, powerful reasons to believe that South African capitalism is unlikely to survive black majority rule unscathed. In part, this is simply because the present economic system is so identified with white supremacy that white industrialists are likely, in the wake of such a change, to find themselves in the same uneviable pariah position as did, come the Liberation, those French industrialists who had collaborated with the Nazis. But more significantly, whichever black party comes to power it will face the same pressure from below to use that power to achieve a sweeping redistribution of social and economic resources. Adam and Moodley argue persuasively that this means that the only type of regime which can guarantee long-term democratic stability is probably a fairly strong form of democratic socialism, and that such a regime, assuming it would still leave a considerable space to free enterprise, may already represent the best hope for enlightened white capitalists. Adam and Moodley speculate interestingly on what the contours of such a regime might be, but on at least one crucial point they fail to carry conviction. It is imaginable that black nationalists, like their Afrikaner nationalist predecessors, may be willing to tolerate for years to come the fact that another ethnic group remains far wealthier than they are, but it is hard to imagine that they, any more than the Afrikaner nationalists did before them, will long tolerate a situation in which their children receive such a grossly inferior education that this economic status *quo ante* can be perpetuated for ever. At present, per capita expenditure on black education is only 10 per cent of the figure for whites. Any progress towards equality in this field can only mean a dramatic levelling down in white educational standards sufficient to ensure that young whites can no longer compete in an international First World labour market, only in a Third World one. Such a prospect would produce large-scale white emigration and a growing, consequential economic destabilisation. This simply is a gut issue – as even Oliver Tambo's own behaviour suggests.

All of this is to leap over the question of how a transition to majority rule can be made in the first place. At present – partly because it makes for such dramatic TV – a great deal of attention has been focused on the emergence of an Afrikaner Far Right, determined to prevent further reform, let alone majority rule. But it is doubtful if the Far Right deserves so much attention. It is, in fact, quite weak. Its main strength lies in its ability to slow reform, not to stop it. In any case, a situation in which the Far Right seemed likely to snatch actual power from the present (or any similar) government is the one scenario in which a military *coup d'état* would be truly thinkable. To be sure, as Kenneth Grundy shows in his brief but admirable study (1986), the power of the military has increased hugely in every sphere of South African life over the past fifteen years – and the military has shown a growing propensity for independent action, even where this meant undermining or disobeying the diktat of civilian ministries. But at the end of the day the important thing to remember is that the SADF is essentially a citizen army. There are only ten thousand professional soldiers in South Africa. It is highly unlikely that the mass of young conscripts would be willing to support their officers in a high-risk political adventure unless nothing less than the physical safety of their families at home was at stake. The social and economic explosion which would be triggered by the emergence of a Far Right regime might, however, provide just such a scenario.

As Adam and Moodley rightly warn, the greatest danger in the present situation is that both the two main protagonists – the Botha Government and the ANC – appear gravely to underestimate the other's strength. The Government appears to believe its own propaganda to the effect that the ANC represents a small group of exiled Communist terrorists, while Tambo professes to be 'not bothered by the strength of South Africa'. 'We don't think they are strong at home. We will prove that on the ground.' All of which is alarming in the highest degree. It is all very well for a political *ingénue* like Winnie Mandela to make stupid and deplorable speeches about 'give us the matches, give us the necklace', but Botha and Tambo are both professional politicians. Tambo has to recognise that if he puts AK-47s into the hands of the township militants he could end up by watching helicopter gunships and Mirages in operation over the townships. All that Botha has to remember is that while there are 21 million blacks today, there will, on present trends, be 47 million by the year 2000, 79 million in 2020 and 138 million in 2040. Such figures imply majority rule quite conclusively in each and every imaginable scenario. They also imply something else: South Africa only has sufficient water resources to support a maximum population of 80 million – black, white and brown. If both sides continue to underestimate the other, the prospect is that of a growing 'Lebanonisation' ending in apocalypse. No one can want that.

The problem is that the Botha Government is in search of further instalments of 'reform' which somehow always stop short of facing up to the real issue of future majority rule. At the very least, this represents a criminal waste of time. Indeed, reform which is offered as a palliative or intended substitute for facing up to that question loses, *ipso facto*, all credibility in the eyes even of its intended beneficiaries. More and more, all such initiatives are stillborn by the refusal to release Mandela. The problem is that releasing Mandela as a free South African citizen implies that he then has to be allowed to move around the country speaking freely to his followers. Within months – such is the man's symbolic power – he would probably rally an enormous wave of black opinion behind him. Politically, that would make him the master of the game in black politics – the ANC-in-exile would instantly count for only as much as he decided it should. If he then decided to ditch his old Communist allies – their darkest fear – there would be little they could do about it. But what could the Botha Government do, faced with that united tidal wave behind the one great leader with historic legitimacy? Either it could negotiate with him on the single-question agenda of majority rule; or it could throw him back in jail and crush his movement, thus losing all international credibility and hugely strengthening the position of the Communist faction within the ANC. So there is no point in releasing Mandela unless the Government is also prepared to sit down with him a few months later and bargain about the terms on which it surrenders power. This is not a decision which would come easily to a politician in any country.

As Adam and Moodley point out, all the available evidence from any number of polls and surveys suggests that free elections in South Africa would produce one of the continent's more conservative governments, with radical minorities to Right and Left and power held by a broad Centre of shifting coalitions of liberals and social democrats. But there is no way of reaching such a dispensation without (probably) a more radical phase in between and (certainly) a similar act of hari-kiri by the present white government.

No part of what I have been saying is outdated, or disproved, I think, by the state of emergency which has just been imposed. When and if that crisis is got over, another will come with Botha's retirement: younger National Party MPs might then bolt the party towards the Left rather than face a further prolongation of the present crisis under the sort of orthodox conservative (F.W. de Klerk?) likely to be chosen. Meanwhile more blacks will get killed every week, foreign pressure will grow, and the economy will stagger on downwards. Extraordinary though it may seem, the moment South Africa is waiting for is when considerations such as these at last outweigh calculations about the internal dynamics of the National Party caucus. The clock ticks on.

References

Adam, Heribert and Moodley, Kogila (1986) *South Africa Without Apartheid* (Los Angeles: University of California Press).

Grundy, Kenneth (1986) *The Militarisation of South African Politics* (London: Tauris).

Lelyveld, Joseph (1986) *Move Your Shadow: South Africa Black and White* (London: Michael Joseph).

Lipton, Merle (1986) *Capitalism and Apartheid: South Africa 1910–1984* (London: Gower/Temple Smith).

Chapter 29

Scenes from South African Life

In 1988 I spent nearly five months in South Africa and was wholly recaptured by the magic of that wonderful country. All four of the articles that follow were written on that trip.

The article below was overshadowed by the municipal elections of 26 October. In the event the Conservatives unwisely talked up their gains to a point where they were somewhat disappointed when they failed, by a single seat, to capture Pretoria. A stay-away from work on 26 October was announced at the last minute by various undeclared UDF sources in conditions of maximum confusion. The trade unions, who would normally expect to be the ones to decide on such things, said nothing and were reported to be less than pleased. No one was really sure what was supposed to happen on 26 October in the black townships, but gangs of youths congregated at the bus-stops there to petrol bomb buses taking other blacks to work. I spoke to some of those who had braved the petrol bombs. You lie flat on the floor of the bus, they said, so as to make it look empty. That way they sometimes do not bother to throw the petrol bomb, or it goes over your head and lands on a seat. They felt that even this was worth it to be sure of keeping their jobs, highly valued in an era of such high unemployment. Everyone assumed that intimidation and counter-intimidation were part of the natural order of things. The Conservatives said they were happy at their gains. The Government said it was happy that Conservative gains had been less than expected. The Progressives and their allies did surprisingly well in the white elections, especially in Durban and East London, and they said they were happy. The UDF and ANC said the stay-away had been a great success, so they were happy too. Everyone was happy.

The thing that really got to me after a while was the prostitutes. As I drove back from Cape Town city centre to suburban Mowbray at night along the old Main Road, I would see dozens of them beckoning to motorists, and sometimes as I waited at the traffic-light at Mowbray bus-station, the pimps would genially slap the side of my car to attract my attention to their Xhosa or Coloured charges. Going to a late-night café in Mowbray, the somewhat mixed area in which I was staying, meant threading my way through clusters of begging small boys and prostitutes who ranged in age from schoolgirls to quite old women. The ambience was such that after a while you got to be curious about how safe it was to be a white café-owner (they are invariably Portuguese or Greek) in such a district. After all, loitering round their shop doorway, however good-humouredly are a lot of decidedly poor people; the shopkeeper is, at night, the only white face to be found in quite a large area; and the shop's goods and till represent not only a tempting but almost the only target around.

Such cafés, I gradually noted, favoured very high counters which served a definite security function, only the owner's head and shoulders being visible above them. Further investigation revealed that most such cafe-owners not only keep guns behind the counter, but fully automatic weapons at that. And since the whole family works in the shop, even the children have been trained in the use of this Ramboidal technology. Given the extraordinary crime rates in and around most South African cities, some of these small shopkeepers are understandably a little trigger-happy. Recently one shopkeeper, looking out of his shop, saw his parked car slowly moving away. Concluding that it was being stolen, he grabbed his rifle and came out of his shop blasting away – shooting dead the policeman who was moving his car off a double yellow line.

This sort of barely contained surburban violence (and near universal gun-ownership among whites) is a basic feature of the way South Africa lives now – I am electronically frisked every time I go to my local shopping arcade and refrisked at the door of the supermarket inside the arcade. People have easily absorbed these new parameters of everyday life and are generally pretty sure-footed about staying out of the way of trouble. There is, for example, a pub in Carletonville, near Johannesburg, where the bartender, a certain Siggie, keeps behind his counter no mere sub-machine gun, but a real machine-gun, replete with bullet belts. It is really quite surprising that anyone would want to trifle with Siggie (short for Sigmund), a gigantic German ex-Legionnaire whose massive forearms are the more pronounced for the tattoos they bear of favourite characters from Wagnerian opera. Siggie's first line of defence against late drinkers who refuse to leave is a pick-axe handle, the gun his ultimate weapon (and the pock-marked rafters over the beer-garden attest to the fact that he has occasionally, as he puts it, 'had to give a few squirts'). When, demonstrating his craft, Siggie lays his monstrous gun on the counter, there is a noticeable stir of unease among the drinkers – though it is only early evening – and several men look in anxious surprise at their wrist-watches. It is really very striking how flexible even the most ingrained social habits become in the face of a well-oiled machine-gun.

To get back to the question of why so many prostitutes: the reasons lie in the tidal wave of demographic growth and urbanisation which are together transforming South Africa before one's very eyes. This wave is not so much destroying apartheid as simply overwhelming it. The perfectly correct notion underlying apartheid was that all power and wealth were ultimately centred on a few great urban citadels: apartheid was, at heart, a system for ensuring white predominance in the cities by making sure that as many Africans as possible were kept in the rural areas – on the farms or in the 'homelands'. Albeit at a terrible human cost, this did work more or less as long as the African population remained relatively small. Odd though it already seems, 1980 was the first year in which, in the cities of South Africa, Africans outnumbered non-Africans (i.e. whites, Asians and Coloureds; Africans outnumbered whites alone by 2:1). And those 7.6 million urban Africans represented only 36 per cent of 1980's total African population. By the year 2000, however, the African population will have increased from today's 25 million to 36.2 million and the African urbanisation rate is set to increase from 36 per cent in 1980 to 75 per cent then. The bottom line to all this is that while there are today perhaps 9.5 million urban Africans, by the year 2000 there will be 27.2 million of them. The projections for 2020, for what they are worth, are for around fifty million urban Africans. Today whites constitute a quarter of all urban dwellers; in 2000 they will form a seventh; in 2020 perhaps a twelfth. (And by 2000 there will also be 1.3 million Asians and 4 million Coloureds.)

Mere numbers are not the whole of it. By the year 2000 no less than 60 per cent of Africans will be aged 20 or under – while the white population, like its counterpart in Western Europe, is a notably ageing one: ads for retirement homes and even whole retirement villages are prominent on all the newspapers' property pages. This age structure – lots of old and very young – means that a relatively small economically active population will have to support a very large number of dependants. But most important of all, there will simply not be enough jobs for all these people. The best estimates suggest that the number of employed persons would rise from 7.7 million in 1986 to ten million in 2000 if there were no sanctions; but that if the present economic sanctions against South Africa are maintained, employment will grow only to eight million in the same period. The extra two million unemployed will, of course, be overwhelmingly unskilled and black, which is one reason why not a few black trade-unionists and Marxist 'workerists' – as well as the Government – are opposed to sanctions. Still, sanctions there will undoubtedly be, and probably tougher ones than at present, so it would be fairly safe to predict that by the year 2000, of a potential working population of 17.8 million, 9.8 million will be unemployed. In depressed areas this 55 per cent rate of unemployment has already been reached. At the height of the 1984–6 urban insurrection, unemployment in Port Elizabeth reached 56 per cent; today it is at 57 per cent and the result is seething townships and massive outward migration to less blighted cities. But by 2000, with a national unemployment rate of 55 per cent, there will be nowhere much to go. Meanwhile Port Elizabeth operates with a permanent curfew.

The result of these trends is already visible – those child beggars and schoolgirl prostitutes are the vanguard: a flood of humanity, much of it unemployed, is pouring into the cities and the townships and squatter camps around them. Those that can, seek work in the modern, formal sector; others participate in a burgeoning 'informal' black economy; but an ever-growing number can live only by preying on others. Thus a huge army is forming of beggars, burglars, muggers, pimps, prostitutes, drug-pedlars, protection racketeers and so forth – many of them children. Mainly, of course, they prey on employed blacks, the target group most accessible to them in the townships, but already more and more whites are reacting to this threat of growing insecurity by living behind virtual stockades. Strolling nostalgically round the areas of Durban where I grew up, I found I could hardly see houses I had once known so well – they are all hidden now behind high walls and remote-controlled iron gates. A pollster friend in Johannesburg told me he had had to give up trying to carry out surveys in the affluent northern suburbs: his researchers found they could seldom establish any form of human contact with their interviewees and were having to put all their questions to intercom boxes in garden walls.

In addition to the fortification of their homes, whites depend for their security on a still impregnable police and military establishment and on the fact that African townships and squatter settlements have been placed at some distance from white cities. For the moment this is enough, and the mayhem which reigns in those townships (by far the world's highest crime rates, dozens of murders every weekend, vigilantism, warlordism, etc.) finds only a faint echo in the white city. But it is difficult to see how this separation can be maintained. Over the last seven years the economic growth rate has averaged 1.3 per cent but the population has grown at about twice that rate. So the population increases, per capita income falls, the number of unemployed swells at a steady rate of 1,000 people a day (with no dole), and there are more and more desperate, hungry people all the time. We have really seen nothing yet, but as the 1990s progress, great waves of humanity are going to wash into the white cities. The children who will make up those waves are already born. I doubt whether the distance from the white city or the power of the state will be enough in the end. People can walk and guns cannot stop a tidal wave. Blacks, incidentally, understand extremely well the unstoppable power of these demographics, which is why Aids is a topic of such obsessive concern amongst black radicals – it is seen as the only phenomenon capable of robbing blacks of their decisive power of numbers.

For the moment the black city and the white city remain different worlds. The contrasts this engenders are breathtaking. Thus, for example, as I sit typing this on my PC at the University of Natal, I can look out at the Valley of a Thousand Hills which forms Durban's hinterland. Among the black townships I can see is Chesterville. Now not long ago, in the Inkatha v. UDF fighting which has so terrorised the townships, the traditional Inkatha elders of Chesterville decided that they would teach some of the UDF militants a good old-fashioned Zulu lesson. So they tied them up to trees and cut pieces off them – fingers, toes, genitalia and so on. Apparently it took all day for them to die. A single glance takes in both my Taiwanese PC and the scene of that 'lesson'.

All of which sounds and is very dire. The feelings of doom and gloom among whites have to be experienced to be believed, but the atmosphere in UDF/ANC circles is not much brighter. Amazingly, in 1984–6 many radicals, black and white, talked themselves into believing that the revolution had really arrived. That this was an illusion is plain enough now, with the resistance movements in pieces all over the floor and bitterly divided against one another in today's exhausted calm. The situation, which is bad now, is undoubtedly going to get worse. It is beginning to dawn even on some of the radicals here (and South Africa is the only country I know where Marxism is spreading like a forest fire) that even 'after the revolution' these problems are not going to go away. Putting the ANC in power – which even many whites are beginning to assume, however reluctantly, is the future shape of things – will hardly solve the problem of the demographic explosion and growing insecurity.

Yet despite all the doom and gloom I find myself pulled back to this country, to its natural beauty, the wonderful complexity and variety and drama of life here. I utterly love being here, will always come back.

The present calm could last quite a while as far as blacks are concerned; Govan Mbeki, the released ANC leader, says he has never seen the black opposition more fragmented than it is now. But the world of white politics will reach a major watershed with the municipal elections of 26 October. There will be elections in Asian, Coloured and African municipalities too, but the recent assassination of one of the African candidates apart, these are not really of much interest. The Asian and Coloured contests are generally one-horse races, and with the parties that count either not allowed to stand or boycotting the occasion, the main interest of the elections in the African townships will be whether even a 10 per cent poll is achieved and whether any more candidates get killed. The white municipals, on the other hand, will really count, for there is no doubt that Andries Treurnicht's far-right Conservative Party (CP) is poised to make sweeping gains. Indeed, the CP has made such remarkable progress in recent months that the idea that the ruling National Party (NP) could actually be voted out of office no longer seems fanciful – though whether P.W. Botha would hand over power in such an eventuality is another question altogether. The NP–CP split has divided Afrikanerdom in a way not seen for the last fifty years. All over the country little Afrikaans-speaking towns are facing the first real political competition they can remember, and in many of them the NP is so frightened of defeat that, rather than put up its own candidates, it is backing independents. In some platteland towns, indeed, the CP presence has already become so overwhelming that the NP simply cannot find candidates. There is no doubt that any white supporter of the ANC should vote CP, for nothing would do more to hasten the demise of white power than a Treurnicht government or, alternatively, a pre-emptive NP coup against it. At the moment, the CP is predicting victory in not fewer than 60 of the 84 towns in the Transvaal – the heartland of South African politics. Already, fear of the CP's advance has brought Botha's programme of reform to a complete halt. If the CP makes anything like the gains it is predicting, the present period, with all its difficulties, will seem like a lost golden age.

The NP–CP split has taken spectacular form in the rival

celebrations of the 150th anniversary of the Great Trek. South Africans have a highly developed sense of humour and there is wide enjoyment of the way in which, in the name of history, the Trek is being commemorated, of the quite wonderful tastelessness of the occasion and the blatant lack of respect for any sort of real history. The Government-sponsored wagon has already left Cape Town on its 2,500 km. trek to Pretoria. The original trek took place over a period of years, not, as is now pretended, in one specific year, 1838. Nor, of course, did the Trekkers go straight – or even mainly – to Pretoria: they wandered all over the sub-continent. They didn't start from Cape Town, but from the Eastern Cape, hundreds of miles away. And they did not, of course, travel on tarred roads which the 1988 Trekkers do quite exclusively.

Today's Trek is led by a couple called Flip and Martie du Plooy, who seem to have grasped this idea of history-less history with relish. Apart from stopping for no fewer than 350 festival dinners at towns on the way, Flip and Martie have decided to do without the tent-and-campfire life, living off microwaved take-aways during the day and staying in motels at night. The idea of actually sitting in the bumpy wagons has, of course, been set aside: Flip and Martie drive alongside the wagons in a Combi van. Well, not quite alongside: Flip goes ahead to meet the reception committee in the next town, while Martie sets up sales points for Great Trek memorabilia. The wagon train is linked by radio and TV to Johannesburg, with one Gracelle Gerber, a Potchefstroom communications graduate, providing the wheel-by-wheel commentary. (Thanks to the Californian glop which fills South African TV screens, there are not a few Gracelles, Charlenes and Chantelles even among the staid young ladies of Potch nowadays.) The only real trekkers in all this will be the twelve black labourers who will walk alongside the wagons all the way to Pretoria and sleep by them at night, just as their forebears did. If the symbolism of this was not enough, three of the oxen were injured on their way to the start and another died at the start. One trembles to think of the possible symbolism if the 1988 trekkers, for all their advantages, do not make it. The rival CP wagons (which will start later) are taking no chances and have dispensed with oxen altogether: their wagons will not be wagons at all but outsize – and motorised – carnival floats.

All of which recalls nothing so much as last year's quincentennial Diaz celebrations, which gave much innocent pleasure. A medieval Portuguese ship was rigged to follow the course down the west coast of Africa that Bartholomew Diaz had taken in 1487 on making the first circumnavigation of the Cape. Just to be safe the ship was equipped with a somewhat un-medieval diesel engine as well as sails. The ship set off in good order, but nervous anniversary officials decided that it was going too slowly to make landfall at the Cape on the appointed date. A South African Navy destroyer was sent to help and, despite the furious protests of the latter-day Diaz (who insisted he was making good time), towed the sailing ship along at a speed which would no doubt have startled the good Bartholomew.

The original Diaz, on landing at the Cape, had found a welcoming party of Hottentots. (Well, actually, the welcome deteriorated: the Hottentots stoned the whites, who in turn shot one of the Hottentots dead – both parties were only setting a precedent for what has been going on ever since. Today, of course, press restrictions would make it impossible to report such an incident.) The Hottentots, or to give them their proper name, the Khoi Khoi, have long since been absorbed into the Coloured population, so appeal was made for a party of Coloureds to assist in a cleaned-up re-enactment of Diaz's welcome (no stones, no guns this time). Coloured leaders pointed out that the beach in question was a Whites Only beach. The Government promised to make it an 'Open' beach for the day. The Coloureds said they would settle for nothing less than permanent 'Open' status. The government refused. Coloured leaders called for a boycott of the whole event and sure enough no Coloureds could be found to participate. In the end, the part of the Khoi Khoi was taken by suitable blacked-up whites. Having to create bogus blacks in a country which, whatever else, is hardly short of real black people seems difficult to beat. This is, though, a land of surprises and it would be foolish to bet that even this symbolic high point will not be surpassed.

To be fair, the old white South African attitude of treating non-whites as so many interchangeable garden gnomes has largely gone. In a host of informal ways blacks are more and more evidently citizens. In the old days the media might report that, for example, a black man had raped a white woman, which had the effect for most whites of making some crimes seem more heinous than others. Nowadays, media reports of accidents and crimes no longer mention the race of either the victim or the assailant, so now all crimes, at least, are equal. Perhaps more striking is the American-style affirmatively multiracial character of most advertising, including TV advertising. Similarly, the desegregation of public facilities has reached a point where one is positively surprised, certainly in Cape Town, Johannesburg or Durban, to find any that are not integrated. At the universities of Cape Town and Natal where I have been teaching, nearly a quarter of the students are blacks and it is assumed that black students will be in the majority at both institutions by the year 2000. (Even this calculation is made on the assumption that present political conditions will continue, which of course they will not.) Black students are treated not just equally but preferentially – for example, in the allocation of places in residences. (The Government looks hard the other way as the Universities break the Group Areas Act.) Twenty-six years ago, as a member of the Student Representative Council here in Durban, I fought hard and unavailingly for a lesser degree of integration than is now easily conceded. It has all taken far too long to come, but the progress is undeniable. The black students, understandably, are slow to trust the change and have a horror of finding themselves in the position of a patronised minority in a land where they are the majority: so they will not vote or stand in student elections and in Cape Town they are even, madly, demanding separate sports facilities.

Oddly, perhaps the most warming experience I have had here was at a lunchtime concert given by Ladysmith Black Mambazo of *Graceland* fame. The university hall was thronged with a capacity audience, black, white and Asian, students and campus workers, Zulu maintenance men in their overalls, women cleaners ululating in their excitement at the band's antics, alongside bearded and ponderous white academics. For once, just for once, there was a completely united enjoyment of a single event: everybody, but everybody, was mixed in, and everybody was happy. One had a tantalising glimpse of a common South African identity and citizenship waiting out there somewhere, if only it can be grasped. But to feel that is also to feel the awful tenuousness of the thing, the only too likely possibility that it will not be grasped, that the whites, having come this far, will regret their 'reforms' and decide, in effect, that they would rather the country collapsed back into separate, warring identities. The results in the white municipalities on 26 October will tell us if such a collapse is taking place. It would be wise to fear the worst.

Chapter 30

Laughing Till It Hurts

People who live outside South Africa are liable to misunderstand you if you say it is a wonderful country. Actually, it is wonderful, sad, beautiful, wicked, cruel and very, very funny. No sooner have you stopped laughing at some new grotesquerie than it is immediately topped. The story below about the bigamous Mr Meynhardt was a case in point. I thought, when I wrote it up, that the fact that Mr Meynhardt had actually been elected to the Pretoria city council was remarkable enough. But I was wrong. The National Party held on to control of the council by the slimmest of margins and, seeking to increase its room for manouevre, its eyes naturally fell on the now somewhat friendless figure of Mr Meynhardt. This had the happy and immediate result that Mr Meynhardt was elected as one of the council's vice-chairmen, putting him only a heart beat away from whatever it is that vice-chairmen of the Pretoria city council are next to. People say that everything will change in South Africa after majority rule. Personally I suspect that alongside the agony and the ecstasy and the drama and euphoria of it all, you will be able to just keep on laughing.

White South Africans frequently complain that their country is misrepresented in the British press, which concentrates entirely on the darker side of life here. There is truth in this. This is, after all, the country that spawned Tom Sharpe's first novel, *Riotous Assembly*. You can feel a lot of anger and sadness and tension in this country but it is also the case that nowhere else in the world do you laugh as much as you do here. Bizarre things happen here, routinely.

Where else, for example, would you get stories about attempts to inflict grievous bodily harm on an ox-wagon? By the son of a former Vice-President of this country, at that, one Kallie Schlebusch, who farms at Hennenman in the Orange Free State. The Voortrekker wagon is the centre-piece of the Great Trek commemoration mounted by the Afrikaner Volkswag, the cultural arm of Treurnicht's far-right Conservative Party (CP). The problem is that the CP wagon is a rival to the official, government-sponsored commemorative wagon making the trek to Pretoria by a different route. The CP wagon is not a very convincing object, being a motor-powered and outsize steel replica of the real thing, but the sight of it was enough to provoke a loyal member of the National Party (NP) like Mr Schlebusch. He and two friends sneaked up on the wagon, hooked it to their light truck, and drove off, hoping to topple it over. Caught red-handed, the three men have been made by the CP to repair the wagon themselves and issue public apologies in the newspapers, though Mr Schlebusch sounds remarkably cheerful about it all and professes himself 'satisfied' by the whole event. One knows what he means.

The CP have come off less well in the case of Louis Meynhardt, one of its municipal councillors in Pretoria. One of Mr Meynhardt's former lovers, who claims she has been looking for him in vain for fifteen years, was thrilled to recognise him at last from his picture on his election posters, and promptly slapped a paternity suit on him. This triggered complaints by another lady who feels that her children too have certain claims on Mr Meynhardt, as does a former wife who has subpoenaed him at the same time. These small domestic difficulties coincided with the circulation of anonymous letters in Mr Meynhardt's ward, making various grave allegations against him. Mr Meynhardt admitted to the letter's charges of convictions for drunken driving and illegal hunting but denied all knowledge of other convictions for theft in 1972 and 1975, assault, fraud and theft in 1975, and then fraud and theft again in 1982. Presented with documentary evidence of these convictions Mr Meynhardt said that they were all a long time ago and that he could not comment further because a police brigadier (yes!) had been involved in some of these things with him and that the matter was under police consideration. 'I have since become religious,' added Mr Meynhardt, 'and I now walk the straight and narrow.'

Mr Meynhardt was elected, incidentally, and it would be unkind to think that this was merely due to the disqualification of his NP opponent for breaking the electoral law. Mr Meynhardt has had to resign from the CP but is adamant that he will not resign from the council. It sounds as if there may be quite a large number of children who could, so to speak, take legitimate pride in the way Mr Meynhardt pursues his path of helping to govern the nation's capital.

One of the government's chief objectives in the municipal

elections was to get non-white voters involved and voting for their own segregated councils. Naturally, the Left – the ANC, the UDF and AZAPO – called for a boycott. The government is crowing over Black turn-out rates of around 20 per cent in many districts, neglecting to note that only a tiny fraction of potential voters were even willing to register, so that really we are talking about 20 per cent of almost nothing. Naturally, the state-owned TV did its bit with a stream of propaganda, including, most notably, ads featuring a cute squirrel squeakily telling everyone to be a good citizen and vote. The good citizen whose voice this really was is a Mr Don Lamprecht, an SABC TV star who, apart from imitating squirrels, dubs lots of English-language films into Afrikaans and also has top billing in such soap epics as *Dokter, Dokter* and *Siener in die Suburbs*. The question being asked now, though, is whether Mr Lamprecht is really quite such a good citizen himself, for he has now been arrested on charges of sodomy, indecent assault on minors and possession of child pornography. Already a senior SABC executive, Mr Tinus Esterhuizen, who manages an entire radio channel, has been arrested on similar charges, and we are told that they are merely the first of a large ring of SABC personnel involved in similar activities. Mr Lamprecht is used to being a star, though, so he happily waves to and poses for photographers as he goes in and out of the police charge office. The notion that the SABC is a vast nest of child abusers and child pornographers has caused a twitch of happy surprise among even its sternest critics, and the Left is keenly hoping that one or two particularly hated news presenters will show up on charges before long.

The richness of the comic experience in South Africa is something of a puzzle. It is tempting to say that it is the collision of cultures or the articiality of the political and racial situation here which somehow produces stories like the above. Personally, I think that the wonderful obliviousness of so much White South Africa has a lot to do with it, but I have no proof. It is equally hard to decide whether this is the world's finest climate for satire or not. Certainly, nowhere else could be better. But the problem for any satirist here is the overwhelming competition he has to endure – from simple everyday life.

Chapter 31
Black on Black

The UDF/ANC objects to the use of the term 'black on black violence', pointing out that nobody talks of 'white on white violence', and that the ultimate culpability of the South African government for the violence is omitted if we just talk about 'black on black'. I pondered this for some time. The first objection is not strong: we probably would talk about 'white on white violence' if there was enough of it to merit the term, and the main reason to talk about 'black on black' is that we all assume that there is an awful lot of 'white on black violence' in South Africa, a supposition with which the UDF/ANC do not, presumably, wish to argue. The second objection is tougher. It is perfectly true that the government's forces do not always adopt a neutral stance between the warring parties, and that the government has helped create a situation in which a great deal of semi-random social violence is likely to occur. But then, the term 'black on black' does not say anything about ultimate responsibility; it simply refers to black people killing other black people. An awful lot of this does go on, and all the indications are that as the struggle for power in a majority rule South Africa hots up, there will be even more of it. I asked a UDF militant what term she would like me to substitute for 'black on black'. She was utterly stumped. So I decided to use it. It is what all the people on the spot call it. And, by the way, blacks who kill other blacks bear some considerable responsibility for it: they are not just pawns of the Government, after all.

'Of course, liberal English-speaking whites like you are really the worst sort', said my dinner guest, Mr Precious Tshabalala, glaring at me with real hostility. 'Most of us black revolutionaries' – he broke off to complain to the wine waiter that his claret was slightly corked – 'actually prefer straight talk with Afrikaners. At least you know where you are with them.' Actually, Precious (despite the opening gambit we were quickly on first-name terms) seemed to know just where he was with me – he knew his way round the plush hotel we were in as if he lived there, the hotel staff greeting him with deferential familiarity wherever he went. Precious had been a personnel manager in a large firm, but was now in business on his own as a personnel consultant. An articulate, educated man, he is in great demand, taking part in any number of the where-do-we-go-from-here conferences that white business anxiously sponsors. Before the end of the month he was due to give talks about South Africa's future in Toronto, Washington and New York, for the coming South African revolution has frightened many people with large financial or political interests here into creating an international jet-set circuit of concern on which able and intelligent blacks are much sought after.

Like so many other educated blacks, Precious is a strong believer in Black Consciousness (BC). Indeed, one of the many traps facing the interested white here is that the blacks he talks to belong to the intelligentsia, and it is easy to come away from these conversations with the notion that BC and its political wing, AZAPO, has massive support. 'We control the Eastern Cape and at least half Jo'burg,' said Precious firmly, 'and our comrades in the Unity Movement and the National Forum run things in the Western Cape.' Precious spends a great deal of his time talking to white businessmen, exhorting them, usually in vain, to put black directors on their boards.

> They're such fools, these people: can't they see how they will look when there's a black government? What they need is to have a few black rising stars on their boards. There could be a revolution any time. How can these white people know when the revolution will take place? It is no good planning like a white man, you have to understand the black mind. Whites think they can strategise it all, but the black man acts on instinct, which outwits all this strategising. Only a black man can understand that, can know that instinct, can understand other blacks. The whites haven't any idea what their workers are thinking. They could be taken by surprise at any moment: an incident could break out because a black child is run over, a riot will start – there's no strategising for that. Whites must realise they are no longer the rising star and that the rising star is the black man now.

I asked Precious if anyone had put him on their board of directors. 'Not yet,' he said, somewhat sourly, 'but it will happen. Definitely.' He spoke of his contacts with various white captains of industry – mentioning them all by their first names – and then spoke with particular feeling about what was for him the central issue, Black Economic Empowerment (BEE). He and some of his friends, he told me, had a scheme to take over the distribution of the major South African brands of beer to African townships – a megacontract if ever there was one. But why, I asked, should the breweries hand over such a flourishing business to them? At this Precious pounded the table and said that it really was time for all these white businessmen who said they wanted to help blacks to prosper to put their money where their mouths were. It was some time before he mentioned what I had rather suspected: that word had been dropped to the breweries that if they did not hand over the contract they might find their delivery lorries being set on fire when they went into the townships. (The important word there was 'might' – there is room for doubt as to how far people like Precious can control what goes on in townships or squatter camps.)

Finally, we came to the inevitable question of sanctions – responses to which serve as recognition signals between the contending factions of the South African opposition. The African National Congress (ANC) and the South African Communist Party (SACP) favour sanctions, which means that many of the community organisations affiliated to the United Democratic Front (UDF), which has acted as a loosely-structured ANC internal wing, also favour them. Chief Buthelezi's Inkatha movement is against sanctions, as are virtually all whites and a majority of both Asians and Coloureds. But while the inheritors of the old Pan-Africanist Congress and Unity Movement traditions (i.e. those opposed to the ANC's Congress Alliance), which today means organisations such as AZAPO and the National Forum, generally try to outbid the ANC and UDF in theoretical (Marxist) radicalism, the sanctions issue is sometimes different. The point is that the trade unions have strong, if seldom-voiced, doubts about sanctions: hence the 'workerist' critique of UDF 'populism', the sharp end of which is the suggestion that bourgeois groups within the UDF wish to use the sanctions weapon to defeat, not only the Government, but the power of organised labour too, making the ultimate triumph of a black middle class all the more certain. The most radical workerists, such as the National Forum's Neville Alexander, argue that (a) the South African revolution must be won by the black working class, (b) that sanctions inevitably inflict large-scale unemployment, weakening the black working class, so (c) sanctions are bad. This inevitably leads on to the question of whether the South African revolution is supposed to be a one- or two-stage affair: that is, whether the working class and socialism are going to win right away (one-stage) or later (two-stage). Thus to ask someone whether they are for or against sanctions is less a matter of suggesting that they might have some influence on the international movement towards sanctions (which seems to have a life of its own) than of requiring them to situate themselves within a fairly dense organisational and theoretical context. I had, accordingly, decided to ask Precious this question last.

> 'Well, it is a matter which takes much discussion, much discussion', he said.
> 'You know, we have these children, the comrades, in the townships. They are ignorant, they know nothing – they all went on school strikes and boycotts in 1984, saying: "Revolution Now, Education Later." Now they have no education, no jobs, nothing. They commit any crime and call it a protest. It is terrifying to live among people like them, but that is what apartheid means – that I have to. They say any black businessman is a sell-out and they want to necklace you if you say you're against sanctions. I have to explain that I am in favour of some sanctions, against others. Indeed, I am going to Canada to suggest they only carry out sanctions against companies here which don't have black directors on their boards.'

I could not help liking Precious, with his remarkable entrepreneurial drive to turn everything – township trouble, sanctions, the fear of revolution and the colour of his skin – to financial account. He had done well enough, too, to have his children at an expensive private school in a white suburb, and saw no contradiction in this: it was helping his children to get ahead and they were black, so the whole thing was 'ideologically positive', he explained. The Black Consciousness he espouses is, of course, perfectly constructed to act as the ideology of the burgeoning black middle class. I was quite surprised that Precious could keep a straight face as he made the claim that he somehow had an instinctive insight into the minds of the Xhosa peasant, the Zulu factory worker, the Pedi shack-dweller, the Tswana miner and so on, simply because he was black. Indeed, BC only makes sense as an ideology in a white-dominated society, as a way of uniting blacks against whites, of putting oneself forward as a privileged intermediary between blacks and whites, and as a symbolic representative of all blacks. In a society where blacks start with few resources, it is an attempt to make the possession of a black skin a resource in itself.

Precious's political hero was Desmond Tutu: 'I can definitely see a **rising star rising in the body of that man**', as he put it. This was despite, or perhaps partly because of, the fact that Tutu is a politician in a classically African – that is to say, extravagant – mould: a headline-seeker, a man who makes wild, unsubstantiated and inconsistent charges, goes out of his way to infuriate and inflame even moderate white opinion, and is an egomaniac of historic proportions. Universally remembered is his famous threat to leave South Africa if violence did not stop, as if the fear of losing him would be sufficient to stop the country's evolution in its tracks. The violence went on, Tutu stayed put and more recently has been grabbing headlines with his demands that the Church should not necessarily condemn violence. His antics during the Pope's recent visit to Southern Africa are difficult to explain as anything other than pique at being overshadowed as chief religious 'personality' in the region.

That none of these things can in the slightest shake the widespread black admiration for Tutu is due to two factors. With almost every black leader of significance prevented from playing a public role, attention focuses on the two whose position makes them immune from government harrassment, Chief Buthelezi and Tutu. Since Buthelezi is widely written off as a conservative traditionalist leading an essentially tribal party, Inkatha, this leaves just Tutu, and Tutu has taken the gap. His advocacy of sanctions is a way of signalling that he is anti-Inkatha, and most of his pronouncements are best understood as a careful balancing act between the UDF/ANC, on the one hand, and Black Consciousness movements, on the other. Rather like a bantam cock, he struts and preens, then darts in for a quick attack on the Government – a deliberate personification of the 'cheeky kaffir'. The next moment he has darted back and is the serene but slightly mischievous churchman, invoking God with a smile, and the moment after that he is off on yet another whirlwind foreign tour. Hence the second source of Tutu's popularity with blacks: he is seen as the ultimately successful entrepreneur, who, like any black who makes it, has done so against the system. With his tele-fame here and abroad, his Nobel Prize and other awards, his international jet-set existence, the accoutrements of wealth and immune political status as well, it is no wonder Precious sees Tutu as a role model. As head of the Anglican Church in South Africa, Tutu has what Precious wants so much – a seat on the board: indeed, he is actually chairman of the damn thing, a living example of the delights that Black Economic (well, religious) Empowerment can bring.

The tendency to write off Buthelezi is a mistake. True, the terrible fighting between Inkatha and the UDF in the townships and squatter camps around Pietermaritzburg and Durban has lost Buthelezi the sympathy of many liberal whites, who have been appalled at the disciplined savagery of the Inkatha impis and local Inkatha war-lords (or 'community leaders', as Inkatha calls them). Similarly, the rejection of Buthelezi by black students on the Natal campus where I am working has hardened into a passionate and understandable hatred – for some have had homes burnt down and families hacked to death with pangas in the township fighting, which has claimed well over a thousand dead to date. It is also true that Buthelezi's claim to non-Zulu black support is thinner than it was. But, as Buthelezi pointed out at the Shaka Day celebrations I recently attended, nearly one South African in four is a Zulu and no group in the country is bigger. Inkatha (strictly, Inkatha ye Nkululeko ye Sizwe, or National Cultural Liberation Movement) claims over one million members. (Its dues-paying membership is probably only 250,000, but this is still many times what any other black political organisation in South Africa has ever achieved.) Whatever goes on in the townships, nobody disputes that Inkatha has the rural masses of Zululand locked up solid – and the large numbers of Zulu workers on the gold reef make Inkatha a force there too. Buthelezi somewhat disingenuously claims that one cannot have black unity without first having Zulu unity and points out that the Zulu tradition is one of incorporation, so that anyone who accepts Zulu tradition and culture can become a Zulu – there are even precedents for white men becoming Zulu chiefs.

When Buthelezi launched Inkatha in 1975 the ANC, the victim of more than a decade of ruthless repression, had little grass-roots support inside South Africa and existed mainly in the shape of its External Mission – the exile group in London led by Oliver Tambo. Buthelezi had been an ANC supporter in his youth and was, at least at first, keen to stay on side with the ANC, securing their blessing, for example, before he accepted the position of Chief Minister of the KwaZulu Bantustan. In seems likely that Buthelezi hoped Inkatha would fill the vacuum, that it might even become the effective – and autonomous – internal wing of the ANC. The ANC's colours, flag and anthem were deliberately taken on by Inkatha, which spoke of the ANC as 'great black patriots' and tended to depict Buthelezi as the natural successor to Albert Luthuli, the last really well-known ANC leader and a Zulu chief. In addition, the movement adopted the philosophy of *Ubuntu-botho* (humanism), the official doctrine of the ANC when it was founded in 1912. At this stage it did not appear to worry either side that Buthelezi was an outspoken proponent of both non-violent tactics and a capitalist solution, while the ANC tended to be socialist and was, via its military wing, Umkhonto we

Sizwe, committed to the armed struggle. But whatever hopes the ANC may have entertained of building a patron–client relationship with Buthelezi could not have lasted long: it soon became clear that he was building a wholly independent power base.

The Soweto uprising of 1976 caught the ANC badly off guard. The events owed nothing to them and the Soweto students were quoting, not Mandela or Tambo, but the Black Consciouness writings of Steve Biko: it seemed – nightmarishly – that the situation within South Africa was simply escaping them. Moreover, the new generation of black radicals within South Africa reviled Buthelezi as a collaborator with apartheid and found a ready audience for their denunciations. There is no doubt that the ANC viewed Biko and his BC colleagues as threatening rivals – Biko's repeated attempts to set up meetings with Tambo (of the sort Buthelezi and his representatives frequently had) were always turned down. But while the emergence of the Biko group saw the ANC gravely embarrassed by its links with Buthelezi, it also meant that, if the ANC wished to resist BC on the ground, it needed the Buthelezi alliance more than ever. Today Inkatha will tell you that the ANC heaved an immense sigh of relief when Biko was murdered in September 1977, and that this left the ANC free to confront Inkatha. (The ANC, of course, dismisses this as a gross libel.) The ANC's relations with Buthelezi had never been easy: Buthelezi wanted to build his own power base and saw himself as a future president of South Africa, while the ANC felt that Buthelezi was free-riding on the ANC's historic legitimacy and had to prove himself a disciplined (i.e. subordinate) part of the liberation struggle. Buthelezi was happy enough to call himself part of the liberation struggle, but took orders from nobody: he is, after all, the great-grandson of Cetshwayo, who humbled the British Empire at Rorke's Drift and Isandhlwana, and the great-great-grandson of Dingaan, who massacred the first Boers to venture into Natal. Buthelezi's invocation of that formidable history annoys the UDF, partly because the UDF would like to claim Shaka, Dingaan and Cetshwayo as national figures of resistance to white rule.

In 1979 Buthelezi attempted, unsuccessfully, to get the ANC to adopt his 'multiple strategy' – you do your thing, and I'll do mine – and in 1980 the relationship broke down entirely when Buthelezi refused the ANC's demand that he prove once and for all his bona fides in the liberation struggle by allowing KwaZulu to be used as a guerrilla base for Umkhonto infiltrators from Mozambique. In fact, Buthelezi had already given shelter to some such guerrillas and the Pretoria Government had remonstrated furiously with him when it found Umkhonto arms caches in KwaZulu. It was perfectly clear that to accept the ANC's demand would lead to the South African Army (the SADF) running riot all over KwaZulu and the complete destruction of Buthelezi's power base, perhaps even of Buthelezi himself – an event which might cause the ANC to cry only crocodile tears. Buthelezi, who in 1980 was running better than 2:1 ahead of Mandela in opinion polls among blacks, felt he had far too much to lose and said no.

From 1980 on, Buthelezi was in a state of cold war with the ANC and must have watched with some chagrin the remarkable popular rediscovery and hero-worship of Mandela. But the formation of the UDF in 1983 raised the stakes very considerably. In one sense, the UDF, an unco-ordinated federation of hundreds of community and student organisations, with twelve presidents, no visible constitution and no individual membership, was hard to take seriously. While it followed the ANC line on most things, it was both more and less than the ANC: it enjoyed the support of many associations which had had nothing to do with the ANC, but it lacked any sort of coherent structure. In Natal, where it had to confront Buthelezi, it enjoyed the additional disadvantage of being dominated by the minority Asian community. The UDF did, though, have several things going for it: it was genuinely multiracial and genuinely national in its reach and its base in a way that Inkatha could never be; it had the implicit support of the biggest trade union confederation, COSATU; and there was a clear public understanding that it was the legitimate inheritor of the Congress tradition. The strength of that tradition is such that it is impossible to believe that any black movement can succeed outside it – that is, after all, why even Buthelezi tried to situate himself within it.

The attempt to set up UDF organisations in the great African townships and squatter camps in the Durban-Pietermaritzburg strip was a frontal challenge to Buthelezi and Inkatha. If they allowed the UDF to capture these, the most dynamic and fastest-growing areas of Zulu settlement, Inkatha would be confined to a shrinking and 'backward' rural world. Buthelezi almost certainly saw this as the ANC's riposte: if he would not become a subordinate he would simply be displaced. The result has been a ferocious battle for political control of these areas, with the fighting quickly taking on a momentum of its own and incorporating battles over land, the looting of possessions and the settling of blood feuds. A typical conflict will involve squatters on the lower slopes fighting those with superior sites on the upper slopes and taking their land and possessions if they can – perhaps the most elemental form of class conflict imaginable.

The inevitable product of this long period of bloodshed has been warlordism, with each area living in terror of its own petty feudal lord, who (often in cahoots with the Police) runs a small private army, guarantees protection to those who obey him and drives out all intruders – whether political or just new would-be squatters. The very fact of black-on-black conflict, let alone the savagery of the fighting, gravely embarrassed the exiled ANC, but it was only in September that COSATU (acting for the banned UDF) finally signed a peace pact with Inkatha at Pietermaritzburg, Inkatha taking care to ensure the thirty-nine local Inkatha warlords also signed.

Buthelezi has enormous support among the white middle-class, has indeed a far broader racial base than any other black leader, but he has, as they say, very few friends on campus; the students here in Durban will not allow Inkatha speakers on to the campus, and the (white) National Union of South African Students is a formal UDF affiliate. UDF radicals – and they are, as it were, my people, my friends – tell you that Inkatha has lost enormous ground in the townships and that the UDF is still gaining. My impression is that Inkatha – far better organised than the UDF and perhaps (it is a fine judgement) more ruthless too – has won the battle for turf. Not only has it not been dislodged from its previous redoubts but Inkatha membership, which always increases in the wake of trouble, is now rising. Much of this membership will doubtless be only semi-voluntary – the average township-dweller is far more frightened of the Inkatha impis than he is of the white police. (Even the SADF can seem a welcome presence to the township-dwellers at the end of their tether – there are many cases of SADF troops playing cheerful soccer matches with the township youths who are their once and future enemy.) But Inkatha is also the law and order party and the longer trouble goes on, the more attractive it seems to many.

Inkatha is condemned by a broad band of 'progressive' opinion as being primarily responsible for the terrible bloodshed in Natal. It is certainly true that Inkatha has inflicted far more casualties on the UDF than vice versa, but that may just be because it is a better fighting machine. It is worth pointing out that down in the Eastern Cape (where Inkatha does not exist) the UDF used similarly brutal tactics to smash AZAPO's hold on the townships. Black political culture is often a very violent one – a knife culture, as it were. You can see this even in the rarefied air of university campuses. On the Natal campus, from which I write, an argument between a white student and some of his black peers not long ago resulted in the white being rescued in the nick of time from a necklacing. Inkatha has no monopoly on the use of violence. It also enjoys the support of my old friend, Rowley Arenstein, by far the most senior Communist living in the country – he was a CP Parliamentary candidate as long ago as 1943. I remember only too well standing guard against the Ku Klux Klan night after night outside Rowley's house. In fact, that is how I spent my nineteenth birthday; and the moment when the Klan finally came remains, happily, the only time I have ever been shot at. Rowley had just been expelled by the Party for his Maoism then and would preach Lenin at us while we were on guard. It is weird hearing him arguing for Inkatha now.

Inkatha is also condemned by both BC and UDF for being irredeemably capitalist and bourgeois, an assessment with which it cannot really quarrel. COSATU, is, of course, strongly socialist, as are large sections of the UDF, while the various BC movements and the National Forum attack the UDF for being insufficiently radical in its socialism, or anything else. All these movements, however (even, to some extent, the unions), are led by middle-class élites. In particular, one notes that lawyers and clergymen are taking the same leadership roles in black nationalist politics that their Afrikaner counterparts took in Afrikaner nationalist politics fifty years ago. Those Afrikaner nationalist ideologues and their children have by now grown into very fat cats, proving that radical nationalist politics are very good for you if you can only get on the right side of them. The black middle-class élites have taken note.

That black middle class is growing apace and so is the world of black business. The most prominent example at the moment are the black taxi-drivers, a whole class of bustling entrepreneurs created by bus deregulation, and now organised by SABTA – the South African Black Taxi-Drivers' Association. It is not an uncommon sight to see hundreds of black taxis lined up at bus or train stations, and stealing their clientele wholesale: it is cheaper and far quicker to go by black taxi than it is to travel third-class on the train, even on the 400-mile Johannesburg–Durban run. The only real competition to black taxis comes from other black taxis, which is why every taxi has a bouncer who fights any rival who tries to steal his business or parking spot.

It is quite symptomatic that SABTA, at its recent conference, should have announced that it wished to be considered as 'part of the liberation struggle'. For everybody can see that the day of black majority rule is coming. SABTA, for the sake of what one might euphemistically call the enhancement of their business environment, want a seat on the platform with the political bigwigs when that day dawns and will no doubt make handsome political contributions to that end. Happily for them, there will be plenty of people on those political platforms like my friend, Precious Tshabalala, only too happy to accommodate them via some mutually beneficial arrangement.

There is no doubt that the pickings will be terribly good for some, come the Big Change-over. After all these years of being spectators at the feast of white privilege, there should be no doubting the black élite's enormous appetite for immediate enrichment, nor the frustration it feels that the said Change-over cannot happen right away. I have a bad feeling that the élite will find a way to feather its nest whoever comes to power. As Precious would say, you cannot stop a rising star from definitely rising.

Chapter 23
Via Mandela

The article below was one of the first to draw attention in the British press to the problems attaching to Winnie Mandela and Mandela FC. To a degree which I found decidedly unhealthy, the foreign correspondent corps in Johannesburg knew much of the truth about Winnie but had decided to say nothing in deference to established liberal shibboleths in their home countries. Within the UDF, let alone the ANC, the situation was much the same. Only when Soweto residents began to make an unquellable fuss about the death of a small boy at the hands of Mandela FC and the Minister of Justice announced an inquiry into the affair did the UDF and the foreign correspondents charge into action.

Winnie is an alarming figure: even most blacks hope she never has the power to influence events. Her behaviour added an extra, almost unbearable dimension to the calvary poor Nelson Mandela has had to undergo. He is indeed a heroic figure, as is the perhaps even more remarkable Walter Sisulu. The day will come when Jan Smuts Airport in Johannesburg is renamed Nelson Mandela Airport, when D.F. Malan Airport in Cape Town is rechristened in Sisulu's name, when millions of South African schoolchildren read their names with pride in their history books as the fathers of a modern, non-racial South Africa. But we all get only one life and no amount of monuments when we are dead really compensates for having one's life wasted in prison. I pay homage to both of them and also feel that that is not enough.

Nelson Mandela, incarcerated for over a quarter of a century, writes frequently to his wife, Winnie, about his vivid and often rather frightening dreams.

> I dreamt I was with the young men of the kraal. They gave me herbs to strengthen me against you. They were saying that I should fight with

you so that you would run away. And you were shouting at me to throw away those leaves, they were bad medicine. A whole audience was listening to this conversation. I threw the leaves away.

On the night of 21/9 you and I were driving the Olds at corner of Eloff and Market when you rushed and spewed out porridge. It was hard and old with a crust on top. Your whole body quivered as each lump came out and you complained of a sharp pain on your right shoulder. I held you tight against my body, unmindful of the curious crowd and the traffic jam.

All the wonderful thrills I have missed. A lady sat on the floor with her legs stretched out as our mothers used to relax in the old days. Though I can't remember the actual words, she sang with a golden voice, the face radiating all the affection and fire a woman can give a man. She turned and twisted her arms. That lady was none other than our darling Mum.

'I don't know how to interpret these dreams', Mandela writes. 'But at least they indicate that there is far less steel in me than I had thought, that distance and two decades of separation have not strengthened the steel in me.' There is a terrible sadness to many of his letters. 'I've plans, wishes and hopes', he writes at another point. 'I dream and build castles. But one has to be realistic.' Or again: 'Sometimes I feel like one who is on the sidelines who has missed life itself.'

Mandela may be released soon. If so, a new biography, with his full co-operation, may be possible. Fatima Meer's book (1988) is full of interest, but it is not worthy of the man: it stops and starts several times, is full of gaps and factual errors and is clearly a rushed job. Misspellings and errors litter the pages to such a degree that one wonders if the book was proof-read at all – one word is spelled three different ways in the space of ten lines. Mrs Meer also writes in an over-heated style. Of the Government's actions in 1953, for example, she says: 'The Nationalists, insatiable in their need to dominate and mad with anxiety that they might not be able to do so eternally, extended the frontier of oppression.' This sort of thing is simply nonsense – the Government could hardly be said to be mad with anxiety even today, let alone in 1953. But the book contains hundreds of Mandela's letters, has benefited from Winnie's full co-operation, contains many photographs and, for all its faults, is pretty much compulsory reading for anyone who wants to understand this tragic and remarkable man. Most people are aware of the major public landmarks of Mandela's life: his role as ANC organiser, the Treason Trial, the Defiance Campaign, the Rivonia Trial and his long incarceration on Robben Island and at Pollsmoor. The private man is less known.

Mandela was born the son of Nosekeni, one of the four wives of a Tembu chief, Henry Gadla. He lived in Nosekeni's hut, sleeping on mats, eating mealie meal and playing in the dust like any other little African country boy. He cannot have seen his father much, since Henry Gadla had to divide his time between his four families and in any case died when Nelson was only ten. Nosekeni was worried about her son – the chieftaincy would go to a son of the first wife. Paramount Chief Jongintaba stepped in, assumed fatherly responsibilities and decreed that since Nelson could not be a chief, he had better at least get a good education. Jongintaba paid for everything, coaxed and urged Nelson along, and set him on the road which led to his establishing (with Oliver Tambo) the first African law partnership in South Africa. Little wonder that Mandela has always looked back so fondly on his rural roots or that in 1962 he could speak so lovingly from the dock of the rural idyll of Tembuland before the British came. 'Then, our people lived peacefully under the democratic [sic] rule of their kings and moved freely and confidently up and down the country without let or hindrance. Then the country was our own.' To read of Mandela's concern for the conservative countryside and the world of the chieftaincies is to marvel at Pretoria's squandered luck at having so moderate a man to deal with. Despite what the British had done to Tembuland, Mandela remained something of an Anglophile: 'I regard the British Parliament as the most democratic institution in the world', he said at his trial. (Mandela had visited the Commons to meet Hugh Gaitskell and Jo Grimmond on a secret trip out of South Africa in 1962).

Arriving in Johannesburg in 1941, Mandela was quickly recruited into the ANC by the remarkable Walter Sisulu, the grandfather of a whole ANC generation. Sisulu (who, at 76, is still in jail and well worth a birthday celebration or two) was the son of a white father who had quickly abandoned his mother, a black washerwoman. He had little education, and had worked as a miner, a domestic servant, a factory worker, a baker and an estate agent. He was also endlessly genial, resourceful, and an instinctive radical. He adopted the young Mandela, put him up in his house, got him a job, got him into university, and paid his fees, while his wife, Albertina, found him a wife in their young cousin, Eveline. The other member of the trio was Mandela's law partner, Oliver Tambo. The three men formed a tight little nucleus which dominated the ANC for decades, though, predictably enough, it was the two younger but better-educated men, Mandela and Tambo, who were to assume the leadership. 'Tambo, I could never lay my finger on', a contemporary observed.

'He was the perfect diplomat. Both he and Nelson had a way of hiding their feelings . . . .. Walter was the most open of all of us when it came to working with other race and ideological groups.' Only Mandela's nephews, Kaiser and George Matanzima, were as close to Mandela as Tambo and Sisulu: to Mandela's great pain, they were later to betray the cause by leading the Transkei Bantustan to its spurious independence.

It was to Kaiser Matanzima that poor Eveline turned for help a few years later when it was clear that her marriage was in ruins: but even he could do nothing. Part of the problem was simply that Mandela was quite overpoweringly attractive to women and enjoyed their attentions. Partly it was a matter of temperament – Eveline was a quiet, devoted and dutiful wife, while Nelson had now met the beautiful, fiery and headstrong Winnie. Nelson was himself a handsome, dynamic and athletic young man – a keen runner, boxer, golfer and baseball player – and something in Winnie's passionate character called to him. In the end, Eveline read in the paper that Nelson was divorcing her. Tembi, the eldest of her three children, was devastated, but Eveline has always insisted that Nelson was a wonderful husband and father and that she has no reproaches. Mandela himself writes that 'Eveline is pleasant and charming and I respected her as the marriage was crumbling. It would be quite unfair to blame her for the breakdown.'

Winnie was something of a Xhosa aristocrat, the great-granddaughter of the ferocious Chief Madikizela. Her mother, a teacher, had come under continual heavy criticism from her mother-in-law for being too much the modern, educated woman and not enough a good African wife. Winnie, spending equal time with each woman, was acutely and unhappily aware of this tension – and aware, too, that her mother had wanted her to be a boy. Winnie responded by becoming a complete tomboy and a wilful, troublesome child, which in turn led to savage beatings. Finally, her mother died having the boy she had longed for and Winnie had to nurse this killer man-child. The terrible scars of this childhood doubtless do much to explain Winnie's impulsive and 'difficult' temperament. She decided to become a social worker and at college quickly fell in with the Non-European Unity Movement (NEUM), whose root-and-branch radicalism suited her temperament. It was only after she met Nelson that she drifted into ANC circles.

It has become fairly conventional to see the politics of the 1950s as consisting essentially of the rise of ANC mass action and the state's ever stronger resistance to it, culminating in Sharpeville. But there was another complicating factor which dogged the Mandelas.

This was the ANC's increasing embarrassment in the face of the NEUM and Pan Africanist Congress's attacks on the support the ANC gave to white candidates who would act as Native Representatives in Parliament and to traditional rural structures – the Bunga, the Transkei chiefs' council, the Native Representative Council – and to state institutions such as advisory boards and local councils. All of this the NEUM and PAC denounced as collaboration, alleging that the ANC's tactics effectively handed leadership over to the small handful of white liberals and Communists willing to act as its representatives 'within the system'. For the NEUM and PAC this was mere Uncle Tom-ism and thus to be rejected: non-whites must be led by non-whites and all state structures must be delegitimated by the practice of boycotts. The past forty years have seen the complete triumph of this line of thinking in black South African politics. Mandela, Sisulu and Tambo had no answer to the boycott strategy – and they spent many anxious hours worrying how to avoid being outflanked, as in fact they continually were.

The turning-point was Sharpeville. The massacre left Mandela trembling, sick, and bitterly aware how Uncle Tom-ish it made the ANC look: how could you carry on preaching non-violence when the other side was shooting your people down in scores? The ANC set up Umkhonto we Sizwe as its armed wing – the crime for which Mandela and Sisulu went to jail – and ANC policy hardened across the board. Inevitably, part of this hardening was the ANC's complete capitulation to the boycott psychology, to the point where today it has become the chief orchestrator of anti-apartheid boycotts of every kind right across the world. There are considerable ironies in this. The first non-white intellectuals, the Cape Coloured schoolteachers of the NEUM, decided on the boycott tactic out of weakness: if non-whites could not stop the whites from winning across the board and setting up all the structures they wanted, at least non-whites could withhold their consent from such arrangements. Thus a tactic born of impotence gradually grew into a worldwide movement, expressing itself in a whole series of anti-South African boycotts (of goods, in sport, culture, etc.), which have now culminated in economic sanctions – a very potent force indeed. In the process, people have forgotten that the boycott was only a tactic. Now, crazily, it has become a principle in its own right, with results that are sometimes so ludicrous that the ANC, which once saw only too well the pitfalls of the boycott tactic, can find itself having to defend what was in fact their opponents' philosophy.

Another factor to bring much anguish to the Mandelas was the defection of Nelson's kinsmen, the Matanzimas, and the great rural revolt of 1959 in Pondoland. Winnie's father sided with Matanzima, while her brothers sided with the rebellious Intaba movement against him. In the bitter fighting that followed, Winnie's grandmother was stabbed and left paralysed and her father narrowly escaped in the course of an attack on his house. Winnie relates how, just after this happened, she and Nelson had to host an ANC meeting at their home. As a woman, she was strictly relegated to the kitchen, but after a while one of the guests came through and sat chatting with her about the attack on her father's house.

> Your father is a lucky bastard, we shall get him yet. We just don't know how he escaped through such a small window – such a big man. He must thank his lucky stars. He won't be so lucky next time.

Poor Winnie, dogged by one traumatic event after another. She was mercilessly harassed after Nelson's imprisonment. Between 1966 and 1969 she was charged three times and detained for a total of 491 days. In the next ten years she was charged another three times and spent another six months in jail, and in 1977 she was summarily banished to the remote Free State hamlet of Brandfort – the Police simply arrived in the early morning and started loading her furniture into a van to take it and her to a place she knew nothing about. Winnie did wonderful work at Brandfort, setting up a clinic and giving new confidence to the oppressed and demoralised black population of the town. Her house was repeatedly burgled, attacked and vandalised. On one occasion she was interrogated by the infamous Major Theunis Swanepoel while having to listen to the cries of a man being tortured in the next room. It was during this period that she learnt that her son had been killed in a car accident. Her daughter, Zindzi, who has stuck closely to her mother and says, 'I felt I was more or less raised by the Police', has suffered terribly and endures continual bouts of depression. The other daughter, Zeni, has behaved more like the Xhosa aristocrat that she is and has married Prince Thumbumuzi of Swaziland.

Of all Mandela's sufferings in jail, none was worse than his agony over what was happening to Winnie: 'Although I always put a brave face on it,' he writes to Winnie, 'I never get used to you being in the cooler. Few things disorganise my whole life as much as this particular type of hardship, which seems destined to stalk us for quite some time.' Moreover, as Mrs Meer somewhat awkwardly points out, rumours of Winnie's alleged infidelities were and are rife. Mrs Meer knows Mandela well (indeed, she was in the select group with him on his last secret meeting before his capture) and we can probably rely on her account: Mandela, she writes,

> ... blamed himself for her victimisation ... he had a keen sense of his patriarchal obligations and his impotence was unbearable, and finally because he could not experience it in reality and know its reality, he apprehended it in his mind where it took on limitless proportion, and gruesome forms.

Mandela emerges from his letters as a very considerable figure, a man who writes well and reads widely and voraciously – visitors credit him with a striking knowledge of international affairs as well as a considerable literary and historical knowledge. He has, too, a clear independence of mind – on trial in 1959, he even declared that he personally would settle for sixty African seats in Parliament and a review of the situation after five years, adding that he did not know what the ANC would say, but that was what he felt all the same.

For many people Nelson Mandela has, in effect, become a living saint, and it is difficult to get a more human view of the man. The symbol he has become, the African Christ on the cross, always blots out other perceptions.

Winnie, on the other hand, is at once lionised *and* unpopular. She now lives in considerable style – several houses, a large silver Mercedes, and the Mandela 'football team'. Mandela FC consists of a gang of young toughs who act as her bodyguards (and were recently alleged to have tortured, at her behest, some other young boys suspected of burning down one of her houses). Winnie repeatedly says or does things which she then has angrily to deny: the famous speech about 'give us the matches, give us the necklaces' is said to have been 'misquoted', though it exists clearly enough on videotape. Similarly, she wrote a foreword not long ago for an extreme free-market book on South Africa, only to issue a somewhat unconvincing disclaimer later on. Her attempt to hand over the rights to the use of the Mandela name to Robert Brown, a Reaganite American businessman, brought her into headlong conflict with Nelson. All this highly erratic behaviour is a large political problem for the ANC, who would much prefer that she live the exemplary life of an Albertina Sisulu. Mrs Sisulu, a more modest woman whose life is filled with good works, is widely loved and respected in a way that Winnie simply is not.

Winnie is exciting, however. She draws the crowds. When I went to hear her speak ('The Mother of the Nation, Our First Lady') at the launch of Mrs Meer's book, there was standing room only, with the comrades from Mandela FC doing their war-dances in the foyer.

Winnie was quickly into her stride, bringing us 'greetings from the people's army, Umkhonto we Sizwe'. Departing wildly from ANC policy, she spoke of attacks on 'soft targets' as a 'regrettable necessity' and went on to instance the sort of targets that were OK – hanging judges, National Party MPs and community councillors. Those who had exposed her dealings with Robert Brown, including the now-suspended *Weekly Mail*, on which the whole Left here relies, she condemned as 'gutter journalists and traitors', an open invitation to a necklacing. 'The boiling kettle of Afrikaner domination', she went on, 'has finally blown its lid . . . the apartheid regime is panicking to unproportional dimensions . . . the Government is manipulating our children.' (The last of these remarks was an attempt to suggest that ordinary township youth could not have been responsible for the arson on her house: but I have not met a single person who believes the Government were behind this. The township crowd watched the fire sullenly, and although Winnie issued a statement thanking them for their assistance, the fact is that nobody gave any assistance.)

I sat through all this trying to think that anyone who had been through what Winnie had been through might act like this. When she got to the bit about bombing soft targets, an African about three feet away from me shouted: 'Amandla!' (The ANC cry is 'Amandla Wethu' – 'Power to the People.') I looked at this man. The strength of his features and the bitterness of his expression spoke quite clearly of the centuries of oppression, exploitation, torture and killing. What it meant was: I am so full of hatred for what has been done, and is being done, to my people that the more extreme and outrageous things you say, the more I like it. It was the sort of face you have to respect. And that is a good part of Winnie's secret. The detail of what she says does not really matter, because what she is always saying in different ways is: 'NO, NO, a thousand times NO.' And after all that has been done in this country, after all the torture, the brutalisation, the denial of humanity, there is a fair-sized market for that. The whole point of the boycott psychology was that it offered a way of saying No to the whole system. That is what made it irresistible. (I cannot help feeling Zindzi's decision to call her son Gadafi was made in the same spirit. Who's the guy the whites dislike most? Gadafi. Right then . . ..)

During Winnie's speech, an uproar could be heard in the foyer and members of the Mandela FC were dispatched to sort it out (i.e. beat people up). In the end, however, dozens of angry young Africans burst in with placards denouncing Fatima Meer. Their quarrel had to do with the Phambili school which Mrs Meer set up with US Embassy money for children expelled from township schools in the 1984–6 uprising. Mrs Meer is an old Congress hand, but she is also a Muslim and an admirer of Ayatollah Khomeini, who she believes is a force for the liberation of women. Indeed, the book launch was financed by an organisation called the Iranian Interest Section. (Yes, the US and Iran coexist here. The competition to influence the future is open to all outsiders, even if insiders are somewhat more constrained.) One problem is that Mrs Meer, who has both a maverick and an authoritarian reputation, accepted six hundred children into a school for two hundred, and that not all of those children had been expelled from their previous schools for no reason. Before long, pupils and teachers had united against Mrs Meer and the way she ran the school, while she herself was denouncing 'a small minority of trouble-makers' – a turn of phrase we seem to have heard before. Anyway, the angry Phambili pupils ran in, seized the microphone and started denouncing Mrs Meer. The result was a riot, with generalised fighting between the pupils and Mandela FC. Winnie then took the mike, sided strongly with her old friend Fatima Meer, denounced the pupils as a disgrace to the African race and said she would see them afterwards. Mrs Meer closed the school down the next day, on the eve of exams, and was thereafter systematically unavailable for comment.

What sticks in my mind is not all the shenanigans at Phambili but the face of the man who shouted 'Amandla'. There is a lot of talk among radicals of holding Nuremberg trials here after the Changeover, and the UN has already thoughtfully provided a legal framework for this. On moral grounds, let alone those of retributive justice, such trials are clearly warranted. Up on the university campus where I taught for the past six months I looked down on what had once been the warm and vibrant African community of Cato Manor. Today some of that land is occupied by affluent white housing, but mainly it is just bush. All those people were forcibly removed, simply so that the land they occupied could be turned back to what it was before Vasco da Gama came this way. Today they live in the modern township of Kwa Mashu, but the ferment in that township begins with the fact that the scar of forced removal has never stopped hurting. I looked down there every day, and each day I found that tears filled my eyes as I looked. What was done down there was so wicked. Why should anyone forgive? I cannot. Try the bastards who did it? Why the hell not?

One reason would be that it would be nice if a future black government decided on a new era of humanitarianism, forgiveness and reconciliation. No revenge, no more torture, no more executions. But that may be a pious hope. A stronger reason is simply that of managerial competence. Almost the most worrying thing about this country is the terrible damage done by Verwoerd's Bantu Education Act and the simple lack of resources for African education. The result is a terrible dearth of skilled, competent blacks. I taught African students for two terms and could see only too well the size of the problems ahead. Mandela is one of the very few men of real intellectual stature in the ANC. So a future black government, if it has any sense at all, is going to want as many whites as possible to stay here and contribute their educated expertise in every area of life. But that means not holding Nuremberg trials. However well deserved they might be, they would be interpreted by most whites as an act of revenge. The result would be even greater white emigration and a drain of skills which the country simply cannot afford. One would like to think that the ANC leadership stationed in Lusaka have had a thorough look at the way a quarter of a century of independence has destroyed Zambia. A steady flow of educated Zambians are fleeing the complete disaster their country has become. Not a few are quietly coming to South Africa, preferring to put up with racism and township life rather than live with what poor leadership and a general lack of honest, competent administration have done. If a similar collapse into shambles occurred in South Africa's far more sophisticated economy, where there is so much more to go wrong, not only would the carnage be far worse but the demoralisation of Africans about what has happened in independent Africa would be complete. It is easy in most African states to find people who look back nostalgically to the years of colonial rule when things were better run; who regret that the British or French ever left; who feel that Africans like themselves are somehow no good.

At the moment black politics in South Africa are all about resistance, defiance, struggle, about saying NO. It has to be that way. But a terrible burden rests on the black leadership of the future. Unless that leadership is of a decidedly higher calibre than we have seen elsewhere in Africa, the awful possibility looms that Africans here too might come to look back on a lost golden age of white minority rule. Which brings me back to Nelson Mandela – undoubtedly the ablest black leader of his generation. What South Africa has lost through his incarceration goes beyond injustice and personal tragedy. The country has needed Mandela as a leader. It needs him now.

Reference

Meer, Fatima (1988) *Higher than Hope: 'Rolihlahla we love you'* (Cape Town: Skotaville Publishers).

Index

Abu Hassan, 209-10
academic boycott (South Africa), 132-3, 134-5, 280
Académie Française, 216
Accuracy in Media movement, 198
Acheson, Dean, 186
Adam, H., 287-8, 289, 291, 294-7 passim
Affair of State, An (Knightley and Kennedy), 257
African National Congress, 135, 285
  black on black violence, 310, 312, 314-18
  Mandela and, 321-8, 330
  'Reform' era, 291, 292-3, 295-6
  terrorism, 205, 206, 207
  UDF and, 298, 302-3, 309
Agca, Ali, 202, 235
Age of Terrorism, The (Lacqueur), 204-5
Aka Bud Han, 195
Al Fatah, 209
Albert, Carl, 197
Alexander, Neville, 312
Algeria, 2-3, 15, 20, 28, 173, 261
Algérie Française, 88, 92, 95
aliens (in USA), 181, 182
Allen, Richard, 200
Allende, Salvador, 261
Alliance, 56-7, 60, 65, 70
Althusser, Louis, 144, 166, 167
American Legion, 184
American Right, 196, 197, 198, 202, 203

Ami du Peuple, L', 31
Amsallem, Walter, 109
Andrew, Christopher, 228, 229
Angleton, J. J., 243-4, 245, 247, 250, 252-3
Animal Farm (Orwell), 10
anti-Semitism
  Doriot, 42, 43
  Dreyfus, 25, 27, 28, 29-30
  France, 85, 88, 91, 93-4
  golf-club (UK), 70-1
  Johnson on, 122-3
  Mendès, 16, 17, 21, 22
apartheid, 289, 290, 293-4, 300, 316
Arenstein, Rowley, 319
Armée de l'Air, 222
arms industry
  France, 222-7
  United States, 52-3
Armstrong, Sir Robert, 239, 250, 251
Army Counter-Intelligence Corps (USA), 186
Arrighi, Pascal, 112
Arvad, Inga, 188
Atkin, Sharon, 61
Auden, W. H., 10
Aurore, L', 27
Aust, Stefan, 207, 212
Avril, Marie-Louise, 15
Azapo, 291, 292, 309, 311, 312, 318

Baader, Andreas, 204, 207-9, 211-12

Badinter, Robert, 105, 106
banks (support for Doriot), 41, 42
Bantu Education Act, 330
Bantustan, 2
Barba, M., 225
Barbé, Henri, 41
Barbie, Klaus, 44, 201, 214, 220–1, 260
Barnett, Anthony, 140
Barre, Raymond, 110, 113–14
Barrès, Maurice, 26, 28, 29, 30
Barthes, Roland, 167
Baudis, Dominique, 107
BCRA, 259–60
Beaverbrook, Lord, 161
Beaverbrook press, 163
Belvisi, Armand, 264
Ben Barka affair, 264
Ben Bella, Ahmed, 261
Benn, Tony, 57–61, 125
Bergman, Susan, 197
Best, Geoffrey, 98
best-seller cult, 170
Bettaney, Michael, 247
Bhutto, B. and Z., 2
Bidault, Georges, 215
Biko, Steve, 316
Black Consciousness, 291, 292, 309, 311, 312–14, 316, 319
Black Economic Empowerment, 312, 314
Blackburn, Robin, 143
blacks and whites *see* race
Blanc, Emile, 225
Bloch, J., 233
Blue Plan, 260
Blum, Léon, 17, 29, 42, 260
Blunt, Anthony, 33, 230, 238–9, 241, 244
Bo Hi Pak, 195–6, 199, 200, 201, 203
Boesak, Allan, 287, 290–1
Bokassa, 265
Bolshevism, 42, 181, 240–1
Bombacci, Nicola, 35
Bonaparte, 102
Bonnefoy, René, 217
Boris, Georges, 17

BOSS, 233, 247–8, 264, 285
Botha, P. W., 127, 286–7, 289, 292–3, 295, 296, 297, 303
Bottomore, Tom, 136
Bouchardeau, Huguette, 84
Bourdieu, Pierre, 167–8
Bourguiba, 263–4
boycotts, 132–5, 280, 309, 325, 328
Boyer, Jean-François, 193, 196–7, 201
Bradlee, Ben, 121
Braudel, Fernand, 164
Break-Up of Britain, The (Nairn), 147
Bredin, Jean-Denis, 24, 25, 27, 30
Bretton Woods summit, 18
Breytenbach, Breyten, 9
Britain
    Dreyfus Affair (lessons from), 32–3
    intelligence service, 233–4, 236–51
    left-wing intellectuals, 136–46
    monarchy, 147–56
    see also Conservative Party, Labour Party; MI5; Thatcherism
British Aerospace, 222
British constitution (lack of), 254–5
Brittan, Leon, 72, 73
Brodhead, Frank, 202
Brown, George, 59, 60, 242, 246
Brown, Robert, 327, 328
Brunet, Jean-Paul, 35
Bryan, W. J., 55
Buchanan, Pat, 199
Bulgarian Connection, 202
BUPO, 263
Burgess, Guy, 33, 230–1, 233, 238, 241, 242, 244
Burke, Edmund, 102, 103
Burns, William, 183
Bush, George, 53
Buthelezi, Gatsha, 284–6, 291–3, 312, 314–18
Byron, Lord, 274

Callaghan, James, 59, 60, 76, 246-8
'Cambridge Comintern', 230
Campbell-Savours, Dale, 248
Camus, Albert, 133, 169, 217
Candide, 31, 33
Canard Enchaîné, Le, 19, 215
Cape Times, 280
Capitalism and Apartheid (Lipton), 293-4
Capone, Al, 182, 183
Caramanolis, Richard, 112
Carignon, Alain, 109
Carrington, Lord, 68
Carter, Jimmy, 54, 232
Casanova, Laurent, 173
Casey, William, 52, 232
Castro, Fidel, 175-6, 205
Catholic Church, 122-3
    O'Brien's attitude, 128-32, 133
Caute, David, 174
Ceaucescu, Nicolae, 2
Cecil, Robert, 230
Central Intelligence Agency, 131, 205, 263, 266
    activities, 228, 230-6, 243, 249-50
    Moonies and, 195, 202
    Reagan and, 52, 202, 232-3
Centre-Right *see* UDF (France)
Cetshwayo, 316
Ceyrac, Pierre, 201
Chaban-Delmas, Jacques, 107
Chalfont, Lord, 119, 238, 245
Chambers, Whitaker, 187
Channon, Paul, 73
Charles I, 152
Charles-Roux, Edmonde, 111, 112
Chevalier, Maurice, 218
Chevenement, Jean-Pierre, 222
Chichibu, Prince, 160-1
Chirac, Jacques, 28, 171
    arms policies, 222, 226, 227
    electoral system and, 80-90, 96
    Hôtel de Ville, 99, 100
    intelligence services, 267, 268, 269
    Le Pen and, 92, 96
    municipal elections, 108, 111, 113-15
Church
    French intellectuals and, 169
    see also Catholic Church
Churchill, Winston, 1, 122
'Cicero' case, 230
civil rights, 181, 188-9, 190, 191, 288
'class against class', 38, 39
Clegg, Johnny, 100
Clemenceau, Georges, 29
Cline, Ray, 198
CND, 137, 145
Coady, Matthew, 120
coal industry (South Africa), 283
Cockburn, Leslie, *Out of Control*, 52
Cohn-Bendit, Daniel, 174-5
Cold War, 236, 242
collaborators (and the purge), 214-21
Collomb, Francisque, 110, 113-14
Combat, 31, 170
Cominform, 8
Comintern, 8, 35-40, 44-5
commitment, 4, 7, 8, 10, 11
Communism, 2, 8, 18, 19-20, 30
    France, 81-2, 84, 89, 91, 93-4, 99
    Doriot, 34-42, 44-6
    local elections, 108-9, 111, 112
    secret service, 260-2, 265
    MI5 and, 239-43, 245
    Moonies and, 194-6, 201
    South Africa, 312, 319
    United States, 181-2, 186-92 *passim*
Conable, Barber, 197
Conquest, Robert, 75
Conservative Party
    Britain, 32, 33
    South Africa, 298, 303, 304, 308
contrarianism, 133, 134, 135
Conway v. Rimmer (1968), 256
Coors, Joseph, 198
Cosa Nostra, 180, 192
COSATU, 317, 318, 319

336 Index

Counter-Intelligence Corps (USA), 186
Counter-Intelligence Program, 188–90
counter-revolution (France), 102–3
Cowley, Sam, 184
Cresson, Edith, 84
crime (in USA), 180, 182–5, 192, 202
Criminal Investigation Office, 210–11
Croix, La, 27
Crosland, Susan, 58
Crosland, Tony, 58, 65
Cross, Rupert, 160
Crossman, Richard, 59, 65, 120, 121, 124, 256
Crozier, Brian, 236
Cultural Revolution, 172, 173
culture, internationalization of, 171
Culture and Society (Williams), 137
Cummings, Homer, 182, 184–5
Currie, Edwina, 73
Czechoslovakia, 6–7

Daily Express, 257
Daily Mail, 31, 257
Dalyell, Tam, 121
D'Annunzio, Gabriele, 35
Danton, G. J., 98, 100, 103–4, 214
Darlington, Cyril, 160
Darwin, C., 164
Dassault, 222, 223, 226–7
Dassault, Marcel, 109, 226
Dassault, Olivier, 109, 113
Dassault, Serge, 226
Davanzati, Archbishop, 273
Davidson, Basil, 136
de Beauvoir, Simone, The Mandarins, 220
de Borchgrave, Arnaud, 200, 202, 203, 236
de Gaulle, Charles, 2, 81, 88, 104, 114, 223, 233
  intellectuals and, 173–4, 175
  intelligence service, 244, 259–61, 263–4
  Le Pen and, 92, 95
  Mendès and, 17–18, 20, 21–2
  purge by, 216, 219
de Gaulle, Jean, 84
de Jouvenel, Bertrand, 41, 42
de Marenches, Alexandre, 264, 266
Déat, Marcel, 30, 219
Death on the Rock (documentary), 238
Debray, Régis, 168–70, 176, 209, 266
Debré, Bernard, 84
Debré, Michel, 263, 264
Decter, Midge, 200
Défaite de la pensée, La, 171
defence policies (France), 222–7
Defferre, Gaston, 15, 18, 111, 112
Delon, Alain, 83, 96
dementia Footica, 145–6
Denning, Lord, 256, 257
Derrida, 166
DGER, 259
DGSE, 259–60, 261–8
Diaz, B., 304–5
Diderot, Denis, 130
Dikko kidnapping, 233
Dilks, David, 229
Dillinger, John, 184–5
Dingaan, 316
Diplock, Lord, 255
disinformation campaigns, 202–3, 235–6
dissidents, 4
Donoghue, Bernard, 71
Doriot, Jacques, 34–46
Dracula (Stoker), 271–2, 274
Dreyfus, Alfred, 16, 24–33, 169
Drieu La Rochelle, 41
DST, 259, 268
du Plooy, F. and M., 304
Dubois, René, 263
Dufoix, Georgina, 84
Dulles, John Foster, 19
Dumas, Alexandre, 274
Dumont, Gérard-François, 87
Dupuy, Anne-Marie, 109, 113
Duverger, Maurice, 41
Dyson, John, 266

Eagleton, Terry, 138
Ecole Nationale d'Administration, 18
education (South Africa), 305–6
Edward VII, 148–9
Einstein, Albert, 31
Eisenhower, D. D., 51, 52, 187, 196
elections
  Britain (1987), 63–6
  France, 80–90, 96
  France (municipal), 107–15
Eluard, Paul, 217
Elysée, 100, 115, 259
Encounter, 133, 200, 230
END, 137, 145
ENEs, 87, 88
Enigma, 240
Enlightenment, 7, 130
Ensslin, G., 208, 209, 211–12
espionage *see* intelligence services
Esterhuizen, Tinus, 309
Etrangers Non-European, 87, 88
European Advanced Technology Fighter, 222, 226–7
European Defence Community, 19
Express, L', 18, 170

Fabius, 86
Fabre-Luce, Alfred, 41
Faligot, R., 259
false consciousness, 146
Falwell, Jerry, 197
fame, 3
fascism, 242
  Doriot, 34–46, 91
  Dreyfus, 30, 31
  Grey Wolves, 202, 235
  Le Pen, 91, 95, 97
Fassbinder, Werner, 208
Federal Bureau of Investigation, 179–92
Feltin, Archbishop, 216
feminism, 29
Fernandel, 218
Ferry, Luc, 171
Figaro, 85, 87
Finkielkraut, Alain, 171
Fisher, Alan, 76

Fitzgerald, P., 233
Fitzgibbon, Constantine, 245
FLN, 206, 207
Floud, Bernard, 245
Flynn, William, 183
Flynn's Weekly, 183
Foccart, Jacques, 233, 244, 259, 263, 266, 268
Foot, Michael, 121, 145–6, 161–2, 163
forces of history, 1–2
Ford, Gerald, 54
Ford, Henry, 288
Forward March of Labour Halted, The (Hobsbawm), 140
Foucault, 166, 167
France
  arms industry, 222–7
  Chirac, 80–90
  Doriot, 34–46
  Dreyfus, 24–33
  intellectuals, 4, 27–8, 31, 166–76
  intelligence service, 259–67
  Le Pen, 91–7
  Mairies, 107–15
  Mendès, 15–23
  Revolution *see* French Revolution
Franco, Francisco, 217, 242, 260
Franco-Soviet Treaty (1935), 40
Frankfurt School, 166
Fraser, Donald, 198
Frazer, J. G., *The Golden Bough*, 272
freedom fighters, 204–5, 206
Freedom of Information Act, 190
French Revolution, 7
  bicentennial, 99–100
  effects and attitudes to, 98–106
  Terror, 214–15
Fronde, La, 29
Front National, 82–3, 85, 88–9, 91–7, 111–12, 201
Fuchs, Klaus, 187
Furet, François, 104

Gadla, Henry, 323
Gaitskell, Hugh, 245, 323

Gallimard, Claude, 217
Gandhi (film), 122
Gandhi, Indira and Rajiv, 2
Gang of Four, 56, 65
gangsters, 182, 183-5
Garaudy, Roger, 166, 167
Garner, J. N., 99-100
Garvey, Marcus, 180
Gaudin, Jean-Claude, 111-12, 113
Gaullists (RPR)
   Chirac, 81-5, 88, 96
   defence policies and, 224, 226
   intelligence service and, 261, 267
   municipal elections, 108-10, 112, 114
GCHQ, 247
Geismar, Alain, 175, 176
Gerber, Gracelle, 304
Gestapo, 43
Gidley, Isobelle, 267
Gilder, George, 121
Gilmour, Ian, 75
Giscard d'Estaing, Olivier, 201
Giscard d'Estaing, Valery, 86, 88, 114, 215, 224, 264-5, 268
Glees, Anthony, 240-1, 242
God Land: Reflections on Religion and Nationalism, 128-9
gold, 279, 282, 283
Goldman, Emma, 180
Goldsmith, Jimmy, 198, 245
Goldwater, Barry, 51-2, 198
Golitsyn, Anatoly, 243-5, 250
Gorbachev, Mikhail, 200
Gorz, 166
Gould, Bryan, 65, 66
Gould, Chester, 184
Graham, Daniel, 198
Gramsci, Antonio, 7-8, 10-11, 166
Grasset, Bernard, 217-18
Great Crash, 183
Great Men of History approach, 1-2
Great Trek, 304, 307
Greater London Council, 61, 62-3
Greenpeace, 226, 259, 266-9
Grey Wolves, 202, 235

Griffiths, Brian, 75
Grimmond, Jo, 323
Gringoire, 31, 33
Grundy, Kenneth, 295
Guardian, 163, 172
Guèsde, Jules, 261
Guevara, Che, 173, 176
guilt, moral, 4-6, 7
Guitry, Sacha, 218

Habermas, J., 166
Habsburg, Empire, 150, 154
Hailsham, Lord, 246
Halsey, A. H., 136
Hammond, Eric, 60
Hamon, Hervé, 172-3, 175
Hamon, Léo, 16
Hansen, George, 197
Hatch, Orrin, 197
Healey, Denis, 65
Heath, Edward, 75, 248
Heavy Dancers, The (Thompson), 145
Helms, Jesse, 197
Helms, Richard, 232
Henze, Paul, 202, 203
Herman, Edward, 202
Hermier, Guy, 111, 112
Hernu, Charles, 226, 265-6, 268-9
Herold, Horst, 211
Herriot, Edouard, 16, 17, 110
Hersant, Robert, 84-5, 88, 90
Hersant press, 215
Herzl, Theodore, 30
Heston, Charlton, 200
Hill, Christopher, 136, 137, 164
Hindess, Barry, 144
Hirst, Paul, 144
Hiss, Alger, 187, 189, 239
history, individuals in, 1-4
Hitler, Adolf, 1, 39, 40, 41, 43, 44, 77, 205, 240
Ho Chi Minh, 18, 19, 37, 261
Hobsbawm, Eric, 8, 56, 136, 137, 140, 164
Hodgkin, Thomas, 136
Hoffman, Abby, 171
Hollis, Roger, 242, 244, 252

Hollywood
  crime and, 183, 184
  pseudo-royals, 154-6
Holoch, George, 16
Homann, Peter, 212
Home, Lord, 57, 139
Home Office v. *Harman*, 256
Honeyford, Ray, 75
Hoover, Herbert, 182
Hoover, J. Edgar, 3, 179-92
Hoskyns, John, 75, 76
Hôtel de Ville, 99, 100
Hottentots, 305
Humanité, L', 218

illegal immigrants, 85, 86, 87
IMF, 239
immigrants (France), 85-92
  passim, 94
imperialism, American, 173-4
impossible situations, 4-7
independence (France), 222-7
Independent, The, 250
Independent Broadcasting
  Authority, 238
individuals, politics and, 1-12
Indo-China, 18-19, 261
industry *see* military-industrial
  complex; miners' strike; trade
  unions
Ingham, Bernard, 75
Inkatha movement, 291, 312,
  314-19
intellectuals
  French, 4, 27-8, 31, 166-76
  individualism and, 7-11
  Johnson, Paul, 119-26
  Nairn, Tom, 147-56
  O'Brien, Conor Cruise, 127-35
  Taylor, A. J. P., 157-65
  Thompson, E. P., 128, 136,
    137, 144-6
  Williams, Raymond, 10, 136,
    137-44
intelligence services, 3
  DGSE, 259-60, 261-8
  Federal Bureau of Investigation,
    179-92
  KGB, 228, 234-5, 239, 243-5,
    247, 250, 267
  OSS, 186, 231, 260, 262
  see also Central Intelligence
    Agency; MI5; MI6;
    spycatching
Intellocates, Les (Hamon and
  Rotman), 172-3
International Monetary Fund, 239
International Times, 255
IPSOS poll, 103-5
IRA, 249
Irangate, 52, 53
Iranian Interest Section, 329
Ireland, 127-8, 129, 131-2, 249
Irvine, Reed, 198

Jakobovits, Immanuel, 72
Jarry, Robert, 108
Jaurès, Jean, 29, 102, 104
Jellico, Earl, 260
Jenkins, Roy, 65, 69, 75
Jews
  in British politics, 70-3
  see also anti-Semitism
John Paul II, 129, 130-1, 202,
  205, 235
Johnson, Douglas, 99, 101
Johnson, Lyndon, 179,
  180, 188
Johnson, Paul, 75, 119-26
Johnson, R. W. (*Shootdown: The
  Verdict on KAL 007*), 228
Joint Intelligence Committee, 247
Jongintaba, Paramount Chief, 323
Joseph, Keith, 72, 76
Journal, Le, 27
Joxe, Pierre, 108
'Judaeo-Bolshevism', 42
judges, 252-8
July, Serge, 175, 176
Jünschke, Klaus, 210

Kadar, Jan, 6
Kagan, Lord, 245
Kamenka, Eugene, 100
Kaouah, Mourad, 88-9
Kastenbaum, Léon, 261
Kaufman, Gerald, 120
Kaunda, Kenneth, 283

340 Index

KCIA, 195-6, 198, 200
Kennedy, Bobby, 188, 244
Kennedy, Edward, 291
Kennedy, John, 179, 188, 192, 195
Keynes, J. M., 18, 33
KGB, 228, 234-5, 239, 243-5, 247, 250, 267
Khoi Khoi, 305
Khomeini, Ayatollah, 167, 329
Kiernan, V. G., 136, 137
Kim, Mickey, 196
Kim, Steve, 195
Kim Il-Sung, 2
Kim Jong Pil, 195
King, Martin Luther, 179, 180, 188, 189, 191
Kinnock, Neil, 56, 66-7, 70, 149
Kirkpatrick, Jeanne, 121, 200
Kissinger, Henry, 52
Klerk, F. W. de, 297
Knatchbull-Huggessen, H., 230
Koestler, Arthur, 12
Kolodziej, Edward, 223-5, 227
Korea, 193, 194-7, 198
Korsch, 166
Krasucki, Henri, 86
Krop, P., 259
Kun, Béla, 35
Kuomintang, 37

La Rocque, Colonel, 40
Labour Government, 32
  in 1964-70, 58-60
Labour Manifesto (1983), 121
labour movement, 8-9, 124-5, 141-2
Labour Party
  Benn's diaries, 57-61
  Kinnock, 56, 66-7
  M15 and, 245-50 passim
  monarchy and, 148, 154
  1987 election, 63-6
  Wainwright's account, 57, 60-3
Lacan, J., 166
Lacouture, Jean, 16, 19, 21
Ladysmith Black Mambazo, 306
Lamprecht, Don, 309
Lang, Jack, 167

Laqueur, Walter, 204-5
Laval, Pierre, 45, 77
Law Lords, 252-8
Lawson, Nigel, 72-3, 75
Le Bon, Gustave, 151
Le Carré, John, 33, 231
Le Pen, Jean-Marie, 113, 114, 119, 123
  Chirac and, 80, 82-3, 85-6, 88-9, 92, 96
  Front National, 28, 91-7, 111-12, 201, 261
Le Roy Ladurie, 41
Leclerc, Evelyne, 109
Ledeen, Michael, 202, 203
Lee, Sidney, 149
Left-Centre coalition (France), 81
left-wing intellectuals, 9-10, 136-46
left-wing regimes, 2
Légion des Volontaires Français, 43
Lehmann, John, 54
Lekganyane, Bishop, 292
Lelyveld, Joseph, *Move Your Shadow*, 288-9
Lemaître, G. E., 28
Lenin, V. I., 2, 34, 35, 36, 45
Léotard, François, 109
Levi-Strauss, C., 166
Lévy, Bernard-Henri, 170, 171
Lewis, C. S., 159, 160
Leyser, 161
Libération, 170, 172
Libre Parole, La, 27
Life of Brian, The (film), 274
Ligue d'Action Universitaire Républicaine et Socialiste, 16
Lindbergh kidnapping, 182
Lipton, Merle, 293-4
Livingstone, Ken, 62-3, 149
Lloyd George, David, 150
Lodge, Henry Cabot, 52
London Review of Books, The, 157, 253-4
Long Revolution, The (Williams), 137
Longford, Lord, 125

Lottman, Herbert, 215, 217
Louis VI, 101-2
Luce, Claire Booth, 198
Luchaire affair, 225-6, 269
Luthuli, Albert, 315

McCarthy, Joe, 179, 186, 239
McCarthy, Mary, *The Group*, 124
McDonald, Larry, 198
McFarlane, Bruce, 160, 161
McFarlane, Robert, 200
McGehee, Ralph, 236
MacGregor, Ian, 75
Machel, Samora, 203
Maclean, Donald, 33, 230-1, 233, 238, 242, 244
Macmillan, Harold, 54, 69, 72, 75, 248
Madikizela, Chief, 324
Mafart, Alain, 266, 268, 269
Mafia, 180, 192, 202
Magenta network, 263-4
Mairies (municipal elections), 107-15
Maitland, Olga, 121
Making of the English Working Class, The (Thompson), 137, 144
male voters (1987 election), 63-4
Malraux, André, 217
Mandela, Eveline, 323, 324
Mandela, Nelson, 3, 285, 292, 293, 296, 317, 321-31
Mandela, Winnie, 296, 321, 322, 324, 326-9
Mao Tse-tung, 2, 100, 172, 173
Marat, Jean Paul, 98, 103
Marion, Pierre, 266
Marschal, Marcel, 39, 41, 43, 44
Marshall, Mr Justice, 257
Martin, Kingsley, 120, 124, 151
Marx, Karl, 2, 99, 122, 273
Marxism, 8, 36, 122, 123, 167, 172, 293
Marxists, 2, 136, 301, 302, 312
Matanzima, Kaiser and George, 284, 324-6
Matra (arms manufacturer), 223, 225-6

Mauroy, Pierre, 109
Maurras, Charles, 28, 30, 216
May Day Manifesto (Williams), 143
Mbeki, Govan, 303
Medawar, Sir Peter, 160
Medecin family, 107
Medina trial, 187
Meer, Fatima, 322, 326, 328-9
Meese, Ed, 52, 200
Mégret, Bruno, 95
Mehaignerie, Pierre, 107
Meinhof, Ulrike, 207, 208, 209, 211-12
Mellon-Scaife, Richard, 198
Mencken, H. L., 182
Mendès-France, Pierre, 15-23
Mengistu Haile Meriam, 129
Meynhardt, Louis, 307, 308
MI5, 230, 233-4, 236-7
  history of, 238-51, 267
MI6, 233, 236, 239-40, 247, 250, 260, 261, 267
Michel, Robert, 197
Miliband, Ralph, 136
'militant particularism', 140-1, 142-3
military-industrial complex
  France, 222-7
  United States, 52-3
Miller, Eric, 245
Miller, Jonathan, 69, 77
Millerand (Minister of War), 29
miners' strike, 61-2, 139-40, 246, 247
Minute (newspaper), 95, 97
missionary role, 8-9
Mitchell, John, 52
Mitterrand, François, 100, 104, 167, 214, 215
  Chirac and, 80, 81, 87-9, 96, 100
  in Government, 29, 80-1, 87-9, 92, 96, 152
  intelligence service and, 259, 265-9
  Mendès and, 19, 21
  municipal elections, 109, 114
Mollet, Guy, 8, 20

Molotov, V. M., 19
monarchy, 147–56
Mondale, Walter, 54
Monde, Le, 167, 170, 215
Moodley, Kogila, 287–8, 289, 291, 294, 295, 296–7
Moonie Tong II group, 196
Moonies, 95, 193–203
moral choice, 4–7
Morand, Paul, 216
Morris, John, 160
Morrison, Herbert, 62
Moss, Robert, 200, 202, 203, 236, 249
MOSSAD, 233, 261
Motlana, Dr, 284, 285
Mouillot, Michel, 109
Moumié, Félix, 262
Mounier, 30
Mugabe, Robert, 279
Mulhern, Francis, 170
muncipal elections (France), 107–15
Munzenberg, Willi, 8
Murdoch, Rupert, 121, 258
Murdoch press, 250
Mussolini, Benito, 35, 41, 205
Muzorewa, Bishop Abel, 285

NAACP, 187, 190
Nabarro, Sir Gerald, 72
Nairn, Tom, 147–56
Nallet, 166
Namibia, 281–4
Napoleon, 1, 43, 150, 153, 154
Nasser, Gamal, 242, 261–2
National Coal Board, 62
National Forum, 311, 312, 319
National Front, 96–7
National Party, 303, 307, 308, 328
National Union of Mineworkers, 61–2, 139–40
National Union of South African Students, 318
nationalism
  Britain (Ukanian), 147–56
  France, 28, 29, 30, 102, 152
  Ireland, 129
Native Representative Council, 325
Native Reserves, 3
NATO, 128, 222, 223, 244
Nazism, 17, 240–2
  collaborators, 214–21
  Doriot and, 43, 44, 45
Neave, Airey, 248–9
Neustadt, Richard, *Presidential Power*, 47
New Deal, 124, 186
New Left, 137, 143
New Left Review, The, 144, 166
New Lies for Old (Golitsyn), 250
New Right, 196, 197, 198, 202, 203
New Statesman, 120, 121, 122, 124
New York Times, 198, 200, 202
News World, 198, 199
Newsweek, 200
Nguyen Ai Quoc *see* Ho Chi Minh
Nguyen O Phap, 37
Nicaragua, 129–30, 200, 232
1984 (Orwell), 10
Nixon, Richard, 199, 232, 236
  Hoover and, 179, 180, 186–7, 189–90, 192
  Watergate, 52, 190, 197–8
Nkrumah, Kwame, 2, 128
NKVD, 186
NLF, 206
Noir, Michel, 110, 113, 114
Non-European Unity Movement, 324, 325
Nosekeni (Mandela's mother), 323
nouveaux philosophes, 170
Nouvel Observateur, Le, 170
Nouvelle Revue Française, 217
Nouvelles Littéraires, 170
Novak, Michael, 200
Nyerere, Julius, 2, 133

OAS, 15, 92, 231, 260, 262, 264
Obando, Cardinal, 129
O'Brien, Conor Cruise, 101, 102, 127–33
Observer, 133, 138, 163
Official Secrets Act, 238
Oldfield, Sir Maurice, 244, 249
Operation Chaos, 243, 250

Ordre Nouveau, L', 31
Organisation de l'Armée Sécrête,
    15, 92, 231, 260, 262, 264
Orwell, George, 10-11, 12, 130
OSS (later CIA), 186, 231, 260,
    262
Owen, Will, 245
Oxford University, 157-63
Ox, 255

Paisley, Ian, 249
Palmer, Mitchell, 181-2
Pan Africanist Congress, 312, 325
Papon, Maurice, 215
Pardoe, John, 71
Paris Commune, 129
Park Chung Hee, 195, 196
Parker, Lord Chief Justice, 257
Parti Populaire Française, 41-4, 45
Parti Socialiste, 81-2, 83-4
Passion and Cunning (O'Brien),
    127, 129-30
Paul VI, 131
Pauwels, Louis, 28
Pazienta, Francesco, 202
Pearl Harbour, 186, 191-2
Péguy, Charles, 30
Penne, Guy, 266
personality cult, 2, 149-50, 170
Pétain, Philippe, 43, 45, 77, 105,
    216
Peterson, Sir Maurice, 230
Petit Journal, Le, 27
Petit Parisien, Le, 27
Peyrefitte, Alain, 88
Peyrefitte, Roger, 215
Pezet, Michel, 111, 112, 113
Philby, Kim, 3, 33, 230, 231, 233,
    238, 240-2, 244, 245
Piaf, Edith, 218
Piat, Vann, 96
Pinay, Antoine, 262
Pincher, Chapman, 239, 241
Pinkerton, Allen, 183
Pinochet, Augusto, 201, 249
Pipes, Richard, 53
Pius XII, 123, 215-16
Plans, 31
Pleven (Finance Minister), 18

Podhoretz, Norman, 133
Point, Le, 84, 170
Polanski, Roman, 274
Politburo, 36, 38, 39, 41
political organisations, 7
politicians, 3-4
    municipal elections, 107-15
    Revolution (effects/atttitudes
        to), 98-106
    see also individual politicians
politics
    individuals and, 1-12
    as moral choice, 4-6, 7
    South Africa (in 1980), 279-86
    South Africa (Reform era), 287-
        97
Pompidou, George, 16, 88, 104,
    264
Poniatowski, Michel, 86
Popis, Claude, 112
Popper, Karl, 119
Popular Front, 17 *bis*, 30, 40-1,
    216, 217
populism, 9, 32
Pordéa, Gustave, 201
Porsche, Ferdinand, 260
Porter, Melinda Camber, 171-2
Poujade, Pierre, 91
Poujadism, 91, 95, 114
Poulantzas, N., 166, 167
Poverty of Theory, The (Thompson),
    144
Powell, Enoch, 2, 75, 153, 249
Powers, Richard G. P., 180
Pradel, Louis, 110
Presidential Power (Neustadt), 47
Prest, Thomas, 271
Prieur, Dominique, 266, 268,
    269
Prior, J., 75, 77
Prohibition, 183
proletarian literature, 10
proportional representation, 80-6,
    89-90, 96
Protestants, 130, 131
Provençal, Le, 112
purge, collaborators and, 214-21
Purvis, Melvin, 179, 184, 185
Pym, Francis, 75

Quotidien de Paris, Le, 170

race
  black on black violence, 310–20
  immigrants in France, 85–92, 94
  Mandela, 321–31
  moral guilt and, 4–6
  South Africa (1980), 279–86
  South Africa (as comic experience), 307–9
  South Africa (Reform era), 287–97
  South African life, 298–306
  see also anti-Semitism
Radical Party (France), 18, 20, 40
Rafale project, 222, 226–7
Rainbow Warrior affair, 226, 259, 266–9
Ransom, H. H., 231–2
rapprochement, 40
Raspe, Jan-Carl, 212
Reader, Keith, 168
Reagan, Nancy, 200
Reagan, Ronald, 47–55, 68, 119, 172
  intelligence services and, 198–200, 202, 203, 232–3, 235
realpolitik, 22, 176
Rebatet, *Les Décombres*, 31
Reece, *The Vampire*, 271
Reed, John, 180
Rees, Goronwy, 230
Rees-Mogg, William, 148, 155, 156
'Reform' era (South Africa), 287–97
Regan, Don, 199, 200
Reid, Lord, 256
Renaut, Alain, 171
Republican Front, 20
Resistance, 4, 28, 43, 169
  collaborators, 214–21
Resources of Hope (Thompson), 137, 138, 139, 143
Reston, James, 121
Revel, Jean-François, 200, 201
revolutionary intellectuals, 7–11
Revue du Siècle, 31
Revue Française, 31

Rex, John, 136
Rhee, Syngman, 195
Rhodesia, 286
Rifkind, Malcolm, 72
Rise and Fall of the Bulgarian Connection, The (Herman/Brodhead), 202
Rising Tide (newspaper), 198
Rives, Jean-Pierre, 109
Robbe-Grillet, 166
Robert, Maurice, 259, 268
Robespierre, M., 98, 102, 103–4, 214
Rocard, Michel, 114
Roncalli, Monsigneur, 216
Roosevelt, Eleanor, 179, 186
Roosevelt, F. D., 1, 186, 190
Rosenberg, Ethel, 179, 187
Rosenberg, Julius, 187
Rotman, Patrick, 172–3, 175
Roudy, Yvette, 83–4
Roux, Jean-Pierre, 112
Royal Joke phenomenon, 149
'Royal Socialism', 148
RPR *see* Gaullists (RPR)
Rubin, Jerry, 171, 174–5
Ryle, Gilbert, 160

Saatchi brothers, 72
SABC, 309
SABTA, 319
SADF, 295, 317, 318
'Safari Club', 265
Sage, Anna, 185
St John Dorset, *The Vampire*, 271
Salisbury Review, 245
sanctions, 312–13
Sandinistas, 129–30
Sang Kil Han, 195
Sapphire network, 244
Sartre, Jean Paul, 28, 167, 217
SAS, 260
Sasha network, 244
SAVAK, 208, 233, 265
Scargill, Arthur, 61, 62, 140
Schafly, Fred and Phyllis, 198
Schelm, Petra, 210
Schlebusch, Kallie, 307–8
Schneider, Romy, 260

Schratternbach, Cardinal, 273
Schulz, George, 52
Schuman, Maurice, 16
Schuschnigg, Chancellor, 260
Scruton, Roger, 245
SDECE, 261–6
SDI, 50–1
Sebe, Colonel Charles, 284
Sebe, Lennox, 284
Seberg, Jean, 179, 189
Secret Intelligence Service see MI6
secret service see intelligence services
Senghor, Léopold, 16
Seoul regime, 195, 196–9 passim
Sergent, Pierre, 92
Servan-Schreiber, Jean-Jacques, 18
Servin, Marcel, 173
Shah of Iran, 208, 233, 265
Shakespeare, William, 1, 152, 153
Shanghai massacre, 37
Sharpe, Tom, *Riotous Assembly*, 307
Sharpeville massacre, 283, 324, 325
Shaw and DPP (1961), 255
Shears, Richard, 267
Sherman, Alfred, 72, 75, 119
Shop on the High Street (film), 6–7
Sihanouk, Prince, 263
Silone, Ignazio, 8, 9
Simon, William, 198, 199
Sino-Soviet conflict, 236, 244, 250
Sisulu, Albertina, 323, 327
Sisulu, Walter, 321, 323–4, 325
Sixty-Eight: Year of the Barricades (Caute), 174–5
Slovo, Joe, 292
Socialist Party (France), 20, 94, 217
  Doriot, 35–6, 39–40, 41, 45
  intelligence service and, 260–1, 265, 268–9
  Mitterrand Government, 29, 80–1, 87–9, 92, 96, 152
  municipal elections, 108–9, 111–15
solidarity politics, 11, 136
Somoza, 129

Soulier, André, 110
Soustelle, Jacques, 16, 110
South Africa
  as comic experience, 307–9
  life in (scenes from), 298–306
  Mandela, 321–31
  moral choice, 4–6
  in 1980, 279–86
  O'Brien's account, 132–3, 134–5
  Reform era, 287–97
  violence (black on black), 310–20
South African Black Taxi-Drivers' Association, 319
South African Communist Party, 312
Soviet Union
  disinformation, 202–3, 235–6
  KGB, 228, 234–5, 239, 243–4, 245, 247, 250, 267
Speakes, Larry, 52
Spycatcher (Wright), 69, 70, 252–4, 257
spycatching, 3, 252–8
  Dreyfus affair see Dreyfus, Alfred
  FBI role, 182, 186, 188–9
  see also intelligence services
Stalin, Joseph, 1, 2, 37, 38, 39, 40
Stalinism, 10, 40, 130
Star Wars (SDI), 50–1
Steiner, George, 102
Stendhal, 101–2
Sterling, Claire, 202, 203, 236
Sternhell, Zeer, 30–2
Stevenson, Adlai, 190
Stirbois, Jean-Pierre, 95, 96
Stirling, Colonel David, 249
Stirn, Olivier, 29
Stoker, Bram, *Dracula*, 271–2, 274
Strang, William, 241
Strategic Defence Initiative, 50–1
Strauss, Franz-Josef, 210
Strauss, Norman, 76
Stroessner, General, 201
Struggle for Mastery in Europe, The (Taylor), 164
subversions (MI5), 238–51

Suez Canal, 262
Suhard, Cardinal, 216
Sullivan, William, 191
Summers, Montague, 270, 272
Sun, 257-8
Sun Myung Moon, 33, 194-5, 197-201, 203
Sunday Times, The, 201, 236, 238, 250, 255-6
Sunday Tribune, 281
Swanepoel, Major Theunis, 326
SWAPO, 282

Talleyrand, 215
Tambo, Oliver, 293, 295, 296, 315, 316, 323-4, 325
Tapie, Bernard, 112
Taylor, A. J. P., 157-65
Taylor, Charles, 157-8
Teachers, Writers, Celebrities (Debray), 168
Team B, 53
Tebbit, Norman, 75, 77, 245
Teitgen (Minister of Justice), 215
terrorism, 204-12
Terry, Edward, 271
'thalidomide trial', 255
Thatcher, Margaret, 63, 65, 148, 203
  economic policies, 77-9
  election, 56, 60, 70-1, 248-9
  family background, 49-50
  intelligence service and, 248-9, 250-1, 267
  Jewish community and, 70-3
  Paul Johnson and, 119, 121, 124
  trade unions and, 76-7
  Young's biography, 68, 69-70, 72-3, 75-7
Thatcher Government, 32, 33, 52, 238
Thatcherism, 68, 120, 154
  economic policies, 77-9
  left-wing intellectuals and, 137, 138-9, 141
  origins, 73-7
Thayer, Paul, 53
Third World, 172, 225, 242, 267

Thomas, Dylan, 159
Thomas, Keith, 164
Thompson, E. P., 128, 136-7, 144-6, 151, 164
Thorez, Maurice, 8, 37, 39, 44-5
Through Parisian Eyes (Porter), 171-2
Time, 202
Times, The, 133, 134, 202
Todd, Olivier, 172
Tolson, Clyde, 180-1
Tolstoy, Leo, 9
Tombalbaye, 265
Tong II group, 196
Touré, Sékou, 2, 262
trade unions
  miners' strike, 61-2, 139-40, 246-7
  movement, 141, 142-3
  South Africa, 291-3, 298, 301, 317-19
  Thatcher and, 76-7
Traitors: the Labyrinths of Treason (Pincher), 239
Trautmann, Catherine, 114
Travels of Three English Gentlemen, The, 273
Treurnicht, Andries, 303, 308
Tricot Report, 267
Trotsky, Leon, 36, 37, 180
Truman, Harry, 186-7, 190, 196
truth, 8-9, 136
truth-telling, 10-11, 12
truthfulness, 140
Tshabalala, Ephraim, 290
Tshabalala, Precious, 310-14, 320
Turk, Alex, 109
Turner, Stansfield, 232
Tutu, Bishop Desmond, 284, 285, 287, 290-1, 292, 313-14

UDF (France), 82-3, 85, 89, 109-10, 113, 114
UDF (South Africa), 291-2, 298, 302, 309-10, 312, 314, 316-19, 321
Ukanian state, 147-8, 150-1, 154-6
UN, 128, 133, 262, 329

Index 347

unemployment (South Africa), 301-2, 312
UNITA, 266
United States *see* Central Intelligence Agency; Federal Bureau of Investigation; Reagan, Ronald
Unity Movement, 311, 312
universal culture, 171
universities (South Africa), 305-6

Vaizey, John, 69
Valeri (Papal Nuncio), 216
Vallat, Xavier, 216-17
Valois, 30
vampire myth, 270-5
Van Den Berg, H. J., 264
Van der Post, Laurens, 75, 119
Verwoerd, H. F., 2, 293, 330
Vichy regime, 17, 27-8, 31-2, 43, 44, 95, 215-17, 260-1
Vidal, Gore, 134
Viens, Gaston, 108
Vietnam, 48, 173-4, 206, 261
Vigouroux, Robert, 111, 112, 113
violence (black on black), 310-20
Violet, Jean, 262
Viviani, 29
Volkov (defector), 230
Voltaire, 130
von Hayek, Friedrich, 74, 119
von Mises, Ludwig, 74, 119
Vorster, B. J., 264, 293

Wainwright, Hilary, 57, 60-3 *passim*
Wallace, Captain Colin, 249
Walsh, Tom, 182
Walters, Alan, 75
Walzer, Michael, 8
Ward, Stephen, 256-7
Warnock, Lady, 76
Warren, 160-1
Warren Commission, 192
Washington Post, 198, 202
Washington Times, 195, 198, 199, 200
Watergate, 52, 190, 197-8
Watts, Jim, 199
Weber, Eugen, 98, 99
Weekly Mail, 328
Weightman, John, 24-5
Weinberger, Caspar, 48, 52
Weldon, Harry, 160, 161, 163
Westland affair, 250
Wharton, Harry, 248
Whelan, James, 199
White, Harry Dexter, 239
Whitelaw, William, 72-3
Wilberforce, William, 1
Wilde, Oscar, 160
Williams, Raymond, 10, 136, 137-44
Wills, Garry, 49, 50-1, 54
Wilson, Harold, 60, 65
  Government, 57, 59, 124-5, 150, 242
  intelligence service and, 242, 245-8
Wilson, Woodrow, 180, 181, 229-30
women voters (1987 election), 63-4
Wonderland of Knowledge, The, 98
World Bank, 239
Wright, Peter, 239, 248, 258
  Spycatcher, 69, 70, 252-4, 257
Writers and Politics (O'Brien), 127
Writing by Candlelight (Thompson), 144

Yom Kippur war, 264
Young, Hugo, 68, 69-70, 72-3, 75-6, 77
Young, J. Z., 160
Young Myung Mun, 3, 194, 197-201, 203

Ziegler, Ron, 52
Zilliacus, Konni, 229
Zinoviev, G. Y., 36, 37
Zola, Emile, 25, 27, 28
Zügun, Eleonore, 271